THE MONUMENT GUIDE

GUIDE

TO ENGLAND
AND WALES

DEDICATED WITH AFFECTION
TO MY FATHER BOB DARKE
AND, IN FOND MEMORY,
TO MY MOTHER BETTY DARKE

Queen Victoria (1819–1901). Sculptor: Sir Alfred Gilbert (1903).
Location: St Nicholas Square, Newcastle upon Tyne.

THE MONUMENT GUIDE

GUIDE

TO ENGLAND AND WALES

A National Portrait in
Bronze and Stone

JO DARKE

PHOTOGRAPHY BY
JORGE LEWINSKI AND MAYOTTE MAGNUS

Macdonald Illustrated

A MACDONALD ILLUSTRATED BOOK

ⓒ Macdonald Illustrated 1991
ⓒ Text: Jo Darke 1991
ⓒ Photographs: Jorge Lewinski and Mayotte Magnus 1991
ⓒ Additional photographs: Jo Darke
  pp. 8, 66, 69, 71, 95, 121, 129, 131, 136, 137, 139, 170, 173, 177,
  178, 179, 200, 220, 225(r), 231, 235.

First published in Great Britain in 1991
by Macdonald and Co (Publishers) Ltd, London and Sydney
A member of Maxwell Macmillan Pergamon Publishing Corporation

British Library Cataloguing-in-Publication Data
Darke, Jo
  The Monument Guide to England and Wales.
  I. Title
  725

  ISBN 0–356–17609–6

Typeset by Butler & Tanner Ltd,
Frome and London
Printed and bound in Great Britain by
BPCC Hazell Books,
Paulton and Aylesbury.

Editor: John Wainwright
Designers: Debbie Holmes. Mick Harris. Peter Champion.
Production: Caroline Bennett
Indexer: Hilary Bird

Macdonald & Co (Publishers) Ltd.
Orbit House
1 New Fetter Lane
London EC4A 1AR

Acknowledgements

In compiling this first nationwide survey of our outdoor commemorative
statues and memorials, their history and the heroes they commemorate,
I have relied on the following standard works:

The Buildings of England series by Sir Nikolaus Pevsner (Penguin);
Dictionary of British Sculpture, 1660–1851 by Rupert Gunnis (The Abbey
Library); *Discovering Statues in London and in Southern England* by Mar-
garet Baker, *in Central and Northern England* by J. D. Bennett (Shire);
London Statues by Arthur Byron (Constable); *London's Open-Air Statuary*
by Lord Gleichen (Cedric Chivers); *The New Sculpture* by Susan Beatty
(New Haven); *Patronage and Practise: Sculpture on Merseyside*, edited by
Penelope Curtis (Tate Gallery Publications); *Sculpture in Britain, 1530–
1830* by Margaret Whinney (Penguin); and *Victorian Sculpture* by
Benedict Reid (New Haven). Since completing research, John Black-
wood's *London Immortals* (Savoy Press) has appeared.

Library information on the monuments and their dedicatees has come
from standard biographies (and the invaluable *Dictionary of National
Biography*); locally published volumes by local writers; contemporary
accounts from local newspapers; informative booklets published by
various major cities and towns, notably Birmingham, Bradford, Coventry, Leeds, Liverpool, Manchester, Portsmouth and Southampton, and
publications such as *Country Life* and *Country Quest*.

Most valuable and warming has been the assistance received fom
numerous county or local librarians, museum curators and County
Record Office archivists; directors and employees of commercial firms;
archivists or estate managers or owners of historic homes; regional
Historic Buildings representatives and local officers of the National
Trust; members of local history societies and city planning departments;
parish councillors; fellow writers; monument buffs, and friends and
acquaintances. I have also received particularly valuable assistance from
Ian Leith of the Royal Commission on the Historical Monuments of
England.

I would also like to offer special thanks to the following local experts
who gave their time to meet me or escort me around their localities:
Tom Bennett (West Midlands); Professor Christopher Brooke (Gonville
and Caius College, Cambridge); Michael Brook (Nottingham); Philip
Browning (Liverpool); Norman Cook (DoE); Theo Crosby; Carl De'Ath
(Essex); Peter Fairweather (Lincolnshire); Allan Howard (Telford);
Terence Leach (Lincolnshire); members of Leeds City Art Galleries;
David McLaughlin (Bath); Catherine Moriarty (Imperial War Museum,
war memorial archive); Andrew Naylor, and Naylor Conservation; Peter
Naylor (Derbyshire); Cyril Pearce (W. Yorkshire); Benedict Read (then
of the Courtauld Institute); William H. Senior (S. Yorkshire); Lee Waite
and Christopher Williams (City of London Blue Guides); Annabelle
Walker; Dorothy Wright (Isle of Wight).

In addition, I much appreciated talking to Kevin Atherton, Janet
Barry, Greta Berlin, Richard Cowdy, Vicki Craven, John Letts, and André
Wallace about their work.

I should also like to record my gratitude to those who made available their
personal archives, or lent me books or papers: these include Sir Edward
Ballam; Brenda Bishop (Cambridgeshire); Ian Bleasdale (Cheshire); John
H. Boyes; Bill Brindley (Stockport, Cheshire); Mike Cave (Cambridge);
Edna Dale-Jones (Carmarthen); Philip Deakin (Alnwick); Reginald Dosell
of Larkins Ltd (steeplejacks); Michael R. Hills (Sudbury); Alison Kelly
(Coade stone statues); P. R. Lee of Rattee & Kett (restoration); Dr
Neil McIntyre; Judy Medrington (Westmorland); Andrew Pierssene
(Norfolk); David Pill; Harry Rowland (Northumberland); Cliff Williams
(Clay Cross); John Wyatt (Cumbria); Marion Zealand Lowndes (Cleve-
land, Teesside).

Published articles were lent me by Katharine Eustace (on Bristol's
equestrian statue of William III by Michael Rysbrack); Dr Jack Harris
FRS (on monument conservation); Richard Hewlings (on the Ripon
obelisk). Clare Midgley let me read her dissertation 'Public Monuments
to Women, 1850–1930'. And thanks are due to Jon Parry, of the
Working Men's College in London, for translating Welsh texts into
English. Extra research undertaken by Gwynedd County Libraries was
much appreciated.

Thanks should also go to the many friends who put me up whilst
researching their locality; to hostel wardens, and bed and breakfast hosts
who offered information and directions; and to the numerous pedestrians
who gave detailed directions, sometimes when rudely hailed from the
car, to monuments in all corners of the landscape. People's friendliness
and courtesy seem limitless. Without it, this book would not have been
written.

Finally I should like to thank my excellent agent Jennifer Kavanagh
for having the idea in the first place; the publishers, Macdonald, for their
patience; to the stalwart photographers Jorge Lewinski and Mayotte
Magnus for following my directions to monuments in obscure locations;
and to the editor John Wainwright, for overseeing the final product
with great skill and patience.

Last but not least, thanks must go to my friends and family, and
daughters Tamsin and Morwenna for their forbearance; and to my
husband Richard Pearce, a fount of encouragement and knowledge, for
running the house whilst supporting *Monuments* with his unstinting
good humour.

**Despite the ready help and encouragement of many experts, there
will be errors and misconceptions which I acknowledge as my
own.**

Contents

The County Boundaries of England and Wales

Most English and Welsh monuments were erected when travel was difficult, when land-owning county families were closely identified with their locality, and when local populations retained long, strong allegiancies to their county. The extensive boundary changes of 1974, which created new administrative counties from the old, meant that, for example, the 19th-century Shap granite boulder erected to the geologist Adam Sedgwick (1785–1873) in his Yorkshire dale town, Dent, now belongs to the new county of Cumbria – created from Cumberland and Westmorland, and from parts of Lancashire and of Yorkshire's West Riding.

The map opposite shows the administrative counties. Throughout the book a featured monument's county of origin, where changed, is indicated in its heading.

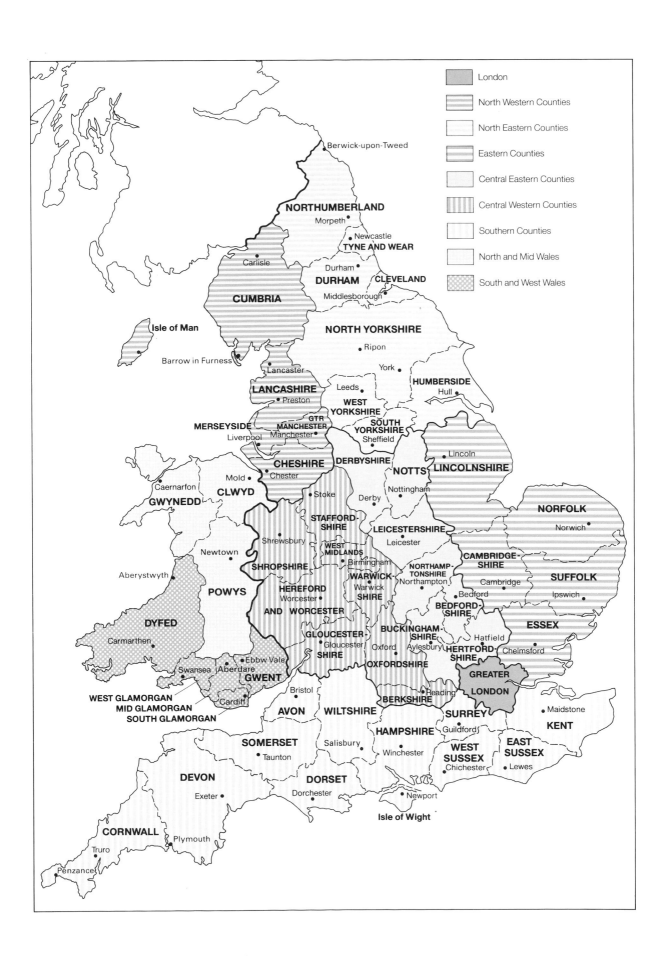

Obelisk to Admiral Sir Harry Burrard Neale (1766–1840) Architect: George Draper (1840).
Location: Monument Hill, Walhampton.

Introduction

His Name, to whose Memory
This Testamonial is Inscribed
Is so deeply graven on the hearts of all who knew him,
That while any of those survive
There needed not the Record of Stone or Marble
To preserve it from Oblivion,
But, because from this changeable scene
All living records swiftly pass away,
It is here Written,
As a more Durable Memorial,
That He was One
Of whom "When the ear heard, it blessed him";
Whom, "When the eye saw, it gave witness to him";
For he delivered the Poor and Fatherless
"And him who had none to help him",
And "caused the widow's heart to sing for joy".
In all the relations of life he was perfect,
(According to the measure of human imperfection).
In his daily walk with God, exemplifying the virtues of the Christian Character,
Above all, in the largeness of his charity and in the beauty of his humility.

(Inscription on the north face of the obelisk to Admiral Sir Harry
Burrard Neale baronet, GCB and GCMG, erected at Walhampton,
Hampshire 'in the 4th Year of the Reign of Queen Victoria By Her
Majesty Adelaide the Queen Dowager, Their Royal Highnesses
the Duchess of Gloucester and Princess Augusta, A large circle of
Distinguished, Professional, and other Friends, and the
Inhabitants of Lymington and its Vicinity')

Not every monument speaks for itself as gladly as Admiral Burrard Neale's obelisk, a shadowy needle on the skyline overlooking Lymington Harbour. Yet the same impulse that so lauded his 'exalted character (kind but undaunted, mild but determined)' raised the pyramids, the Colossus of Rhodes, Nelson's Column, and the humblest gravestone in a village churchyard.

These rich archives of British social history are particularly well-preserved in the Welsh or English quarrying villages such as Altarnun in Cornwall, where Nevil Northey Burnard's first attempts at his father, George Burnard's, craft can be measured against many other simple, but strongly-decorative stone carvings in the church and chapel grounds.

On the old Methodist chapel is the sculptor's carved profile of John Wesley in a roll-curl wig, sharp-nosed and watchful; his portrait of 1834 belongs to the kaleidoscopic collection of statues and equestrian figures, obelisks and classical columns, inscribed stones, carved crosses and other monumentalia that make the British Isles a great open-air gallery of sculpture and stonework.

England's collection of outdoor monuments may

Flora Thompson. Sculptor: Philip Jackson (1981). Location: Liphook Post Office, Hampshire.

be seen as a focal core, whilst other parts of the former Union – Wales, Scotland and Ireland – have an equally rich monumental tradition, in this book explored through the statues and stones of Wales.

An open-air treasure house

The exhibits in this topographical gallery are unevenly distributed, counties and regions being loosely classifiable in terms of monumental quality and style, and in choice of dedicatee.

Most familiar in public perception is the 19th-century statue of a local politician, benefactor, social reformer or industrial captain; these patriarchal pillars survive in bronze or stone as bushy-bearded icons of the past in the altered townscapes of England's industrial cities.

Other famed or forgotten worthies, local landowners, historical figures, military leaders or monarchs, lend their images to market squares or high streets throughout the land. Some towns shelter their statues under a Gothic canopy; a popular alternative was the commemorative clock tower or drinking fountain, prodigiously carved in varied stone. These should be examined for the personal touch, as at Horncastle in Lincolnshire, where a bronze profile of Edward Stanhope (local MP from 1874–93), waxed-moustached and sardonic, is embedded in the stonework.

Regional variation

London's pre-eminence as the national capital is reflected in its rich offering of wall plates and busts, and its extensive collection of portrait memorial statues making roughly quarter of the English total, which numbers around 730, with Wales counting around 50.

London and Wales have few columns, obelisks and beacons, but English country estates, and hilltops, number over 100 eye-catching columns and towers, with some statues or belvederes (but not counting First World War 'Victories'). Obelisks, large and small, also appear as decorative memorials in gardens, parks and town squares. 'Celtic' or 'Anglian' crosses and inscribed megaliths date from periods of historic, romantic or nationalistic revivalism, most popularly in Wales and in Victorian England.

A random selection

Certain categories of monument proliferate in certain counties, commemorative towers being *de rigeur* in Somerset whilst Gloucestershire and Dorset, apart from their county towns, seem barren places for the monument seeker. Hampshire's *richesse* includes a fibreglass bust of Flora Thompson; a square-cut boulder carved with the archaic bat and ball of the celebrated Hambledon Cricket XI; and a Marochetti bronze of the Duke of Wellington on a Corinthian column. One suspects an obscure logic in such random selection, but settles for the hand of chance.

This is borne out in Ormskirk, where Primrose League funds left over from an 1870s Flagday purchased a stone statue of Disraeli, not wanted in Wigan. It is now a traffic hazard at the top of the market place, and a beacon for visitors. Its removal would make a sad void. A Portland stone statue of

Lord John Scott (d.1860), agreeably executed by Joseph Durham, was erected with definite intent on the green at Dunchurch in Warwickshire 'by his tenantry, in affectionate remembrance', 1867.

Small, but diverse

Britain's landscape has nothing to compare in majesty with the Grand Canyon or the Matterhorn, and our monuments reflect this intimacy; even 'Albert Dda' in soldier's uniform, his marble image prominent on the headland at Tenby, is modestly scaled in comparison with the Statue of Liberty in New York or *Christ the Redeemer* extending his arms over Rio.

Anything really big is rebuffed. The great engineer Richard Trevithick in 1832 drew plans for a 1,000ft, gilded, cast-iron Reform Column, but his biographers Dickinson and Titley in 1933 'could only express satisfaction' that it had come to nothing. In 1987 the architect-designer Theo Crosby and others, proposing a 500ft Battle of Britain Docklands monument, provoked a shoal of 'No's' in the *Times* correspondence columns.

As our monuments belong in their small scale landscape, so they reflect its diversity: statues in England and Wales account for a broad range in style and quality, including works by the great eighteenth-century master Michael Rysbrack (see his superb equestrian bronze of William III, 1736, in Queen Square, Bristol); the stiff, formal bronzes of popular mid-Victorian sculptors like Matthew Noble; or the more naturalistic approach to portraiture introduced at the end of the 19th century by New Sculpture practitioners such as Sir Hamo Thornycroft or Sir William Goscombe John, whose bronze portrait statues illuminate his native Wales.

Added to this rich mix are the unclassifiable offerings of the native mason, and finally the more informal portrait sculpture practised in the present century. Belonging to a scattered and eclectic collection, these exhibits can be assessed not so much as works of art as corporate tribute to individual worth. They reward inspection by local and social historians and by students of art, architecture, masonry, landscape, or any one of myriad subjects associated with a particular dedicatee.

Starting points

Britain's heritage of statues and sculpture dates from long before Saxon or Roman times. Surviving from before the Conquest are inscribed stones of British kings, carved Celtic, Anglian or Norse crosses and hogback coffin lids, menhirs or dolmens of pre-Saxon Britain, and Roman inscribed stones, customarily set up at the roadside after burial.

From the Norman age comes the tradition of church building in stone, with zestful ornamentation of carved foliate, grotesque or human images. Small stone figures of College patrons inhabit medieval gateways in Oxford; surviving market crosses like Winchester's feature royal or saintly figures.

These are national treasures, but perhaps the earliest true starting point for study of English public commemorative sculpture is the Eleanor cross, of which three examples survived the Cromwellian purges. Two in Northamptonshire display the original 13th-century statues of the resourceful Eleanor: head demurely bowed, she has occupied her decorative niches since Edward I placed a spired, stone-carved tower, surmounted by a cross, at each resting place of his Queen's cortège from Harby, Northamptonshire, to Westminster.

Another important marker in the history of English public statuary is Charles I's bronze bust of

*Charles I. Sculptor: Hubert Le Sueur (erected 1660).
Location: top of Whitehall (Trafalgar Square).*

1630 (now in fibreglass replica) made by Hubert le Sueur, erected over the Square Tower at Portsmouth to mark the King's return from his European quest for a bride, accompanied by the Duke of Buckingham. Having failed in wooing the Infanta of Spain, the King at last succeeded with Henrietta Maria, daughter of the French king Henry IV.

More importantly for England's landscape, sculpture and local history, Charles returned inspired by Continental antique and classical statuary. He brought to England three European sculptors whose training in academic anatomical drawing was far superior to that of English craftsmen still bound by a long tradition to apprenticeship in the master mason's yards.

Of the three, Francesco Fanelli and François Dieussart are less well known than Hubert Le Sueur, who re-introduced the use of bronze casting in English sculpture, and promoted the idea of the portrait bust. The Diana Fountain, much altered but thought to be by Fanelli (1636), survives in Bushey Park near Hampton Court. Made for Somerset House as part of the king's fine collection of classically-inspired garden sculpture, it was moved from Hampton Court early this century.

After the Restoration, Charles II pointedly installed his father's equestrian statue, made by Hubert le Sueur for Charles I's Lord High Treasurer, at the head of Whitehall on the last site at which an Eleanor Cross had been erected, and where later the Regicides were cruelly executed.

From this period can be traced an unbroken tradition of public statuary and monument building. Early manifestations brought ornamental statues of royalty garbed as Roman emperors out of the private landscapes, and into public view.

The unbroken tradition

Copies or originals of classical statuary, collected for the great 18th-century country estates, were artfully placed in Arcadian landscapes so that cultured visitors, fresh from their Grand Tours, could appreciate their host's learning and cosmopolitan style.

As at the Stowe estate in Buckinghamshire, improved for the powerful Whig politician Viscount Cobham (d.1749), or on the Wentworth-Woodhouse estate, built on coal in mine-scarred South Yorkshire, commemorative or ornamental monuments also signalled political allegience – sometimes through long, obsequious inscriptions.

In many instances, from this period, a carved inscription in lichened, archaic letters makes the monument. At the site of the battle of Lansdowne (1643) above Bath, a much-repaired stone pillar, 1720, quotes the historian E.H. Clarendon's record of the mortal wounding of the Royalist Sir Bevil Grenville 'which would have Clouded any Victory'.

East of Leek Wootton near Warwick, above the A46/A429, a wood-shrouded hillside cross by J.C. Jackson (1832), raised on piers, makes bitter reading:

> In the Hollow of this Rock,
> Was beheaded,
> On the 17 Day of July, 1312,
> By Barons lawless as himself,
> PIERS GAVESTON, Earl of Cornwall;
> The Minion of a hateful King:
> In Life and Death,
> A memorable Instance of Misrule.

(But further south on the Welcome Hills near Stratford, the Philips family's obelisk erected 1876 above their mansion, now a hotel, fulfils a hotel doorman's promise of 'a good read'.)

A good – and verbose – read appears on 'the pillar called Mail Coach Pillar' beside the Brecon-Llandovery road in Powys, where the drunken driver Edward Jenkins, speeding on the wrong side of the road, met a cart and plunged over the 121ft precipice: '... at the bottom near the river he came against an ash tree when the coach was dashed into several pieces ...'

Towers or obelisks sent political signals from afar, but were equally revealing through close inspection of inscriptions such as 'Sacred to Liberty' which informs 'The Needle' overlooking Kendal from Castle Howe, erected in 1788 to commemorate the centenary of William III's landing. A dark obelisk to William Pitt, 'the pilot that weathered the storm', was raised above the Kendal-Windermere road (A591) by James Bateman of Tolson Hall; the inscription was not engraved until a century later (1914), 'Owing to Napoleon's escape from Elba'. These urgent messages satisfy the most arduous scramble over rough terrain, or up the steepest hill.

The pace quickens

The most famous of the Napoleonic monuments, Nelson's Column, appeared over 20 years after Pitt's. By then obelisks, columns or towers, erected nationwide to the great Napoleonic heroes Nelson and Wellington, or simply echoing the inspiring name 'Waterloo', had created a momentum in monument raising which gathered pace after the death of Sir Robert Peel in 1850, and quickened further at the demise of Albert, Prince Consort, in 1861.

Sir Francis Chantrey and Sir Richard Westmacott, working at the beginning of the 19th century, were amongst the first to create statues marking the achievements of public figures, commissioned by public rather than private patrons. Chantrey's work is exceptionally fine: Westmacott could not rival Chantrey in his *forté*, portrait busts after the 18th-century masters, but was to build his prolific and eminently successful career on commissions for open-air statues as well as funerary monuments. Both sought inspiration from Rome. They followed the ancient custom of raising their public statues on pillars: Chantrey's Duke of Sutherland, 1836, a repeat of that in Dornoch, is a grand waymark off the A34 at Trentham Park; Westmacott's Duke of York was elevated 'higher in the public eye Than he was ever known before' on a Tuscan Column, at Carlton House Steps, London, in 1834. Following sculptural tradition, Westmacott based Liverpool's equestrian bronze of George III, and Chantrey his of George IV in London, on the statue of Marcus Aurelius (*c.*175 AD) at the Capitol. (This can be seen in replica crowning the triumphal arch entrance at Wilton House, in Wiltshire.)

The earliest public statue of Lord Nelson was made by Westmacott for the city of Birmingham. The ensemble, erected in 1809, shows the hero of Trafalgar in his uniform with his empty sleeve, and is an early departure from Sir Joshua Reynolds's dictum, laid down in his 10th Discourse, that a contemporary appearance might look odd to future generations whilst the garb of a Roman Emperor or senator would place a statue's subject on a timeless, therefore universal plane.

The Victorian gentleman

This convention seemed equally odd to laymen of later generations, confronted with statues of over-weight Hanoverian monarchs or Whig politicians draped in togas, with sandals and laurel crowns. Most Victorian sculptors, in their passion for roman-tic realism, recreated their notables in standard poses as smooth-modelled establishment figures with uniform and decorations, ceremonial robes, the mayoral chain, or gentlemen's modes presented in the finest detail of side whisker, collar and cravat.

Sir Robert Peel's sculptor, Edward Hodges Baily, maintained that the wrong-sided buttoning of the waistcoat was a foible of the amiable Peel, immor-talised in his native Bury where his father, John Peel, built the town's cotton industry and reputedly 'stole' Samuel Crompton's idea for the spinning mule.

Peel's death in 1850 brought a flood of feeling in the northern towns. His first public statue, carved by Thomas Duckett, was installed at the sculptor's native Preston in 1852. Bronze statues appeared later that year in Leeds and Bury, with later unveilings in Manchester, Salford, Tamworth, Oldham, Birmingham and Bradford, and an afterthought appearing at Huddersfield in 1873. This statue by William Theed the Younger has since been scrapped, its pedestal reputedly used as motorway hardcore.

Peel's public statues exemplify the problems of faithfully recreating the fashionable Victorian gen-tleman's attire, if Robes of the Garter, or other ceremonial robes, were omitted: 'tight trousers' was the recurring cry of sculpture critics and writers. London's statue by William Behnes, erected in Cheapside and now sited at Hendon Police College, was assessed by Lord Gleichen in 1928: 'his trousers, according to the fashion of those days, are woe-fully tight and display his powerful muscular development'.

Meanwhile the Peel Tower was begun outside Bury in 1851, predating all the statues, and is now a landmark on the moors beyond the town.

Henry Hornby (1805–1884). Sculptor: Albert Bruce-Joy (1912). Location: Blackburn.

The continuing tradition

Tributes to Peel, Wellington, James Watt and other national figures firmly established the practise of raising public monuments, an activity perfectly attuned to the Victorian age of Empire building, prodigious manufacturing, bureaucratic finagling and swaggering civic pride. Commemorative work was generally funded by public subscription, sometimes 'the pennies of the poor'. It was also gifted by individuals or by colleagues, comrades-in-arms, the local squire, or – 'in affectionate rememberance' – by the tenants and family of the landlord himself.

Valuable collections made by institutions such as universities, or the prestigious town halls, continued the practise of private patronage that had already established superb collections of 18th-century public sculpture, notably at the universities of Oxford and Cambridge. Also now on public view, are rich private collections of garden statuary after the Antique, or portrait busts by 18th-century masters, made for libraries and orangeries of the nobility: these augment our wealth of church monumental sculpture dating from before the Dark Ages.

A Victorian convention

Victorian public statuary rapidly established stylistic conventions in adornment and inscription, based on classical practise. Heraldic emblems, or symbols such as Minerva's owl for wisdom, were favoured pedestal enrichments; sea motifs embellish monuments in ports like Hull or Bristol. Pedestal *bas*-relief panels recall the subject's life and symbolise his achievements, providing precious, detailed visual recordings of people, machines and implements in domestic or work interiors, historical scenes, smoky industrial panoramas and the odd rural idyll.

Bronze allegorical figures around the base of a statue exemplify the subject's achievements, interests and noble aspirations. On Wellington's big monument in Manchester by Noble, 1856, the helmeted warrior-figures, possibly Mars and Minerva, look like Mr and Mrs Normal in uncomfortable fancy dress, but the Oldham MP John Platt's Grecian-draped muses by D.W. Stevenson make graceful, if unlikely, company in Alexandra Park.

Victorian self-aggrandisement

The rapidly-entrenched Victorian practise of forming a Memorial Committee (in the Swan Inn or Dog and Duck, depending on social status), of setting up Subscribers' and other Sub-Committees, choosing an appropriate monumental style (for which was formed a Committee of Taste), selecting the sculptor (generally by competition), finding the site, appointing masons and founders, and at last ceremonially laying the foundation stone, often with its 'Time Capsule' of coins, newspapers and household objects, afforded endless opportunities for self-advancement and bureaucratic intrigue, all in the blameless cause of perpetuating a revered local name.

A mayor instigating a memorial might become Committee Chairman, and later see his own name immortalised on a pedestal inscription, recording the mayorality in which the statue was raised. Local luminaries who performed unveilings were later unveiled posthumously, as statues, by succeeding luminaries. Hull's extensive collection of statues by local sculptors, and those in Bradford (Leeds's old rival) by more eminent sculptors, perfectly exemplify these beguiling phenomena.

Robust civic rivalry no doubt fuelled Wolverhampton's application in 1865 to erect a statue of the Prince Consort, to which Queen Victoria acquiesced, stipulating a military equestrian figure. She even loaned Albert's uniform and favourite mount to the sculptor, Thomas Thornycroft (a royal favourite), but caused panic and confusion by unexpectedly agreeing to perform the unveiling: she had, after all, turned down Manchester and Liverpool.

Nine days of furious activity produced ceremonial arches, one built with coal, and several grades of lavatory at the station for relevant ranks in the royal entourage. Further consternation was caused when the Queen, accompanied by John Brown, knighted the wrong man. The knight erratus later apologised to the deserving mastermind of the project, Alderman Underhill, who had given generously to the subscription fund totalling £1150.

Public ceremonial

Whether performed by a national or a local notable, unveilings occasioned mutual back-slapping by the city fathers, and a show of loyalty by the multitudes, who were rewarded with pomp and speechifying in stupendous processional pageants orchestrated with solemn Victorian industry. Months, or years, earlier, the vast, festive crowds would have stood silent at the dedicatee's black-draped funeral procession.

These rituals were not wholly a Victorian phenomenon. At the ceremonial laying of the foundation stone for Lord de Dunstanville's 90ft granite cross in 1836, a crowd of 30 thousand witnessed the

Masonic procession as it climbed the mine-scarred slopes of Carn Brea in Cornwall, along a path flanked with 1,000 Roskear miners.

The elaborately-staged unveilings, and foundation-layings performed with silver trowel and mallet, were often preceded by unseemly wrangling. The noble impulse to immortalise the far-famed innovative agriculturalist William Thomas Coke, 2nd Earl of Leicester – activated on the day of his death (July 2, 1842) – also activated hot debate over the term 'farmers' or 'agriculturalists'; the style of monument; the level of subscriptions; the site – whether at Holkham Hall, or in the county town, Norwich. This was won by setting a subscription of 10/- (50p), which introduced large numbers of eligible local voters.

The disputatious designer, W.I. Donthorn, caused endless holdups which by swelling the interest on the £4000 fund at least allowed him to order a bronze plate for W.B. Donne's fulsome inscription (the Committee wanted cheaper, less durable, stone). But murkier waters were revealed when committee member Mr R.N. Bacon, originator of the scheme, claimed authorship of the rough sketch on which Donthorn had based his winning design.

The resulting 120ft column with its crowning wheatsheaf, carvings of bulls kneeling in foliage of turnips and mangel-wurzels, of lifesize farm implements and Coke of Norfolk's 'special breeds', and massive base with relief panels carved by John Henning the younger, is indeed 'equal to any in the kingdom' as specified, and can be seen on Holkham Hall's open days. As well as featuring the 'great and good' Coke with his Southdown sheep, his drainage scheme and his fortunate tenants, one panel shows the committee members who so zealously directed the manufacture of his column.

Hiccoughs

Some monuments were thwarted from proposal stage. Oliver Cromwell's birthplace, Huntingdon, early in 1899 (the tercentenary of his birth), refused an offer to buy his statue from the celebrated Coalbrookdale foundry, one alderman at least wishing to dissociate himself from 'one who unfortunately was guilty of the death of his sovereign'. A further appeal was abandoned at £100 after six months – at which neighbouring St Ives (predominantly Nonconformist where Huntingdon was Anglican) set up a fund; when F.W. Pomeroy's brooding bronze of the Protector was unveiled in St Ives market place, 1901, the £1168.7s:6d was about £50 short.

Oliver Cromwell (1599–1698). Sculptor: John Bell (1899). Location: Bridge Foot, Warrington.

Early in 1899 Warrington, then a Lancashire town, was rowing over a cast-iron statue of Cromwell by John Bell. Bridge Head, scene of Cromwell's decisive victory at the Battle of Preston (1648), was felt to be 'an inconvenient corner' for a gift 'unwillingly accepted'. The donor, a local industrialist, had Coalbrookdale connections. This firm's gift of golden gates for Buckingham Palace was supposedly refused by Queen Victoria, piqued at seeing Cromwell's statue displayed *en suite* with the gates at the Great Exhibition. 'Old Noll' still stands in Warrington; the town hall rejoices in a pair of glorious golden gates.

Queen Victoria, unamused by Cromwell's statue, was honoured at her Jubilees and after her death with a great volume of statues throughout England, those of the manufacturing centres far outclassing almost any other in scale and design. Showing the Queen in haughty old age, some have been banished to parks (among them Leeds), some relegated and later revived (Wakefield); some have seen tower blocks replace their townscape (Manchester); some match in grandeur their original majestic surroundings (St Helen's).

At Bradford, a fine bronze of Victoria by Alfred Drury (1904) forms a successful grouping with the town's Great War memorial, set between the modern Museum of Film and the old Alhambra. The Queen's heavy, luxuriant robes fold over the pedestal, her orb supports a winged Victory, a small crown pins down her head drapery, and her jowly countenance is imperiously unamused.

Southward on the dark moors above Huddersfield the Jubilee Tower, conspicuous on Castle Hill, is just one of countless beacons and clock towers that celebrate Victoria's long reign.

Pompous Victoriana

Down in Bradford's centre, on banks and civic buildings, carved portrait heads and statues from national or local history — notably 'the City Hall Monarchs' and the 'Wool Exchange Celebrities' — exemplify the vigorous tradition of sculptural decoration which enriches the surviving architecture of Britain's old manufacturing centres, and numerous county towns. Bradford's patriarchal statues of entrepreneurial and reforming industrialists epitomise the profoundly local roots in our Victorian public monuments.

These bronze or carved images may be dismissed as pompous, but locally they can be familiar and fond objects; the present siting of 'Honest John' Fielden's statue in a Todmorden park brought pained comment from a market trader: 'They've put him down there in a cloomp of trees, he belongs oop there at 't'side of 't'Town Hall'.

This restrained figure by John Foley (1863) commemorates Fielden's 'Perservering Efforts' towards obtaining the Ten Hours Act. More importantly for some, the Fielden family, mill owners, gave amongst other buildings Todmorden's fine Town Hall, its sculptured pediment showing figures of both 'Lancashire' and 'Yorkshire'.

Flesh and bone, clay, plaster, bronze and stone

The peculiar art of public monumental sculpture established the names, eminence and fortunes of the many sculptors whose works still ornament our towns. Much as stoneyards of monumental masons flourished next to the great cathedrals, and workshops of decorative sculptors, from the 17th century, turned out garden statues, fountains, and exquisite house interiors, so the huge studios of leading 19th-century sculptors and their pupils (some studios having their own foundries) became established in London and other major cities.

The names of sculptors such as Baron Carlo Marochetti, J.E. Boehm and Alfred Drury span the Victorian and Edwardian eras. Familiar to memorial committees, as were their contemporaries - Royal Academicians and others — they entered their models for the selection competitions by which most important commissions were won. Reputation, studio visits, and a fair degree of personal angling accounted for other work.

Most public statues were specified to be in bronze (some in marble, or other stone). The master sculptor would make a small-scale, then a full-scale model, commonly from clay supported on an armature, or framework, of flexible metal piping. From this would be cast the 'original plaster model', ready for the expensive and skilled process of bronze casting. Using sand that would cement together and solidify when baked, the shape of the plaster model was taken in the form of an inner core and an outer mould; these would be held apart by pins to the desired thickness of metal, and the liquid bronze poured between. Casts were made in sections, reunited and finished at the final stage.

Sculptors sometimes ordered a number of bronze casts before the clay and plaster models and the moulds were pulverised for re-use. G.F. Watts's equestrian figure 'Physical Energy', in Hyde Park, and his impressive statue of Tennyson at Lincoln, are rare in retaining the original plaster models kept at the Watts Art Gallery in Compton, Surrey.

Modern artists like André Wallace also make limited editions, either in bronze or fibreglass. The ancient *ciré perdue*, or 'lost wax' process, reintroduced here late in the 19th century — and use of materials such as rubber in place of plaster — are superficial changes in an age-old process. The expertise and skill of the founder is vital, and the bronze base of most Victorian or Edwardian statues carry the foundry's name on one side, complementing the sculptor's name and date of completion on the other.

Also basically unchanged is the art of carving in marble or plainer stone. Measurements in three dimensions were transferred from a small-scale clay model to the great lump of stone by means of a pointing machine, which drilled holes to the appropriate depth. The stone was then hewn by professional stone masons or pupils until the image was close enough to be worked by higher-grade masons and, in the final stage, the master himself.

The speaking likeness

Some sculptors, among them Thomas Brock and Albert Toft, began as modellers in ceramic factories – Worcester and Wedgwood respectively. George Tinworth and John Broad of Royal Doulton modelled public statues in terracotta; Broad's roseate figure of Queen Victoria glows rudely against the green of a Newbury park. It was erected, 1903, in a lion-guarded ensemble by A.E. Pearce, for the circus proprietor 'Lord' George Sanger on the site of his father's market stall.

Victorian sculptors got 'speaking' likenesses. John Cassidy, who practised in Manchester, overheard two passers-by appraising his statue of the dialect writer Ben Brierley (1898): 'Why bother putting his name, anyone can tell that's Owd Ben!' At the unveiling of the Earl of Dudley's marble statue beneath his castle walls (C.B. Birch, 1888), an onlooker seeking the identity of a female dignitary was told 'That's the statue's missus'.

Studios and schools

The studio system prevailed until the sculpture schools in London, Liverpool, Sheffield and other towns became popular at the end of the 19th century. Godfrey Sykes, a pupil of Alfred Stevens and later a tutor at Sheffield School of Art, is commemorated by a pretty pillar at Sheffield's Weston Park; designed by his friend and assistant James Gamble, it is enriched with Sykes's terracotta work, including some of his designs for the South Kensington museums. The affectionate bronze relief of Sykes in an artistic floppy bow was made by South Kensington students in 1871. The white paint dates from the 1960s.

The schools system, encouraged by Frederick Leighton, and influenced by teachers such as Dalou and Lantéri from France, nurtured the 'New Sculpture' movement that inspired more naturalistically modelled and textured bronzes by sculptors like Hamo Thornycroft, Onslow Ford, Alfred Gilbert, and George Frampton. Apart from Ford, all these sculptors received knighthoods, as did other turn of century sculptors.

Thomas Brock was knighted at the unveiling of his colossal monument to Queen Victoria outside Buckingham Palace in 1911, and George Gilbert Scott, architect, was honoured for his *tour de force* the Albert Memorial, – as *The Builder* called it, a 'piece of monumental jewellery', after its inauguration in 1872.

The end of an era

The 'New Sculpture', and Edwardian statues, with their rich Art Nouveau pedestal decoration, mark the end of a prolific era of public statuary, which was universalized by world conflict. National grief after the Great War set up monuments in nearly every parish, varying in scale and style from small personal crosses on remote waysides, or statues of soldiers in Welsh villages, to classical edifices with sculpture and statues, like the Mercantile Marine Memorial designed by Sir Edward Maufe in the City of London's Trinity Square gardens, in 1955.

The rich diversity of styles, many retaining an Edwardian flavour, encompass familar forms like the Calvary Cross at Hooton Pagnell near Doncaster, or the helmeted St George at Ramsey, Cambridgeshire; and they popularised the image of the winged Victory, elevated on a column, erected at locations as disparate as Burton on Trent, Denbigh in Clwyd, and Lewes, East Sussex.

Glamour and realism

The adaptation of traditional designs brought some rich juxtapositions, amply shown in Hereford's county war memorial by L.W. Barnard (1922), sited opposite the Shire Hall – near Marochetti's bronze statue of 1864, commemorating the politician and writer Sir George Cornewell Lewis. The Gothic 'Eleanor Cross' carved in warm stone by J. Thompson & Son shelters, in recesses under canopies crocketed with trails of hops and tracery, white stone statues of World War One heroes, including a goggled fighter pilot and a uniformed nurse.

Boys' Own figures, idealised images of clean-cut soldiers, as is dashingly epitomised at Station Road, Cambridge – 'R. Tait McKensie Fecit', 1921 – are said to mirror the recruitment posters that stirred nationalistic valour before the carnage of the trenches. These and other forms were also used as monuments of the Boer War.

Perhaps more than any building or monument since the Albert Memorial, First World War monuments provide examples of collaboration between architects and sculptors as equals. The stately, inscribed cenotaphs are augmented with bronze figures symbolising grim heroism in battle; uniform, weaponry and kit are reproduced in fine detail. In contrast, aproned mothers with babes in arms stand as symbols of stoic sacrifice on the home front. Local surnames are spelt out on Rolls of Honour, typically in upraised letters on metal panels. Bronze relief panels show soldiers in combat, or carrying wounded comrades from the scene of conflict.

Amongst the most outstanding and unusual is that made by Sir William Goscombe John, for the model village Port Sunlight. It is centred on a massive stone cross, its circular stone podium carrying statues of school age children, as if to show what was at stake. They and their mothers, the 'people next-door', stand firm with soldiers, sailors and airmen of varying ranks.

A new beginning

After the Second World War, the idea of raising new monuments seemed futile. The dates 1939–45 (ignoring the Far Eastern theatre), and Rolls of names, were added to those of 1914–1918/19. In almost every case the space chosen for the later inscriptions seems, uncannily, to balance the original design. Some monuments recall the Korean and Falkland conflicts.

In 1989, the Imperial War Museum and The Royal Commission on the Historical Monuments of England embarked on the immense and important task of listing and describing all the United Kingdom's various categories of war monument, dating from before and after the First World War.

The names of between-wars sculptors such as Hermon Cawthra, Gilbert Ledward and Lady Kathleen Scott, who contributed some impressive war monuments, mark a tentative regeneration of public sculpture in the 1930s. In their memorial statues, adhering to Victorian technical formality but more freely modelled, they expressed their subjects' individuality rather than public status.

Post-war rebuilding saw resiting (usually still at the centre), storage, or scrapping of Victorian statues that obstructed motor traffic or the development of new shopping precincts. The current quest for a local identity in the face of this '50s and '60s uniformity is, as in the Victorian period, reviving interest in local heroes. Thus, Thomas Chippendale has returned as a bronze statue to his native Otley, and John Ray to Braintree in Essex. Neither statue shows the technical mastery of the '30s artists, whilst each represents the enduring impulse to immortalise our betters, combined with a prevailing rejection of the 'pompous' in preference for such subjects as Ray the

great 16th-century botanist (by Faith Winter), and Chippendale the master craftsmen, presented by Graham Ibbeson as a youthful carpenter.

Modern heroes

Confronting the onlooker eyeball-to-eyeball from low pedestals, they are examples of 'democratic sculpture', of which the ratepayer is patron – not always to the ratepayer's satisfaction. Poets and writers, or great engineers like Brunel and Thomas Telford, are among the subjects selected, perhaps because they practised gentler disciplines than the warrior heroes and statesmen recreated in Victoria's Empire-building days. The armed services are still favourite subjects for honour, although generals no longer claim the local loyalty of a county regiment, as they did when landowner, general, and MP were often from one family and sometimes were one person. As ever the new images exhibit varying degrees of sculptural talent, combined with a quest for artistic originality that promises a new collection of great diversity within a few years.

Community art

The new age of leisure and tourism has sparked projects such as the Bretton Hall Sculpture Park in South Yorkshire, the Grizedale Forest Sculpture Trail in Cumbria and the Powys Sculpture Trail; commissioning agencies, regional art councils, city planning departments and commercial groups organise landscape art in neon sculpture, ceramic pavings and other sculpture-related media. Architecture and sculpture again meet in schemes such as the 'percent for art', where property developers allow part of a project's budget for sculpture or artwork.

Sculptures may be in a variety of materials, bronze being ever-popular, but expensive. Cement, particularly dark *ciment fondu*, and polyester resin – sometimes given a metallic finish – are also used. More and more works appear in colour; near the old canal route at the Brunel Centre in Swindon, John Clinch's sculpture 'The Great Blondinis', cast in aluminium alloy of sugar pinks, yellows and blues, brings memories of the fairground and the rude postcard. Made in collaboration with six craftsmen from Swindon's British Rail Engineering Workshop in 1987, it also marks the lost skills of a former workforce – 14,000 strong – as part of Swindon's community art programme initiated in 1975.

Like Swindon, most new towns, from Welwyn Garden City begun in 1920, incorporate sculpture

'The Great Blondinis'. Sculptor: John Clinch (1987). Location: Brunel Centre, Swindon.

programmes into their planning: Basildon town centre's Mother and Child fountain by Maurice Lambert (1959) has been adopted as the town symbol. Works by artists as varied as Henry Moore, Franta Belsky, Liz Leyh and others brighten the boulevards from Stevenage to Milton Keynes.

Present convention

The present-day practise of raising monuments remains basically unchanged, attended as ever by alarms and diversions, self-interest, and the simple desire to mark worth. Ceremonies once involving a cast of thousands now draw lesser crowds, not always with much pomp or glamour. At the unveiling of London's Seven Dials Pillar as part of the

William and Mary tercentenary celebrations in 1989, there were energetic street performers and a Balloon Ascension, but Queen Beatrice of the Netherlands, limply introduced by a Camden official, pulled the ribbon without a word.

The old pomposities would have marked the fine creation of architect A.D. Mason, engineers, astronomical consultant, construction workers, youth trainees and others in copying (to original plans) Edward Pierce's cream-painted Doric column, with blue and gold sundials, in 1984–9. Erected 1694 as part of Thomas Neale's property plan, scrapped in 1773, it was reconstituted as a Weybridge memorial to the Duchess of York in 1820. Camden's 'cheeky' request to Elmbridge District Council for its return, in 1987, was rebuffed forthwith.

Saving souls

The Seven Dials monument was claimed as the first London pillar to be raised since Nelson's in the 1840s. Many other statues and monuments have followed, among them the simple granite and Portland stone pier in St James's Square, erected by the Police Memorial Trust to WPC Yvonne Fletcher, heroine of the Iranian Embassy Siege in 1984. The Trust was formed after its present chairman, the film director Michael Winner, promoted the memorial to WPC Fletcher through a press campaign. Other deserving members of the police force have since been honoured, in London and elsewhere, by individual granite monuments based on George Cook's handsome design.

Memorials follow as a matter of course now after such catastrophes as the Lockerbie Air Disaster (1988), or the Hillsborough football tragedy of 1989. Police, fire, and other services are traditionally represented; lifeboat memorials mark willing valour along our coasts. The career of Superintendant fireman Howard Beckwith, killed in 1926 when his fire engine plunged off the parapet of Stockport Bridge, is recorded on a tablet: 'WELL DONE THOU GOOD AND FAITHFUL SERVANT'.

Near London Bridge, a marble tablet depicts the Great Fire of Tooley Street (1861). High on a wall of No. 33, the carving by S.H. Gardner commemorates London Fire Brigade's first Chief Officer, James Braidwood, killed on duty. He is said to have had the largest civilian funeral in Victorian England.

At Bexhill in Sussex, a lifesize marble figure of fireman Sydney Albert Wise is shown holding the firehose left-handed, recalling the theory that he fell to his death when a hose coupling dislodged a clutch

*'Flaming Heart' headstone. Stonemason: not known (1727).
Location: Burwell Churchyard, Cambridgeshire.*

on the telescopic ladder, which collapsed. His is one of many monuments raised in a local churchyard; amongst the most beautiful is the canopied effigy of Grace Darling, lying with her coble oar at Bamburgh in Northumbria; particularly poignant is a headstone at Burwell, near Cambridge, recording a fire in 1727 which killed 78 villagers and children at a puppet show in a barn. The stone with its plump, flaming heart was cleaned and recut in 1901.

Death and disaster

A gravestone is not strictly a public monument, which can be categorised, and even associated with certain types of dedication. Death and disaster go with Gothicky stone monuments, or the Celtic revival crosses such as that erected in 1904 near Brampton in Cumbria on the site of the 'Capon' tree from which were hanged six men 'for adherence to the Cause of the Royal Line of Stewart', in 1756.

The Marian martyrs, burned in the Protestant cause during Bloody Mary's reign of 1553–8, received many monuments in the Victorian and Edwardian period, some renewing earlier stones. Typically, these are based on the Eleanor or 'Celtic'

Crosses; or they may be small, churchy pillars in polished granite, as in Haverfordwest, Dyfed. Here was demonstrated the astonishing freshness of memory in which deeds long past, marked by public monuments, are popularly held. Asked for directions to the Balmoral-granite column (1912) marking the last public burning and commemorating William Nichol, 1588, a townsman remarked, 'that's old Bill Nichol you'll want'.

Good examples of this touching trait are the battle monuments, like 'Mortimer's Cross' in Herefordshire (restored 1988), which appears on the sign of the pub outside which it stands with its battle saga spelt in stone. These too are likely to have been erected centuries after the event, and some are the scene of regular re-enactments by historical societies. Others, predictably, attract the Heritage industry's worthwhile Interpretation schemes, as at the lonely roadside location marking wholesale carnage at the Battle of Hedgeley Moor, April 1464.

The old stones sited at 'Percy's Leap' are obscured by a large Interpretation Board in jarring colours, explaining the course of battle across the adjoining fields. Presented less brashly, these invaluable facts would preserve the joy of personal discovery and contemplation, whilst leaving this lonely site some dignity. It could be argued that any monument is an intrusion – but monuments, signalling public appreciation, tell their own story. It is a question of taste, for which there can be no arbiter.

Who claims this objet d'art?

Most monuments, once erected, promise potential embarrassment and shilly-shallying on the part of local authorities faced with problems of acid rain, traffic fumes and vandalism. Few towns have a proper repairs programme; the rot is met with varying colourful solutions, from another coat of cover-all paint to the scrap heap. Ownership of minor but distinctive works is consistently denied; at Tooting Broadway a proud bronze of Edward VII, by L.F. Roselieb, was encrusted with pigeon droppings until 1988, when it was cleaned in the face of a royal visit after being disowned in various corners of Wandsworth town hall. The borough's Amenity Services Department now answers for King Edward.

Jacking and spalling

Apart from pigeons and vandals, the main threat comes in weathering and pollution wherever corrosive metals are present, for example as supports within bronze castings or as clamps on stonework. Rusting can cause expansion and distortion (called jacking) and, thereby, extensive though superficial cracks (called 'spalling') in stonework. Faced with repairs costing thousands of pounds, many authorities understandably resort to 'laissez faire'; some simply remove the monument. One suspects that the images of large numbers of forgotten grandees have ended up as motorway infill.

Some provincial local authorities do effect expert repairs. William III in Hull, Britain's oldest obelisk at Ripon, Sir Robert Peel outside Tamworth Town Hall, the Wade Monument in a Cambridgeshire field, Queen Anne on her colonnade in Barnstaple, 'Eros' in London and many other monuments were refurbished in the 1980s. In Wisbech, Cambridgeshire, on the Gothic Clarkson Monument (by George Gilbert Scott), James Hackwood's worn sandstone relief, the 'Slave in Chains', is preserved and sealed but not renewed. Paul Guidici of Kettering, in a weather-protective Polythene cubicle, also conserved the other panels portraying contemporary anti-slavers

(these have kept their crisp detail). Any cleaning process is here considered a form of erosion, and the memorial is allowed to weather naturally.

London's maintainence programme involves regular repair inspection, described in his book *Steeplejacks and Steeplejacking* by William Larkin, who gave a fearful description of laddering Nelson's column in 1905 without spikes or nails, on instruction from the Office of Works, by means of ladders and slings. He negotiated the cornice near the top which, covered in an inch of soot, was 'probably the heaviest projection of throw-back work in the whole of Britain', by climbing up and over it with his back to the crowds on the ground 'like a fly on a ceiling'. The firm still sends men sky-high to inspect and repair; an unusual recruit in 1990 was the daughter of Reg Dosell, the present Larkins chief.

Many bronzes in the metropolis are maintained by a scheme dating from the 19th century, with regular coatings of lanolin wax to prevent repatination, which promotes pitting and corrosion. This has been criticised for losing original patina and

Martyrs' Memorial: to nine Protestants martyred between 1538–1555. Design: H. T. Edwards (1903, restored 1980). Location: Christchurch Park, Ipswich.

looking too uniform, but it is simple, inexpensive and protective, and is better than 'bronze' paint. Considered aesthetically if not practically, even livid-green verdigris, or honest soot, is better than paint.

Stones of contention

Despite all this, monument raising continues unabated. Amongst the most spectacular is Middlesbrough's £50,000 30ft, listing steel bottle-form, the brain child of Claes Oldenburg, who once also proposed the erection of a monster lipstick to replace 'Eros' in London. The bottle, representing Captain Cook, has been as contentious as other modern works in the city's extensive public collection.

Contentious also was Richard Cowdy's sculpture for Calne in Wiltshire, to mark the passing of its bacon factory (1979). A tree had been planted but repeatedly vandalised, and Cowdy's bronze low-level composition of wallowing, beatifically grinning pigs are claimed to be vandal-proof in shape and construction. Within living memory the red-brick factory, with stone pigs-head corbels and a carving of Circe (reputedly modelled by one of the early Sausage Queens) was the destination of pigs driven from the station through Calne, but not every townsman wanted this aspect of local history immortalised in the market place.

Rivalries and imbroglios

Following the Victorian tradition, the new municipal art excites local rivalries and imbroglios. In 1974 Robert Thomas's 7½ft bronze of 'a typical shopper', erected by the developers of a central Blackburn shopping precinct, caused a rumpus for lack of a wedding ring on the mini-skirted mother with baby. At Lewes, Sussex, 'Brian the Snail' – a £20,000 Portland stone Spiral Form sculpture by Peter Randall-Page, set at the Cuilfail Tunnel entrance – was burned in effigy at one of the town's stupendous, fiery 5th November rituals. William Redgrave's 'Call of the Sea', a bronze fisherman, was pilloried for posing violently outside Tuttles at Lowestoft, but also – far worse – for wearing a Cromer jersey.

More tactless still was Ivor Roberts-Brown's Portrait of the Artist donated to Fordingbridge by the Augustus John Society in 1974, when residents of this well-behaved Hampshire town were trying to forget their former illustrious neighbour's annoying foibles, manically mirrored in this marvellous bronze of John barefoot, bearded and misspent, lurching misanthropically across the municipal park.

The broader view

These brave new images combine with those of old to provide a brilliantly ill-balanced open-air view of national heroes of every shape and repute. Representation of national talent is erratic, there being no outdoor statue of Abraham Darby, ironmaster, whose discovery of coke-smelting made his Ironbridge works the *fons et origo* of the Industrial Revolution, whilst at Stockton-on-Tees, in 1977, Jose Sarabia was commissioned to make a bust of the town's most famous son, John Walker, the unassuming inventor of the match. Suffolk has a statue to the painter Thomas Gainsborough (1727–88), but none to his near-contemporary John Constable.

Dramatis Personæ

Royals, top brass, statesmen, local tub-thumpers, industrialists, philanthropists and reformers loom large in the national pantheon; science and the arts are less evident, and unevenly covered to boot. Shakespeare, Byron, Brooke and Housman are about the only major poets to get lifesize statues; Christopher Marlowe (1564–1593), playwright, gets Onslow Ford's adorable Muse (locally, 'Kitty Mar-

John Walker (1781–1859). Sculptor: Jose Sarabia (1977). Location: John Walker Square, near High Street, Stockton-on-Tees.

lowe') in the Dane John Gardens at Canterbury. Her stone support holds statuettes of Sir Henry Irving, who performed the 1891 unveiling, as Tamburlaine, and other figures of Marlovian actors added in 1928 by Ford's pupil Charles Hartwell. Stolen in the 1970s, they take the form of fibreglass copies by Ken Dixon of Hythe (1987).

An Onslow Ford muse attends the sculptor's memorial at St John's Wood in London; Sir Francis Chantrey's friend Philip Hardwick designed a sombre obelisk of Cheesewring granite (brought to Hull from Cornwall by sea) for the green at Norton near Sheffield, the great sculptor's birthplace; G.F.Watts's small wood-carved image adorns a City of London park; Henry Moore and Barbara Hepworth sculptures ornament their birthplaces Castleford and Wakefield in Yorkshire, and Hepworth's later Cornish home, St Ives.

Harlow New Town's market place statue of a young woman entitled 'Portrait Figure', bought in 1957, standing near Ralph Brown's bronze 'Meat Porter' (1960), looks like a brash and bonny stall holder but is in fact F.E. McWilliam's vigorous portrayal of the popular sculptor Elizabeth (later Dame Elizabeth) Frink: her bronze 'Boar', of the same period, and a Henry Moore 'Family Group', were vandalised, and removed from the Town Centre in 1988. A cast of Frink's statue stands outside the Herbert Art Gallery, Coventry.

Women's work

Monuments to women are not entirely rare; by women more so, unless one counts the public art of the late 20th century. Countess Feodora Gleichen (1861–1922) and Princess Louise, a daughter of Queen Victoria, made public monuments for Derby and Hyde Park, London, and in Kensington gardens, respectively. Frances Darlington's market square statue of Joseph Priestley (1912) stands in his native Birstall. Mary Thornycroft, daughter and wife of sculptors, and Mary Grant, also practised in the 19th century. A Miss Delahunt carved the stone war memorial at Westfield Village, near Lancaster, 1922; Lady Scott, later Lady Hilton Young, made expressive portrayals of individuals as various as Lord Northcliffe (bust, Fleet Street, 1930) and her husband Scott of the Antarctic, whose statues stand in London and Portsmouth.

Public statues to women are as unselective as their male counterparts, concentrating on royalty, medicine, social work and literature; obelisks or crosses to women are rare, despite the queenly

The Marlowe Memorial ('Kitty Marlowe'): statue and ensemble to Christopher Marlowe (1564–1593). Sculptor: Onslow Ford (1891, resited 1921, original statuettes added 1928). Location: Dane John Gardens, Canterbury.

Eleanor. At Wentworth Castle South Yorkshire (now part of Northern College), a plain obelisk commemorates Lady Mary Wortley Montagu, wife of the Ambassador in Constantinople, who was scarred by smallpox; she brought to England in 1720 the live serum method by which she had successfully innoculated her children, predating by over 70 years Dr Edward Jenner's pamphlet on cowpox serum. The Prince of Wales was said to have been one of many innoculated by live serum.

Children, understandably, appear rarely as public statues, and then from legend or literature (although Dorothy Wordsworth appears as a child on a fountain at her birthplace, Cockermouth). Fine renderings – apart from Peter Pan – include Goscombe John's 'Girl' in Llansannan, Clwyd (commemorating five male writers), and Rudyard Kipling's heroic band boys, Jakin and 'Piggy' Lew, the work of the 8th Earl of Albermarle, set outside the Council Offices in Woodbridge, Suffolk. Other striking portrayals, both by Frampton, include bronze figures of Lord Hailsham's protégés in Langham Place, London, and of children accompanying Dr Barnardo's privately-owned monument at Barking.

The private domain

Some fine outdoor commemorative monuments are on private land. Amongst these is Onslow Ford's marvellous study of General Gordon in his fez, on camelback: one cast is outside the Royal Engineers' Library at Chatham, and one at the Gordon Boys' School, Woking. A farm near Haverfordwest has a most stately monument (c.1918) featuring marble statues of an elderly farmer, born at the house in 1846, and his wife, who had no children but wanted their farm to remain in the family: it is now owned by a nephew. At Ryston Hall in Norfolk, home of the Pratt family, 'Kett's Oak' on its grand, twisted trunk carries a 19th-century tablet which replaced the original, dating from the period of Kett's Rebellion, 1549: *'Mister Pratt your Shepe are very fat ... We have left you the skynns To buy your lady pinnes ...'* Wymondham oak near Norwich is a better known, but lesser, specimen.

The Barningham obelisk (1872), put up on the grouse moor to celebrate a record bagging of 2070 was stolen in 1987 but returned in two pieces, and re-erected on the family's estate. G.F. Watts's equestrian statue of Hugh Lupus raising a falcon on his gauntleted wrist, can be contemplated on open days at Eaton Hall, in Cheshire. Lupus's *Gros Venator* (Big Hunter, root of 'Grosvenor') was modelled on a horse specially bred from a Percheron mare and an English thoroughbred; this was said to reflect the 3rd Marquis's twin passions, family lineage and horse breeding. The statue inspired Watts's final passion, his sculpture 'Physical Energy', sited in Kensington Gardens.

Other exotica

Race horses, the White Rabbit at Llandudno, an otter on Cardigan Bay, Misty the vixen at Stowmarket, various pet dogs, and numerous British Lions feature among other beasts in this unclassifiable collection, which in human terms represents all stages of social elevation from Queen Victoria to top-hatted Blind Joe the Bellman, his poor carved face eaten away, ever sounding his knell in an Oldham park.

It seems only human to immortalise the memory of the great and the good in the unsettling event of their mortality, and even more human to neglect or remove their monuments thereafter, or to utilise them as waymarks or meeting places. Some are put up as landmarks: *pace* Lord Collingwood's statue at Tynemouth. As time passes, the monument takes on its own identity and symbolism, often featuring in local myth; Queen Anne, and William III at Bristol, descend their pedestals at dead of night, but the most widespread story features a sculptor's *faux-pas* and resulting suicide.

Thomas and Hamo Thornycroft, father and son, are said to have got the spurs back to front on Prince Albert's equestrian at Wolverhampton, and Oliver Cromwell in Westminster, respectively; Rafaelle Monti supposedly omitted the horse's tongue from Durham's statue of Lord Londonderry (the tongue is visible through binoculars) – all lived productively after their statues' unveiling.

The fate of fame

A statue often takes on public significance contrary to original intent, as the world saw during the momentous events in China, Eastern Europe and South Africa, 1989–90. Massive statues of Stalin, Lenin and other Communist leaders were toppled; the Chinese students' plaster Statue of Liberty, created in Tiennanmen Square, was a potent symbol before hope turned to bloodshed; after President de Klerk announced the unbanning of the ANC, the British press portrayed a euphoric ANC supporter photographed astride the huge stone head of Jan Smuts. In 1956, Nelson's Pillar in Dublin was reduced to a neat pile by the IRA. A victim of the Great War was a statue of Albert, Prince Consort, which stood outside God's House Tower in Portsmouth and was smashed up by soldiers on leave because Albert was a cousin of the Kaiser.

The bronze and the passer-by

All these belong with the typical market square statue as part of a large, amorphous assemblage in which a small hawkish statue of Lord Nelson, marooned in a lily pond at the foot of Corby Castle's red cliffs, can be catalogued with Rodin's portrayal of Balzac, immensely powerful and energetic in its public presentation of the private man. One of 12 casts, this work of art occupies a corner of the office forecourt at the Kodak Headquarters, Hemel Hempstead. Its sprawling surroundings of roads, petrol stations and edge-of-town architecture merely heightens the sense of engagement between the anarchic vitality of the bronze and the passer-by.

Public art demands this engagement between the piece, the surroundings and the spectator. It is doubly appealing to see a statue in outline at the end of a street, and soon to confront a faint sneer or a grave smile, and to read history's assessment of the cloaked hero on the pedestal.

Any monument fancier should cross Hardwicke Circus roundabout at Carlisle, enter the central gardens, approach the foolish stone column — an overgrown hatstand carrying a St George — and confront, at the stone base, the moustached features of James Robert Creighton, local councillor and mayor in the 1880s, staring owlishly from behind wire-rimmed spectacles in a bronze roundel by the ever-expressive Lucchesi. This admirable Creighton brought water and gas to the town; his monument was erected two years after his death in 1896.

Meanwhile Admiral Burrard Neale's distant obelisk welcomes boats and ferries into Lymington harbour, whilst its immediate surroundings provide a site for picnics or courting couples, beneath the white, soaring stonework with its powerful Egyptian motifs, its iron plaques and fulsome inscriptions, gently mouldering in their grove of twisted oaks. The trees were planted at the same time as the foundations, and they and the big stepped obelisk on its mound (architect George Draper, builder George Banks) make the climb up Monument Hill worthwhile for anyone who appreciates a haunting location, stone carving, and the small ironies of local history.

Admiral Lord Nelson (1758–1805). Sculptor: not known.
Location: Corby Castle, Cumbria.

Bronze lion, one of a pair, overlooking south lawn at Kingston Lacy. Casting: by Comperot, c. 1850.
Location: Kingston Lacy, Dorset.

Sir Winston Churchill (1874–1965). Sculptor: Ivor Roberts-Jones. Location: Parliament Square.

London

The High and the Mighty

*'AN EXAMPLE TO HIS ORDER
A BLESSING TO HIS PEOPLE'*

(Part of the inscription on the Shaftesbury
Memorial Fountain (*Eros*), Piccadilly Circus)

London, capital city, the seat of government, royalty and the established Church, ranks effortlessly as statue capital of the nation; there are more statues per acre than in any city throughout the United Kingdom, immortalising royalty, military leaders, statesmen and other national or more shadowy figures.

Some are forgotten and best forgotten and some, like Ivor Roberts-Jones's frowning Churchill outside the House of Commons, make a unique fusion of local and national history. Others have a parochial presence, closely associated with buildings or localities the communities of which have long dispersed; the statue of Richard Green, ship builder, for example, on East India Dock Road, bears silent witness to a former local community. All were once illustrious names, nationally or in their neighbourhood, and together they form a distinguished company of mainly English heroes. London monu-

ments do not as a whole reflect glory on other parts of the Union.

Their monuments are distributed over Westminster, the City of London, Holborn or Bloomsbury, while others stand in the older localities at the edge of the metropolis, from Heathrow to Walthamstow.

Portrait statues prevail as the means of commemoration, obelisks and columns being few, although these make a vital contribution to London's marvellous variety which places the internationally-known sights of Eros and Nelson's Column in the same collection as the Panyer Boy, chubby cherubic infant, a small stone-carved high relief on the wall of Panyer Alley. For its collection of outdoor medallions and wall busts alone, London would stand apart from the rest of the country.

London's development over the centuries has created few vistas or set-pieces which make natural sites for display. The great names are parked, rather than presented, in squares or public gardens, on odd corners, and along some of the old processional ways. Some correspond with their surroundings in scale, the monumental buildings of Whitehall being matched by bronze military leaders on lofty pedestals, and – nearer Westminster – by the austere but subtly-curved planes of the stone Cenotaph.

But they also contrast with the more human proportions of Inigo Jones's Banqueting House opposite Horse Guards Parade, where a lead portrait bust of Charles I smiles meaningfully from over the main entrance. It was from a window of the Hall that the King stepped to the scaffold in 1649, as he said, 'from a corruptible to an incorruptible Crown, where no disturbance can be'.

This portrait, and others, are formal pieces, but their visual contribution to the townscape seems incidental, and although their companionable presence would be missed if removed, the passer-by might not necessarily be sure of what had altered. Even so London statues make a focus, forever caught in the same attitudes, telling a changeless story whilst the city around them imperceptibly changes.

Sovereigns or soldiers on horseback make familiar silhouettes when the sky turns ultramarine and buildings darken, the starlings gather and the city lights razzledazzle. In wet weather the dark bronze gleams, drops drip from noses and chins and from declaiming fingers, the reflections waver on the pavings. In strong sunshine the burnish brings out human qualities in a furrowed brow, a wing collar supporting a heavy jowl, or – as in David McGill's 1909 bronze of bushy-bearded Sir Wilfrid Lawson, temperance advocate, in the Embankment Gardens – a pair of spectacles suspended from the waistband.

This is true of any of our cities, but London allows the statue fancier to plot the development and sculptural conventions of public commemorative monuments from their gradual emergence in the 17th and 18th centuries, through surviving works representing sculptors such as Le Sueur and Cibber, Peter Scheemakers, and the great Rysbrack. Victorian sculpture is represented in all its phases, flowering with the stiff, accurately-representational works of popular mid-period sculptors such as Noble and Marochetti, and crossing into the 20th century with the less formal, more lifelike approach of Hamo Thornycroft, Onslow Ford, George Frampton, and other practitioners of the New Sculpture.

Sculptures on buildings and in public spaces show works of major calibre by Epstein, Moore, and Gill among others, and the lesser-known but always humanistic talent of post-war sculptors like Siegfried Charoux, whose 'Neighbours' are seated in rugged companionship on a small Highbury housing estate. London's casting of the famous 'Burghers of Calais' was originally sited, under Rodin's supervision, in the Victoria Gardens, Westminster.

These 20th-century sculptures emphasise the ornamental role of public commemorative monuments, dating in London from the late 14th-century statue of a 'King' known as King Alfred, London's oldest public statue of any size or prominence. Decorating Westminster Hall, it was removed and later installed as a free-standing figure in Trinity Church Square, Southwark, laid out between 1824–32.

Other early statues, such as the stone figure of Queen Elizabeth I (probably from Ludgate) at St Dunstan-in-the-West, Fleet Street, and that of her father Henry VIII in Smithfield, were made to complete the design of important gateways such as proliferate in medieval Oxford (with their original stone statues) and to a lesser degree in Cambridge.

London has no medieval market cross like the well-preserved examples at Winchester, or Chichester. The last of Queen Eleanor's crosses to be erected, where her cortège approached Westminster,

Elizabeth I (1533–1603). Sculptor: probably William Kerwin (1586). Location: St Dunstan-in-the-West, Fleet Street.

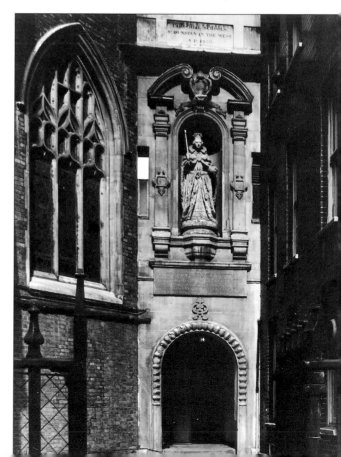

was destroyed in 1647. E. M. Barry's version of 1863, with statues by Thomas Earp, stands outside Charing Cross station. Copiously carved, it is a monument to a monument.

Charles II erected two important and moving monuments, amongst the earliest now surviving erected to commemorate an historic event. The 202ft Monument, designed by Wren (1671–7), marks the rebuilding of the City after the Great Fire, and is the predecessor of eyecatchers and belvederes that grace country estates throughout England. These were intended as adornments and also as commemorative gestures, some with a sharp political symbolism.

Charles II's commemorative zeal led him to purchase (for £1,600) the charming, charmed equestrian figure of his father, Charles I, which he installed at the top of Whitehall, on the site of the Regicides' executions carried out where Westminster's original Eleanor Cross had stood. Hubert le Sueur's piece of garden art, the Martyr King on his 'Horsse in Brasse', was commissioned in 1633 for the Lord High Treasurer's Roehampton estate, and it represents a step from decorative royal statuary towards commemorative statues erected as public declarations of personal and historical worth. Stuart supporters still lay wreaths on the anniversary of Charles's death (January 30th, 1649).

Other 17th- and 18th-century London statues are personal and decorative, standing in town squares with gardens, or domestic sites such as hospital courtyards and other buildings closely associated with the sculptors' worthy subjects. They are rare outdoor examples of commemorative work of the period; John Nost's lead statue of Sir Robert Geffrye on his Shoreditch almshouses is now in replica, but Scheemakers's bronze statue of Sir Thomas Guy, 1734, still stands at the entrance to his hospital. Sir Thomas is buried in the chapel.

Other early works anticipate the mid-18th-century convention first for presenting royalty, and later non-royal subjects, in Roman garb: this continued into the 19th century. C.G. Cibber's carved relief of Charles II on the base of the Monument shows the Merry Monarch in Roman military costume but parading the fashionable full-bottomed wig as first observed by Pepys in 1663. The fine bronzes of the King and his successor James II, presented by Tobias Rustat from Grinling Gibbon's workshops but thought to be the work of his assistant Arnold Quellin, are fully clad as Roman generals. Originally set up at Whitehall they show the brothers lean and haughty, laurel-crowned, muscles rippling under skin-tight armour.

Sir Joshua Reynolds (1723–1792). Sculptor: Alfred Drury (1931). Location: Burlington House, Piccadilly.

In the late 18th century the style was discussed by Sir Joshua Reynolds in his Discourse on sculpture: '. . . even supposing no other objection, the familiarity of the modern dress by no means agrees with the dignity and gravity of sculpture'. The sartorial style of this great portrait painter's own period was recreated in a fine bronze of Sir Joshua by Alfred Drury, 1931, showing the first president of the Royal Acadamy (established 1768) elegantly poised in the forecourt with palette and brushes, wearing his tie wig and tight-waisted, flared coat, knee breeches and hose, buckle shoes, and ruffles at neck and cuffs.

London's first non-royal statues to be set up in public places, dating from 1809 and 1816 and both the work of Sir Richard Westmacott, are classically draped, but that of the agriculturalist Duke of Bedford in Russell Square is lavishly endowed with putti, a plough, produce, farm animals and other rustic symbols. At the edge of Bloomsbury Square the bulky, thoughtful bronze of Charles James Fox, his toes protruding from sandals over a big, cuboid pedestal, reverts to the neo-classical.

A statue by Sebastian Gahagan of Queen Victoria's father the Duke of Kent appeared at the top of Portland Place in 1825, and was perhaps the first to combine all elements of commemorative outdoor sculpture as practised, at its peak, from the mid 19th century. A bronze statue with a smooth finish, it portrays a public (not a sovereign) figure in contemporary dress, with intricate detailing of medals and trimmings, elevated on a tall pedestal carrying a plaintive inscription; the work visible from the public highway. Statues of Nelson showing Westmacott's work in Liverpool and Birmingham predate this by a decade and more, respectively, but each forms part of an ensemble.

From this period, public commemorative sculpture has established itself as a minor art with history, quirks and conventions, all of which can be traced in the capital's monuments erected to our illustrious forbears in large numbers by the end of the 19th and the beginning of the 20th centuries, hardly at all during the world wars, and in appreciable numbers between-times.

London reflects the national trend with works by sculptors such as Sir Henry Moore, Franta Belsky, William Pye, David Wynne, George Segal, Karin Jonzen and many other postwar names, all accessible within a comparatively small circumference, some prominent, like Paolozzi's robot-like man incorporated into a new building in High Holborn, some more local, like Kevin Atherton's lifecast self-portrait 'On Reflection', in a Holloway park. Today's convention retreats from extolling the high and the mighty, in favour of 'ordinary', revolutionary, or colourful characters: John Doubleday's Charlie Chaplin, the familiar baggy-trousered clown, shares the limelight with Shakespeare in Leicester Square, and the monumental bronze bust of the great black African nationalist leader Nelson Mandela — then a political prisoner — by Ian Walters, unveiled by the African National Congress leader Oliver Tambo on the South Bank in 1985, powerfully stated the anti-apartheid commitments of the late Greater London Council, at the same time as Mandela's own more urgently expressed: *"The Struggle is my life"*.

Sculptors' and critics' preoccupations with style come down from early statues like those of Sir Francis Chantrey (1781–1841) who favoured minimal ornamentation and a high pedestal, to the informal presentation of statues like Oscar Nemon's 'Monty' in Whitehall (1980), standing at ease in battle fatigues and beret, supported on a low wedge-shaped plinth. The architectural critic, Gavin Stamp noted that the plinth supporting Franta Belsky's 'stiff

and wooden' figure of Lord Mountbatten, erected near Horse Guards Parade in 1988, 'has all the interest of an upended shoe box'.

In this he prolongs the tradition of colourful carping practised since the early days (not always so well-informed), when Punch printed doggerel, it seemed, about each new statue, including Matthew Cotes Wyatt's representation of George III in Cockspur Street. Originally commissioned in 1822 it was much vilified, even before its erection in 1836. The King's hurrying figure appears in contemporary dress, his pigtail tied in a bow and his horse with a sharp, swishing tail. (The old surroundings have given way to early 20th-century buildings.)

George III's favourite sculptor John Bacon fared no better with an earlier statue of the King classically draped, languidly leaning on a ship's rudder and accompanied by a lion and Father Thames, erected at Somerset House. It provoked Queen Caroline's famous remark 'Why did you make so frightful a figure?' to which Bacon replied 'Art cannot always effect what is ever within the reach of Nature — the union of beauty and Majesty'.

Even Chantrey got cold feet about the pedestal for his statue of William Pitt in Hanover Square, writing in 1831 to Sir John Soane, 'is it high enough, or too high?' But he threatened to resign his commission rather than reduce the height. Like so many, this has been declared 'the best statue in London'.

Amongst the worst — and cheapest, according to Gleichen — is a Sicilian marble figure of Richard Cobden, subscribed at £320: 'Napoleon III was the principal contributor'. The statue was raised on the old turnpike near Camden Town in 1868, three years after Cobden's death, and less than a decade after his efforts in Paris had checked another French war.

Unlike most other regions, London can define as a group its portrayals of women. Apart from Sarah Siddons and Boadicea, most made their mark in social reform. They include Florence Nightingale, Mrs Ramsay MacDonald and the prison reformer Elizabeth Fry (1780–1845), whose medallion portrait balances that of John Howard over the entrance to Wormwood Scrubs prison.

Even more unusual as a grouping is that of foreign nationals whose names have crossed world boundaries. Presented by their respective countries, mostly the United States, they also include the statue of the Venezuelan born liberator Simon Bolivar, in superbly detailed uniform; Gandhi cross-legged in Tavistock Square, and the Emperor Haile Selassie, a stone-carved head and shoulders, on Wimbledon Common. At Gray's Inn, a relief head of Sun Yat Sen (1866–

'Jété'. Sculptor: Enzo Plazzotta (1975). Location: Millbank.

1925), 'Father of the Chinese Republic', was lost during the Blitz.

There is a sizeable collection of outdoor sculpture, prominently sited, like Wendy Taylor's Sundial near Tower Bridge (1973) or the smooth, stainless steel, ever-popular Zemran by William Pye (1972), near the Festival Hall. A beautiful representational work, 'Jété', by Enzo Plazzotta stands outside a residential terrace overlooking the Thames on Millbank. Just north, opposite the Tate Gallery, Sir Henry Moore's 'A Locking Piece' overlooks the brown Thames.

Some prestigious names have works tucked into corners, including Elizabeth Frink's Blind Beggar and his Dog, her first public commission (1957), in a Bethnal Green housing estate. A Frink horse with its nude male rider emerging from Dover Street into Piccadilly conveys the idea of the relationship between man and horse, explained the sculptor, which 'is primitive in essence'. It seems also to remind us of man's place in his environment.

London's multifarious animal statues include E. Bainbridge Copnall's rearing aluminium stag in Stag Place, Victoria, and two small, hugging bears on a drinking fountain at Marlborough Gate, Kensington Gardens. Favourite curios include Shakespeare's painted head and shoulders idly leaning out of a

niche from a pub in Foubert's Place, and at Blackfriars on the Arts and Crafts pub The Black Friar, the friar himself; in a corner at Horse Guards Parade is a fiery bronze dragon, part of the Cadiz Memorial, supporting a massive mortar 'cast for the destruction of that great port with powers surpassing all others'. Presented in 1814, this frightful creature is still crisp in detail.

London shares with the provinces fate's wilful disregard for balance, erecting as many statues of soldiers and sailors, or of statesmen or royals, as of practitioners from all the arts combined. Explorers, the medical profession and religious figures come next, scientists last. Jenner and Lister appear in statue and bust respectively, and an image of Joseph Priestley by Gilbert Bayes (1914) appears over the Royal Institute of Chemistry entrance in Russell Square.

Big frowning stone portrait heads of illustrious chemists including Priestley, and early directors, line the third storey of ICI on Millbank. There is no statue of Michael Faraday, nor of James Watt, but Euston Station features Robert Stephenson by Marochetti, now dramatically silhouetted against a glass and concrete block. Richard Trevithick's bronze relief profile by L.S. Merrifield was fixed to the wall of University College, Gower Street, in 1933, the centenary of the great mining engineer's death.

Dr Johnson expiates outside St Clement Danes, his oddness and exuberance recreated by Percy Fitzgerald, but too loosely modelled to show the characteristic shabbyness of his wig, its front permanently singed by candle flame. Pepys appears in Seething Lane Gardens as a bronze by Karin Jonzen (1983), but other London chroniclers, such as John Stow or Dickens, are not represented by statues, nor is Pepys's fellow-diarist John Evelyn. He claimed to have introduced the wood carver, Grinling Gibbon to Charles II and to Wren.

This unevenness, repeated in all the varying groups, confirms the pleasing idea that a monument is raised not because Jones has one but because Smith is thought to deserve one. It recalls the time-honoured inscription on Sir Christopher Wren's monument in St Paul's: *Si monumentum requiris, circumspice* ('If you would see his monument, look around you').

Deserving   or   undeserving,   'frightful'   or handsome, London statues like their provincial counterparts add vitality to the streets and squares. If the nation's notables were to melt in the sun – as George Bernard Shaw wishfully imagined on seeing the Prince of Wales carved in butter at the Wembley Exhibition – one might tire of London, and of life.

Inner London Gazetteer

The West End

West End Feature:

Anthony Ashley Cooper, 7th Earl of Shaftesbury
(1801–1885); the Shaftesbury Memorial Fountain
Bronze fountain on stepped base: octagonal main
basin with corner basins supported by figures of
mer-babies and fishes, surmounted by octagonal
base with decorative corner fountains, carrying
aluminium figure *'Eros'* on a conch shell
Sculptor Alfred Gilbert RA
Location Piccadilly Circus

The statue of *Eros* is world famous, a sight and
symbol of London. The aluminium archer flying
over the tiered bronze fountain with its sinuously-
intertwining water forms shows the extraordinary
talents of Alfred Gilbert as innovative artist and
metalworker *par excellence*.

It is typical of the sculptor's fascination with
symbols and fantasy that the work should commemorate a much-loved reformer through a mythi-
cal image, in this case Anteros God of selfless love
(but commonly known as 'Eros', God of Love). It is
a demonstration, too, of fate's unsteady hand in
selecting dedicatees for monuments, since *Eros*,
world-famous, recalls no warrior hero or momentous

*'Eros', part of Shaftesbury Memorial fountain. Sculptor: Sir
Alfred Gilbert (1892). Location: Piccadilly Circus.*

*Bronze horses, moquette for part of fountain, Sculptor: Rudy
Weller (c.1991). Planned location: Piccadilly Circus.*

national event, simply the politician and his unceasing crusade on behalf of the disadvantaged in Victorian England. He was illustrious in his day, but only the more zealous will cross the street now to read the reforming name 'Shaftesbury' on the inscription, which was composed by a political rival, W.E. Gladstone.

The work was unveiled in 1893, eight years after Lord Shaftesbury's death and seven years after completion of his marble statue in Westminster Abbey by the influential sculptor J.E. Boehm. It was Boehm who recommended his pupil, Alfred Gilbert, to the memorial committee headed by Lord Grosvenor. Gilbert's repudiation of 'coat and trousers' statuary resulted in a monument to Shaftesbury's philanthropic works as well as his name, and as Gilbert insisted, 'rather than the glorification of his tailor'.

A master craftsman, Gilbert revived the 'lost wax' method of casting, using it on Eros to achieve sharper definition of outline and detail. He worked closely with the founders, George Broad & Sons, on the fountain and its winged, mercurial figure, the first ever to be cast in aluminium. The statue's wing feathers were separately created, expertly joined and finished by the sculptor himself.

The immediate result seemed to be a costly failure. The committee had caused technical and design hiccoughs by ordering drinking facilities for man and beast; council regulations required Gilbert to add a parapet, a job he entrusted to his lifelong friend, the architect Howard Ince; Boehm's lifesize bust of the earl was added to provide a figurative dimension (it was soon removed, and the inscription relocated); the government did not after all provide gun metal, and Gilbert had to buy the copper for the base of the fountain. After the unveiling, the decorative drinking cups were vandalised and all disappeared inside a week.

The memorial strikingly displayed Gilbert's unsettling imagery and his fascination with contrasting materials and colours, but where a gallery audience might have acclaimed its artistry, to the man in the street and the newspaper letter-writers, the green-and-gold patinated fountain was 'a dripping, sickening mess', whilst the silvery, speeding archer's semi-nudity provoked outrage. Gilbert, unstable and brilliant, was wounded, and thereafter his career was beset with money and delivery problems. Later (1901) he was to retreat, discredited, to Bruges, and ten years after Eros, he was suggesting a new way of helping the poor: 'Why not pull down the whole work, and reduce it to copper ...?'

The irony of raising a costly ornament to a champion of charity – the perennial dilemma of memorial committees – was not lost on the public. And there were other contradictions: in the nickname Eros; in the spent arrow or 'buried shaft' which Gilbert variously declared was, or was not, a pun on the name 'Shaftesbury'; and in the 'impossible site', Piccadilly, chosen only as a lesser evil than Cambridge Circus (created when Shaftesbury Avenue was cut through between 1877–86).

Despite these vicissitudes, the flying figure of Eros has become part of London and of England. It was absent in the world wars, also during construction of the Piccadilly Line station, and for its own restoration in 1986. This was carried out for an Edinburgh firm by the sculptor-caster George Mancini, whose father had assisted the 'beautiful craftsman' Gilbert on the original sculpture. After this complicated and costly enterprise, Eros should now last for another 100 years – Mancini having suggested annual polishing with linseed oil as the best form of maintenance.

The memorial can still cause dispute. English Heritage reportedly accused Westminster Borough Council of mishandling after the £1 million restoration, and art experts argue, as ever, that Piccadilly is too tacky a site for such a jewel. However, it can be argued that tackiness was the lot of Lord Shaftesbury's raggle-taggle followers, London's chimney sweeps and ragged-school pupils, Shoe Shine Brigade and Barnardo Boys and Peabody-homers, in whose cause 'our earl' was reduced to living on borrowed money, and whose company he preferred to that of his social or political peers. Lord Shaftesbury was indeed 'an example to his order', but his privilege lay in the values he received, as a neglected child, from a family servant who reared him as her own.

His funeral was attended by people of all 'orders', one floral wreath bearing 'the loving tribute of the flower-girls of London'. The flower girls remain only as a memory and Lord Shaftesbury's name has faded in time but Piccadilly Circus and Eros are inseparable in their fame.

Note: Meanwhile the most outré modern plan for Piccadilly has been Claes Oldenburg's proposal to erect, in place of Eros, a giant extending and retracting lipstick, its mechanism to be driven by the tidal Thames. Wildly differing from the 'coat and trousers' image, this does recall Gilbert's sense of the fantastic.

A less fearful scheme adopted by private developers in 1990 will raise a team of mettlesome horses in bronze composition, part of a fountain by Rudy Weller, originally intended to crown the roof of the

£170 million neo-classical Criterion development at the top of Haymarket. A similarly spirited nude who was to have driven the horses from a *quadriga* will still occupy the heights. Admirably, the deal includes daily cleaning and maintenance. This farsighted, sensible and cost-effective arrangement is still largely overlooked by planners and monument committees outside London. Perpetuation of a symbol, it seems, is more important than the preservation of its physical form.

West End Selection

Long before it was a symbol of West End junketing, Piccadilly Circus – then Regent's Circus – was a pivotal point on the majestic route planned by John Nash from the Regent's park via Portland Place to Carlton House, the Prince's palace in St James's Park. In 1956 a replica of William Behnes' marble bust of John Nash was erected just outside his lovely

John Nash (1752–1835). Sculptor: William Behnes (replica, 1956). Location: All Saints Church, Langham Place.

circular, colonnaded porched church, All Saints in Langham Place.

From here, with a sardonic grin, the great town planner surveys what is left of his design as Regent Street traffic rumbles past to Oxford Circus, the route intact, the Regency buildings sacrificed to 1920s commercialism. Like Gilbert, Nash (1752–1835) saw his and others' designs altered or curtailed; Henry Holland's Carlton House was pulled down in 1826, soon after completion of the plan, and Nash's design for Carlton House Terrace was begun in 1827. *Listed below* are some of the statues to be seen along the route, most erected after Nash's time.

Monuments to the Prince Regent's brothers, the Dukes of Kent and York, stand at either end. The Duke of Kent has a conventional bronze statue, perhaps the first, erected in the 1820s in Park Crescent at the top of Portland Place. The regal stance and pudgy Hanoverian features reflect in countless studies, nationwide, of the Duke's daughter Victoria, many made for her 50th and 60th Jubilees, and after her death in 1901.

The most unusual and appealing statue here, at the continuation of Portland Place into Langham Place, is the bronze group featuring Quintin Hogg (1845–1903) by the creator of Kensington Gardens' Peter Pan, Sir George Frampton. Like Gilbert, Frampton was a brilliant exponent of Art Nouveau who could also deliver an effective commemorative portrait. This one has the founder of The Regent Street Polytechnic seated, poring over a book with two of his protégés in knitted pullovers, one boy with a football under his arm. It dates from 1906 and has an added inscription to Quintin's wife Alice, described by their grandson, Lord Hailsham as 'a Scots Presbyterian and a saint'. A third tribute goes to polytechnic members lost in both world wars.

In Langham Place, carvings by Eric Gill on the novel BBC building of 1932 brought outrage with artistry. Like Epstein's nudes of two decades earlier on a Strand building, now Zimbabwe House, the BBC's entrance statue of Prospero and Ariel was pruned to accord with public decency (some would say mutilated in the face of public prudery). Just south, over a convent entrance at its top end, Cavendish Square has Epstein's much-loved Madonna and Child in dark lead (1950–52).

At the southern end of the route is Waterloo Place, with broad stairs descending to the Mall from the Duke of York's Tuscan column which augments the view of St James's Park along Lower Regent Street. Sir Richard Westmacott's statue of 1831–4, his last recorded commission, and the column by

Benjamin Wyatt, were paid for by docking a week's wages from each soldier in the British army, commanded by the Duke (who was profligate, inefficient and popular with his men) from 1798.

The Grand Old Duke of the nursery rhyme now commands a gracious parade ground for bronze statues of old soldiers, assembled between 1866 and 1915 against tree-shaded railings lining Waterloo Place between the column and Pall Mall. At centre-street stands an equestrian bronze of Edward VII in Field Marshal's plumes, made by Sir Bertram Mackennal and unveiled in 1921 after long arguments over a suitable site. At the Pall Mall crossing a bronze statue of Florence Nightingale by A.G. Walker, and her hard-pressed champion Lord Herbert of Lea (J.H. Foley), flank John Bell's monument to the Brigade of Guards at the Crimea (1860), a heavy-handed ensemble of soldiery and cannon which, wrote Lord Gleichen, 'looks its best in a fog'.

In her long, arduous career as Crimea veteran, army reformer and mother of British nursing, Florence Nightingale (1820–1910) encountered many crusty old campaigners whose statues now stand in Waterloo Place (or elsewhere in London). Sir John Lawrence, whose statue by Boehm was erected here in 1882, was appointed Viceroy of India only after consultation with Miss Nightingale, who instructed him on the Indian sanitary question before he sailed. General Sir John Burgoyne, however, after Sydney Herbert's death in 1861, remarked that Lord Herbert's 'hobby was to promote the health and comfort of the soldier and his pet was Miss Nightingale'. Burgoyne's bronze as Field Marshal, also by Boehm, was unveiled in 1877.

During her bitter struggle to break away from 'the petty grinding tyranny of a good English family', Florence took rooms in Pall Mall; her father habitually sought refuge in Waterloo Place, in Decimus Burton's Athenaeum with its bust of Pope by Rysbrack (1730), and its gilded Pallas Athene over the external entrance. Next to the Athenaeum is Matthew Noble's stiff bronze of the explorer Sir John Franklin (1856); the pedestal lists the names of his company who 'forged the last link with their lives' in discovering the North West Passage. A relief panel minutely relives the commital of Franklin's body to the ice (1847), one sailor shielding his grief with an arm across his eyes.

Franklin's statue contrasts with Lady Scott's free-modelled image of her late husband, Captain Scott, in Antarctic attire, the famous words from his last diary entry on his pedestal: 'Had we lived I should have had a tale to tell of the hardihood and endurance

and courage of my company which would have stirred the heart of every Englishman'. His statue was erected in 1915.

In the 19th century the Prince Regent's grand route must have made gracious contrast with the surrounding web of West End streets. Their leafy squares were laid out with gardens and perhaps a statue, the scale domestic and intimate. The 17th- and 18th-century buildings have been replaced, whilst the statues themselves bear witness to grand schemes gone awry; Charles II in Soho Square was part of a gorgeous fountain, and it is claimed that the painted lead figure of George II by the younger John Nost, in Golden Square, Soho, was acquired at auction from Canons, the palatial Edgeware mansion of the Duke of Chandos, on an ill-timed nod.

George appeared here in 1753, and almost a century later Dickens in *Nicholas Nickleby* described 'a mournful statue, the guardian genius of a little wilderness of shrubs'. No matter how mournful, however, a statue brings zest to a town square; an animating presence by day, at dusk or during winter its persona takes silent possession of the deserted gardens.

St James's Square near Piccadilly has a regal bronze equestrian statue of William III (1650–1702), but only after decades of procrastination, the pedestal awaiting fulfilment in an ornamental pond. In 1837 a bequest was unearthed from Samuel Travers for a statue 'to the glorious memory of my master, King William the Third'. Cast in 1808, it is the work of John Bacon Junior, but thought to have been designed by his father. They included the mole hill which tripped the royal horse at Hampton Court, breaking William's collar bone and inducing a fatal fever, the inspiration of the Jacobite toast: 'to the little gentleman in velvet'.

St James's is the West End's earliest square c.1660. (Leicester Square was laid out in 1670.) A resident, the Princess of Wales, on her birthday in 1748 'uncovered' an equestrian statue of George I, modelled c.1716 by C. Burchard, assistant to John Nost the Elder who cast and gilded it, originally for the Canons estate. In the 1850s it was reputedly buried beneath the Great Globe, one James Wyld's answer to the Great Exhibition, but was later reinstated, with the horse lacking a leg. An 1866 engraving shows the Elector of Hanover with a dunce's cap and bezom on a polka-dot nag, paint and props by courtesy of the Alhambra.

The square's present appearance dates from its replanning of 1874 by the bogus 'Baron' Grant who placed at its centre Fontana's large, bad, marble

William Shakespeare (1564–1616). Sculptor: not known.
Location: 29 Great Marlborough Street, London W1.

The Mall to Whitehall

Mall & Whitehall Feature:

Horatio, 1st Viscount Nelson, Duke of Brontë
(1758–1805)
17.5ft Craigleith stone statue surmounting Devon
Granite fluted Corinthian column (height from
steps to capital, *c*.150ft); Bronze gun-metal
capital, and reliefs on granite stepped base;
Bronze lion at each corner
Designer William Railton
Statue sculptor Edward Hodges Baily RA
Panel sculptors M.L. Watson, W.F. Woodington,
J. Ternouth, J.E. Carew, supervised by Sir Richard
Westmacott and C.L. Eastlake
Lion sculptor Sir Edwin Landseer RA
Location Trafalgar Square

The most famous and glorious of monuments, Nelson's Column was completed in 1842, almost 40 years after the Battle of Trafalgar. The statue of Nelson in full dress uniform, made from three stone blocks, was raised in November 1843. In 1840 Charles Barry had submitted his scheme for the completion of Trafalgar Square, planned by John Nash after slum clearance in the 1820s at the historic crossroads of Charing Cross. The square had acquired its name by 1830.

Barry feared that the planned column would dwarf the National Gallery (1832–8, by William Wilkins), but objected too late. The Nelson Memorial Committee was already set up and an appeal fund launched (1838, decades behind England's other major Nelson monuments), the competitions were held and selections approved (E.H. Baily in 1840 submitted designs for an obelisk with symbolic figures); the site was granted, the column's proposed height reduced for public safety, the concrete foundations laid down.

Thus, almost a quarter of a century after the project was discussed in Parliament in 1818, England repaid her venerated hero according to his epic triumphs in establishing Britain's naval supremacy in the Mediterranean, and in the eyes of the world. Since the fateful Battle of Trafalgar, and thanks to the 'Nelson touch' in earlier sea battles against France and her allies, Britannia ruled the waves and was to do so throughout the Empire-building Victorian era. This was also the period when statue-building approached its zenith, and London's *penchant* for displaying the images of worthy citizens might well

copy of the Shakespeare statue by Scheemakers in Westminster Abbey, with busts of noted residents by various sculptors at each corner. A century later, the Royal Fine Art Commission pompously advised against siting a bronze statue, 'however good', of Sir Charles Chaplin (1889–1977) in the same square as that of Shakespeare's, whilst petitions were made against any monument to Chaplin, on grounds of his reputed communism.

Planning consent came through on the 91st anniversary of Chaplin's birth, and at a later refurbishment of the square the bronze by John Doubleday was brought into a more central position. Doubleday's caricature style suits Chaplin's famous image of the saggy-trousered, sad-eyed clown tenderly clasping a rose against a pigeon chest. The Bard (his lighting and fountain restored) would most probably approve.

Admiral Lord Nelson (1758–1805). Sculptor: Edward Hodges Baily (1843). Location: Trafalgar Square.

Part of Nelson's success was his ability to inspire loyalty and courage among the people, as those serving below decks were known. His captains, fully briefed before battle on every conceivable eventuality, were encouraged to take individual initiative, no matter how unorthodox; the commanding admiral's objective, annihilation of the enemy line, could thereby be pursued with lethal decisiveness and speed. In this way Nelson, when a subordinate, had built his own reputation.

The vigorous panel reliefs cast from captured French guns, each by a different sculptor, were attached in 1849–52. M.L. Watson's facing the Mall, completed after his death in 1847, shows Nelson after the Battle of Cape St Vincent, 1797, accepting the defeated Spaniards' swords aboard the *San Josef*. Acting against orders Nelson, then a Commodore, had captured two prizes by the unprecedented method of boarding a second enemy ship from one already taken.

His men on this exploit included several of his 'old Agammemnons', and it was from this ship in 1794, during an assault on the Corsican port Calvi, that Nelson's right eye was blinded. His right arm was lost after the St Vincent success, on a buccaneering adventure off Tenerife. The following summer (1798), during the Battle of the Nile, Nelson received a head wound and is depicted in W.F. Woodington's north-facing panel refusing preferential treatment: 'No, I will take my turn with my brave fellows'.

Raised to the peerage soon after, Nelson lost favour with George III through an undisguised affair with Emma, wife of his friend and host Sir William Hamilton, British Minister at the Neopolitan Court. The King of Naples, however, made him Duke of Brontë (1799).

The east-facing panel by J. Ternouth shows Nelson sealing a dispatch to the Crown Prince of Denmark after a protracted gun battle at which, as the Danes were flagging, Nelson's Commanding Admiral signalled withdrawal. Putting his telescope to his blind eye, Nelson declared 'I really do not see the signal', and went on to win the Battle of Copenhagen (1801). Four years later, he achieved his *ne plus ultra* at Trafalgar. The death scene on the fourth panel is the work of J.E. Carew.

Nelson's statue faces the Admiralty, where the hero lay in state after arriving by funeral barge from Greenwich. Forty seamen from the flagship *Victory* hauled his carriage to St Paul's Cathedral, where he now lies directly under the dome in the sarcophagus intended for Cardinal Wolsey before his fall from

have been encouraged by Nelson's Column in its spacious setting – Sir Robert Peel thought it 'the finest site in Europe'.

The scale of the monument reflects Nelson's prestige and achievements, but not his physical presence. Like his adversary, Napoleon, he was 5'2" tall. It is said that he could not swim, and that he suffered from seasickness. The familiar, elevated silhouette of the Admiral of the Fleet, with sword and cocked hat, gives a proper impression of a commanding presence, whilst close detail conforms to Nelson's love of epaulets, ribbons and medals. His prominent features stare starkly from the stone. The original model is on view in the Admiralty building (by arrangement).

grace. Nelson's body is preserved by the same mixture of rum and sweet wine in which his *Victory* carried him home.

The four great bronze lions guarding the foot of Nelson's column were modelled on a lion from London Zoo, which died, leaving the sculptor Sir Edwin Landseer to rely on plaster casts, photographs and hurried studies (as recorded by Benedict Read in his *Victorian Sculpture*) – or on the paws of a family cat (according to London lore). A painting in the National Portrait Gallery is claimed to show Landseer modelling lion no. 3 at Marochetti's studio; Read says, with the sculptor's tool wrongly positioned – but Landseer after all was an animal painter by profession.

Commissioned in 1859 by the Prime Minister the Earl of Derby, they were installed in 1867, long after completion of Barry's square with column, fountains and other bronzes. Four smaller stone lions by Thomas Milnes at Saltaire near Bradford, Yorkshire, are said to have been intended for Trafalgar Square. The poet and civil servant Humbert Wolfe (d.1940) preferred them: '... they have all of Africa under their paws and they guard, not the No 24 Route to Tottenham Court Road, but the No 1 Roadway to Samarkand'.

The Mall & Whitehall Selection

As well as being on the 24 bus route, Trafalgar Square is part of the royal processional way from Buckingham Palace along the Mall, under Admiralty Arch and down Whitehall to Westminster. The Victoria Memorial in front of the palace is part of a commemorative scheme in which Sir Aston Webb refaced the palace, reorganised the space outside its gates, broadened Charles II's Mall, and erected, in 1911, Admiralty Arch at the far end. The Queen's statue was carved from a single block of marble by Thomas Brock, who was knighted by George V immediately after the unveiling in the presence of the German Emperor.

Completed in 1911, Brock's opulant ensemble is now a superior roundabout, but still attracts picnickers and sightseers, whilst Benedict Read has called it 'in its way one of the supreme achievements

The Victoria Memorial: statue and ensemble to Queen Victoria (1819–1901). Architect: Sir Aston Webb. Sculptor: Sir Thomas Brock (1911). Location: Outside Buckingham Palace.

of the New Sculpture'. It works as a focal point along the broad Mall, or close-to where the wealth of decorative stone carving and idealised figures can be admired.

The huge marble statue of Victoria is enthroned beneath a gilded figure of Victory on a high pedestal. On either side stand Truth and Justice, whilst Motherhood sits facing the Palace. Against this dazzling white marble are Brock's other statues and groups in dark bronze, also representing noble ideals such as Progress and Peace, or sterner concepts like War and Shipbuilding. On the outer wall of Aston Webbs's balustraded, circular podium, are bronze or marble reliefs of mermaids, naiads and tritons, and masks spouting water jets.

Typically, small details loom large, including the pliers carried in the apron belt of 'Manufacture' with his lion, or the Queen's wedding ring worn on her right hand out of deference to beloved, German-born Albert. Her beaky nose, vandalised and replaced for the Duke of York's wedding in 1986, has yet to weather and stands out like a sore thumb. Other sculptors, Sir Alfred Drury and F. Derwent Wood, carved ornamental figures for the tall stone gateposts at exits from the roundabout.

Monuments set up along the Mall to Westminster are of particular interest and variety. In Marlborough Gate, near St James's Palace, is Sir Alfred Gilbert's bronze Art Nouveau wall fountain to his friend and patron Queen Alexandra, erected 1932, the water symbolising Alexandra's charity to children. It was Gilbert's swan song after exile in Bruges.

On the shrubby corner of the Mall is Sir William Reid Dick's pleasant portrait medallion of Queen Mary (d.1953) in tiara and pearl choker, with words finely chiselled on a slate surround. A handsome architectural setting in Carlton Gardens has a bronze statue by William McMillan of the diffident monarch, George VI. At the unveiling of 1955, George's daughter Elizabeth II recalled him as 'the living symbol of our steadfastness' in the last war.

Near Admiralty Arch is a bronze of Captain Cook (1728–1779), also the work (1914) of Brock; one unseamanlike foot is placed on a coil of rope, but the eloquent inscription makes up for this sculptural *faux pas*. Around Trafalgar Square a variety of immortalised heroes accompany Nelson's Column, most with a nautical or military history. Busts of medal-encrusted Admirals at the top of the square were provided by Franta Belsky, and by Sir Charles Wheeler and William McMillan whose bronze figures, mermen and mermaids respectively, animate the fountains designed by Lutyens in 1939.

The one-time Lord High Admiral James II, lean and sardonic in Roman armour, was sited outside the National Gallery, after years of neglect, as 'a temporary measure' in 1947. The Ministry of Works lauded the public accessibility of the site, but a *Times* leader doubted whether 'the convenience of being able to inspect a work of art without even getting off the bus leads to keener appreciation'. This fine statue from Grinling Gibbon's workshop is matched by a replica bronze 18th-century statue of the first American President George Washington, by Jean Antoine Houdon, placed to the east of the gallery steps in 1921; the State of Virginia also donated a ton of earth, in respect of Washington's vow never to set foot on English soil.

James II is billed on his pedestal as King of England, Scotland, France and Ireland. In the square itself (southeast corner), General Havelock's pedestal proclaims:

"SOLDIERS!
YOUR LABOURS
YOUR PRIVATIONS
YOUR SUFFERINGS
AND YOUR VALOUR
WILL NOT BE FORGOTTEN BY
A GRATEFUL COUNTRY"

Other pedestals are occupied by Lord Napier near Havelock's statue, on the southwest of the square, and by George IV on London's first figure of a static horse. The King's dithering over choice of a pose caused the sculptor Francis Chantrey to compromise. His bronze statue in semi-classical garb, intended for Nash's Marble Arch, was later placed here 'temporarily' on a typically-high Chantrey pedestal; its companion at the square's northwest corner has yet to be filled, and is the subject of sporadic speculation which might well inflame the correspondence columns if a candidate were put forward.

In St Martin's Place is the Cavell Memorial of 1920 showing Sir George Frampton's pallid stone portrait statue of Nurse Edith Cavell (1865–1915) with his colossal sculpture of Humanity Protecting the Small States (a woman and child) towering above. It was unveiled before angry and tearful crowds soon after Nurse Cavell's execution for assisting the escape of British and Allied soldiers whilst serving as Matron in a Brussels hospital at the onset of the Great War.

Her famous avowal, 'Patriotism is not enough ...' was added later but considered jingoistic, although her words were recorded by the prison chaplain from whom Nurse Cavell received the Sacrament, and with whom she repeated the words of the hymn

*Cavell Memorial: statue and ensemble to Nurse Edith Cavell
(1865–1915). Sculptor: Sir George Frampton, RA (1920).
Location: St Martin's Place.*

Abide With Me on the eve of her execution by firing squad. She declared that her treatment in prison had been kind: 'I expected my sentence and I believe it was just'.

South of this monumental reproach, at the top of Whitehall, stands Hubert le Sueur's engaging bronze equestrian statue of Charles I. It was fixed with grim irony by Charles II at the site of Edward I's Eleanor cross, torn down by Puritan parliament decree to 'a great shoute of People with ioy', as inscribed on a contemporary etching; later the regicides were

cruelly punished here, and since 1675 Le Sueur's work has silently proclaimed the Jacobite cause.

The statue was commissioned from Charles I's sculptor by the Lord Treasurer Baron Weston for his Roehampton garden: 'The saide Sueur' was directed to 'take the aduice of his Maj. Ridders of great Horsses, as well for the shaepe of the Horsse as for the graesfull shaepe and action of His Maj . .' This Le Sueur did, seating the king bare-headed, long-booted and in demi-armour, on a Flemish horse with arched neck and long knotted tail. The date of completion appears around the left forehoof: HVBER LE.SVEVR [FEC]IT 1633.

The statue's sale to a local brazier for scrap in the Civil War, its apparant transformation into trinkets and souvenirs, its reappearance and its restoration, belong to London lore. The ornamental Portland stone pedestal, with the Royal Stuart arms, was made by Joshua Marshall, master mason to the Crown.

From its vulnerable traffic-island site, the horse trots towards Banqueting House, Whitehall, which was built by Inigo Jones for Charles's father James I, and adorned by Charles with ceiling paintings by Rubens. Later, a plaque records, the king 'passed through this hall and out of a window' to the scaffold. His lead bust, staring out of a niche over James Wyatt's entrance, was one of three salvaged from a Fulham builder's yard by the Secretary of the Society of King Charles the Martyr. Presented and installed in 1950, it neatly fuses local and national history.

The long stretch of Whitehall and Horseguards provides a proper parade ground for statues of Britain's top brass, bellicose veterans of 19th-century colonial campaigns, and their successors whose names still ring familiar from the World Wars: Field-Marshals Kitchener and Haig; Earl Mountbatten; and in April 1990, unveiled by HM the Queen outside the Ministry of Defence, Field Marshal Viscount Slim (1891–1970) in his bush hat, a companion for Oscar Nemon's bronze, rough-modelled 'MONTY' (1887–1976) in the familar beret. Slim's bronze, typical of the work of its creator Ivor Roberts-Jones, was commissioned by the Burma Star Association; both subject and sculptor won the Burma Star. The inscription is carved by David Kindersley.

The later bronzes shown standing, some bare-headed, make amusing contrast with the earlier equestrian figures of grim old Field Marshals in their extravagent headgear, the best of which is Adrian Jones's archetypal portrayal of the Duke of Cambridge (1819–1904). Greatcoat flying, supremely arrogant and peppery, he trots briskly down Whitehall near Horseguards, whilst Field Marshals

Roberts (1832–1914) by Harry Bates (1924), and Wolseley by Goscombe John (1920) flank Horseguards' Parade arch; their dates of birth and death coincide to within one year, and between them they patrolled the Victorian Empire from Ireland to Tel-el-Kebir.

Booted and spurred, moustaches bristling on stiff upper lips and war wounds concealed under braided uniform, all three seem to epitomise the Wolseley family motto, *Homo Homini Lupus* ('Man is a Wolf to Man').

A contrast is the bronze of Clive of India (1912) with pigtail and high boots, commanding the stairs that descend from King Charles Street to the park; his pedestal reliefs have intriguing cameos with titles ('Clive in the Mango Tope on the Eve of Plessey, June 22 1757'), and he gives the scene an atmospheric touch. His creator John Tweed, another military sculptor, also made the statue of Lord Kitchener (1926), on Horseguards' Parade.

On Whitehall's approach to Westminster, in counterpoint to the military men, the Cenotaph by Sir Edwin Lutyens makes its plain statement of loss and remembrance at the centre of the street. This too was placed here temporarily, in plaster cast, for the Victory march-past of 1919 led by Marshal Foch whose fine equestrian statue, a cast taken from Malissand's bronze in France, stands in Grosvenor Gardens at Victoria.

The Portland stone Cenotaph, installed the following year as the nation's memorial 'To the Glorious Dead', is one of four by Lutyens to be erected after the Great War. Its altar shape, symbolising sacrifice, represents the empty tomb erected in ancient Greece to honour a warrior who fell overseas and who had no burial place at home. Carrying no identifyable effigy, this was considered by many the most fitting monument to Britain's stupendous losses in the War to end all Wars.

Westminster

Westminster Feature:

Queen Anne (1665–1714)
Full-length stone statue on ornamental bow-fronted pedestal
Sculptor Not known
Location Queen Anne's Gate

'More comely than majestic' was Smollett's idea of Queen Anne, and despite the small crown and the

Queen Anne (1665–1714). Sculptor: not known (c. 1707). Location: Queen Anne's Gate.

sceptre and orb, the Collar and George of the Order of the Garter, and the ermine mantle over a ruffled, brocaded gown, so the good Queen appears in this and other stone-carved statues commemorating her eventful reign. Protestant-reared daughter of James II, and younger sister of Dutch William's Mary, Anne succeeded to the throne following the outbreak of the war of Spanish Succession in 1702, to preside over Marlborough's devastating and brilliant campaigns, which concluded in the Peace of Utrecht of 1713, and a period of national stability and expansion. (Although by 1711, Marlborough had been removed from his command.)

At a time when Britain's two-party political system was emerging, Anne actively involved herself in affairs of State, choosing ministers from Whig or Tory party according to preference and finally resisting the influence of her childhood friend and confidante Sarah, Duchess of Marlborough and supporter of the Whigs, over a period of bitter disaffection. In her personal life she suffered with fevers and gout, and was shadowed with the loss of all but one of her numerous children in infancy. Her son the Duke of Gloucester lived for nine sickly years. Her statue by Francis Bird in front of St Paul's Cathedral inspired the rhyme:

> Brandy Nan,
> You're left in the lurch,
> Facing a gin bar,
> Your back to the church.

Wren's cathedral was completed in Anne's reign, an 'Augustan Age' so-called, in which the London literati included Dryden, Pope and Swift, and architects created majestic piles such as Vanbrugh's Blenheim Palace near Oxford, Anne's gift to Marlborough after the famous victory. Anne herself preferred the great outdoors, avoiding London theatres and neglecting the court for the turf; she was described at the Windsor Stag Hunt in Swift's *Journal to Stella* as a portly figure in a close-fitting one-horse chaise, driving 'furiously, like Jehu'. Her statue's setting of graceful town houses, first planned partly as a square, was created in Anne's reign (*c*.1704) and the statue known to be sited by 1708.

A generous patron of the Church, Anne was charitable to her old soldiers and to the poor, and continued to pay her late husband's servants 'providing they kept no public houses'. She was not clever or witty, but was single-minded and obstinate. In her last years she was accurately, though spitefully, described by the Duchess of Marlborough as 'exceeding gross and corpulent'.

Statues of Queen Anne were erected throughout England as decoration, and to celebrate her reign. This one, its back left rough as if intended for a niche, appears in Hatton's *New View of London* (1708) against the east wall of Queen's Square. It now stands outside No.15, where the old wall divided the square from Park Street on the east – or Abbey – side until 1873. A former resident of Queen Anne's Gate, then the Master of the Worshipful Company of Gardeners, presented the statue (rather run-down) to the Company who gave it to the nation in 1974.

Despite changes of ownership and of surroundings the queen's statue, so it is said, persists in stepping off its pedestal at dead of night to patrol the street. The houses with their odd keystone heads, some grimacing and some smiling, are no longer family dwellings, and the children are gone who pelted the queen with missiles and shouts of 'Bloody Mary' when she refused to do this in the daytime.

Westminster & Victoria Selection

Other statues in Victoria and Westminster also have a quiet, more domestic setting, but the best known are the Parliament Square set, bronze statues of politicians and statesmen who directed momentous national events from the Victorian expansionist era to Churchillian bulldog days of the Second World War. They inhabit the green opposite the Houses of Parliament, isolated by London traffic.

The pre-1939 statues number four Tory politicians (Canning, Lord Derby, Disraeli and Peel), with Palmerston representing the Whigs, and Abraham Lincoln the outsider; the absentee, Gladstone, stands aloof in the Strand, and the square has no Socialist. Like Disraeli's, Lincoln's gaunt features make a striking portrait. The statue, standing in front of the Presidential chair, is a replica of that in Chicago by the French-born sculptor Augustus Saint-Gaudens.

Benjamin Disraeli (1804–1881). Sculptor: Mario Raggi (1883). Location: Parliament Square.

Disraeli's statue of 1883 by Mario Raggi is decorated with primroses on his birthday. Canning's, by Sir Richard Westmacott, toppled over in the studio and killed one of the Gahagan brothers (Vincent) who was working on it in 1832. Matthew Noble's statue of Peel (1876) was cast from one by Marochetti, which was rejected and melted down. Lord Derby's, by Noble (1874), has exceptional pedestal reliefs, in deep perspective like stage sets, showing the House of Commons interiors before the fire of 1836, and before its rebuilding by Barry and Pugin, whose designs included the present astonishing wealth of detail inside and out. The prolific carving was superintended by Barry's protégé John Thomas.

Churchill's vaguely-contorted bronze bulk at the front of the square, recognisable as the work of Ivor Roberts-Jones, conveys the menacing but reassuring persona which with the growl, the cigar and the V sign became a constant image of the war years. His overcoat flaps around him and he leans on a stick; like Epstein's tilted figure of Smuts further back — is the Field-Marshal on roller skates? — the image hints at human weakness as well as strength.

The sculptor was selected after a limited competion and the site facing Big Ben was Churchill's choice. As she had on other occasions, his widow objected, provoking letters to *The Times* which included the *cri de coeur* 'a man is best remembered by his acts'. The statue was floodlit after various requests, including that of a local beat policeman who thought it proper.

At time of writing, the Fountain Society has applied for planning permission to install on Parliament Square a Royal Fountain in tribute to Her Majesty Queen Elizabeth II. Designed by William Bertram working closely with HRH Prince Charles, its central sculpture, a bronze unicorn with gilded horn and coronet, will be supported on a 25ft plinth of Balmoral rock centred on a raised circular pool. An elaborate system of water jets, illuminated at night, will enhance the sculpture by James Butler RA, winner of a limited competition held in 1989. Construction and maintenance will be the subject of an Appeal fund. (At present, however, London Transport also have plans to use the square when building an extension of the Jubilee Line, in which case the Parliament Square Set is likely to be disturbed for some time.)

Historical characters near here include Marochetti's bronze equestrian statue of 'RICHARD COEUR DE LION', corseted in chain mail and unveiled in 1860 in Old Palace Yard; the cost of

Richard I (1157–1199). Sculptor: Baron Carlo Marochetti, RA (1860). Location: Old Palace Yard, Westminster.

over £3,000 and the pedestal at £1,650 was paid by Parliament. Oliver Cromwell, shown 'warts and all' by Sir Hamo Thornycroft, was presented by the Liberal leader Lord Rosebery in 1899 for the 300th anniversary of Cromwell's birth. The Lord Protector's potato features have been strengthened and the hair thickened, but this bronze is probably the most thoughtful public statue of Cromwell. (Others stand in St Ives, Cambridgeshire, Warrington, and Wythenshawe Park near Manchester.)

Exactly across the street in a small niche is a bust of Charles I, 'this man against whom God hath witnessed', according to Cromwell. Charles was buried with dignity at Windsor but Cromwell's body, after the Restoration, was retrieved from Westminster Abbey to be hanged at Tyburn, and his head displayed outside Westminster Hall near the present site of his statue. Just southward stands George V (1865–1936), bareheaded and in Field-Marshal's robes, by Sir William Reid Dick, Sculptor in Ordinary to the King. His stone statue on a high pedestal by Sir Giles Gilbert Scott RA was unveiled by George VI in 1947.

Another rebellious character, disrupter of parliamentary debate, was Mrs Pankhurst (1857–1928), whose bronze statue stands at the entrance to the Victoria Tower Gardens. She suffered imprisonment and hunger strike for the Suffragette cause but is portrayed by A.G. Walker RA in a modish fur-trimmed coat (1930). A graceful profile of her daughter, Dame Christabel, was added in 1959, when the ensemble took the site of Rodin's famous 'Burghers of Calais' – this casting came down off its impossibly-high pedestal (the sculptor's choice in 1914) and now occupies the centre of the gardens. Its present low plinth recalls a *Times* letter quoting Rodin's disapproval of the Calais original's low base '"aussi disgracieux que superflu"'.

In the southwest corner of the gardens, formerly in Parliament Square (1865–1949), is S.S. Teulon's Buxton Memorial Fountain, a broken down Gothic fantasia holding statuettes of historical figures and described by Arthur Byron as 'magnificently ugly and complete with dog bowl'. Pevsner, on the other hand, calls it 'pretty' and describes it as 'a little house of stone, with some enamel-work'. (Nearby, *see* a pretty, white stone seat and fountain carved with sheep, typical modernistic London work 'Erected for the children' by the Harry Gage Spicers in 1923, but now sadly dilapidated.)

Westminster's best architectural sculptures, by Sir Jacob Epstein, Henry Moore, Eric Gill and others, are integrated into the design of the London Underground headquarters near St James's Park and Queen Anne's Gate. Most conspicuous are Epstein's 'Night' and 'Day' which sit low over the street, whilst horizontal relief figures of the winds appear on high. Like other Epstein work in London, 'Night', a mother passing her hand across her child's eyes (but bordering on the grotesque), was tarred and feathered for being too extreme after the sculptures' début in 1929. Unlike gallery art their contours, lit by day or street light, change with the hours and seasons; they are a far cry from Queen Anne's statue, but they too add zest to the street and to the architecture's flat planes.

Chelsea

Chelsea Feature:

Thomas Carlyle (1795–1881)
Bronze seated statue on polished pink granite pedestal
Sculptor Joseph Edgar Boehm RA
Location Cheyne Walk (Embankment Gardens)

An intense figure looking every inch the Sage of Chelsea, brooding over the Embankment and the river, his life starkly contained on the pedestal: 'Thomas Carlyle. Born Ecclefechan. Died Cheyne Row'. The historian and essayist sits cross-legged with his overcoat reaching his ankles, hands clasped in his lap, his books stacked beneath the chair. Directly north, along Cheyne Row, his frowning portrait head in a decorative surround announces

Thomas Carlyle (1795–1881). Sculptor: J. E. Boehm, RA (this cast, 1882). Location: Cheyne Walk.

No. 24, where he and his wife, Jane Welsh Carlyle, 'spent our two and thirty years of hard battle against Fate'.

The house was purchased by public subscription 14 years after Carlyle's death, and has received visitors ever since. It is cared for by the National Trust. The stone portrait over the door was designed by C.F.A. Voysey, and modelled by Benjamin Creswick, protégé of John Ruskin who was an admirer and visitor.

The Carlyles moved with a maidservant to 'unfashionable Chelsea' from Scotland in 1834, carrying their goods and chattels and a canary through Belgravia in a Hackney carriage. The son of a stonemason, Carlyle was by then a man of letters, a learned teacher and tutor, but still impoverished and ignored; it was said of him at the time that no man knew so much, or had seen so little. His wife of eight years was the dutiful and hard-pressed housekeeper, with a knack of attracting and entertaining distinguished friends and neighbours. Her own brisk wit, clarity of expression and vivid, descriptive writing are evident in facsimiles of her letters, displayed with those of her husband in the Attic Study.

This clever and difficult pair lived here in aggravated concord for the rest of their lives. After hard beginnings, Carlyle completed and published his history, *The French Revolution* (1837), which received unexpected acclaim and was to bring him and his later works lasting renown. Earlier, to relieve their poverty, friends had arranged a series of lectures for Carlyle, whose odd but expressive style of delivery, and individualistic ideas − the former lapsing into broad Annandale speech when the latter gripped him with special passion − brought him enthusiastic audiences 'composed', as he reported, 'of mere quality and notabilities'.

Carlyle's influence and prestige as writer, critic and historian, his vociferous, doomy outlook and singular appearance, and Jane's *conversazioni* brought distinguished friends and admirers to Cheyne Row. Visitors included Dickens (who drew inspiration from *The French Revolution* for his *Tale of Two Cities*), Tennyson and Darwin, the revolutionary Mazzini (an admirer of Jane), and their neighbour, the painter, Leigh Hunt.

In a particularly testing moment, John Stuart Mill had to be consoled after his tearful confession to the accidental burning of Carlyle's only manuscript for the first volume of *The French Revolution*. With Jane's support − the housekeeping spent and the original notes destroyed − Carlyle eventually overcame this monumental setback, and began anew.

The house is full of pictures, some original furnishings and personal mementoes. The living room where Carlyle first worked, where Mill confessed, where friends and followers were entertained and where Carlyle was to die, has a plaster head of the writer by John Tweed, and other relief portraits by Boehm and Woolner. The least changed room is the Attic Studio, built to free the cantankerous Carlyle from various street annoyances, including a neighbour's 'demon fowls'. Here over 12 years he wrote his lengthy biography of Frederick the Great, hindered by unforeseen river noises and the same street sounds scarcely reduced by the new arrangement.

Carlyle would probably have scorned such memorials as the house, and the statue of which castings can also be seen in Edinburgh and in his birthplace, Ecclefechan; this was unveiled by the donor's granddaughter, a great-great niece of the Sage, in 1929. The Arched House where Carlyle was born has Boehm's original terracotta maquette modelled from life (1875), showing the same hunched figure, but formally suited with waistcoat and wing collar. The house belongs to the National Trust for Scotland.

Carlyle's Chelsea statue was unveiled in 1882, at a time when his friend A.J. Froude was writing his four-volume biography which was to cause uproar by its un-Victorian frankness. In 1883 Froude also published Jane's letters, given to him by Carlyle after her shattering and sudden death in 1866 which effectively brought Carlyle's writing output to an end.

In his biography, Froude records Carlyle's remark: "If I had been taught to *do* the simplest useful things, I should have been a better and happier man. All that I can say for myself is, that I have done my best". Most people, whatever their particular ability, would find this an acceptable epitaph.

Chelsea Selection

Ranging in rarity and scale, monuments along this reach of the Thames are rewarding for their local associations. They include, near Carlyle's statue, a lamp post ornamented with athletic cherubs and the names of Sir Joseph Bazalgette, Chief Engineer, and his Chairman of the Board of Works, who began work on the Chelsea Embankment in 1866. It opened in 1874, the year before Carlyle's 80th birthday. In Roper's Gardens on the site of Epstein's studio, a slab of warm stone carries an unfinished Epstein nude relief figure, unveiled by Caspar John, son of Augustus, in 1979. Nearby is Gilbert Ledward's 'Awakening', a nude carved in stone. His beautiful

Charles II (1630–1685). Sculptor: Grinling Gibbon's workshop (1676). Location: Chelsea Hospital.

bronze Venus Fountain (1953) stands in busy Sloane Square.

'Roper', Sir Thomas More's son-in-law, laid out the Gardens on the site of More's orchard. Outside Chelsea Old Church, which Sir Thomas improved, is an unusual seated bronze showing Henry VIII's Chancellor with gilded face and hands, and the chain of office resting on his knees (1969). The sculptor L. Cubitt Bevis included More's signature on the base, and on the stone pedestal are carved the words, SCHOLAR: STATESMAN: SAINT.

Sir Hans Sloane (1660–1753), buried in the churchyard (his monument by Joseph Wilton), left chained books for the church and the Chelsea Physic Garden for botanical study; his marble figure in 18th-century dress by Rysbrack stands in replica at its centre. Sir Hans, physician, naturalist, historian and collector, endowed the gardens in 1722, and in 1733 his statue was ordered 'With grateful Hearts And general Consent' by the master and wardens. Erected in 1737, the original is on loan to the British Museum, which was largely founded on Sloane's collections.

Charles II founded Chelsea Hospital, laying the foundation stone in 1682, and ten years later his excellent bronze statue, presented by his servant Tobias Rustat in 1676, was erected in the central court of Wren's colonnaded building. Like its companion statue of James II, sited outside the National Gallery, it is from Grinling Gibbon's workshop and shows James (when Prince) in Roman armour, sombrely handsome. The hospital still shelters old and disabled soldiers, and on Oak Apple Day (Founder's Day, May 29), when the pensioners receive double rations, Charles's statue is wreathed with oak leaves.

Between here and Westminster are other statues with a garden or courtyard setting, some with medical associations, the most rewarding group sheltering against the massive new frontage of St Thomas's Hospital, along the north wing terrace. The weather-bitten, 'restored' but charming stone statue of the hospital's founder, Edward VI, was made for Nathaniel Hanwell's gateway of 1682 by the hospital's contractor, Thomas Cartwright the Elder. (His four small stone figures of crippled patients which stood on the old gate now stand in the Hospital entrance).

Next in line is a marble statue of Sir Robert Clayton, Lord Mayor, carved by Grinling Gibbon in Clayton's lifetime (1709). It shows the munificent President of the Board of Governors in his periwig, with a small pigtail. Peter Scheemakers's bronze of Edward VI, after Holbein's portrait at Kensington Palace, was originally erected for the hospital treasurer, Charles Joye in 1737, when the hospital still stood in Southwark.

All were associated with the Southwark premises, displaced by railway building in 1860, when Florence Nightingale's approval of the present Albert Embankment site was sought — and given after characteristically thorough research. A bronze statue of Lady and Lamp, by Frederick Mancini, was stolen in 1970 and later replaced in composite at the end of the row. It accords with the popular notion of the nurse, 'devoted and obedient', which Miss Nightingale in her booklet *Notes on Nursing* (1859) stated might do for a horse, but not for the more taxing moral and practical demands on a Nightingale nurse.

At this time, as ever against opposition, she founded the Nightingale Training School at St Thomas's, intended to turn out nurses capable of training beginners who were then having to learn nursing skills on the ward. No Nightingale statue shows her grit and practicality, but she refused to sit for artists in any medium apart from the sculptor John Steell, whom she met and liked. His bust made from two sittings, completed in 1862, is now at Derby Art Gallery; the National Portrait Gallery has a replica. Miss Nightingale was the first woman to receive the OM, delivered as she lay uncomprehending and in decline, three years before her death at 90 in 1910.

Close to St Thomas's, on a big bow-fronted pedestal at the northeast corner of Westminster Bridge, is W.F. Woodington's massive Coade Lion which 'stood from 1837 on the parapet above the river front of the Lion Brewery', survived the Blitz, was removed when the site was cleared for the Festival Hall and was 'preserved in accordance with the wishes of His Majesty George VI'.

Woodington modelled this admirable lion in 1837 for William Croggan, who had taken over the artificial stone works of Coade & Sealy in 1813; the Lambeth factory was founded by Eleanor Coade (another redoubtable woman) c.1769. She, her nephew and later partner John Sealy, their successors and a team of well-known artists including Rossi and Flaxman, can be thanked for crisply-preserved ornamental and commemorative Coade stone sculptures throughout England.

Victoria Embankment

Embankment Feature:

Cleopatra's Needle (c.1500 BC)
68½ft pink granite obelisk on 18ft base and steps;
19ft bronze sphinxes on either side
Sphinx designer G.J. Vulliamy
Modeller C.H. Mabey
Location Opposite Savoy Place

London gives space to parks and wildernesses but not to formal townscapes, so there is no satisfactory site for our oldest and most exotic monument. Cleopatra's Needle was brought to England in 1877

and erected on the newly-constructed embankment, with big stone steps descending to the ebb and flow of the tidal Thames. It is now a famous landmark on the riverside dual carriageway linking Westminster with Blackfriars.

The obelisk was quarried at Syrene, and set up by Pharaoh Thothmes III at the third Sed-festival in Heliopolis. This is recorded, with Thothmes's oblations and petitions, by hieroglyphic inscriptions in the centre of each face. Rameses II later carved his victories along the needle's sides. The Roman Emperor Augustus Caesar brought it to Alexandria, 'the Royal City of Cleopatra', and raised it seven years after his defeat of Anthony and Cleopatra in 30 BC.

Bronze plaques on each face explain the inscriptions, and give a partial account of the needle's

Bronze Sphinx, part of Cleopatra's Needle ensemble.
Design: G. J. Vulliamy; Modeller: C. H. Mabey (1882).
Location: Victoria Embankment.

history between the time of Thothmes's Heliapolis c.1500 BC and Queen Victoria's London, where it was erected in 1878, the 42nd year of her reign. The male sphinxes, cast by H. Young & Co, copies of basalt sphinxes from Thothmes's time, were added in 1882.

Like Ozymandias, the obelisk lay 'prostrate for centuries on the sands' before discovery in 1801 by Sir Ralph Abercrombie's troops, who wanted it for a trophy having repeated Nelson's rout of the French. The base stone was hollowed out for the Earl of Cavan, and a tablet recording principal events of the campaign was sealed within. Transport of the 186-ton obelisk proved impossible, however, and by 1819, when the Viceroy of Egypt presented it to Britain as 'a worthy memorial of our distinguished countrymen Abercrombie and Nelson', the base stone had vanished.

The plaque facing the river lists the names of six seamen who perished whilst assisting the crew of *The Cleopatra*, which was towing the lead-encased Needle to England 'through the patriotic zeal of Erasmus Wilson F.R.S.'. The ship met with a storm in the Bay of Biscay and the obelisk was abandoned, but was recovered and at last erected 'on this spot' by John Dixon, set in a bronze sheath designed in the Egyptian style

An array of objects sealed into the pedestal included Dr S. Birch's official translation of the hieroglyphics, written on parchment; several translations of the Bible, and the Hebrew Pentateuch; a *Bradshaw* and a *Whitaker's*; a pipe, a shilling razor and portraits of Victorian England's 12 prettiest women, together with one of Queen Victoria. These curios are contained in earthenware jars.

London is rich in Roman sites but this is her bit of Ancient Egypt — companion obelisks stand in New York, Paris, and in Rome. Few other outdoor monuments in England or Wales combine as many known commemorative and symbolic gestures; even the big sphinxes have a plaque marking bomb scars from the First World War. (*Note*: Also over Sotheby's, No. 34 New Bond Street, the lion-head and shoulders of Sekhmet, war goddess carved in diorite c.1320 BC; discovered on Waterloo Bridge after an antiquary sale in 1835, she was purchased for the selling price, £1, and has been the firm's mascot ever since.)

As for the Viceroy's grand gesture, this was forgotten 20 years later when he was causing trouble over the Dardanelles, and Palmerston was threatening to 'chuck Mehmet Ali into the Nile'. Improved relations were evident when in 1979 an Arab businessman anonymously contributed towards cleaning Cleopatra's Needle, to reveal the mellow pink of ancient Syrenian stone.

Embankment Selection

Thothmes, Rameses and Abercrombie may be shadowy figures to most passers by, but no more than the once-illustrious citizens assembled along the Victoria Embankment, from Westminster to Blackfriars, as bronze statues or busts. They feature on the anonymous green spaces behind Whitehall, and in the public gardens behind the Strand. Like the RAF war memorial with its golden eagle, a few accompany Cleopatra's Needle on the river side of this long stretch, across the dual carriageway that divorces the rest of London's north bank from its 'liquid 'istory'.

Over 25 monuments have been erected since 1871, following completion of the Victoria Embankment. Their marvellous variety of typical styles are encompassed between Blackfriars Bridge, where a sound portrait bronze of Queen Victoria (1893) by C.B. Birch faces the City, and Westminster Bridge, where Thomas Thornycroft's heroic group of Boadicea and her daughters ride their scythe-wheeled chariot under the shadow of Big Ben. Their monument begun in the 1850s, but not completed until much later, was unveiled in 1901.

Matthew Noble's statue of General Outram, a hero of Lucknow (1871), was first to appear behind Whitehall. General Gordon was moved here from Trafalgar Square in 1953. His sculptor, Sir Hamo Thornycroft, son of Thomas, also made the statue of Cromwell at Westminster, another portrait of a maverick leader. The full-length bronze of 'Chinese Gordon' recalls the 'strange and single-minded hero' recorded by G.M. Trevelyan; Thornycroft gives us the meditative soldier. The statue was erected in 1888 three years after Gordon's death at the hands of Sudanese rebel forces during the Fall of Khartoum, which had provoked public outrage and a sense of martyrdom. Pedestal reliefs represent Fortitude and Faith; Charity and Justice.

These, and other Victorian statues sited here, make interesting contrast with those of Air Marshals Viscount Trenchard and Portal, key figures respectively of the First and Second World Wars, by William McMillan RA (1961) and Oscar Nemon. Portal's rough-textured figure, 1975, looks fixedly skyward from a wedge-shaped plinth.

Quirks of sculptors and their subjects are best appreciated in the Victoria Embankment Gardens, a favourite being the Imperial Camel Corps Great War Memorial (1920), between the brass band platform and the tea kiosk. Major Cecil Brown's small-scale statue shows a soldier on camelback, the pedestal carrying a roll of names, and relief scenes of desert battles against Turkish troops in Egypt, the Sinai and Palestine.

Further along is a bronze head and shoulders by Goscombe John of the neatly-bearded, diffident Sir Arthur Sullivan, collaborator with W.S. Gilbert in the Savoy Operas but also composer of 'Onward Christian Soldiers' and 'The Lost Chord'. He is looking steadfastly ahead. The semi-naked muse draped melodramatically against his pedestal was modelled in Paris between 1890–9, and added as an after-thought. Voted 'the most erotic statue in London', it has inspired the rhyme:

> Why, O nymph, O why display
> Your beauty in such disarray?
> Is it decent, is it just,
> To so conventional a bust?

Lines by WS Gilbert are cut into the pedestal:

> Is life a boon?
> If so it must befall
> That death when'er he call
> Must call too soon

A new monument near here, marking the centenary of the Savoy Theatre which was built for Gilbert and Sullivan, is formed from a stainless steel globe with the couplet:

> Every season has its cheer,
> Life is lovely all the year

A bronze bust of W.S. Gilbert, who died attempting to save a drowning woman, is mounted on the river wall near Hungerford Bridge. Dating from 1913, it is one of three in this area made by George Frampton (1860–1928), its backing panel bearing Gilbert's family arms, figures of 'Tragedy' and 'Comedy', and other decoration with a distinctively art nouveau flavour. Frampton's signature also appears, mysteriously, on the edge of a classically-ornamented bronze wall plate above a drinking fountain by Basil Champneys, near Sullivan's monument. This has Mary Grant's medallion portrait of the blind Liberal Postmaster General, Henry Fawcett (1833–1884), and was erected in 1886 'by his grateful country-women' – the lettering in Arts and Crafts style.

This small incongruity is a feature of the gardens, which aspire to elegance but are endearingly seedy. The dedicatees' vocations and professions come as variegated as the sculptural styles. The poet Burns has a large, treacly statue (1844), by Sir John Steell; the political philosopher John Stuart Mill, who

Sir Arthur Sullivan (1842–1900). Sculptor: Sir William Goscombe John, RA (1902). Location: Victoria Embankment Gardens.

loomed large in Carlyle's fortunes is thoughtfully seated in a bronze of 1876–9 by Thomas Woolner; the novelist Sir Walter Besant, 'Historian of London', appears bushy-whiskered and bespectacled in an informal Frampton bust. Brother-in-law of the Theosophist Annie, Besant founded the Society of Authors (1884) and inspired the foundation of the People's Palace at Mile End.

A monument closely associated with the river is the 17th-century York Water Gate, attributed to Sir Balthasar Gerbier the architect of York House, which stood on the river bank. Erected in 1626, it shows influence from the Fontaine de Medici in the Luxembourg, Paris, c. 1624. It survives near the Victoria Embankment Gardens' band stage and, like 'Queen Mary's Steps' near General Gordon's statue, shows the width of the river before the Embankment's construction. The lions *couchants* are the work of Nicholas Stone.

The Embankment is as much a monument to its creator, Sir Joseph Bazalgette, as St Paul's Cathedral is to Wren, but Sir Joseph has a wall bust (near Samuel Plimsoll's decorative panel with bust) by F.V. Blundestone, 1929, in a desolate stretch opposite

Northumberland Avenue. Chief Engineer to the Board of Works, Bazalgette was ordered to repair centuries of river pollution after the hot summer and Great Stink of 1854, which had severely discomfited the House of Commons.

As his dedication recalls, FLVMINI VINCVLA POSVIT (he placed the river in chains) by creating London's sewerage system and laying out the Embankments, richly augmented with seats (given by W.H. Smith in 1873) and the famous dolphin lamps. Cast-iron figures supporting the seats are possibly the work of C.H. Mabey who modelled Cleopatra's sphinxes. Westminster's seats have sphinxes, the City has camels (shamefully dilapidated), and across the river at Lambeth are swans. A firm in Queen Anne's Gate sells reproductions — at a price.

Bazalgette (1819–1891) was knighted in 1874 and his bust installed in 1899. Dome-headed and heavily-moustached, he looks faintly amused, perhaps at his carved, pedimented marble surround. His sculptor George Simonds, as first Master of the Art Workers' Guild, was instrumental in establishing the Arts and Crafts movement; his portrait shows the flesh and blood touch.

Monuments showing Arts and Crafts influence take their place amongst more formal Victorian statues, and late 20th-century figures, between Westminster and Blackfriars. Not all these have been mentioned, but each awaits — and rewards — inspection. (*Note*: Westminster Council supplies a useful statues trail leaflet for this stretch of the Thames.)

The Strand

Strand Feature:

The Gladstone Memorial
William Ewart Gladstone (1809–1898)
Full-length bronze statue on Portland stone
pedestal with bronze allegorical figures;
cruciform base on stepped platform
Sculptor (Sir) William Hamo Thornycroft RA
Location St Clement Danes, Aldwych

W.E. Gladstone's fellow elder statesmen, including his arch-rival Disraeli, convene in Parliament Square, but the English national monument to Gladstone takes pride of place on the paved expanse outside

St Clement Danes. Unlike Wren's church the statue survived the Blitz, witnessing the church's restoration and also the build-up of London traffic which surges round its island site.

Flanked by the Virtues 'Courage', 'Brotherhood', 'Education' and 'Aspiration', the 16ft statue was erected in 1905 when the Aldwych and its monumental buildings (some with sculpture) were newly planned. Scarcely a decade earlier, the Grand Old Man had taken office for the fourth and last time at the age of 83, still intent on Home Rule for Ireland. A Gladstone National Memorial Fund was set up in 1898, the year of his death.

Gladstone Memorial: statue & ensemble to W. E. Gladstone (1809–1898). Sculptor: Sir W. H. Thornycroft, RA (1905). Location: St Clement Danes, Aldwych.

Gladstone was one of England's greatest statesmen in an era of great statesmen, amongst them Palmerston, Peel and Disraeli. His father, a Liverpool merchant, had dissuaded him from entering the Church, and Gladstone's crusading fervour coloured Victorian politics for 63 years, roughly corresponding with Victoria's reign. His statue shows him in Chancellor of the Exchequer's robes, a post he held as a young politician during Peel's first Tory ministry.

After Gladstone's Free Trade budgets culminated in the repeal of the Corn Laws, the Tory party was riven, with Disraeli leading the revolt. When Peel died in 1850, Gladstone as a 'Peelite' joined the Whigs. He began his first ministry in 1868 at the age of 59, leading a grouping of Peelites, Whigs and Radicals, and created the Liberal party which he was to dominate until the end of the century.

His first and most successful premiership disestablished the Anglican Church in Ireland, and brought national reform by abolishing class privilege in education, the Civil Service and the Army; after six years, compared by Disraeli to 'exhausted volcanoes', Mr Gladstone and his ministers were voted out of office. Over his three later terms, Gladstone continued the Reform of Parliament, failed in foreign policy and unsuccessfully attempted his 'mission', as he had declared it in 1868, 'to pacify Ireland'. When Disraeli took leadership of the Conservatives, their bitter and brilliant clashes in the House of Commons were as much public spectacle as politics.

The rivals' dissimilarities are scarcely mirrored in their London statues, or in statues elsewhere; both take dignified poses in Parliament Square (Disraeli in his peer's robes) and the Aldwych (Gladstone as Chancellor of the Exchequer). Gladstone is shown in stiff discourse in Bow Churchyard, also in Manchester and Blackburn, but no sculptor has successfully shown him in fiery, moralistic, complex oratory, blazing out facts and appealing to reason. Disraeli the inscrutable, with his barbed wit, his recourse to patriotic, popular, not always principled policies, his political panache, and his discernible human weaknesses, had the charismatic edge.

This was evident in their dealings with Queen Victoria. Devout and respectful, Gladstone never overcame the Queen's hostility to his uncomfortable presence or, as she saw them, his revolutionary policies. Her friend Disraeli commented, 'Gladstone treats the Queen like a public department; I treat her like a woman'.

The Gladstone Memorial was one of a group of three destined for London, Edinburgh (by P. Mac-

Dr Samuel Johnson (1709–1784). Sculptor: Percy Fitzgerald (1910). Location: St Clement Danes, Aldwych.

gillivray) and Dublin. Ireland's, by John Hughes, was eventually refused, and in 1925 it was warmly received in Liberal, Nonconformist Wales. It stands in Hawarden, the Clwyd birthplace of W.E's wife Catherine, and the Gladstones' family home.

Strand Selection

The newest work is Faith Winter's bronze of Lord Dowding, misused hero, whose leadership triumphed at the Battle of Britain in 1940. In 1988, almost 20 years after Dowding's death, his statue was unveiled by Queen Elizabeth the Queen Mother outside the RAF church of St Clement Danes, as a lone Spitfire flew overhead.

Behind the church, where a brass plaque marks Dr Johnson's pew, is a vigorous, stumpy bronze statue of the Doctor. 'The gift and handiwork of Percy Fitzgerald', it was erected by the Rector of St Clement Danes in 1910. In Gough Square, off Fleet Street, can be seen the attic where Dr Johnson compiled the first *Dictionary of the English Language*, published in 1755. A lexicographer features as 'a writer of dictionaries, a harmless drudge'.

A figure of Boswell by the same sculptor stands in Lichfield, Staffordshire, where Johnson set out for London accompanied by Garrick 'with twopence halfpenny in my pocket, and thou, Davy, with three halfpence in thine'. The great actor-manager's bronze medallion by H.C. Fehr survives on his house, No. 27 Southampton Street. Dr Johnson's attic now has a far view of the Old Bailey's 'Justice', made without blindfold by F.W. Pomeroy in 1907. Near St Clement Danes, the Law Courts are said to be the only secular building in London carrying a figure of Christ; He is accompanied by King Solomon and King Alfred. Inside is Armstead's seated statue of the Law Courts' architect, G. E. Street (1886).

Behind the Law Courts, the corner of Serle and Carey Street has a lifesize stone niche statue of Sir Thomas More, Henry VIII's Lord Chancellor; it makes a handsome ensemble with its building half of red brick, half of the same stone. Carved by Robert Smith in 1886, it bears the somewhat reproachful inscription '... the faithful servant both of God and the King'.

Temple Bar marks the city boundary of Westminster and London with a big carved pedestal (mid-street) supporting a City of London griffon; designed by the City architect Horace Jones, it was erected in 1880 as an unpopular replacement for the Temple Bar built by Joshua Marshall and Thomas Knight in 1670–2. This was declared a traffic hazard and removed in 1878, and erected in Theobalds' Park in 1887, complete with its statues of Stuart kings by John Bushnell, and spikes for traitors' heads, all faithfully depicted in relief on the replacement - except for the heads.

Mabey and Kelsey made the bronze relief panels, Boehm made marble statues of Queen Victoria and her son Edward, Prince of Wales, among much carved decoration. The detailed inscription wrongly ascribing the earlier Bar to Wren, and vivid images of contemporary scenes, make absorbing study best done at dead of night, when one is less likely to be crushed by a bus. The griffon, which has been likened to 'an animated corkscrew', is by C.B. Birch, whose statue of Queen Victoria stands on Blackfriars' Bridge. (She was blown into the bushes in the Great Storm of 1987, but re-erected.)

Bloomsbury and Holborn

Bloomsbury Feature:

Lord Brockway (1888–1987)
Full-length bronze statue on plain stone pedestal
Sculptor Ian Walters
Location Red Lion Square (west entrance)

Erected in his 97th year, this exuberant statue projects all the vigour and optimism with which Fenner Brockway pursued his socialist, pacifist and internationalist aims to the last. With his jacket flapping and trousers hitched up by braces, and his eyes seeming to glint in glee from behind the familiar thick-framed spectacles, 'the Member for Africa' thrusts up a hand in greeting. He could be acknowledging any of numerous friends gathered from Europe where he led anti-fascist, peace and socialist movements, or from Asia and Africa, where he was active as a life-long anti-colonialist and present at more than one country's Independence celebration. His links with India were sustained from his childhood in a family of Calcutta missionaries.

Universally known as 'Fenner', Lord Brockway deemed himself a rebel from early years, and a 'reverent agnostic'. Tony Benn saw his role as that of 'a prophet, forever preaching against the abuse of power'. At the statue's unveiling in Fenner's presence ('I feel very humble'), Stan Newens, chairman of the peace movement Liberation, described him with relish as an agitator and trouble maker: 'a great radical and a great man'. He entered the Commons as Labour MP in 1950.

The statue was unveiled by a veteran unveiler of socialist monuments, Michael Foot. Lord Brockway would have preferred the £12,000 appeal fund to have been spent on other campaigns, but in a speech he also called for the square to be filled with statues of socialist figures, from his own to the bust of Sir Bertrand Russell at the top end. This would certainly help to redress the absence of socialist statesmen from the famous political statuary convened in Parliament Square.

It was as a bust that the socialist sculptor Ian Walters first envisaged Lord Brockway's portrait; he himself initiated the work, modelled from life, but was later commissioned by Liberation (which Lord Brockway founded). Aided by a GLC grant, Walker evolved the work from a *Morning Star* photograph

Lord Brockway (1888–1987). Sculptor: Ian Walters (1984). Location: Red Lion Square.

of the veteran campaigner delivering a peace petition to No.10 in 1980. Bearing millions of signatures collected world wide, the petition makes a bulky bundle balanced on the statue's left arm.

Among other singular qualities the statue is probably unique, as Lord Brockway noted, in having been not only erected but demolished in the lifetime of its subject; it was toppled in the Great Storm of 1987, only months after its unveiling. Deprived of the jubilant right arm, and once again the subject of a fundraising appeal, it was stored in the Ladies' at Conway Hall, the humanist centre, and brought out for the 99th birthday celebrations held in the newly-named Brockway Room. (The Hall, where Lord Brockway gave lectures, was built in 1929 further up the south side of the square. *Note* over both entrances the vitality of stone-carved relief panels by A.J.J. Ayres.)

The statue was eventually 'reinstated 1989 by Irene Chamberlain and others in memory of her father W.J. Chamberlain and all opponents of War'. Lord Brockway's late secretary and companion Joan

Hymans, who encouraged and aided the sculptor in initiating the project, is also commemorated. Chamberlain and Brockway, both conscientious objectors, had shared a cell during their imprisonment, with other members of the Independent Labour Party, in the First World War. Brockway then declared 'no power on earth can make me do what I believe to be wrong'. His small, exuberant statue, reflecting the affection of numerous fellow MPs, campaigners and friends, makes it hard to imagine otherwise.

Bloomsbury and Holborn Selection

Even more than in the West End, Holborn and Bloomsbury squares contain their watchful statues, all of bronze, many portraying reforming politicians or thinkers, and all dating from either side of the Victorian era.

Red Lion Square, at its west end, has a bust by Marcelle Quinton of the pacifist philosopher Sir Bertrand Russell (1872–1970), who marched with

Margaret MacDonald (1870–1911). Sculptor: Richard Goulden (1914). Location: Lincoln's Inn Fields.

Fenner Brockway and other CND leaders, supported many political and social causes, and in 1950 won the Nobel Prize for literature. Brockway was involved in erecting his monument. Russell's bronze, aquiline features seem to watch the world; Lord Brockway's statue at the far end of the square excitedly hails it.

Lincoln's Inn Fields commemorates Mrs Margaret MacDonald (1870–1911), wife of the Labour leader, who lived at No 3 on the north side. The founder of the Women's Labour League reclines graciously along the edge of a stone memorial seat with a bevy of bubbly infants far removed, one imagines, from any wretched urchin encountered as she 'quickened faith and zeal in others ... and took no rest from doing good'. The sculptor was Richard Goulden (1914). At the south end of the square, near the Royal College of Surgeons, is a huge head of John Hunter (1728–1793), surgeon extraordinary, by Nigel Boonham. It was taken from his death mask (so does not convey his irascible nature) and was set up in 1979 by the RCS, which also has a bronze statue (1805) of Hunter by Weekes, and a bust (1805) by Flaxman.

A mystery queen occupies Queen Square, her ornamented leaden figure (*c.* 1775) variously named as Queen Anne, or as wife of one of the Georges. (Gleichen makes a case for Queen Caroline, but Byron notes 'the statue's face is pretty, which should eliminate them all'.) A character of the same era, but recreated by William McMillan in 1963, is Thomas Coram (d. 1751), jovial outside his old Foundling Hospital in Brunswick Square. The statue is based on a portrait by Hogarth, one of many famous names who aided the old sea captain in establishing the hospital after 1739.

Handel performed his *Messiah* on an organ which was his gift. Organ, inmates, and an earlier (1852) stone statue of Captain Coram, by William Calder Marshall, were moved to Berkhamstead in 1926. The Hogarth can be seen in the same building, now the Thomas Coram Foundation for Children; Coram's relief portrait by D. Evans (1936) is sited over the door.

Tavistock Square has an unusual double bust of Dame Louisa Brandreth Aldrich-Blake (1863–1925) by A.G. Walker (1927), whose back-to-back portrait heads are part of a stone memorial seat by Sir Edwin Lutyens, cramped into the square's southeast corner. Long inscriptions detail her impressive career as Dean of the London (Royal Free) Hospital School of Medicine for Women, and as a consultant surgeon; there are religious texts, but no words on Dame Louisa's formidable boxing and cricket skills. Lutyens, whose wife was an ardent Theosophist, designed the Theosophist headquarters (now BMA House) nearby.

Fredda Brilliant's bronze figure of the Mahatma Gandhi sits crosslegged on a beehive-shaped stand, a receptacle for flowers; he wears the symbolic loin cloth adopted as an act of penance for the too-violent actions of some of his followers. A statue of Nehru, who planted a tree nearby, is planned for Montague Place.

Outside the squares, Charles Bacon's equestrian statue of the Prince Consort, raising his cockaded Field-Marshal's hat in Holborn Circus, is rated 'the politest statue in London'. Costing £2,000, it was presented by Charles Oppenheim to the City Corporation in 1874. It rewards venturing to its traffic island for close appreciation of 'The Prince laying the first stone of the Royal Exchange', and 'The Exhibition of All Nations, 1851', in minutely-detailed high relief bronze side panels.

London's oddest statue, that of George I, crowns St George's Church in Bloomsbury, on London's oddest steeple. John Boson, employed on Hawksmoor's church (1716–31), may have been creator of the statue. The steeple is said to emulate the stepped pyramidal tomb of King Mausolus at Halicarnassus, one of the seven wonders of the ancient world, and viewable, in part, in the British

Museum. The statue is not strictly a monument, but with its steeple it is one of the wonders of London, portraying King George in toga and billowing cloak, seemingly reaching for his sword. His style is somewhat cramped by a spiked lightning conductor. Without it, he would be at home in any of London's homelier squares.

Monument & the City

City Feature:

The Monument
202ft fluted Doric column of Portland stone supporting a square balcony with drum, dome and bronze urn; large base and pedestal with carved pedestal inscriptions and carved allegorical relief panel on west side.
Column Sir Christopher Wren
Sculptor C.G. Cibber
Location Fish Hill Street

The Monument is local history solidified in stone. Other monuments in England give the name to their locality, but none is so grand in gesture or design as the City of London's, raised to mark the Great Fire of 1666 and the immediate rebuilding which took place at the command of Charles II. The frightful details of the fire, and the sensible rebuilding specifications, were recorded in Latin by Dr Thomas Gale, Master of St Paul's School and Dean of York, and carved into the north and south sides of the pedestal. Each has a later translation beneath, on upraised metal letters.

The Monument was constructed (1675–78) by Joshua Marshall, master-mason to the Crown, for a fee of £1,500. Its design is attributed to Wren, possibly in collaboration with his friend Robert Hooke. The sculptor C.G. Cibber, imprisoned for running up debts, worked on the pedestal relief of Charles II succouring the City of London, whilst on daytime parole.

The translation includes lines that were added in 1681: 'BUT POPISH FRENZY, WHICH WROUGHT SUCH HORRORS, IS NOT YET QUENCHED'. A madman had confessed to arson, whilst Titus Oates's 'Popish Plot' had wrought frenzy and terror of a return to Catholicism under Charles's brother and heir apparent James, Duke of York. The Latin lines, erased when James did succeed,

The Monument: erected to mark the Great Fire of London, 1666. Architect: Sir Christopher Wren (1678). Location: Fish Hill Street.

were carved more deeply under William III but finally eradicated in 1830 following the Catholic Emancipation Act. A similar inscription was removed from the Pudding Lane bakehouse and presented to the Guildhall Museum in 1871. Pope made an allusion in his *Moral Essays*: 'Where London's column pointing at the skies, Like a tall bully, lifts its head and lies'.

The Great Fire raged for three days, consuming '89 churches, gates, the Guildhall, public edifices, hospitals, schools, libraries, a great number of blocks of buildings, 13,200 houses, 400 streets' ... and leaving ashes over 436 acres. The previous year,

1665, had been the year of the Great Plague. Dr Gale's long account includes the King's ideas for rebuilding: with Parliament, he imposed a tax on coals to pay for it, then decreed that City churches and the cathedral be rebuilt 'with all magnificence; that the bridges, gates, and prisons should be new made, the sewers cleansed, the streets made straight and regular, such as were steep levelled and those too narrow made wider . . .'.

But the various proposed plans could not be imposed in time on a flattened city whose higgledy-piggledy layout delineated ownership, and whose owners survived to exploit need (the fire destroyed property but on the whole spared people). Wren, one of the three Commissioners for Rebuilding the City of London, submitted plans within days of the disaster and his churches and the Monument are all that materialised of a proposed street layout centred on St Paul's and the Royal Exchange.

Cibber's relief carved in 1674 employs the vigorous symbolism then in mode (the accounts record payment for carving 'hieroglifick ffigures'), but it clearly exemplifies one building specification as set out by the Commissioners, 'that all house walls should be strengthened with stone or brick'. Whilst a female London sits in ruins supported by Time; whilst Charles clad in Roman habit and periwig directs Architecture and Design (as Arthur Byron notes in his book on London statues, with his fingers resting 'not for the first time, on a naked breast'); whilst the city burns and Plenty hovers ready to declare victory, and whilst Envy beneath a stone gnaws at a heart, a London brickie with his hod, in the top right hand corner, can be seen getting on with the great rebuilding.

The fate of the great rebuilding echoes in the plaintive rider on the south face: 'Haste is seen everywhere, London rises again, whether with greater speed or greater magnificence is doubtful, three short years complete that which was considered the work of an age'. In the heart of the 20th-century City, rebuilt after the Blitz in the same opportunist manner (albeit more slowly), Wren, Cibber and Gale are here to remind us that history repeats itself.

Under the relief, a modern inscription includes the Monument's claim as 'the loftiest isolated stone column in the world'. Over 300 black marble steps lead to the fenced balcony, with a panorama of river and city. Beneath its flaming gilded urn, the column's 202ft is claimed as equal in distance from Farynor's bakehouse in Pudding Lane where the 'fire broke out in the dead of night, which, the wind blowing, devoured even distant buildings, and rushed devastating through every quarter with astonishing swiftness and noise'.

Wren's reputed plan for the monument, as for the city, was abandoned, otherwise we should have had a huge interior telescope, carved flames issuing from slits in the exterior, and a phoenix, or a statue of the king, on top; all in glorification of what was, and might have been.

City Selection

Unlike the City of Westminster which deals in affairs of state, the City of London with its Lord Mayor and Corporation, Livery Companies and archaic customs commemorates local rather than national history. Even its equestrian monument to the Duke of Wellington (by Sir Francis Chantrey d.1841, completed by Henry Weekes), given a prime site outside the Royal Exchange, was erected not as a tribute to Wellington's victories but to his political good will which secured an Act of Parliament for the rebuilding of London Bridge in 1844.

Also on this site is Sir Aston Webb's Great War monument of 1920, with sculpture by Alfred Drury, and J. Whitehead's fountain of 1911, with a bronze water-pouring nude maiden under a red granite canopy, erected to mark the Jubilee of the Metropolitan Drinking Fountain and Cattle Trough Association.

Recent additions to City streets, such as Karin Jonzen's bronze bust of Samuel Pepys in Seething Lane Gardens, 1983, and Fetter Lane's bronze statue of a past Lord Mayor John Wilkes (1725–1797), politician, Radical agitator, journalist and publicist, by James Butler (1988), have the local touch – like the City selection listed below.

Queen Anne's statue outside St Paul's Cathedral celebrates the cathedral's completion in 1710, two years before Francis Bird made this ensemble for which the Queen provided the marble. Symbolic figures represent England and Ireland, together with English colonies in France (so Anne believed) and America – notably an Indian squaw with her foot resting on someone's head.

Mutilated by a madman, the original work was replaced, and this group of 1886 is by the inferior sculptor Richard Belt in conjunction with Louis Auguste Malenupre. The original Anne ('Brandy Nan'), repaired by John Henning the Younger (c.1825) stands in a convent school at St Leonard's, Sussex. Francis Bird was one of many who worked on St Pauls's fine stonework; Bird also carved the

Captain John Smith (1580–1631).
Sculptor: William Coupar (replica,
1960). Location: St Mary-le-Bow.

figure of Henry VIII, founder of St Bartholomew's (1703), for the hospital gateway facing Smithfield.

Beneath St Paul's south face in a narrow public shrubbery is a rare memorial, honouring St Thomas à Becket (born on the corner of Ironmonger Lane and Cheapside) not by a conventional image but in a bronze sculpture by E. Bainbridge Copnall (1979), which evokes a recumbent, contorted martyr. In the Great Storm of 1987, the head was severed by a falling branch and later replaced by the sculptor, but to a different shape. On the north of St Paul's, a stone replica of a statue of John Wesley by Samuel Manning Junior was unveiled in 1989. Near here Wesley's heart was 'strangely warmed' on receiving enlightenment at a religious meeting in 1738.

In a Cheapside court by St Mary-le-Bow stands a stone replica statue of Captain John Smith (1580–1631), founder of Virginia, 'Citizen and Cordwainer'. This is indeed Cordwainer country, one of 25 administrative City wards named after the various guilds. William Coupar's figure shows Smith in his boots of Spanish leather, fashionable in the late 17th century

only after new leather-dressing techniques from Cordoba, practised by Cordwainers, allowed their crafting. It was presented in 1960 by the Jamestown Foundation of the Commonwealth of Virginia.

In the small, cavernous garden behind the Royal Exchange, among other monuments, an imaginative memorial of the 'good read' variety shows the frowning stare, domed brow and flowing forked moustache of Paul Julius Reuter (1816–1899) emerging from a column of words. It was carved by Michael Black in 1976, for the 125th anniversary of Reuter's news agency founded at No 1 Royal Exchange Buildings on October 1851. Nearby is the beautiful fountain by the French sculptor Jules Dalou, influential as assistant professor of modelling at the National Art Training School, South Kensington (later the Royal College of Art). His bronze group represents Charity but shows all the untidy bounty of 'Motherhood'.

West of St Paul's in Postman's Park, near the King Edward Street post office depot (*note* Onslow Ford's statue of Sir Rowland Hill erected in 1881, the sculptor's first major assignment), a wall monument assembled for the 1887 Jubilee catalogues the 'heroic sacrifice' of ordinary citizens. It was installed by the painter and sculptor G.F. Watts, and later his energetic widow, who placed a miniature wood carving of Watts by T.H. Wren on the wall with its series of ceramic tile panels. The coloured tiles vividly record names, dates, and deeds of personal bravery: 'Saved a lunatic woman from suicide at Woolwich Arsenal Station. But was himself run over by the train ...' 'Rushed into a burning house to save the neighbour's children and perished in the flames ...' It is endlessly absorbing and stirring. Michael Ayrton's Minotaur (1973) brings brooding intensity to the same park, a redundant graveyard.

In Giltspur Street is a bronze wall bust by William Reynolds-Stephens of Charles Lamb (1775–1834) who made his old school, Charterhouse, the subject of one of his essays. His boyish portrait with a floppy bow is just one of the City's collection of busts or medallions, from Trinity Square to Fleet Street, each as expressive as any statue.

Subjects include Lord Northcliffe (at St Dunstan-in-the-West, in the company of the City's oldest statue, Elizabeth I), made by Lady Scott in 1930 to a Lutyens design. Across Fleet Street is a portrait from the same period showing journalist and politician T.P. O'Connor: 'His pen could lay bare the bones of a book or the soul of a statesman in a few vivid lines'. F. Doyle Jones's bust is worthy of this image.

Hyde Park & Kensington Gardens

Kensington Gardens Feature:

The Albert Memorial
Albert, Prince Consort (1819–1861)
Bronze seated statue under square-section canopy of carved Portland stone, surmounted by ornamental metal flèche; podium with carved marble relief frieze and symbolic groups of marble statuary groups at base corners; stepped, paved platform also with symbolic groups at corners
Designer (Sir) George Gilbert Scott RA
Sculptor of Prince Albert John Foley RA
Sculptors of platform groups John Bell, John Foley RA, Patrick Macdowell RA, William Theed

Sculptors of base groups John Lawlor, Calder Marshall RA, Thomas Thornycroft, Henry Weekes RA
Sculptors of podium frieze H.H. Armstead, J.B. Philip
Canopy stone carving William Brindley
Bronze statues for canopy H.H. Armstead, J.B. Philip
Bronze statues for flèche James Redfern
Ornamentation & construction of metal flèche (filigree, enamel & gem setting) F.A. Skidmore
Tympanum & spandrel mosaics: (Design) J.R. Clayton & Bell; (Execution) A. Salviati, Venice
Construction John Kelk
Co-ordinator (Sir) George Gilbert Scott RA
Location The gardens between Alexandra & Queen's Gates

This colossal, hand-crafted *objet d'art*, raised in honour of the nation's Prince Consort, represents the high peak of the Victorian Gothic Revival as exemplified by the memorial's creator George (later Sir George) Gilbert Scott. Queen Victoria helped the memorial committee to choose Scott's design, one of six submitted by selected architects, and monitored each stage of the work, even inspecting the massive brick-built vaults that form the foundations. 'It is terrible for me, who do not thoroughly understand severe and correct art, as my beloved one did', she wrote, 'to have to decide on what is best'.

The Queen was closely involved in the committee's choice of a sculptor for the Prince; they first approved Carlo Marochetti, but his model was rejected, and he died before another could be completed. The commission then went to John Foley, who caught a chill whilst working *in situ* on one of the attendant sculptures, and died before seeing his sculpture cast.

Scott in promotion of his idea had evoked the medieval Eleanor Cross, the pure example of English Gothic art. Both designs honour steadfast consorts, being personal, as well as public, tributes. Cross and Memorial have since informed monuments up and down the land, but the biggest, the most sumptuous and the most complex of them all belongs to Albert.

The memorial consists of an outsize seated bronze statue of the prince, holding the catalogue of the Great Exhibition, under a carved Portland stone Gothic canopy supported by clustered granite columns, and surmounted by a metal, filigréed flèche. The canopy has bronze statues of the practical arts and sciences; higher, on the flèche, come statues of

Albert Memorial: statue, canopy & ensemble to Albert, Prince Consort (1819–1861). Architect: Sir G. G. Scott (1872). Albert's Sculptor: J. Foley, RA. Location: Kensington Gardens.

the Christian and moral virtues, with figures of angels on the upper stages. Glass mosaics in the tympana show the Arts of music and poetry, of painting, sculpture, architecture. The flèche carries a gilded cross. Much gilding of stonework and statuary, (including the prince's) was removed in 1914.

The marble-clad podium beneath Albert's bronze figure is carved on each side with a frieze depicting practitioners of the Art that appears above. At its base corners, groups of marble statuary represent Engineering, Agriculture, Commerce and Manufacture, while the stepped platform, paved in variously-coloured stone, has flanking corner groups of marble statuary showing Europe, Asia, Africa and America. The memorial in construction was a triumph of co-ordination. An admirer, Edmund Gosse, called it 'a national effort in art'.

The prime mover in organisation was the architect, George Gilbert Scott, who provided plans for statues and ornamentation, commissioned sculptors and craftsmen, and supervised the work. The cost came close to £150,000 shared by the Queen, Parliament (which haggled), Mansion House, which had originated the idea, and others. Work commenced in 1862 and inauguration came in 1872, the year that Scott received his knighthood, and four years before the statue was installed. Scott even added the last eight words to the mosaic tribute:

QUEEN VICTORIA AND HER PEOPLE. TO THE MEMORY OF
ALBERT PRINCE CONSORT. AS A TRIBUTE OF THEIR
GRATITUDE. FOR A LIFE DEVOTED TO THE PUBLIC GOOD.

Albert's stooped form under its carved and bejewelled canopy seems subtly at odds with his monument's intended grandeur, but this is its charm and its true unwitting symbolism, for Albert and Victoria were less taken up with the glittering pageantry of monarchy than with its huge and oppressive responsibilities to which, earnestly and diligently, they devoted their lives. Albert's arrival from his beloved Germany, as husband of England's young and headstrong queen, was later recalled with irony: 'Peel cut down my income, Wellington refused me my rank, the Royal family cried out against the Foreign interloper, the Whigs in office were only inclined to concede me just as much space as I could stand upon'.

Patiently, Albert carved out a role as Prince Consort. The title was formally conferred only in 1854, but by then he had long been acknowledged the queen's prime political and personal adviser; his were the directives from behind the throne: Albert and Victoria occupied twin desks, and worked as a team. In addition he brought administrative order to the royal household and estates, co-designed family homes at Osborne and Balmoral, promoted and furthered the arts and sciences, espoused Lord Shaftesbury's social reforms and encouraged reform in the army. He also introduced the Victoria Cross, designed by himself, for all ranks.

All this was performed with stoicism in the face of implacable public cold-shouldering. He was presumed dull, since he was stiff and remote in public, yet the private Albert, as Carlyle remarked, was 'jolly and handsome'. The Great Exhibition of 1851, which Albert inspired and masterminded, was considered his finest achievement. 100,000 exhibits from all corners of the globe were procured for display under Paxton's spectacular glass hall, erected close to the spot on which the memorial now stands.

Recalling the exhibition, the platform corner groups — 'four quarters of the globe' — were carved from H.H. Armstead's models to Scott's designs, 1864–70. Australasia, destination of convict ships and gold-seekers, was omitted. The United States, then fighting a Civil War, was shown with Indian America on a bison, flanked by the Dominion of Canada (formed 1867) holding the English Rose. Livingstone was then making his third great exploration of Equatorial Africa, here shown as Nubia being instructed by Egypt, whilst the marble version of Bismarck's Europe has France as the military power and Germany the home of science and literature. The mutual atrocities of the Indian Mutiny (1857) were vivid and bitter memories, but Foley's partly-clothed 'Asia' astride her elephant was meant to convey a 'feeling of repose'.

Like a cathedral the memorial needs a guide, since the details are many, and some mysterious. Bomb damage renovations in 1954 revealed that some figures (such as the virtue 'Fortitude') have a double image, with only one face visible from the ground. A bird's eye is required to appreciate this, and Prudence wearing a tiger's head, or the spandrel mosaics showing artists at work.

The podium reliefs, carved *in situ*, caused much brow beating over the hardness of the durable 'campanella' Carrera marble, especially sought out by Scott. Much research went into likenesses; acquaintances of Beethoven and Goethe were produced, Phideas was declared to have been bald. Scott declined to appear as the only living artist, but was overruled by the Queen.

Albert in his lifetime had rejected any idea of a statue, 'as it would both disturb my quiet rides in Rotton Row to see my own face staring at me, and if (as is very likely) it becomes an artistic monstrosity, like most of our monuments, it would upset my equanimity to be permanently ridiculed in effigy ...' Critics of his national memorial would say he had spoken prophetically, yet he would have applied himself with characteristic vigour to the feat of creating this massive work from such a rich diversity of materials, by such a multitude of hands.

Public response has veered between pride and ridicule, and it has been claimed that the memorial, artistically, is impossible to take seriously. But, continued the writer Tancred Borenius, in his book on London Statues (1926), 'looking upon it merely as an episode in the landscape of Kensington Gardens — especially in the mellow light of the late summer evenings, when the masses of foliage are full and rounded — the Albert Memorial is not without its *raison d'être*'.

Hyde Park & Kensington Gardens Selection

Whether 'vulgar' or 'gorgeous' or, as Scott intended, emulating the preciousness of a medieval shrine, the Albert Memorial has rusted at the core, and is now in need of expensive repairs. Government agency proposals of 1987 dismayed the Victorian Society with their 'white elephant' approach. One option, demolition, was rightly declared unthinkable, but all were unacceptable. A restoration is now under way, and the monument may yet survive as the biggest and best, if only in aspiration. It makes an intriguing standard by which to contemplate other monumental 'episodes in the landscape' of Kensington Gardens and Hyde Park.

Outside Kensington Palace is a rare figure of Queen Victoria, youthful and queenly at her accession carved in marble by her daughter Princess Louise, a pupil of Boehm. It was erected in 1893. The Princess, when a budding talent of 16, had submitted useful advice on sculptures under production for the Albert Memorial. On the Palace's south lawn stands a bronze of William III, 'presented by William II, German Emperor and King of Prussia' in 1907.

In Kensington Gardens the most famous and most popular, and scarcely more tasteful than Albert's gaudy Gothic, is the bronze statue of Peter Pan by Sir George Frampton. Frampton's commemorative work typically combines truthful characterisation of his subject with spirited expression of art nouveau themes on pedestals or surrounds. Here, in immortalising the immortal, Frampton gives free rein to the fantastical elements in his art, creating a fusion of innocence and underlying sophistication to be acknowledged on either level.

It is children and nannies who respond to long-legged Peter sounding his pipes from his tree stump inhabited by bunnies, birds, mice and snails, and sleek, knowing sprites poised in Arts and Crafts liberty gowns. Since the work appeared in 1912, they have been polished smooth by generations of small hands.

Commissioned anonymously by Sir James Barrie, creator of Peter Pan, the monument's mysterious and unplanned appearance in a royal park provoked a question in the House, but the immortal boy's appeal quickly established him as a permanent feature. He calls across the Long Water from the west shore, where he landed from his island home in the Serpentine. The model was Nina Boucicault, star of the first annual production at the Duke of York's Theatre in 1904.

Unlike the Albert Memorial, 'Peter Pan' is more a display piece than a commemorative monument, and this accords with other sculptures in the park; some of the most striking show a vigour and individual style more readily accepted in the art gallery. The earliest belongs to the painter G.F. Watts RA (d.1904), whose remarkable rough-modelled horse and rider, 'Physical Energy', prances at a focal point on Lancaster Walk between the Albert Memorial and the Long Water. This ebullient piece, begun in 1883, was not intended for casting; modelled on a jointed armature, it could be (and was) altered at will.

Among other distinguished visitors, Millais saw the 'wonderful equestrian piece' in Watts's studio and remarked 'the dear old boy doesn't know if it's finished'; but it seems to have been the finish of

Peter Pan. Sculptor: Sir George Frampton, RA (1911). Location: Kensington Gardens.

Watts who, struck by 'a stroke of genius', as he said, on the train to Clapham, had the model moved to the garden to be worked. The resulting chill was too much for the 88-year-old Watts, who died within a fortnight. By then, a cast had been taken as a centrepiece for the Rhodes monument in Cape Town (1902–3); the Kensington Gardens bronze was recast from public funds in 1906 and a third cast of 1960 is in Bulawayo. 'Physical Energy' is a variant of Watts's bronze equestrian figure of Hugh Lupus, made for the Earl of Westminster's Cheshire seat, Eaton Hall, between 1876–83.

Even more than in the gallery, a public work of art can provoke outrage, as London's earlier outdoor works by Jacob Epstein, including his nude figures

'Pan'. Sculptor: Sir Jacob Epstein (1961). Location: Edinburgh Gate, Hyde Park.

on the Strand's British Medical Association, and his sculptures for London Transport in St James's, did in 1910 and 1929.

In 1925, Epstein contributed to Lionel Pearson's design for a bird sanctuary in memory of W.H. Hudson, just north of the Serpentine boat houses in Hyde Park. Carved on a waterside panel of Portland stone, his relief image of Rima, beautiful jungle heroine of Hudson's novel *Green Mansions* (1904), owes more to Epstein's powerful and stylistic symbolism of the Spirit of Nature than to the South-American born naturalist's original characterisation. Hudson's book became a best-seller, but Epstein's Rima was twice tarred and feathered.

A century earlier near Hyde Park Corner, a tribute to the Duke of Wellington and his brave companions-in-arms from 'their countrywomen' was unveiled to reveal a colossal, muscular bronze nude, *Achilles*, which provoked blushing consternation despite the fig leaf that poses a perpetual challenge to souvenir seekers. A subscription was begun by the Ladies of England in 1814, and Sir Richard Westmacott's sculpture was uncovered in 1822. Cast from captured guns, the work was adapted from one of the antique Dioscuri on the Monte Cavallo in Rome, which Westmacott provided with a sword and shield.

Near it (across Park Lane north-bound) is Richard Belt's bronze of Byron, unveiled in 1880 and acclaimed as the worst statue in London. 'Byron'

ponders on a rock, attended by his adoring dog. The pedestal of richly-veined marble was given by the Greek Government, and the commission was won in a competition, it is said, over the head of Rodin.

At Wellington's death in 1852, England mourned him as the last of the great heroes but made no national monument to compare in scale and siting with Nelson's Column, or the Albert Memorial. The moment had passed; Waterloo's glorious memory (marked by monuments throughout England) was long superseded by the Iron Duke's political career.

Wellington's earlier equestrian monument of local value, erected in the City, was so fiercely contested by leading sculptors that another commission was suggested, and won by Matthew Cotes Wyatt in 1846. His enormous cloaked equestrian figure, modelled from life, was hoisted with dire misgivings on to Decimus Burton's Arch, part of the processional way *via* Constitution Hill from palace to park.

The statue's obvious failings caused a furore. The current joke was 'What's High Art?' with the reply, 'Wyatt's Duke', and when the arch was realigned in 1883, Wellington, stiffly pointing his baton, was banished to an obscure site in Aldershot.

Boehm's subsequent bronze group of 1888 stands on the site of the arch opposite Apsley House, Wellington's residence and now his memorial museum. It shows Wellington astride his charger Copenhagen, flanked at the corners of the base by uniformed regulars from regiments at each quarter of the United Kingdom. Beneath the outlandish headgear, each has a soldier's war-lined face.

Wellington's monument and two regimental memorials occupy a vast, grassed island with the arch at its centre, divorced from the life of the streets by Hyde Park Corner's traffic system and a complex of pedestrian subways. The arch now carries the 'Quadriga of Peace', Adrian Jones's forceful image of Peace as a heroic female descending on a Roman triumphal war chariot. The massive sculpture succeeds in skyline – memorably from the Serpentine Bridge – and also on neck-craning approach. The boy driver, gritting his teeth between the hooves of the furiously galloping horses, was modelled by Captain Jones's son.

The original was exhibited at the Royal Academy in 1891 and admired by the Prince of Wales, later Edward VII; he had offered his famous racer Persimmon as a model after his friend, the Liberal financier Lord Michelham, commissioned the large-scale work for Hyde Park to the displeasure of Academicians.

The sculptor built up his career after retiring from active Army service as Veterinary Surgeon, and his lack of scholarship made him suspect. Thanks to the better judgement of his clients he could inform his statues and reliefs, including his Duke of Cambridge in Whitehall (1907), and the Cavalry St George at Stanhope Gate, through his knowledge of military men and horses.

Raised in 1912 the Quadriga brought vehement criticism, notably over the outsize winged figure. In 1925, the year of the Rima outrage, the Royal Artillery Memorial was unveiled near the Quadriga to a similar storm. The sculptor was Charles Sergeant Jagger, and the designer of the Portland stone base, which supports a massive stone-carved 9.2in howitzer, was Rima's Lionel Pearson. Like Adrian Jones's work, C.S. Jagger's revealed a first-hand experience of battle in the Great War.

Guarding the carved faces of the base are statues of soldiers, accurately modelled to the last grenade or water carrier. Confrontation with these dark bronze sentinels reaffirms the shock of wastage in the fourth recumbent figure, covered with his cloak and bearing his tin helmet on his chest. Above are the regimental arms and the motto, 'Ubique', and the words: 'Here was a royal fellowship of death'.

A roll of honour reposes in a chamber beneath, and on the sides of the base are listed the theatres of war. The carved reliefs show gunners operating every kind of ordnance used in battle, but the memorial is sombrely reflective rather than warlike, and

Machine Gun Corps Memorial ('David'). Sculptor: F. Derwent Wood (1925). Location: Hyde Park Corner.

it is now recognised as a solemn tribute to almost 50,000 dead and 6,700 missing. Jagger himself, holder of the Military Cross, had been wounded at Gallipoli and later in France. Trained as a salon sculptor, his experiences at Gallipoli were to bring a weighty realism to his idealised war heroes.

The memorial was unveiled by the Duke of Connaught, who had performed the same ceremony earlier that year for Derwent Wood's Machine Gun Corps Memorial. This is a bronze David (without the fig leaf), holding a large sword, and flanked by wreathed tin hats and machine guns, now standing near the Duke of Wellington's statue. Other monuments (including Donald Potter's granite-carved Lord Baden-Powell OM, Chief Scout, as an old man – the only London statue wearing shorts) inhabit the parks and their periphery; some may be more conventional, but each has its distinguishing detail or design.

Outer London Gazetteer

Paddington & Northwest London

Paddington Feature:

Sarah Siddons (1755–1831)
Marble seated statue on Portland stone pedestal
Sculptor Léon Joseph Chavalliaud
Location Paddington Green

Like Albert in Kensington and Churchill in Parliament Square, the great tragedienne is honoured with a single explanatory inscription: SIDDONS.

This is how she was recalled by the acting profession, and was known in her lifetime. Her marble statue owes something to her portrait as the Tragic Muse by her friend Reynolds, but the finger cocked against her cheek, the intense stare as if from centre stage and the large dagger in her right hand owe all to Chavalliaud. His statue was damaged in the blitz and has received two restorations, the most recent in 1987. (The Reynolds portrait hangs in the picture gallery at Dulwich College, and the National Gallery has one by Gainsborough.)

The Green (which had a pond in Mrs Siddons's lifetime) and St Mary's Church where she worshipped, now look over Westway, the motor-route to the West, and to Wales where she was eldest

Sarah Siddons (1755–1831). Sculptor: L. J. Chavalliaud (1897). Location: Paddington Green.

child in Roger Kemble's family of strolling players. Two of her brothers and her niece Fanny made their names on the stage, but as the tragic actor John Philip Kemble declared, whereas his performances were controlled art, his sister's were art itself. She is buried in the disused churchyard, her tomb shared by her companion and dresser, Pattie Wilkinson. Sarah's son John is also buried here (as is the sculptor Joseph Nollekens, d.1823).

Further along Westway is the site of Siddons' first retirement home, then in rural surroundings, where she settled in 1817 with her daughter and dresser to do gardening and clay modelling (the V & A stores a plaster self-portrait). From here she ventured to London through footpad territory, entertained literary and theatrical society, and received the Prince Regent. His father, George III, once commanded Mrs Siddons to repeat her most famous role, Lady Macbeth, at which the king had to distract Queen Charlotte from the most dramatic parts. At these powerful and impassioned performances the audiences, packed to suffocation, were said to shriek, sob and swoon.

The Drury Lane audience brought her retirement performance to a halt after the famous sleepwalking scene, to which Mrs Siddons as Lady Macbeth brought intensity where others evoked stupor. Almost four decades earlier, as a friend of the actor-manager David Garrick, her first London part had been a 'conspicuous failure', but as Sir Henry Irving recalled in 1897, after unveiling her statue, 'she went back to the hard school of the provincial theatre, and matured her powers by unflagging industry'.

At her next appearance in Drury Lane after a gap of six years, Siddons took London by storm. She recalled sitting down afterwards with her father and husband to 'a frugal neat supper in a silence uninterrupted except by exclamations of gladness from Mr Siddons'. Sarah was tall, with dark eyes and brows, a full mouth and the long Kemble nose; modest and sensible in private, as noted by Walpole, her stage presence was awesome and terrifying. For the dramatic critic William Hazlitt, she was Tragedy personified.

Her shapely hands belied early years as working wife of a minor player, when she taught the world, said Dame Sybil Thorndyke, that 'domesticity was not incompatible with art'. Personal tragedy touched her in the death of two grown daughters, and a son. At her own funeral, which she requested should be small and private, 5,000 people followed the cortège from her last home in Baker Street to her church on Paddington Green.

Paddington & Northwest London Selection

On Paddington station, the powerfully-built figure of a C.S. Jagger 'Tommy' stands easy against the wall of Platform One. His tin helmet is at an angle, his haggared features are momentarily eased over a letter from home. The idealised physique and gaunt expression, combined with a brutally-accurate reproduction of combat uniform, is a hallmark of Jagger's sculptural work on Great War monuments, of which he was one of Britain's most outstanding exponents. The memorial recalls the '3312 men and women of the GWR (Great Western Railway) who gave their lives for King and Country'.

Also worth finding at the platform entrance, on the same wall, is a *bas*-relief depicting the great GWR engineer I.K. Brunel, designer and builder of the glass-vaulted station. He is cocksure (as well he might be) with top hat and cigar. The plaque signed by E.R. Bevan was unveiled on the station's centenary of 1954. In 1982, Brunel's seated statue by

I. K. Brunel (1806–1854). Sculptor: John Doubleday (1982). Location: Paddington Station.

John Doubleday was inaugurated at the top of the Underground staircase in a unique twinning with Bristol's unveiling of Brunel's full-length bronze, also by Doubleday.

In St John's Wood, at the Zebra crossing immortalised by the Beatles, the Arts are represented by an obelisk to a practitioner of the 'New Sculpture', Onslow Ford (1852–1901). A bronze roundel by Lucchesi shows Ford's keen profile with waxed moustache, and an early example of a flat-top haircut. At the front of the obelisk, designed by Sir J.W. Simpson in 1903, is a casting of a seated Muse from Ford's dramatic Shelley Memorial at Oxford (1892); for those with florid tastes, this guarantees a bright moment along the North London commuter route to Paddington and the M40. Ford's first important commission, a bronze of Sir Rowland Hill (unveiled in 1882), stands in the City.

At the back of the Swiss Cottage Library, on Adelaide Road, is a tense portrayal by Oscar Nemon of Sigmund Freud (1856–1939). The seated figure was unveiled by young members of the Freud family in 1970. The great psychoanalyst, who sat for Nemon, lived near here in exile from Vienna, and his house in Maresfield Gardens can be visited. In amiable contrast, on loan outside the Camden Arts Centre and visible from Finchley Road, sits a fibreglass edition of André Wallace's 'The Whisper', in pale pastel colours.

The original was exhibited at the RA in 1983, and the next year was installed at Sainsbury's Homebase store on a landscaped island in 'Peter Pan's pool', Beckenham Road, Catford; and these two hefty, gossiping girls perch (in bronze) outside Milton Keynes Library.

In Waterlow Park at Highgate, a conventional commemorative statue by Frank Taubman shows Sir Sydney Waterlow (1822–1906) Lord Mayor, with hat and umbrella. The park occupies his estate, a gift in 1891: 'A garden for the gardenless'. The statue was erected the following year.

Farther out on the North Circular (Regent's Park Road) is another brawny heroine, locally known as the 'Naked Lady' in a jubilant tip-toed pose, holding up a sword; her name Déliverance appears across its hilt. Inevitably she caused a stir when unveiled by David Lloyd George in 1926, but the inscription explains: 'This statue by Emile Guillaume symbolises the emotion inspired among the Allied nations when the armies of Britain and France defeated the invading German armies at the Battle of the Marne, September 1914'. It was called one of the decisive battles of the world, but the abyss was yet to open.

Islington & Northeast London

Islington Selection:

Sir Hugh Myddleton (1560–1631)
Full-length marble statue on stone pedestal, and fountain with ornamental sculptures
Sculptor John Thomas ·
Location Islington Green

The entrepreneurial Sir Hugh Myddleton, goldsmith, banker and MP for Denbigh in his native Wales, appears in marble image with Elizabethan trunk hose

Sir Hugh Myddleton (1560–1631). Sculptor: John Thomas (1862). Location: Islington Green.

and ruff, accompanied by stone cherubs whose pitchers once poured water. The chief donor of this set piece was the Victorian entrepreneur Sir Samuel Morton Peto, patron of the arts, contractor for the Houses of Parliament and for Nelson's Column, and an influential force behind the Great Exhibition. The sculptor, John Thomas, produced private works for Peto at Somerleyton Hall in Suffolk, and his Islington fountain is a reminder of the New River by which 'Myddleton's Water' supplied north London and the City until the late 1980s.

On an island near the man-made river's source at Amwell, a beautiful backwater near Ware in Hertfordshire, a small 18th-century pillar bears the chiselled words:

> From the Spring of Chadwell,
> two miles West
> And from this Source of Amwell
> the Aqueduct meanders
> for the space of XI Miles:
> Conveying
> Health, Pleasure and convenience
> to the Metropolis
> of Great Britain

The scheme was devised by Edmund Colthurst but it was Myddleton, member of a Government Committee on London's water shortage, who backed it, with Colthurst acting as his partner and overseer. Starting in 1609, the 10ft channel was constructed to follow contours, maintaining level ground whilst covering almost twice the distance from the source to the River Head near Islington. Engineering problems and aggrieved land-owners brought holdups and financial hardship, relieved in 1611 by a loan from James I, who also forbade any further hindrance against his 'highe displeasure'. Myddleton's technical achievements included underground conduits and, at Enfield where he had a house, a boarded overground flume.

A reservoir, the Round Pond, was built over 'an open idell pool' at the River Head, and from here the water was piped *via* a series of cisterns and elm-trunks to various parts of North London. At the New River's inauguration on Michaelmas Day in 1613, watched by Sir Hugh with the Lord Mayor, the Lord Mayor elect (Myddleton's brother) and other dignitaries, the flood gates were opened with 'drummes and trumpets sounding in triumphall manner', and the stream 'ranne gallantly into the cisterne'.

Myddleton received a knighthood, and later a baronetcy; in 1614, the Myddleton's Head inn opened opposite the Round Pond, amongst fields belonging to the water company. The inn, with Sir Hugh's portrait along with his conduit on its sign, appears in Hogarth's painting, 'Evening'. Later it was popular with performers from the Sadler's Wells Theatre, where the three-year-old Joseph Grimaldi first trod the boards. (His burial place is now a pretty park, named after Grimaldi, bordering Rodney Street and Pentonville Road. His shapely headstone, and grave sewn with forget-me-nots and geraniums, has been railed off, and wrought-iron theatrical masks affixed, with a bronze plaque: '... From his debut in 1806 at Covent Garden in Mother Goose he was adored by all and could fill a theatre anywhere. The name Joey has passed into the language to mean a clown ...' The monument just post-dates the demolishing of the house, nearby, where Grimaldi died.)

'Myddleton's Water' system has been successively enlarged and updated, one of the first additions being the Water House, Clerkenwell, built at the terminus with stopcocks and a counting house, replaced by the Thames Water Company offices in the 1920s.

Other reminders near the site of the New River Head, now part of Rosebery Avenue, include streets and squares carrying names of Myddleton, Amwell and Chadwell. They were developed by the Company surveyor William Chadwell Mylne, who altered the Water House to accommodate company offices, and made other improvements. Chadwell succeeded as surveyor his father, the architect Robert Mylne (1733–1811), who raised the pretty pillar dated MDCCC at Great Amwell (and one at Chadwell) to mark Myddleton's endeavour:

> An immortal Work
> Since men cannot more nearly
> imitate the Deity
> Than in bestowing health

The gifted and versatile Robert is listed as 'Architect, Engineer, &ca'. The New River Walk between St Paul's Road and Canonbury Walk brings a green stretch to Islington, but Sir Hugh Myddleton's New River faces redundancy through Thames Water's construction of a new deep water link system, and a new Action Group seeks to preserve the old water course with its picnic sites and bird sanctuaries, bridges, and other fine structures such as Chadwell Mylne's 'Castle' Pumping Station – a Stoke Newington landmark. These, too, are monuments to the 'Genius Talents & elevation of mind' that created Myddleton's Water. (Sir Hugh's effigy by Samuel Joseph, 1814, with Sir Thomas Gresham's and Dick Whittington's, also ornaments the City's Royal Exchange.)

Northeast London Selection

As if to form a trio, statues in this part of London honour two others who set out to bestow health, one for the body, one for the spirit: John Wesley's bronze statue welcomes Methodists to his City Road Chapel, built in 1777, and Sir Robert Geffrye (1613–1704) stands in lead effigy over the entrance to his almshouses in Kingsland Road (since 1911 a museum).

The original, and a model, by John Van Nost (1723) belong to the Ironmongers' Company, and this £40 copy by James Maude & Co., with its fine detail of the full-bottomed wig, and the brocading on the municipal robes, was installed in 1913. It shows 'SR Rob Geffryes KnT Alderman and Iron-

John Wesley (1703–1791).
Sculptor: John Adams–Acton (1891).
Location: City Road Wesleyan Chapel.

monger' holding a glove, as in the original briefing to Nost, 'with ye proper ornaments of a Lord Mayor'. A GLC booklet of 1979 amply describes Sir Geffrye, his statue and the Almshouses.

In the chapel is a fine marble monument to Geffrye, a City merchant, and his wife, probably by a City woodcarver Richard Saunders. The front gardens once had a bust of Sir William Cremer, MP for Haggerston, who fought for their retention as a public space after the almshouses were sold by the Ironmongers' Company in 1911. The building had retained its original use since its construction in 1715 from money left by Sir Robert.

Still in use as a chapel is 'the mother church of world Methodists', built by John Wesley in 1777 to replace his smaller Moorfield headquarters in a converted cannon foundry. Wesley's dwelling next door is now a small museum, and his bronze statue in the chapel forecourt bears the message, 'The world is my parish'. Wesley did indeed spread his fervour wide, preferring life on the road to a settled existence, travelling in all weathers, reading, on horseback with the reins slack, until he was 70, when he took to a chaise with bookcase and desk. His diaries include notes on the countryside, and Wesley's stern values bear upon each scene, as at Stourhead where the statue of the River God and others are 'images of Devils'.

His statue by John Adams–Acton was erected by the 'Children of Methodism' in 1891, the centenary of Wesley's death. He holds his small field bible. The sculptor has not managed to record his diminutive stature – Wesley was only 5'3". Nearby is a small handsome obelisk ('Albert Dunkley, stonemason') to Wesley's mother Susannah (d.1742), who is buried in Bunhill Fields across the road.

In Victoria Park East, Bow, near the bandstand, the fabulous riches of the remarkable banking heiress, the Baroness Burdett-Coutts (1814–1904), are reflected in the variety of stone and stonework on her sumptuous Victoria Fountain, designed by H.A. Darbishire and opened 1862 by the baroness in the presence of large gathering of nobility and gentry, and a crowd of 10,000. Erected 'for the love of God and Country', it is now boarded up against vandalism and awaiting refurbishment that Bow cannot afford. The baroness directed her fortunes to the needy in all parts of the world; conducted a *Grand Amour* with the Duke of Wellington; was the first woman to be created Baroness (1871) rather than inherit the title, and was the last person to be buried in Westminster Abbey. She represents a grand era, long past.

Poplar & East London

Poplar Feature:

Dock Road
Richard Green (1803–1863)
Bronze seated statue on granite bow-fronted
pedestal with bronze reliefs
Sculptor Edward W. Wyon
Location Poplar Public Baths, East India Road

A big impressive monument showing the shipowner seated at ease, his foolishly-adoring Newfoundland dog, Hector, resting its head on his knee: this impression of domesticity and power recalls Green's philanthropy and concern for the individual which won him the affection of East Londoners. The Poplar Hospital which he assisted, and the Sailors' Home which he founded, stood near the site of his statue outside the Poplar Baths and Laundries. His death was noted in *The Illustrated London News* as 'little less than a calamity'.

On the west face of his pedestal, in strong relief, is an ugly-looking frigate under production for the Spanish government at the time of Green's death. On the east face is shown the first ship dispatched by Green's Blackwall shipyard on the China run. His father George, also a prominent local figure, had built the business by fitting out whalers; Richard, born in Blackwall, entered the partnership in 1829 and at his father's death continued independently with his brother Henry. Together they perpetuated their father's tradition of public generosity which according to older local people, being still remembered, needs no monument.

Their company built East Indiamen and supplied ships during the Gold Rush. Green, a generous employer with sound business sense, had a knack for quick decision making. He explained that he had 'no time to hesitate', but found time to improve his men's conditions and, more broadly, the Merchant Service, as well as for local good works. His major role in founding the Merchant Service training ship, HMS *Worcester*, later secured him its first Chairmanship; he was also involved in forming the Royal Naval Reserve at the time of his death. Green's statue, proposed within days, was subscribed by admirers both local and from the far continents plied by his ships.

The London docks no longer operate; the readership of *The East End News* which carried black rules between its columns to mark Richard Green's

Richard Green (1830–1863). Sculptor: E. W. Wyon (1863). Location: East India Road.

passing, and the same community that raised his monument, are largely gone. The Baths' utility by the poor and needy has given way to more high-spirited usage: in 1965, firemen freeing a schoolboy trapped while reclaiming a swimsuit from the statue, saved the boy's leg at the expense of the dog's ear. Hector's master is buried in the nearby grounds of Trinity Chapel, founded by George Green, destroyed in the Blitz and rebuilt as Trinity Congregational Church.

East London Selection

East London monuments, some neglected and abused, hark back to former communities now dispersed. Outside the London Hospital in Whitechapel Road is the remains of an elaborate fountain to Edward VII, whose monuments dominate the locality. W.S. Frith's bronze bust of the king has been torn off; the bronze figures over side basins, cherubs holding a car and an aeroplane, should be conserved as period curios, if not for their charm.

The Angel of Peace prevails, and so does the inscription 'In grateful and loyal memory of Edward VII, Rex et Imperator, erected from subscriptions raised by the Jewish inhabitants of East London'. The community has dispersed, leaving its £800 fountain to new settlers with other memories.

In the courtyard of the London Hospital is a fine statue of Edward's wife, Alexandra, by George Wade

*Queen Alexandra (1844–1925); statue pedestal panel.
Sculptor: G. E. Wade (1908). Location: London Hospital,
Whitechapel Road.*

(whose statues of Edward stand in Reading and Bootle). Relief panels show grim scenes of the Princess visiting a female ward where patients receive from goggled nurses the Finsen Light Cure for Lupus (a form of skin tuberculosis). Needless to say the 'cure' itself was later found to be highly dangerous. Edward is in attendance, uniformed, holding his plumed helmet. Alexandra, as Princess of Wales, presented the country's first Finsen Lamp in 1900, and the statue dates from 1908.

Past Cambridge Heath Road on a green alongside Mile End Road, north side, is a fine bronze bust of Edward in his medals and tassels: PEACE HATH HER VICTORIES NO LESS RENOWNED THAN WAR. This was raised in 1911, the same year as the Whitechapel fountain,'by a few Freemasons of the East district of London'. Also at either end of this stretch are vandalised casts of Wade monuments to General William Booth, who founded the Salvation Army here in 1865, preaching his first sermon in the disused Quakers' burial ground.

Nearby at Trinity Green are ornamental gate piers with stone sailing ships and medallions commemorating Captain Henry Mudd's gift of land to Trinity House for 'This Almshouse Wherein 28 decay'd Masters & Comanders of Ships or the Widows of such are maintain'd'. (Inside, but formerly behind the chapel, is Jasper Latham's marvellous image, 1683, of Captain Richard Marples (d.1680) who left £1,300 towards construction of the almshouses; also by an unknown sculptor a stone statue — 'very poor', according to Gleichen — of Captain Robert Sandes, erected 1746.)

Facing the river in King Edward Memorial Park, Shadwell, a big stone pillar carries Bertram Mackennal's bronze portrait medallion of Edward VII, 'in grateful memory'. It was funded with extra money from the London memorial, an equestrian statue by the same sculptor (*see* West End), and resulted from the Bishop of Stepney's idea for a people's park to replace the old Shadwell fish market. Inaugurated in 1922 by King George V for 'the use and enjoyment of the people of East London for ever', it is indeed enjoyed by successive local communities.

Also in the park, near the old Rotherhithe Tunnel rotunda, a pretty shipping scene in coloured tiles is signed 'Carter & Poole, 1922'. Erected by the LCC, it commemorates 16th-century navigators and explorers whose tall ships set sail from this reach of the river.

The latest East London statue, standing outside the Limehouse Library in Commercial Road, continues the tale of dispersal and renewal. It is a bronze figure of the Labour leader Clement Attlee, who became Prime Minister immediately after the Second World War. It was commissioned from Frank Forster for Mile End Park not by Jewish residents or Freemasons, but by the Greater London Council. Part of the £23,000 cost was still unpaid at the demise of the GLC in 1987, and the statue was offered to any of the newly-formed local neighbourhoods willing to pay £3,000. It was finally erected near Attlee's former residence in the Wapping Neighbourhood, and unveiled in 1988 by Sir Harold Wilson, then the last living member of Attlee's post-war Cabinet of 1945–1951.

Crystal Palace & South London

Crystal Palace Feature:

Sir Joseph Paxton (1801–1865)
Outsize marble bust on dark red brick pedestal with
bronze relief of Crystal Palace
Sculptor W.F. Woodington ARA
Location National Sport Centre Entrance
(Ledrington Gate)

How are the mighty fallen! Paxton's great leonine, Victorian-classical marble head, set on a brick stalk, well as a friend, travelling companion and business adviser to the improvident duke.

Paxton applied his own flair and influence in property and railways development, and grew in brilliance not only as a landscape gardener, but as designer and engineer of Chatsworth's famous fountains and superb conservatories in conjunction with Decimus Burton. These were built to Paxton's new glass and metal system, the largest, completed in 1840, being 300ft long.

This Victorian whizz-kid shot to fame by saving Prince Albert's Great Exhibition of the Works of Industry of All Nations, doomed to the Executive Committee's turgidly-designed exhibition building. Paxton offered a 'notion', and with his Chatsworth team, completed plans from a blotting-paper sketch doodled at a Railway Board meeting in Derby.

This revolutionary scheme, a colossal version of the Lily House at Chatsworth, caused committee dithering but was publicly acclaimed after appearing in the *Illustrated London News*. Acceptance hung on saving three lofty elms but I. K. Brunel who, like Charles Barry, acted as an adviser to the architect, suggested roofing the trees, and the palace's vast vaulted transept was born. 'It will be more curious than anything that can be seen in it', was the Duke of Wellington's prediction.

The Exhibition and its Hall, constructed by the railway engineers Fox and Henderson, were a success; Paxton was knighted, and entered Parliament. After the Exhibition, he formed a company to buy the Hall for £70,000 and re-erected it at Penge Place, also specially purchased. It was enlarged to include three transepts displaying, among other features, sculpture galleries with busts of the powerful and famous. The sloping, 349-acre woodland became a People's Park with lakes, sunken gardens, tea maze, rosery, fountains and statuary.

When the Crystal Palace was burned in 1936, the Victorian Imperialistic vigour that created and maintained it had long died; like so many grandly-conceived monuments, the Palace became a costly white elephant, neglected and abused.

After the fire, the park's beauties were buried beneath a sports centre and fun machines. Many statues lay among the weeds, still guarded by the great stone sphinxes at either end of the Italian Terraces. Works by Rafaelle Monti, by Marochetti and others, were dispersed in the mammoth statuary sale of 1957, whilst some selected specimens were stacked away.

No one bothered to remove the educational, geological 'swamp' where 'Paxton's Monsters' roamed.

Sir Joseph Paxton (1801–1865). Sculptor: W. F. Woodington RA (1856). Location: Ledrington Gate, Crystal Palace.

peers like Mr Wot over the turnstile gates of the sports arena which was built in the grounds of the defunct Crystal Palace in 1964. The GLC made a concrete seating area just outside the gates, and put Paxton in the space between, where he remains as an example of the 'institutional vandalism' noted in a report by Bromley Council on transfer of the Crystal Palace site from the GLC in 1986.

The bust was recorded in the Crystal Palace statuary sale catalogue of 1957, which described 'the Paxton Memorial Garden, with its Triton fountain reminiscent of Bernini, ringed by putti centred on a colossal marble head of Paxton, architect of the Palace'. It was specially carved for this setting at Paxton's Crystal Palace in Sydenham, 101 years earlier.

The Crystal Palace was the *chef d'oeuvre* of Joseph Paxton, farmer's son, whose youthful employment in the Historical Society Garden at Chiswick had entailed opening the gates for the 6th Duke of Devonshire. Head-hunted, Paxton was to become Chief Gardener at the Duke's Chatsworth estate, as

These famous lifesize prehistoric animals had been constructed of stucco-covered brick and iron by Waterhouse Hawkins to the instruction of Professor Richard Owen, originator of the name Dinosaur. A feast was held in the belly of the Iguanodon on New Year's Eve, 1853. An Irish guest drank himself insensible, awoke in prehistoric Britain, and escaped trembling to Penge.

Paxton's palace still lives in public memory, acclaimed as a triumph of architectural innovation. It was the world's first large-scale prefabricated building of iron and glass that had 'taught the world how to roof in great spaces', according to Prince Albert's co-organiser of the Great Exhibition, Henry Cole. To Queen Victoria, the palace was 'one of the wonders of the world'. In both its locations it was a thing of beauty, its reflections from Sydenham Hill visible on the South Downs. Its spectacular end was watched by Londoners throughout the night of the mysterious fire.

Bromley Council has taken possession during a revival in public awareness of design and style. They are slowly, surely, commendably, recreating the park. A palace-inspired hotel is being built on the original palace site, near the BBC transmitter. The tea maze was restored in 1988. There is new hope for the noble portrait of Paxton, erected by public subscription in 1873 and still sharply defined, and so reminiscent of Woodington's other large, leonine sculpture, greeting travellers from north London at Westminster Bridge – his majestic Coade Lion.

South of the River Selection

Just by the lake and behind the cafe at the Penge entrance on Thicket Road is 'Guy the Gorilla', carved from dark marble by David Wynne in 1961. Guy came via Paris from the French Cameroons aged 18 months, and for over 30 years was a favourite at London Zoo until his early death in 1978. His realistic and curiously-agreeable statue, showing Guy on all fours on a rough wedge-shaped pedestal, is an audience-participation work since children pat, stroke and climb as well as look.

Other curious, agreeable statues can be admired in south London, most of them belonging to buildings which are still standing. On Champion Hill, the Salvation Army's training college lawn has bronze statues of the Army's first General, William Booth, and the Army Mother Mrs Catherine Booth; she is serene and matronly in her bonnet, but her husband is an Old Testament figure with eyes ablaze, beard flowing, finger pointing, medals mustered, and a

Guy the Gorilla. Sculptor: David Wynne (1961). Location: Crystal Palace Gardens.

small prayer book in his hand. His tunic bears the Army motto, 'Blood and Fire'.

He was 'Promoted to Glory August 20th 1912', and she in 1890; the College installed the statues by G.E. Wade on the centenary of their birth (1929). The Booths began their first Mile End mission with bands, banners, uniforms and hymn singing to attract the poor from the gin palaces. The Army is now part of a worldwide organisation and fellowship.

Further west at the top of Brixton Hill, Thomas Brock's bronze bust of Sir Henry Tate (1819–1899) stands outside the Tate Central Library, one of many national and local gifts of this 'VPRIGHT MERCHANT, WISE PHILANTHROPIST' and south London resident who started work as a grocer's boy and made a fortune from developing the sugar cube. The original of his 'speaking likeness' is stored in the Tate Gallery on Millbank, given with Sir Henry's collection of English paintings built around the finest works of Millais (whose statue is in the Tate's forecourt). This bust, unveiled in 1905, was given by Lady Tate.

Across the road, a church monument of the Budd family now forms the apex of a small public park created from St Matthew's Church graveyard. A big Portland stone sepulchre, rich in classical and Egyptian carved symbols, it is the work of R. Day (1825) and grade II* listed.

Catherine Booth (1829–1890); Sculptor: G. E. Wade (1929). Location: Salvation Army Training College, Champion Hill.

William Booth (1829–1912). Sculptor: G. E. Wade (1929). Location: Salvation Army Training College, Champion Hill.

Described in Allen's History of Lambeth (1826) as the finest of its kind in London, it would have been removed in 1953 when the park was planned, but for Captain Bentinck Budd who withheld permission, despite the suggested replacement tablet which it was 'not unlikely' Lambeth Council would fund. Captain Budd's ancestor Richard Budd (1746–1821) was physician to Bartholomew's Hospital but, says the Dictionary of National Biography, 'did not exert himself greatly in private practice, having married the only child of a wealthy merchant'. He definitely does not deserve a Lambeth Council replacement tablet.

Brixton railway station, platforms 1 and 2, definitely does deserve Kevin Atherton's 'Platform Piece', comprising three extraordinarily strong and effective bronze figures of Brixton commuters. Lifelike in the extreme, they stand waiting on the platform (which serves as the pedestal) like any other traveller, two on one side, gazing across the track at the third. This unusual work, funded by British Rail and Lambeth Council, shows a harsh but handsome realism which confronts, but does not corroborate, Brixton's public image of urban deprivation and unrest.

In a technique popularised among others by the sculptor George Segal, moulds were taken from local volunteer models using hospital plaster bandages. Clothing of the models' choice was added to the casts taken from these moulds, and another mould of the whole was made. Within this mould, the clothing (and with it the first cast) were burned away leaving a second mould from which the final bronzes were made.

The installation ceremony performed by Sir Hugh Casson marked completion of a £1 million painting and refurbishment to station, market shops and viaduct. Since 1986 the figures in their vulnerable position have, on the whole, been unmolested.

A piece of South London exotica stands in Cannizaro Park on Wimbledon Common, behind the Cannizaro Hotel. It is a large, grey stone bust of the Emperor Haile Selassie, who 'visited Wimbledon when he took refuge in this country' as Italian troops entered Abyssinia in 1936. His image was carved by his hostess, Hilda Seligman, and in 1958 when the family house was sold and demolished, Mrs Seligman's work was given to Wimbledon Council in memory of the Emperor's visit. Its presence causes minor embarrassment through the potentially energetic interest of the Rastafarian community, but adds to the silvan pleasures of a clearing to the left of the Rhododendron Walk.

Admiral Lord Nelson (1758–1805). Sculptor: F. Brook Hitch (1951). Location: Pembroke Gardens, Portsmouth.

Southern Counties

'Soldier, Sailor . . .'

Sleep after toyle
Port after
Stormy seas
Ease after war
Death after life
Doth greatly
Please

(Edmund Spenser's lines quoted under the
bronze statue of Admiral Robert Blake
(1599–1657) by F.W. Pomeroy, at Bridgwater
near the Parrett Estuary in Somerset)

M en and women are known for the company they keep, and a region may be known for the men and women it commemorates. So it is in England's rural counties south of the Thames estuary and the Severn Sea, in the seaside resorts, and the old battle-scarred seaports facing the Continent across the English Channel. The statues and monuments are wide-ranging in style, scale and subject, but there is a bias towards admirals and generals, forgotten battles and global wars. Royalty who caused or encouraged the battles, and the landed gentry who provided admirals and generals, also make their mark.

The military and naval aspects come together in Bridgwater's statue of Admiral Blake, who showed his mettle as a Cromwellian soldier before exercising his outstanding sea skills as Commonwealth sailor. The Admiral appears in sea boots and wind-whipped coat, pointing over-dramatically at some far horizon whilst history is relived on pedestal *bas*-reliefs, one showing Blake's flagship in Plymouth Sound after his spectacular action against the Spanish at Santa Cruz. The lines from Edmund Spenser's poetry quoted on the pedestal aptly evoke Blake's death from fever within sight of Plymouth.

Born at Bridgwater and educated at Oxford, Blake

Admiral Robert Blake (1599–1657)
Sculptor: F. W. Pomeroy, RA (1900).
Location: Cornhill, Bridgwater.

followed his father's occupation as a trader, joining Cromwell's army in his late forties. He was given command of the Commonwealth fleet against Prince Rupert's navy, 'doubtless', wrote G.M. Trevelyan, 'because his knowledge of ships and seamen was at least greater than that of other soldiers'. Within a decade, Blake's brilliantly effective actions against the French, the Spanish, and the mighty Dutch had restored English superiority on the high seas.

Blake's naval pre-eminence has placed him alongside Drake and Nelson, and all three have statues on the southern shores facing the Atlantic and the Channel, the Continental powers, the Mediterranean, the far-flung oceans and the Main.

Most prominent in its landscape is a bust of Nelson, his medals and his empty sleeve across his chest, staring over Portsmouth and the Solent from a lofty white pillar on the Portshead ridge. It was erected (1807–1814) by his comrades of Trafalgar 'to perpetuate his triumph and their regret'.

In Portsmouth near the sea front, F. Brook Hitch's bronze figure of Nelson (c.1959) shows him hawkishly handsome in undress uniform, including the coat in which he received his fatal wound. It is correct 'to the smallest detail', states one of many inscriptions – 'you who tread his footsteps remember his glory'.

Drake's bronze statue on Plymouth Hoe has a single inscription: DRAKE. The Elizabethan adventurer commands the Hoe and the Sound, whilst Nelson in Portsmouth's Pembroke Gardens, marking a spot passed embarking for Trafalgar, confronts a run-down pleasure park. This may be a question of period, our own lacking a certain reverential concern for quality and worth, or it may be that Drake belongs to Devon whilst Nelson was a Norfolk man.

In Praise of Waterloo

Nelson's military counterpart Arthur Wellesley, 1st Duke of Wellington, was born in Ireland; like Nelson, his monuments occur throughout England. Amongst those in the south is Marochetti's bronze statue raised on a Tuscan column by Wellington's son the 2nd Duke, and the 'Tennants, Servants and Labourers' at Stratfield Saye, the Hampshire estate given by the nation in gratitude for Waterloo; a gravestone in the grounds marks the burial place of his war horse, Copenhagen, put out to grass here after the battle – a favourite with Wellington's grandchildren. Man and horse, in a big bronze by Mathew Cotes Wyatt (assisted by his son James, 1838–46), were put out to grass at Caesar's Camp near Aldershot after being banished by public displeasure from Decimus Burton's Arch, Hyde Park, in 1883.

The Ladies of Torrington in Devon showed their pleasure in Wellington's triumph by erecting a small pyramidal Waterloo Tower with a seat, overlooking the wooded River Torridge, and a dedication: 'PEACE TO THE SOULS OF THE HEROES!!!' Near Wellington in Somerset a spotlit obelisk on Blackdown, above the M5, recalls the choice of Wellington's name from a gazetteer on his ennoblement after Talavera, by his brother Lord Wellesley. With its strong Egyptian motifs the obelisk was designed by T. Lee in response to plans for a Waterloo Tower at Bulkeley near Beaumaris, Anglesey; it was built – three-sided to save money – from 1817, its present 175ft not attained until 1892.

Somerset Belvederes

Somerset's wealth of 18th- or 19th-century viewing towers, exalting soldiers, seafarers and others from the time of Alfred the Great, may have sprung from such rivalries; perhaps one tower inspired the next. They are amongst the most haunting of monuments, their dark spiral stairs ascending to panoramic views, the minutiae of their dedicatees' deeds, titles and honours carved in marble at the door.

A lonely rostral tower of 1851 near Butleigh, designed by Henry Goodridge, is a tribute to Admiral Hood (d.1814) by his fellow officers, whilst Sir William Pynsent's elegant belvedere at Curry Rival, designed by Capability Brown for William Pitt, is colonised by jackdaws; it deserves restoration, and is the subject of an appeal.

Joseph Jopling's pretty Ammerdown column, emulating the Eddystone Light, stands in memory of T.S. Joliffe (1853). The pear-shaped glass panels of the viewing drum, some still intact, reflect across the arable fields of Lord Hylton's estate, open to the public on certain days. Near Hawkesbury Upton, Vulliamy's fanciful creation of 1843–8 gives a resumé of Lord Edward Somerset's redoubtable military career; the key to his tower is kept at the custodians' cottage. The view reaches to a neighbouring Gloucestershire hill and the Tyndale Tower, erected 1866, a tribute to the translator of the New Testament. A North Nibley villager keeps the key.

Waterloo Tower, to commemorate the Battle of Waterloo (1815). Design: not known (1816). Location: Torrington.

Other counties' half-forgotten heroes are immortalised with towers as disparate as Lieutenant-General Walter Raleigh Gilbert's mighty obelisk and landmark (1856) on Beacon Hill, Bodmin, or the Coote Column with disused viewing platform planted in a Rockbourne cornfield, Hants, where it was used for 1940s target practice by USAF troops. Local people speak of a ghostly servant sweeping leaves from the path to West Park house (now demolished), home of Sir Eyre Coote, extraordinary hero of the Indian campaigns, after his marriage in 1763. His widow erected the column in 1827, also dedicated to Coote's less-illustrious nephew.

Another India hero is honoured by a triangular turreted tower on Haldon Hill near Exeter, built in 1788 by Sir Robert Palk, 'eyewitness of the triumphs in war and the virtues in peace' of his benefactor Major-General Stringer Lawrence. Amongst mementoes of Lawrence's India is a copy by Eleanor Coade (1789) of his marble statue by Peter Scheemakers, made for the East India Company HQ in 1764. The custodians offer old world courtesy, and the stairs are light and broad – the tower was used for parties, and as servants' quarters, for the Palk home nearby. It was brutally damaged in army occupation during the Second World War.

Soldier, Sailor, Adventurer . . .

Soldiers' and seafarers' monuments, with salt and adventure in their joints, stand in all the south's main seaports, from Plymouth to Chatham on the Thames

The Hon. C. S. Rolls (1877–1910). Sculptor: Kathleen Scott (1912). Location: Promenade, Dover.

estuary, to which Sydney March's bronze equestrian figure of Lord Kitchener in replica, made by the Royal Engineers, was returned from Khartoum after Sudanese Independence in 1958. The Sudanese Press Attaché attended the 1960 unveiling, at Dock Road, by the Minister of War Christopher Soames in morning dress and top hat. General Gordon, whom Kitchener avenged, rides eternally on camel back in Onslow Ford's bronze of 1890, at the Brompton Barracks, where he and Kitchener trained.

A familiar landmark to passers by in Railway Street, Chatham, is H.H. Armstead's bronze of Thomas Fletcher Waghorn, 'Pioneer and founder of the overland route' to India in 1829, a chart spread across his knee and a bronze-etched globe on the pedestal. The name 'Fletcher' comes from a long line of local dockyard craftsmen. Nearby on Sovereign Boulevarde is a stuggy clock tower, with drinking troughs (1934), to Will Adams (1564–1620), Gillingham pilot and Samurai whose tomb is in Gillingham's twin town Yokosuka, Japan. A plaque records Adams's shipwreck and lifelong captivity as the Japanese Shogun's salaried designer of ships, and intermediary with the East India Company. The

first Englishman on record to live in Japan, Adams supported his Gillingham family whilst rearing a Japanese one.

More familiar, on the Promenade at Dover, is Lady Scott's fine bronze of the Hon. C.S. Rolls, 'the first man to cross the Channel and return in a single flight'. Even before this exploit within a month of Rolls's death in June, 1910, the Mayor of Dover had mooted a monument in a letter to the *Times*. The bust of the Channel swimmer Captain Matthew Webb (1848–1883), carrying the fatal hero's signature, was 'Presented by MDVE ZO SOTIRAKI', the Greek long-distance swimmer, in 1951.

Rolls was from Monmouth and Webb from Shropshire, but Louis Blériot (1872–1936) made the mistake of being French, and has no statue. His first-ever flight of the Channel in 1909 was urged on by Mme Blériot: 'Where's the risk, except in getting your feet wet?' His lonely monument is specially atmospheric, and should not be neglected. Its monoplane shape is formed from granite pavings set in the grass at Northfall Meadow, Blériot's landing site behind the Castle.

War Heroes

The most conspicuous coastal monuments are those that recall the south's front-line position of both World Wars. They range from the small boulder carved with the Dunkirk small ships under fire, standing on the front in Dover – 'Hellfire Corner' – to Sir Edward Maufe's cathedral-like hilltop pavilion, the Commonwealth Air Forces' Memorial, full of light and poetic detail, overlooking Runnymede (NT) in Surrey. (Maufe's rotunda marking the signing of the Magna Carta, and G.A. Jellico's slab to John F. Kennedy, inscribed by Alan Collins – American gifts – are within walking distance.)

In Chatham, Portsmouth and Plymouth, the Royal Naval Manning Ports, stand First World War sea mark memorials with stone obelisk, carvings and figures of officers and ratings from a single impressive design by Sir Robert Lorimer, and pavilions added after 1939–45 by Sir Edward Maufe. They honour those 'who have no other grave than the sea'. Most affecting is Chatham's on the crest of Great Lines, overlooking a hillside housing estate and the former dockyard. All these imposing edifices attract personal anniversary memorials of flowers in jam jars, or handwritten messages.

Other war monuments, prominent in High Streets or on promenades, include the fine, flamboyant Winged Victory at Lewes, looking across at the

Royal Naval War Memorial: 1914–18/19. Architect: Sir Robert Lorimer (1924); sculptor of heraldic figures: Edmund Burton; 1939–1945/6 Pavillions added by Sir Edward Maufe. Location: Portsmouth.

Martyrs' Memorial on the opposite Hill, and Goscombe John's jaunty bronze soldier in Hussars' uniform of the Bengal Infantry, strutting on the front at Eastbourne. The Sussex villages of Eastergate and Staple Cross pay tribute with big stone lions, their tails hanging over the pillars in indolent menace. A range of small, Gothicky stone obelisks, like a set of chessmen, line Portsmouth sea front and Clarence gardens; rich in variegated stone, they were erected over the last half of the 19th century to record Victorian Empire-building battles, making sombre catalogues of losses from fever or wounds sustained in forgotten conflicts, fought out in disease-ridden trouble spots across the globe.

Royal Pleasures

In more frivolous vein are the statues marking royal patronage in the name of health, and later pleasure, in the seaside towns. George IV's love affair when Prince of Wales, with Mrs Fitzherbert and Brighton which he made 'Queen of Watering Places', is marked by Chantrey's bronze replica of the King in Pavilion Gardens; the prince's father George III, who braved the Weymouth seawater from a bathing

machine to the sound of brass bands, is shown ermine-robed beside a large crown, in a joyfully-painted ensemble rising from the sea front. Created in 1804 at Coade & Sealy's Ornamental Stone Manufactury, Lambeth, on a lofty base by Weymouth architect James Hamilton (1809), this is one of England's most delightful monuments.

George's trotting equestrian figure reveals the chalk on the long green slope overlooking the port; its cutting by 'forty navvies' was witnessed by Anne in Thomas Hardy's *The Trumpet Major*. This primitive form of tribute is quite common on the southern chalk scarplands, the earlier designs taking equine or human form, their purpose and origin as yet unknown. Better documented are the army regimental badges cut by Great War troops stationed near Wiltshire's Fovant Downs alongside the A30, and tended by the Fovant Badges Society. These as well as other chalk figures, and numerous rural monuments, owe their survival to the uninterrupted landowning tradition of the south.

The Landlord Tradition

The seaside resorts themselves were first developed by landowners as speculative ventures, and the clifftop Promenade at Eastbourne records this in its stately bronze by Alfred Drury of the 8th Duke of Devonshire (d.1908). Nearby, his father, who began

7th Duke of Devonshire (1808–1891). Sculptor: Sir W. Goscombe John, RA (1901). Location: Promenade, Eastbourne.

the development in the 1830s, appears slumped in a chair; signed and dated 1901, this statue is an example of Goscombe John's unrestrained approach to portraiture.

In Folkestone further east, Albert Bruce Joy's bronze of William Harvey, physician to Charles I, faces the steep cliff shoreline of his childhood (now the beautiful Leas walks). It is a formula bronze except that the famous diviner of blood circulation stands with his hand on his heart, and a heart (anatomically correct) in his hand. (A statue of Harvey from the same mould erected outside the William Harvey Hospital in Ashford, Kent was reputedly bought by a doctor from a patient, a local scrap dealer. A stone version, said to have come from the Royal College of Physicians demolished in the 1960s, stands outside the William Harvey Pub, Willesborough; it was bought from a builder's yard and restored by the landlord 'and several of his regulars', according to a local newspaper, in 1965.)

The rural towns have statues of landowners, seafarers or soldiers, some illustrious, others local boys made good. The Truro-born explorer Richard Lemon Lander's worn stone statue, carved by the Cornish sculptor Nevil Northey Burnard in 1852, stands on a granite column overlooking Lemon Street; Tavistock commemorates the renowned Sir Francis Drake in a bronze by Boehm, and the 7th Duke of Bedford, whose arsenic and copper mine (which provided the metal) made the town prosperous, by the Exeter sculptor E.B. Stephens. In Salisbury market, Henry Fawcett 'the Blind Postman', whose father was mayor in 1832, stands within sight of his Queen Street birthplace.

Fawcett was blinded reputedly from pellets accidentally shot as his father slipped when shooting on Harnham Hill. A 'reader' was employed to attend his Cambridge studies, and the statue's pedestal records a distinguished career as 'Professor of Political Economy, Cambridge', and MP. Fawcett's sculptor, Herbert Pinker, shows him without his glasses, which he often removed in debate. As Postmaster General, he introduced, among other services, the parcel post (1882) and the 6d. telegram.

Marochetti's bronze statue of Sydney Herbert, 1st Baron Herbert of Lea, also stood here until its removal to Victoria Park. His son, Lord Pembroke, unveiling the Fawcett bronze in 1887, declared 'there is no man, living or dead, I would so gladly see standing by the side of my father's'. Lord Pembroke's statue stands outside the ancestral home, Wilton House, where a stone equestrian figure of Marcus Aurelius crowns the gates.

Royal Allegiance

Royalty graces some market towns, notably Chichester, where Hubert le Sueur's bust of Charles I was installed after the Restoration in a niche formerly containing a figure of Bishop Storey. As with Le Sueur's historical lead gilt bust on Portsmouth's Square Tower, presented by the king in 1635, the original is now in the City museum, and has been copied in fibreglass. In Barnstaple, Queen Anne's Walk with a stone statue of the Queen (possibly by J. Harvey of Bath) was erected to emulate London's Royal Exchange in 1708; she also appears at Minehead, where her effigy attributed to Francis Bird was removed from the church to a columned canopy in Wellington Square in 1893. Her pedestal lists the great military victories of her reign. At Winchester, a High Street statue of Anne celebrates the Treaty of Utrecht in 1713.

At Petersfield in Hampshire, a lead equestrian statue of William III, in classical mode by John Cheere (1757), now rides above the hustle of the market square; it was expertly restored by public subscription in 1913 but not regilded – tarring and feathering during an election put paid to the original gilt. The handsome bow-fronted pedestal proclaims: WHEN THE STATE WAS TOTTERING HE HELD IT FIRM. It has been called 'ridiculous' but also 'magnificent, heroic'; its counterpart, a bronze by Michael Rysbrack in Bristol, is without doubt a masterpiece.

Bath

Bath's cultural history focuses on its spa waters, and its best sculpture is ornamental rather than commemorative; the buildings' warm ashlar blocks are chiselled with street names in Roman letters and the old elegant buildings bear carved figures, like Bath itself seemingly rarer and more precious than in other towns. Lucius Gahagan, who called his house 'Lo Studio', carved 'Commerce' and 'Genius' on No. 9 Quiet Street (1824), also Garrick's head – not very well – for the Garrick Head Hotel in 1831. It is now behind the Theatre Royal; on the front are garlanded masks and lyres, recently recarved by Lawrence Tyndall and Richard Strachey.

Over one of the pedimented residences in St James's Parade is a watchful, helmeted Athene, an antique bust which has been delicately restored as have small, queenly sphinxes on parapets in George Street and Belvedere. In a wall niche of the King's Baths, the statue of Bladud, Bath's legendary founder, has had layers of municipal paint scraped off to reveal rich reds and golds of the 17th century. His head and body are thought to have different pedigrees.

Simon Verity's more recent ornament, a reclining nude nymph, inhabits a riverside grotto belonging to Chatham Row. In the shrubbery by the Botanic Garden looms an outsize head of Jupiter carved from a six-ton block of Bath stone by John Osborne (c.1835), and over the Victoria Library and Art Gallery, imposing though bespattered, stands Her Imperial Majesty, erected in 1901 'with loyalty and love' by the women of Bath. (Inside is a fine plasticine model of William Harbutt, inventor of plasticine in

'Rebecca' Fountain. Sculptor: not known (1861). Location: outside Bath Abbey.

1897. On his former factory in the nearby village of Bathampton is a relief profile showing his domed head, beetling brow and shovel beard, and his name in sausagy lettering.)

Victoria Regina et Imperatrix . . . and Royalty's Odder Subjects

The south did not go to town over statues of Victoria, except for Hove's, solemn and old by Brock (1897), Winchester's by Gilbert (1887), and at Portsmouth where Drury's imperious, heavy-lidded bronze matriarch, installed in 1903, faces Neptune lounging naked in the pediment of the classically-styled Guildhall. Behind her rise dark, tinted windows of the new civic offices. At Maidstone in Kent Victoria appears uniquely, limply Grecian under a Gothic canopy on the Randall Fountain, carved by John Thomas in 1862.

The gentry went to town in some glorious monumental eccentricities, still to be seen in the southern pastoral landscape. Mad Jack Fuller's folly trail is well-known in Sussex, the most exuberantly wilful erection being the 'Sugar Loaf' on the B3096, a witch's-hat spire raised to substantiate Fuller's reckless claim that he could see Dallington Church from his Brightling home. Dallington's sheep-grazed churchyard has the pyramidal mausoleum where, according to a tourist trail leaflet by Michael Barnard, John Fuller MP was buried 'in the usual position' under the floor (1834) and not, as reputed, seated at a table laid with roast goose and wine.

On Farley Mount, now part of a country park near King's Somborne, Paulet St John raised a 30ft pyramid to his hunter Beware Chalk Pit, so-named after the horse had 'leaped into a chalk pit twenty-five feet deep a foxhunting with his master on his back', in 1733. One of the four porches enters a chamber containing a record of the hunter's exploits, and a prospect of the Hampshire downs.

Far southwest in Cornwall, on Worvas Hill above St Ives, John Knill's Steeple is still the focus of a quinquennial ritual in which ten small white-clad maidens and two widows from tinning or sea-going families dance round the pyramidal granite obelisk singing 'All People that on Earth Do Dwell'. The complicated ceremonial was laid down by Knill in a bequest when he was Collector of Customs, and £1 provision was also made for a fiddler to play the Furry Dance whilst in procession to the hill.

Knill's plan for his granite monument to serve as a mausoleum remained unfulfilled on his death at

Gray's Inn (1811), but the curious ceremony of his legacy continues fundamentally unchanged. The St Ives Corporation takes care of the obelisk which was claimed to be a seamark for smugglers in league with Knill – a dutiful, if offbeat, public servant.

Eccentricity emerges in every era, as can be seen on a front lawn near St Merryn, North Cornwall, where Eddie Prinn's bungalow lurks behind lofty stone monuments to the memories of his mother, and other women he has held dear. His tributes are gigantic granite slabs, some supporting other slabs in emulation of the dolmens and menhirs of ancient Cornwall. In the Glynn Valley, at Cornwall's famous cut-price emporium Trago Mills, the handsome riverside walks are lined with locally-modelled fibre-glass 'bronzes' of all pretensions, from the Sphinx to full-length portrait studies, with acerbic inscriptions, of local officials who thwart the owner's plans.

Variety the Spice of the Southern Counties

Every county has its obscurer monuments, mainly away from the town centres, adding zest to the south's seafaring, military flavour. Typically, each feature in the landscape, over-familiar, perhaps, to local people and ignored by the casual passer by, displays at close hand local craftsmanship, or perhaps a wider talent, whilst paying silent tribute to local effort, endurance and achievement. Cornwall's dark granite memorial beacons are visible from afar; others occupy more remote sites like the cliffs above the fort at Readymoney Cove (NT) near Fowey where, beneath a skeletal dome of intersecting granite arches surmounted by a Maltese Cross, William Rashleigh of Menabilly (d.1871), his wife and their daughter lie peacefully in 'the haven where they want to be'.

On St Columb's Red Lion Inn, a stone carving shows the tumbling body of a former landlord, the great wrestler John Polkinghorne, in his celebrated bout against Abraham Cann in 1826. Devon, broad-spread, but bony in parts like Cornwall, is equally broad-ranging in its monuments. All are affecting – the small, rough Jubilee cross near Throwleigh village church, with biblical slogans in childlike letters, no less than the grey obelisk raised in 1860 on Hatherleigh Down, its bronze relief panel by E.B. Stephens depicting Lieut. Col. William Morris, Major of the 17th Lancers, being born away mortally wounded from Balaklava. The distant prospect is of the shapely moors on the Devon horizon.

Devon statues and busts include Joseph Whitehead's marble figure of Charles Kingsley beside the river at Victoria Gardens in Bideford, where he wrote his swashbuckling romance *Westward Ho!*, published 1855. Despite Canon Kingsley's misgivings, the name was given to an 1860s speculative development of the village Northam Burrows; an unlucky speculator was J. Pine-Coffin, Chairman of the Landing Pier Company, whose piers at Westward Ho! were consistently washed away. He was presumably related to the John Richard Pine-Coffin (1842–1890), whose lichened, bearded bust frowns anxiously on a small public garden just across Bideford bridge.

Somerset, with its towers and tors, has some haunting war monuments, amongst them Burrow Mump (NT) near Burrow Bridge, a hill given by A.G. Barrett as a Second World War memorial. Occupied by Romans and fortified by Alfred the Great, its incomplete 18th-century hilltop chapel occupies an earlier ruin.

Even more atmospheric, a granite monolith near Westonzoyland marks the site of the Battle of Sedgemoor, the last to be fought on English soil, under tall trees in Graveyard Field on Bussex Farm. It is cared for, with ceremony, by a local school. On the 300th anniversary in 1985, local societies re-enacted the 'Pitchfork Rebellion' conflict which raged across Bussex Rine, the surprise element lost to Monmouth's untrained peasant force, the drainage ditch savagely held by James II's troops. The final horror of Judge Jeffreys' 'Bloody Assize' is still resented in the locality. Attending this event were members of the Taunton-Barbadian Society, West Indian descendants of deportees.

Wiltshire's many rural monuments include the Robber Stone and Airman's Crosses, obscure roadside memorials, and the sentinel lion saluting travellers on the A342 at Etchilhampton Hill. He also salutes James Long who, in 1768, built the new road by which 'a Tedious & Dangerous Way over the adjacent Hill is avoided, To the great Pleafure and Convenience of Travellers'. In the late 1980s, a much-needed restoration of this agreeable lion took place after prodigious fund-raising based at the *Fox & Hounds* in Nursteed. At Airman's Corner, the junction of the A360 and the A344, unseen hands placed red roses on the small stone cross many anniversaries after a Royal Engineers' Nieuport Monoplane crashed in 1912, killing both its crew, in what is thought to be the first-ever services air fatality.

On Devizes market cross designed by Benjamin

J. R. Pine-Coffin (1842–1890). Sculptor: not known. Location: Bideford bridge.

Dean Wyatt, a metal tablet replaces an earlier 'salutary warning' relating to one Ruth Pierce, who in 1753 protested that she had paid her share of a sack of wheat, and hoped to drop dead if she had not – 'when to the consternation and terror of the surrounding multitude, she instantly fell down and expired having the money concealed in her hand'. Another plaque records the 'grateful attachment' of Henry Viscount Sidmouth, donor of the cross in 1814, to the borough of which he was Recorder for 30 years, and six times elected MP. The market place has a large ornamental fountain by a Mr Woodyear (1879), with a statue of Thomas H.S. Sotheron-Estcourt, 33 years' MP, founder of the Friendly Society; big, carved, Art Nouveau letters add to the richness of vari-coloured stonework.

Dorset's monuments are few, but include Eric Gill's beautiful carved war memorial 1914–19, an elongated cross with Christ on one side, and the Madonna on the other, in the estate village Briantspuddle: '... ALL SHALL BE WELL AND ALL MANNER OF THINGS SHALL BE WELL'. Hampshire like Wiltshire has an *embarras de richesse*, from the rugged stone (1908) marking the immortal Hambledon Cricket Ground on Broadhalfpenny Down ·(note the early cricketing scene on the Bat and Ball

pub sign), to conventional market square statues. Both counties have hilltop stones to local authors, the Hammerman Poet Alfred Williams sharing his on the Liddington Hill Triangulation Pyramid, now pock-marked from 1940s target practice, with his friend Richard Jefferies (1848–1887). Their sarsen stone on Burderop Down, also Wiltshire, quotes lines from their work.

The poet Edward Thomas, who was much influenced by Jefferies' portrayal of the countryside, has an inscribed boulder high in the Hampshire hangers. Completing the hard ascent up Shoulder of Mutton Hill, one arrives, weary, to read:

> *And I rose up & knew*
> *that I was tired*
> *and continued my journey*

Thomas was killed at Arras in 1917, and is remembered for his war poems. Engraved clear-glass windows in the church at Steep imprint his words over the view of the hill, all of which is dedicated to his memory.

At Liphook further north in 1981, outside the new post office, friends of the village writer Flora Thompson unveiled her green-patinated bust on the 34th anniversary of her death – a gift of the sculptor Philip Jackson, who lived locally. The Liphook Community magazine recalled the village post mistress's too-late recognition after her book *Lark Rise to Candleford*, and her love of 'dear, warm, tender Hampshire'. Off the A3 towards Petersfield is 'the Banana Man' in his Indian feathered helmet, Onslow Ford's gung-ho equestrian bronze of Field-Marshal Strathnairn (1801–1885), one-time Commander-in-Chief of the Indian Army, originally unveiled in Knightsbridge in 1895.

The Martyrs' Monument at Lewes in East Sussex features in fire ceremonies around November 5; a granite obelisk on Cliffe Hill, it stands 'in loving memory' of 17 Sussex men and women burned between June 1555 and June 1557, one fire devouring ten including a mother and son. The rebel Jack Cade's fate, 1450, is recalled in a grim roadside stone at Cade Street: '... His body was carried to London and his head affixed to London Bridge. This is the success of all rebels ...' At Rye Harbour, selfless bravery is honoured in a fine churchyard lifeboat memorial comprising a stone statue of a lifeboatman carved within a cruciform. The roll of local names recalls the terrible loss of the *Mary Stanford* in 1928, launched in response to a distress signal, too soon to receive the recall: the sailors were by then safe. The tragedy is still publicly marked on the anniversary Sunday nearest November 15th.

Surrey's few, but notable, public statues include Alan Collins's gilded copper angel, raised on the tower of Guildford Cathedral to commemorate R. D. Adgey–Edgar, killed in training for the Intelligence Corps in 1944. The cathedral, for which Maufe as designer received his knighthood, is rich in stone carvings by Eric Gill, Collins, Karin Jonzen and others.

The prima ballerina, Dame Margot Fonteyn, late in the 1970s unveiled her own bronze by Nathan David in London Road, Reigate. Showing her on points in her favourite role, Ondine, it has since been moved some yards away from the site of the house where she was born in 1919.

Lovingly restored in 1990, is a grey stone statue to Mrs Caroline Stephens (d.1894); 'a most loving and devoted wife', she stands long-skirted by the hedge at Oatlands County First School in Weybridge. 'W. Juleff fecit' in 1895, to accord with Mrs Stephens's wish that her image remain at her Oatlands home when the family moved. When the house was bulldozed (c.1960), Mrs Stephens was spotted in the bushes by an inquisitive child, and salvaged as tangible evidence of local history. Few 'ordinary' individuals receive a public statue.

Other 'ordinary' Surrey characters received tributes: The sailor's stone at Devil's Punchbowl, Hind-head, was 'erected in detestation' at a murder on the grim site of Gibbet Hill; a big, inscribed stone seat on Hydon's Ball, above Godalming, commemorates a founder of the National Trust, Octavia Hill; the big tower on Leith Hill (NT), replacing his belvedere Prospect House, marks the burial place of Richard Hull, while the burial place of Major Labelière, near the Waterloo Tower on Box Hill (NT), is locally famous, since the Major at his own request was buried upside down.

Great Houses and Gardens

The great houses of the Southern Counties can be savoured not only for their architecture and interiors but also for their grounds. Some were laid out by landscape designers and architects such as Capability Brown, others took shape over the centuries, and many are ornamented with sculpture either venerable or humble.

At Poleseden Lacey (NT) near Dorking, sculpture introduced by Mrs Greville in the Edwardian era includes a Roman sarcophagus, vases inscribed with Pope's verses, and a lead statue of Diana on the Croquet Lawn. The avenue of trees along the main drive was replanted in 1956 as a tribute to George Mitchell, 'A man of hope and forward looking mind' and first secretary of the Ramblers' Association. Kingston Lacy (NT), in its garden exotica, includes the Philae Needle discovered by William Bankes in 1815. Marking the exemption from taxes of the priests of Isis, it is reckoned Britain's only ancient Egyptian obelisk apart from 'Cleopatra's Needle' in London. An ex-music hall giant and engineer removed it from the Egyptian island of Philae in 1819; the Duke of Wellington laid the foundation stone (1827); George III gave the granite, from Leptis Magna, for repairs. The story is told at its base, and in the Kingston Lacy guidebook.

The best gardens have a sense of theatre with the visitor a participant, as at Stourhead in Wiltshire, when the circuit with its views of statues, lakes, temples and plantations plunges into a dark tufa grotto with uneven cobblestones, which one crosses to encounter the River God, weirdly white in his watery cavern. His lead statue is by John Cheere (1751). The lead nymph recumbent over a cascade is a copy of *Ariadne* in the Vatican gardens.

In the Pantheon is Rysbrack's marble statue of Hercules, based on the Roman Farnese Hercules and also, according to Walpole, on varying anatomical parts of the strongest men in London, 'chiefly the bruisers and boxers' of the boxing amphitheatre. At

Bristol Cross. Architect: not known (medieval cross re-assembled on this site, 1764). Location: Stourhead.

the head of the circuit near the church stands the medieval Bristol Cross, its renovations dating from various depredations and removals. In 1764, Stourhead's proprietor Henry Hoare collected the bits from Bristol Cathedral and brought them home in six wagons.

Two miles northwest on Kingsettle Hill, site of Alfred the Great's defence in A.D.879 against the Danes, Hoare employed Henry Flitcroft (d.1769) to build a viewing tower in emulation of 'Sn Marks Tower at Venice, 100 foot'. Completed in 1772, its statue of Alfred served as a symbol of loyalty to British values in the Hanoverian era whilst ushering in George III's accession with vain hopes for peace.

King Alfred's Footsteps

Alfred's considerable worth is acknowledged in a fulsome inscription:

To Him we owe
The origin of Juries
The Establishment of a Militia
The Creation of a Naval Force
Alfred the light of a benighted age
was a Philosopher and a Christian
The Father of his People
The Founder of the English
Monarchy and Liberty

A large late-Victorian bronze statue of Alfred appears in Winchester and a small marble one in Pewsey, Wiltshire, where Alfred was 'once a chief landowner in this vale'. It was erected in 1913, two years late to commemorate the coronation of George V 'A King who grandly follows in great King Alfred's footsteps'.

Soldier, sailor, religious and cultural leader — Alfred the Great stands for all the heroes of the Southern Counties.

Southern Counties Gazetteer

(**Note:** The Southern Counties appear in roughly topographical order. Within each county, monuments are listed under their locations, which appear in alphabetical order. The city of Bristol, formerly self-governing, is now administered by the new county of Avon (A), created from part of Somerset in 1974.)

Kent

Gravesend

Town Feature:

Princess Pocahontas Rebecca Rolfe (1595–1617)
Bronze casting of full-length statue on ornamental
textured stone pedestal
Sculptor William Ordway Partridge
Location Pocahontas Gardens, Chapel of Unity and
Pocahontas Memorial Church (St George's)

Set in a tidied graveyard close to the Thames, this figure of Pocahontas as Indian squaw, with feather headdress and moccasins, makes telling contrast with the oval engraving by Simon van der Passe of Rebecca Rolfe in her court dress of lace ruff, brocaded jacket and plumed fan. Made in Pocahontas's 22nd year, this handsome image appears on tourist leaflets and guides to Gravesend where she was brought dying, it is thought of tuberculosis, on board the ship that was returning her with her husband John Rolfe to her native Virginia. The transformation from Cherokee girl to Christian wife had taken just three years.

Fêted in her lifetime as an exotic visitor to England and the English Court, Pocahontas was exalted by the Cherokee nation more than three centuries later when Clarence Tomkins, Ambassador Falling Sky, accompanied by the Cherokee President and Governor, laid down Virginian soil as close as possible to her unknown burial place at Gravesend's former parish church.

Over 30 years earlier in 1952, the church was renamed after Pocahontas, and in 1958 the Governor of Virginia presented this figure of the Princess, which successfully merges the fierce features of her race with the gentle demeanour noted by James I's courtiers. The original stands outside Jamestown parish church, where she was baptized and married.

It is poignant to think that the 11-year-old Pocahontas's actions may have hastened the eclipse of the American Indians. Daughter of Powhattan, chief of Cherokee tribes on the Chesapeake Bay, she was said to have saved the life of the English explorer and trader John Smith, popularly acclaimed as founder of Virginia, who was later erroneously thought to have died in an explosion. In fact, he survived and subsequently returned to England.

Three years later (1612), Pocahontas was brought to Jamestown as hostage against Indian attack; an honoured guest, she was baptised and renamed, and in 1614 married a widower, John Rolfe, who introduced 'Virginia tobacco' seed from Trinidad. In 1616 they sailed for England with their infant son, Thomas, and a small Indian retinue. The planned return to Virginia, according to a courtier, was 'sore against her will'.

She fell ill, and died at Gravesend — romantics claim a broken heart on revival of contact with John Smith. Smith himself wrote the Virginian colony, through Pocahontas, had been preserved from

'Chinese Gordon' leans against a tree trunk; as supervisor of construction of Thames forts (1865–71) he encouraged the poor to grow food in this garden, then part of his residence, Fort House. He also taught Ragged School children and street urchins – his 'Kings'.

Gordon left Gravesend to take up governorship of the Sudan; attempting to rescue the Egyptian garrison besieged in Khartoum (1885) he was executed, and his head presented to the Mahadi. He was later avenged by Lord Kitchener. Both have statues at Chatham in Kent, Gordon's fine bronze by Onslow Ford, erected five years after his death, shows him on camelback, in his fez and gold coat given by the Khedive to impress the chiefs whilst subduing slave traffic.

Another casting, set up in 1904 at the site of his execution, was thrown into the Nile during a local uprising, returned to England, and erected at the Gordon School for Boys in Woking. Recently its return was unsuccessfully requested by the Sudan government.

Princess Pocahontas (1595–1617). Sculptor: W. O. Partridge (replica, 1952). Location: St George's Church, Gravesend.

'death, famine and utter confusion'. In 1644 her son, captain of Fort James in Virginia, held it against Powhattan's successor, his uncle.

Pocahontas's burial ground is a starting point of one among many American Heritage Trails in Britain. Her statue near the grey Thames, and fresh tributes to 'our beloved Algonquin Sister', make food for thought.

Gravesend Selection

Two fine 1890s statues by John Broad were 'made and fired by Messrs Doulton at the Lambeth Works', as inscribed on the cylindrical pedestal of General Gordon's in Gordon Gardens, Khartoum Place. The other, in Darnley Road, shows VICTORIA QUEEN AND EMPRESS uncommonly young and feminine.

Westerham

Town Feature:

Sir Winston Churchill (1709–1784)
Seated bronze statue, rough limestone plinth
Sculptor Oscar Nemon
Location The Green (northwest side)

Siren-suited, Sir Winston looks curiously out of place on Westerham's spacious green, perhaps because the sculptor has successfully fulfilled the brief for a figure in repose by presenting him relaxed but pugnacious in an armchair. Still watchful, the great statesman faces Chartwell two miles south, his home when out of office from 1922 until his death.

It was acquired by Churchill for its view of the Weald, and anonymously purchased for the National Trust, with a residency for Sir Winston and his wife Clementine, after Churchill's electoral defeat in 1945. By this time, as Robin Fedden explained in his guide *Churchill and Chartwell*, the house was 'not an oasis, but a shrine' and Churchill, leader of the Opposition, 'the most respected man in Europe'.

The statue was unveiled by Sir Robert Menzies, a former member of Sir Winston's War Cabinet and his successor as Lord Warden of the Cinque Ports – a tactful choice of a political figure uninvolved in

Sir Winston Churchill (1874–1865). Sculptor: Oscar Nemon (1969). Location: the Green, Westerham.

British politics. At Menzies' request, the ceremony coincided with the Australian Test Series, played in England in July, 1969. Churchill's daughter Mary, Lady Soames, was an organiser of the statue project which, publicly subscribed, was far less costly at £7,000 than a public hall, suggested by some local residents as a more useful monument.

Amongst the family, friends and dignitaries at the unveiling was the Yugoslav Ambassador, a friend of the sculptor Oscar Nemon who had successfully applied to President Tito for the plinth's rough-hewn marble, presented 'as a symbol of Yugoslav soil' (the same quarries had yielded material for the Washington White House). The marble was delivered by two personable Yugoslavs who, having unloaded and asked directions, made off in their lorry for the bright lights of London.

Oscar Nemon made other studies of his friend Sir Winston, and visitors to Chartwell can purchase a small purpose-made bronze replica bust. On show since 1990 is Nemon's bronze of Sir Winston, similar to the Westerham figure but accompanied by Lady Churchill. Nemon himself sat for a bust which stands,

unfinished, in the studio; Churchill's sole attempt at sculpture, it is said to be a remarkable likeness. Churchill paintings hang throughout the house, translations of his histories and biographies are kept in the library, and the garden wall, inspired by the wall at Quebec House nearby, is well known as Churchillian handiwork.

Westerham Selection

Quebec House (NT) was the boyhood home of General Wolfe, whose statue on Westerham Green Oscar Nemon judged to be one of England's three best. It is by F. Derwent Wood who modelled the hero of Quebec in tricorn hat and pigtailed wig, brandishing his sword above his head (1911). A similar portrayal in oils, 'Wolfe at Quebec', can be seen at the house; neither painting nor statue shrinks from revealing the subject's long nose and receding chin, giving an impression of vulnerability combined with strength. The statue is fast deteriorating.

Wolfe died of wounds, smiling at his victory over the French, and was buried at Greenwich, where his bronze statue was presented by the Canadian people in 1930 and unveiled by a descendent of his French adversary, General Montcalm. The slight figure at Westerham Green on its large, shapely pedestal makes a satisfying foil for Nemon's hulking Churchillian form.

It was Churchill's big presence and growling pronouncements whilst directing operations in the Second World War that provided comfort and inspiration, particularly for people in the Southern Counties and in Kent, holding the front line 23 miles across the Channel from Occupied France. At the Pines Garden on St Margaret's Bay, another bronze of Churchill by Oscar Nemon seems to stride from its three-tier plinth of glittering dark Yugoslav granite. Even more imposing than that at Westerham, Churchill's hunched but thrusting stance is recorded in a Pines Garden brochure as 'the epitome of undying resolution'. It was unveiled by Churchill's grandson, Winston, in November 1972.

East Sussex

Brighton

Town Feature:

George IV (1772–1830)
Full-length bronze copy of marble statue, on stone pedestal
Sculptor Sir Francis Leggatt Chantrey
Location Royal Pavilion Gardens

The king's statue stands at the north entrance to the Royal Pavilion, looking towards the public gardens and the busy traffic routes that are as much part of Brighton as its Regency architecture, antique shops, shingle beaches, piers, and distant downs. The extravagant onion-domed Pavilion was created by John Nash, brilliant planner of Regency London. Its transmogrification from 'superior farmhouse' to fantasy palace took most of George's lifetime, employing three eminent architects and numerous master craftsmen, and attracting public distaste at royal profligacy and exotic opulence. The result, as the official guidebook concludes, was a 'single, princely work of art'.

Francis Chantrey's first commission in bronze (1822), the statue is a cut-price copy of a marble

George IV (1772–1830). Sculptor: Sir Frances Chantrey (bronze cast, 1828). Location: Royal Pavilion Gardens, Brighton.

figure at Windsor. The target of £3000 was undersubscribed, and the bronze went up in 1828 two years before the King's death. George's love for Brighton began as Prince of Wales, secretly married to the Catholic widow Maria Fitzherbert and seeking amusement away from his father's stodgy household in brilliant and cultivated society, amid the growing splendours of interior Chinoiserie and the Hindu exterior of his Pavilion. His seaside retreat Brighthelmstone became 'Brighton' in the early years of the 19th century.

Prinny's latter-year, duller, Brighton regime involved sumptuous dinners at 6.30 in the Banqueting Room and performances by the Band, sometimes featuring George himself, in the magnificent Music Room with its lotus gasoliers. Other royal pursuits included conversation or cards in the Drawing Rooms or Saloon; waltzing, or airgun practise; the races; practical jokes.

Brighton pleasures palled but as Prince Regent and as King, by then fat, gouty and dropsical; George continued to take pleasure in personally directing design and decoration of the Pavilion. His successor, William IV, continued to use the palace, but Victoria had the exquisite interiors dismantled, the treasures stored and the shell sold to the Town Commissioners. After successive renovations, Queen Mary between the Wars returned much of the original furnishing, but restorations true to original splendours started only during the 1950s. Now, as in Prinny's day, Brighton's 'princely work of art' continues to be renewed.

Brighton Selection

Various monuments inhabit the public gardens near George IV's plump, cloaked figure. A statue of Queen Victoria, by Professor Nicoli of the Sculptured Marble Company, is dated 1897. Its unveiling was followed by a Military Tattoo. E.B. Stephens's marble statue (1878) shows Sir John Cordy Burrows in mayoral robes, bow tie and cravat. He was a distinguished surgeon ('ever-memorable' according to the *Brighton Gazette* in 1904), and thrice mayor.

The Victoria Fountain (1846), its cast-iron dolphins reputedly on sarsen stone supports, was designed by Amon Henry Wilds (*fl.*1822—46), whose father Amon's work survives in the town's fine Regency terraces. The First and Second World War memorial, with columns and fountain, invites 'prayer and meditation'; a pretty polished pink granite obelisk recalls the Egypt Campaign and the Nile River Expedition of 1884—5.

The south gate of the Royal Pavilion was designed by Thomas Tyrwhitt in 16th-century Gujerati style — more restrained than the Regency Oriental of the building itself — and dedicated to Brighton people 'by H.H. the Maharaja of Patiaba' in October, 1921. It commemorates Indian soldiers who used the Pavilion as a military hospital in the Great War. 'The complexities of caste and religion', says the official guide, 'were catered for by nine kitchens and two distinct supplies of water'. (A walk on the Sussex Downs from Patcham, north of the town, arrives at the Chattri, a domed marble memorial to Indian troops by E.C. Henriques, unveiled by the future Edward VIII earlier the same year.)

Queen Victoria (1819—1900). Sculptor: Professor Nicoli (1897), Location: Royal Pavilion Gardens, Brighton.

Regency Square contributes a freely-modelled great-coated, bare-headed bugler to the noteworthy collection of South Coast war memorials; unveiled in 1904, it honours soldiers of the Royal Sussex Regiment who fell in the Boer War. On the front at the Hove Boundary, the Peace Statue by Newbury Trent (1912) commemorates Edward VII with a bronze relief profile, the pedestal bearing a winged angel facing seaward. The monument's back view is equally fine. The same subscription funded a memorial home for Queen's Nurses.

In Hove's Grand Avenue, facing the bathing huts, is an imposing seated bronze of Queen Victoria crowned, solemn and old, 1899, by Thomas Brock. (Carlisle's casting was the first northern statue of the Queen after her death.) Further up the Avenue is Lutyens's column with a bronze St George (1921), since dedicated to citizens lost 'in the Great War and the World War'.

A Brighton curiosity is the 1887 Jubilee Clock Tower in the North Street Quadrant. Controlled by electricity from Greenwich Observatory, its time ball rose and fell by hydraulic power. Its designer was Magnus Volk, creator of the Brighton and Hove Electric Railway.

Hampshire

Southampton

City Feature:

Louis, Earl Mountbatten of Burma (1900–1979)
Full-length bronze statue on natural Portland stone plinth
Sculptor Greta Berlin
Location Grosvenor Square

Born Prince Louis of Battenberg at Windsor, the last godchild of his great-grandmother Queen Victoria, Mountbatten's personal history was touched by many tumultuous events of the 20th century. His family name was Anglicised near the end of the First World War; at the same time, his maternal aunts and other close relatives were assassinated in the Russian revolution. An intimate of Europe's royal families, military leader and diplomat, Louis Mountbatten saw adventure and high office in almost all parts of the world.

His statue, part of a Timberlaine Properties development, shows him in naval cap and army fatigues as Supreme Allied Commander of South-East Asia (1943–6), a handsome and charismatic leader reputed for getting his men out of tight corners (having first got them there).

Lord Louis' associations with the south coast date from his period as a sea-cadet at Osborne Naval College on the Isle of Wight, and continue through the family home 'Broadlands', outside Romsey. Former home of Lord Palmerston, it was inherited by Lady Mountbatten the year before their marriage; rich, beautiful and socially élite, the couple began their honeymoon there and made it their country base after the Second World War.

A condition of the commission was that the sculptor (who lives near Southampton) should, like Lord Louis, have close ties with the locality. It was Greta Berlin's first major commission and first large-scale

Lord Mountbatten (1900–1979). Sculptor: Greta Berlin (1990). Location: Grosvenor Square, Southampton.

sculpture, and was approached with some trepidation, although executed with considerable conviction and sensitivity.

In the foyer of the newly-built Mountbatten House is Berlin's intensely-expressed bronze bust of Mountbatten in his late years, an honoured and decorated Admiral of the Fleet. Both were completed in 1990, and the full-length statue was unveiled by the Countess Mountbatten of Burma on July 6 of that year.

The plinth, seeming to form a natural part of the surroundings, is of stone selected from the Isle of Purbeck quarries by the sculptor and the master mason Trevor Weeble of Vokes and Beck, a Winchester family firm. Weeble's father worked at Broadlands and often, as master mason, assisted Lord Mountbatten at local foundation stone laying ceremonies. The Purbeck stone, which splits naturally into blocks, had been quarried some years before, and was already weathered. After assembly, it was sprayed with yoghourt to promote growth of lichen.

The sculptor's choice of fatigues for a subject who relished decoration and ceremony subtly evokes Mountbatten's experiences at home as well as on active service in the Atlantic and Mediterranean, or as Viceroy of India travelling with Lady Mountbatten through the heat and dust in the violent, harrowing months leading up to Indian Independence.

He retired, a widower, to Broadlands in 1965, remaining active as spearhead of numerous organisations, and accepting such posts as President of United World Colleges, and Governor and Lord Lieutenant of the Isle of Wight. The mansion with its family archives was opened to the public shortly before Lord Mountbatten's assassination in Ireland whilst staying at Classiebawn Castle.

Periods at Broadlands allowed relaxation with the family, or entertaining distinguished guests as varied as the Queen of England or Charlie Chaplin, or Noel Coward whose film *In Which We Serve* was based on Mountbatten's command of the legendary and ill-fated HMS Kelly. Guests were invited to leave their mark by planting trees on the Broadlands estate. The Mountbatten imprint is as much on his house and locality as on the first three eventful quarters of the 20th century.

Southampton Selection

George III presides indolently over High Street from Bargate, the statue judged 'coarse' by Pevsner while the gate is 'probably the finest, and certainly the most complex', town gateway in Britain. Both are relics of the pre-Blitz city. The Coade-stone king with fringe and laurel wreath, modelled on a Roman statue of Hadrian at the British Museum, replaced a wooden figure of Queen Anne in 1809. This is now kept in the City Museum, which occupies a room above Bargate's arch.

Further down High Street, the ruined Sailors' Church (Holy Rood) makes a peaceful memorial garden 'to those who served in the Merchant Navy and lost their lives at sea'. Other memorials honour The Watch Ashore, and those lost in the Falklands. Under the tower is an elaborate stone fountain to the crew of the *Titanic*, which sailed to her doom from here in 1912, in the heyday of luxury liners.

Memorial to engineers of the Titanic (1912). Design: Whitehead & Sons (1914). Location: London Road, Southampton.

On Western Esplanade is the tapering Mayflower pillar, with its lofty cupola and gold and white mosaic dome. Dedicated to U.S. forces of the Second World War as well as the Pilgrim Fathers, it was designed by R.M. Lucas, and unveiled by the U.S. Ambassador in 1913. Nearby is an octagonal stone fountain marking the 'heroic death' of Mary Anne Rogers, stewardess, who aided the women passengers 'amid the terror and confusion of shipwreck' when the *SS Stella* foundered on the Casquets while bound for Guernsey in 1899.

A handsome, grubby Titanic Memorial, facing London Road from East Park, is formed from a granite semi-circular seat supporting a central carved prow with a 7ft bronze angel. Bronze reliefs depict the engineers 'who showed their high conception of duty and their heroism by remaining at their posts'. The design was by Whitehead and Sons, the unveiling in 1914. Across the road in West Park is the Cenotaph by Lutyens; like the London Cenotaph it is of Portland stone, but this is grander in scale, and bears the recumbent body of an unknown warrior.

The town's Victorian statues are dispersed in this area. Watts Park has Richard Cockle Lucas's marble statue to Isaac Watts (1674–1748), Nonconformist scholar and writer, his life vividly carved on side panels together with a quote borrowed from Dr Johnson: 'He has taught the art of reasoning and the science of the stars'. He faces the Civic Centre, the clock tower of which chimes Watts's best-loved hymn, 'Our God, our help in ages past'. The sculptor, a marvellous eccentric, was a townsman.

Philip Brannon, also of Southampton, was the sculptor of coach builder and mayor Richard Andrews's faded limestone statue, all that remains of an ornate Bath stone fountain, destroyed in 1975 for want of £2000 repair costs. The City architect was later prevented by public outcry from moving the statue indoors. In 1869 Thomas Sharp of London won a court action brought for incomplete payment for an £800 marble statue of Lord Palmerston (1784–1865) as 'Burgess of Southampton'. The work stands in Palmerston Park.

A more nobly sited bronze statue of Lord Palmerston, by Matthew Noble (1867), occupies the market square at Romsey. His debating stance recalls the statesman, but 'Old Pam', born at Broadlands, made his mark locally as a landowner who ran his horses and rode to hounds well into his latter years. From the square can be seen the squat, flint-built tower of Romsey Abbey, scene of Mountbatten weddings and christenings, and resting place of Mountbatten of Burma.

Winchester

City Feature:

Alfred the Great (849–c.899)
Full-length bronze statue on pedestal and base made from two single blocks of Penryn granite
Sculptor Sir William Hamo Thornycroft RA
Location The Broadway

Alfred's National Memorial, a massive statue of the king as Christian warrior and scourge of the heathen Dane, stands at the town's eastern entrance. The helmeted figure in tunic, cloak and thonged sandals

Alfred the Great (849–c. 899). Sculptor: Sir W. H. Thornycroft (1901). Location: lower end of High Street, Winchester.

confronts the winding, rising High Street along Broadway; behind him can be seen the neighbouring green hill, a pleasant feature of many southern towns. He raises his sword in the symbol of the Cross whilst his free hand rests on the emblem of defence, a shield probably no smaller than the 'Round Table' which hangs in the Castle.

Supported by two monolithic rough-hewn slabs, the statue was unveiled in 1901, one year late in marking the millenium of Alfred's death. His burial place at Hyde Abbey above Westgate, which he founded, was destroyed at the Reformation, and in the mid 19th century bones found on its site were reinterred at St Bartholomew's, former parish church of the abbey servants. The installation of his monument was hailed by a local newspaper: 'it will add to the attractions which Winchester offers to the whole of the Anglo-Saxon race'.

Alfred made Winchester his capital, a cultural centre from which he revived the Arts in England, reintroducing the disciplines of English learning and literature after the ravages of the Danish raids. It was Alfred who united south and west England against the enemy after the English victory at Edington in Wiltshire (878), negotiating with the Danish King Guthrum the north and eastern regions, later the Danelaw.

Alfred laid the foundations of a stronger, cohesive England by establishing a system of law, home-based and active armies, and, so it is said, the first English navy. The *Anglo-Saxon Chronicle*, which the King may have instigated or inspired at Winchester, report Alfred's fleet of 'swifter, steadier' warships to meet the Danes, 'full nigh twice as long as the others', with 60 or more oars.

His fortified earthworks, or burghs, were the earliest English towns. He suffered ill health and spent most of his life at war, but taught himself to read and write in Latin and English, translated histories and philosophies, and set up a school at his Court.

His 15ft statue took 11 months to cast at the Singer foundry, in Frome. The 23ft foundations are filled with 400 tons of concrete. The granite blocks, 45 and 43 tons, were delivered by a team of horses. The top block was said to have been winched into position upside down and the mistake instantly spotted, but 'soft-pedalled to avoid the immense labour of reversal', according to the letters page of a local newspaper. If this is so, the inscription ÆLFRED must have been carved on site.

The eye-witness correspondents also reported that Driscoll's, the contractors, scoured the town for coarse brown sugar to form a seating between the plinth and base block, and that subsequently the molasses could be seen trickling over the sides of the base. A brass plate commemorates 'the Founder of the Kingdom and Nation', and also records the names of the sculptor, the orator Lord Rosebery, and the mayor, Alfred Bowker. Alfred's large, stolid warrior figure is one of the sights of Winchester.

Winchester Selection

In the High Street heart of Winchester, near St Laurence's Church, is the 15th-century Butter Cross, restored by Sir G.G. Scott in 1865. Its statue is thought to be of St Lawrence. The cross was sold by the Pavement Commissioners in 1772, but townsfolk chased off the removal men. Outside Lloyd's Bank nearby, the large niche statue of 'Anno Pacifico Anno Regina', with touches of gilding, was given by MP George Bridges in 1713 to mark the signing of the Treaty of Utrecht.

This fine old building was once the Town Hall, its clock and carved timber support the gift of Sir William Paulet. Other figures and carvings, notably the beasts supporting the gable window on the Boots store in the colonnaded Pentice, and dark statuettes of holy men occupying niches in the shop front, contribute to the traditional High Street atmosphere of the county town.

Also to be seen, just below Westgate, are the primal figures of a Frink horse and rider in an ivy-covered, brick-lined enclosure. Gaping heads on Westgate are thought to have supported the draw-bridge chains. Above Westgate is an ordinary obelisk (1759) with marvellous eloquent inscriptions, erected by the Society of Natives, a local apprentice boys' charity, over the stone on which market exchanges were made 'Whilst the City lay under the Scourge of the DESTROYING PESTILENCE' (the plague) in 1666.

Winchester College buildings and gateways have statues, including Cibber's figure of William of Wykeham (1697). On Cathedral Green, not strictly a secular memorial but in the public domain, is an amusing tombstone epitaph to a soldier who died after drinking small beer, while inside the Cathedral is Sir Charles Wheeler's bronze commemorative statue of William Walker in his cumbersome diving suit (1964). Walker saved the cathedral from collapse, from 1906, by laying bags of concrete under the watery foundations. Surviving five years' arduous toil, he died aged 54 in the 'flu epidemic of 1918.

Winchester's best outdoor statue was a brilliant seated figure of the aged Queen Victoria, by Alfred

Gilbert (1887). Presented by a Mr Whittaker, High Sherriff of Hampshire, it was later removed from the grounds of the old abbey and subsequently 'pushed into a corner of the Great Hall', to the irritation of Pevsner. It is less accessible, but probably better-preserved.

Isle of Wight

St Catherine's Down

Island Feature:

The Hoy Monument
72ft stone pillar with ball finial
Designer Not known
Location St Catherine's Down, near
Blackgang Chine

The Hoy Monument. Designer: not known (1814).
Location: St Catherine's Down, Isle of Wight.

This shapely pillar on high land between the villages of Niton and Chale is also a rare monument to the march of history. It originally marked the visit to Britain of Tsar Alexander I, 'Emperor of all the Russias', then popular as saviour of Europe from the Napoleonic Wars which had brought hardship to the poor, and had destabilised foreign trade. The big stone tablet on the pillar's base also recorded 'many happy years residence in his dominions' of the City merchant Michael Hoy (d.1828), who raised the Alexander Pillar, as it was first known, in 1814 on pastureland above his country retreat the Hermitage.

The pillar's badly-weathered inscription tablet has since been replaced by a small inset plate, but an original stone tablet on the converse side was installed by the next landowner, William Henry Dawes, former Lieutenant of the 22nd Cheshire Regiment, in 1857. The ironic carved inscription, now lichened and worn, recalls ... THOSE BRAVE MEN OF THE ALLIED ARMIES WHO FELL ON THE ALMA, AT INKERMAN, AND AT THE SIEGE OF SEVASTAPOL. The tablets' dates measure a span of 43 years between Britain's perceptions (ever ambiguous) of mighty Russia as friend and as foe.

In 1982, Wydcombe Manor handed the deteriorating monument over to Chale Parish Council. Not long before, members of the council and public had contributed to scaffolding and materials so that interim repairs could be carried out by the then Chairman of the council, a local farmer who was experienced in restoration and stone masonry. The new inscription was given by the Director of the Blackgang Leisure Park, then Deputy Lieutenant of the island.

The island, with little industry, has many parishes like Chale, the small-farming population of which is naturally daunted by the large sum required for a full restoration. At Mr Gorbachov's visit to England in 1989, the Parish Council and the National Trust, the present landowner, each wrote to the Russian Embassy inviting a contribution. The letters were passed to the Trust's Russian counterpart, but momentous events have intervened, and this is the sum of Hoy Perestroika at time of writing.

It would be nice to redress the balance of the Crimea, but if ever the monument weathers away, the splendid views west to Freshwater, and north across the island and the Solent to Portishead, will compensate on clear days. A footpath leads up from the carpark above Blackgang Chine; near here on Chale Down is St Catherine's Oratory (the Pepper Pot), a buttressed, octagonal tower built by order of a Papal Bull after shipwrecked wine consigned to the Church was sold by survivors to Walter de Godyton and others in 1323. Local romance makes de Godyton a wrecker, the Oratory his penance.

Trinity House built a light tower nearby in the 18th century. However, sea fogs made it redundant and a lighthouse now stands nearer sea-level, at St Catherine's Point.

Isle of Wight Selection

The island has no outdoor commemorative statue, but the church at Yarmouth has a richly-carved marble effigy of Louis XIV's body topped by the head of Sir Robert Holmes, later the island's Governor, who had captured effigy and sculptor in a ship *en route* for France and Versailles. Instead of the French king's, Sir Robert ordered his own head to be carved. After his death in 1692, the ornate figure was erected at the church under a fine marble canopy, with a long Latin inscription beneath.

Most outdoor monuments are landmarks visible from various spectacular viewpoints on this delectable island. The best known is the granite Celtic cross, raised in 1897 on High Down (NT) to Alfred, Lord Tennyson 'by the people of Freshwater and other friends in England and America'. The poet, then landowner, set up a seat at this viewpoint; he was one of a group of artists and writers who discovered the island, and later settled or visited. One, for a time, was G.F. Watts, whose statue of Tennyson stands outside Lincoln Cathedral.

The site, showing traces of earthworks, was formerly occupied by a wooden structure called the Nodes Beacon. The *Red Guide* mentions a two man ward-and-watch on 'Freschwaltor Downs' in 1638. The Tennyson cross, perhaps by W.G. Collingwood, is maintained by Trinity House; in the year of its installation, Giuglielmo Marconi's transmitting station was set up overlooking the famous Needles at Alum Bay. Marconi's technological landmarks and 'wonders' are recorded on a memorial in the carpark of a colourful, but scenically unsound, modern leisure complex.

Earlier seamarks include an obelisk on Stenbury Down behind Appuldurcombe House, Wroxall, which has a central southern position on Wight. It was raised in 1744 to the prominent landowner Sir Robert Worsley, and reduced to a stump by lightning in 1831.

On Bembridge Down a big, blunt granite obelisk serves as a seamark for Wight's eastern coast. It also commemorates the Royal Yacht Club's first Commodore, 1st Earl of Yarborough and Baron Worsley of Appuldurcombe: AS THE OWNER OF LARGE ESTATES, HE WAS ONE OF THOSE MOST CONSPICUOUS FOR THE QUALITIES WHICH PECULIARLY ADORN THAT STATION. He died on his yacht *Kestrel*, at Vigo, in 1846.

A humbler monument is the rustic fountain (now dry) outside the Crab Inn, Shanklin, bearing lines written by Longfellow whilst staying there. In Church Litten park at Newport, behind the Lord Louis Library, is a sad little obelisk to a ten-year-old chimney sweep, Valentine Gray, who died ill-used in an out-house (1822). '... This Monument Is errected By Public Subscription', protests the dedication, 'In Testimony of The General Feeling For Suffering Innocence '. The story appears as a poem in *Vectis Lays*, by J. Dore.

In 1965 at Ashley Gardens, Ryde Esplanade, Lord Louis (Earl Mountbatten of Burma) unveiled a memorial to seamen lost from the *Royal George*, which sank off Spithead in 1782. Many bodies were washed up on the shore, and buried in the sand dunes. The sea and the land, as well as the people, reside in the island's monuments.

Dorset

Dorchester

Town Feature:

Thomas Hardy (1840–1928)
Seated bronze statue on large limestone pedestal
Sculptor Eric Kennington
Location Top o' Town

Thomas Hardy belongs to Dorset, the 'untamed and tameable' wild heath, rural backwaters and strange stony coast of which inspired settings for the thwarted and fated passions of his novels. His neat bronze figure, perching cross-legged on a tree stump, faces out across a soulless new roundabout at the top of High West Street. The sculptor shows him in knee-breeches and walking boots, but dapper also with moustache, collar and tie. He holds a battered hat, and looks displeased at being disturbed. Hardy stressed that his locations were ideal, but suggested by real ones. Natural features sometimes appear undisguised in his works, and some places, like Dorchester in *The Mayor of Casterbridge*, are fictionalised only in name.

The 'Wessex', or Dorset, backcloth of the novels is made real by Hardy's delight in utilising real or imaginary landscape features, such as the roadside cross near Holywell on which the heroine in *Tess of the d'Urbervilles* is made to place her hand whilst swearing never to tempt her seducer Alec, a converted lay preacher.

The author's childhood village, Higher Bockhampton, appears as Upper Mellstock in his comedy *Under the Greenwood Tree*. It features the cottage where Hardy was born and, in Lower Bockhampton, his first school. This and other early novels were written at his birthplace. They include *A Pair of Blue Eyes*, located in Cornwall where as an architect's assistant Hardy met his future first wife Emma Gifford. *Far from the Madding Crowd* brought success, and with it the means to wed.

After their marriage in London, where Hardy had commenced in architecture and was to return regularly as a writer, they lived in various parts of Dorset before settling at Max Gate. A gloomy house outside Dorchester, it was designed by Hardy and built by his brother who had followed the family trade. Many eminent figures paid visits, but despite success the marriage became bitter, a source of tension being Thomas's village upbringing and Emma's gentle breeding. After her death in 1912 his discovery of her diaries, revealing his heartlessness, brought deep remorse later expressed in some of his most moving poems.

Hardy is remembered as a novelist, but returned to his first love, poetry, after the hostile reaction to his novels *Tess of the d'Urbervilles* and *Jude the Obscure*. His epic-drama of the Napoleonic Wars, *The Dynasts*, was published in three parts in the 1900s. As in other works it draws on Hardy's boyhood experiences of the countryside, here using first-hand accounts of villagers and aged campaigners in vivid vignettes of wartime endurance.

Hardy's Wessex can be explored using trail pamphlets for the novels put out by the Thomas Hardy Society, available from the Dorchester information centre. Hardy's own life is recalled in many of the locations, including the county town where he worked at an architect's office in South Street – a plan of St Peter's Church, drawn by Hardy, hangs in the church's south aisle. The Dorchester County Museum, designed by a Weymouth architect who

Thomas Hardy (1840–1928).
Sculptor: Eric Kennington (1931).
Location: Top o' Town, Dorchester.

had also employed him, now holds an unrivalled Hardy collection and shows a reconstruction of the study at Max Gate as it was at his death.

Hardy's ashes are interred at Westminster Abbey, but his heart lies at the parish church in Stinsford (Mellstock), in the grave shared by Emma and Hardy's second wife, Florence, who saw the later years of honour and adulation. Amongst the distinguished pall bearers at the funeral was his friend Sir James Barrie, who unveiled his statue in 1931. (An effigy by Eric Kennington of Hardy's friend T.E. Lawrence is in Wareham Church. One of the more progressive figurative sculptors, Kennington travelled with Lawrence in Arabia.)

Also in 1931, a heath stone was set up by American admirers at the back of Hardy's birthplace. The cottage has views of Admiral Hardy's 70ft octagonal tower on Black Down, raised as a seamark in 1844. The hill, and Nelson's commander (who is not related), make an appearance in *The Trumpet Major*. It is interesting to reflect that Hardy's characters moved in the Wessex country of his inspiration rather than in today's 'Hardy Country'.

Dorchester Selection

A founder of the County museum was the Dorset dialect writer William Barnes (1801–1886), Hardy's friend and mentor, whose statue of 1888 by Edward Roscoe Mullins stands outside St Peter's Church halfway up High West Street. He wears the scarlet dressing gown which nettled Edmund Gosse: 'Mr Barnes is dying no less picturesquely than he has lived'. Hardy's obituary in *The Athæneum* noted Barnes's 'complete repertory of forgotten manners, words and sentiments'.

The house where Barnes, a sorrowing widower, lived when rector of Winterborne Came, was reached from Hardy's across a field; much earlier, he lived next-door to the South Street architect's office where Hardy worked. The younger writer helped organise the commission for the statue in 1888. The pedestal carries an excerpt from Barnes's work:

ZOO NOW I HOPE HIS KINDLY FEACE
IS GONE TO VIND A BETTER PLEACE
BUT STILL WI' VO'K A-LEFT BEHIND
HE'LL ALWAYS BE A-KEPT IN MIND

Just outside the town, on the South Walks site of the old gallows, is a bronze group by Elizabeth Frink (a local resident). Recalling Anglican, Catholic and Non-conformist martyrs of the 16th and 17th centuries, the work caused a stir when installed in 1986.

Wiltshire

Wick Hill

Maud Heath (fl. 1474). Sculptor: not known (1838). Location: Wick Hill.

Countryside Feature:

Maud Heath (*fl.* 1474)
Seated stone statue surmounting an octagonal column, issuing from a square pillar
Sculptor and designer Not Known
Location Maud Heath's Causeway outside Bremhill village, near Chippenham

This is a precious monument, if only because one can take active delight in the 500 year-old beneficence that brought it forth. Maud Heath's Causeway, 4½ miles of highway and footpath built and maintained from the endowment of a local widow, is best followed from its Chippenham terminus on the corner of Foundry Lane and Langley Road (the A420 to Swindon). Opposite St Paul's Church is a plate affixed to a stone:

Hither extendeth Maud Heath's gift
For where I stand is Chippenham Clift
Erected 1698 but given 1474

The original inscribed stone was found (1969) by builders of Barclay's Bank in Chippenham Market Place, and is now displayed in the foyer. The present causeway's plaque is thought to date from *c.*1894.

Since the causeway's construction in c.1474 across water meadows, to protect the feet of people coming to market, it has been maintained and administered by a body of trustees whose first members were named in Maud Heath's deed of gift. This consigns 'lands and tenements cottages tofts and gardens meadows grazing pastures rents reversions and all their appurtenances', and the £8 yield, to their care. The original Latin deed is kept in a town safe, whilst a copy is displayed at the Yelde Hall (also of the 15th century). Present trustees are drawn from Chippenham and Langley Burrell councils, and hold office for four-year periods.

The ancient route begins at Wick Hill, crosses the Wilts & Berks Canal, descends to East Tytherton, crosses the River Avon near Kellaways (thought to have been Maud's village), passes Langley Burrell, then follows the Swindon road to St Paul's. The best-preserved section, starting at the Kellaways Weir, is supported on 64 arches to allow for river flooding; further west, the London to Bristol railway crosses over a special arch for the causeway.

Various monuments have been erected along the route, the most striking being Wick Hill's lofty grey pillar with a statue of Maud surveying a view which reaches west toward the Bristol Channel. Behind her, the Wiltshire hills roll to the Lansdowne Monument standing above the Cherhill White Horse.

Maud's effigy was erected in 1838, and can probably claim the distinction of being England's earliest surviving public statue to a woman not of royal blood. It is scarcely possible to see her from the front, since the hillside drops steeply from the railed-off pillar. Her strange silhouette with straw basket and staff, and her ample back view, are memorable enough. The design of the medieval head dress 'cost a great deal of research', according to correspondence between Lady Lansdowne and Mrs Bowles, whose husbands erected the pillar at their 'joint expence'. It introduced the market woman image, but Maud was surely a woman of means.

Repairs to the causeway are recorded in the Maud Heath Trust Minute Books, dating from 1753, which log such items as wheeling grist, digging gravel, pitching stone, and barging the hedges. The *Devizes and Wiltshire Gazette* in 1876 printed a 'lamentation' in verse over the causeway's stones which

... once well laid down
In nice even rows,
Now sunk, worn and jagged,
Give pain to toes.

A restoration of the statue, in 1936, replaced corrosive iron clamps and dowels with bronze ones. The winter gales of 1990 blew off Maud's head, but it landed in a bramble bed and survived almost unscathed. It was replaced the same year, with other repairs, at a cost to the Trust of £2000.

The pillar's dedication and inscribed, uneven verse were written by the eccentric Reverend W.L. Bowles, Vicar of Bremhill from 1805 for 40 years, and a former trustee. He claimed to have translated from Latin the couplet now stamped onto a plaque beside the road bypassing the pillar's field, and is also thought to have translated the Latin admonitions that appear on three sides of another pillar which has sundials, standing below the weir at Kellaways:

Hafte Traveller, The Sun if Sinking now
He Shall return again, but never thou

In the intriguing booklet written for the 500th centenary of Maud's benefaction by J.A. Chamberlain, the English runs 'I shall return — thou never'. The pretty riverside pillar, with ball finial, was erected by the trustees of 1698, 'to the memory of the

worthy Maud Heath'. The causeway is her true monument, but she might have approved another of the sundial inscriptions which advises 'While we have time, let us do good'.

Causeway Selection

At East Tytherton, stands a stepped pyramid of stone blocks with incised Roman numerals, and a central gnomon made from a single protruding block, on which appears Maud's name and the dates 1474 1974. The sculptor Joe Tilson, who lives locally, made the ancient form of a ziggurat in modern style to mark the passage of time.

A seat along the back is dedicated to 'past and present members of TOGS, 1792 1974': they are the Tytherton Old Girls Society, and their boarding school by the Moravian Church closed in 1938, so the younger members are now in their 60s and the oldest in their 80s. Reunions each September consist of a visit to the Wick Hill column (the destination of the school walk after church), followed by a church service, and tea in the village hall.

Avon

Bristol

City Feature:

William III (1650–1702)
Bronze equestrian statue,
plain stone pedestal
Sculptor John Michael Rysbrack
Location Queen Square

This supreme example of Rysbrack's artistry, his classically-styled figure of a king based on the antique statue of the Emperor Marcus Aurelius in Rome, bears little relation to history's physical impression of William of Orange. Born at the Hague, Stadholder of the United Provinces, courageous opponent of Louis XIV and the last successful invader of England (albeit by invitation), William was short, slight and asthmatic with bright blue eyes, a humped back and a big, beaked nose.

On Guy Fawkes's day, November 5th, 1688 — with his warships and fleet flying the white flag for peace and the red to discourage opposition — with

William III (1650–1702). Sculptor: John Michael Rysbrack (1736). Location: Queen Square, Bristol.

subjects. He consolidated the Protestant position in Scotland at the Battle of Killiecrankie in 1689, and in Ireland at the Boyne in 1690. His reign saw the founding of the Bank of England and the National Debt and, on the eve of William's death from fever after a fall from his horse, formation of the Grand Alliance prior to the Wars of the Spanish Succession. Marlborough's great victories thereafter heralded a period of peace and stability, and the 'Augustan Age' of literature and art, in which by the mid-18th century, sculpture in England was approaching its zenith.

Bristol in the 1720s, according to Defoe, was 'the greatest, the richest, and the best port of trade in Britain, London only excepted'. St James's Square, King Square, Dowry Square and Queen Square are among the fine developments of the period, the latter becoming a desirable and leafy residential area by 1731, when a poem expressed the prevailing idea:

Henceforth let London blush whilst Bristol shines,
And all the World applaud their great designs;
BRISTOL, by thy Wealth does no such honour
    bring
As will the Statue of so great a King

A site was approved by Bristol corporation; models entered for the commissioning competition, as the art chronicler George Vertue recorded, were 'Viewd by judges of Art & horses'. That of Peter Scheemakers (whose statue of gilded lead and pewter was erected in Hull, 1734) lost to Rysbrack's bronze masterpiece showing the Great Deliverer leaner and harder, and effortlessly authoritative, wearing an athlete's band in place of a laurel crown.

Vertue's 1733 report on the 'Clay horse and man', cast in plaster of Paris, concluded that it was 'by Criticks skilfull in that Art thought to be the best statue ever made in England'. Cast in bronze the following year at Rysbrack's London studio, the statue was erected in Bristol in 1736. The cost, c.£2000, was met by the city Corporation and the Society of Merchant Venturers.

First restored in 1740 and removed during the Second World War, Rysbrack's masterpiece now rides above the traffic that brutally bisects Queen Square.

his armies, and about 4,000 horses – William sailed into Torbay. He was rowed towards Brixham where, standing in the boat, he pronounced: "Mine goot people. I mean you goot. I am come for your goots. I am come for all your goots', to which one of the throng replied 'You'm Welcome!'.

The stone at New Quay, on which the prince supposedly set foot after being shouldered ashore, forms the base of an obelisk (1803), and at the harbour, a large, awkward marble figure by the Wills brothers was installed late in Victoria's reign. The Prince holds a big feathered hat in one hand, and the pedestal proclaims in Dutch: 'England's liberty restored by Orange'. The Middle Street fisherman's house where he spent his first night still stands. A detailed account of this 'invasion of Devon' and the triumphal march for Westminster, based on an army chaplain's diary, is given in a booklet by Joyce Packe published Tre Kemynyon, Newton Abbot, 1984.

James II's vacillation during the month-long march, and his final flight to France, left the throne 'vacant', and in February 1689, the English crown (with reduced parliamentary authority) was offered to William and Mary at the Banqueting House, Whitehall – where William's maternal, and his wife's paternal, grandfather Charles I had been beheaded. Here also Mary's father, James II, had watched the weathercock for the 'Protestant Wind'.

During his able administration of 13 years William neither sought nor won the affection of his British

Bristol Selection

Bristol's centre converging on Bridgehead, scruffy and noisy with traffic and pedestrians, is further livened by an abundance of carved or brightly painted street furniture, weathervanes, and statues cropping up at every turn and within walking distance of Queen Square.

At the Bridgehead is a flabby Neptune, 'God of the Sea', lead-covered with a long trident, 'produced by Joseph Rendall, founder, 1723'. The metal tablet, recording numerous resitings, including this last in the city centre replanning of the late 1940s-50s, gives the Bridgehead compass bearings.

To the east of Bridgehead in Broad Quay, a top-hatted bronze of I.K. Brunel (1806–1859), designer of the Clifton Suspension Bridge and brilliant engineer of the Great Western Railway, dates from May 26 1982. The same sculptor, John Doubleday's, seated bronze of Brunel was inaugurated at London's Paddington station that morning, and later Bristol's mayor unveiled this one outside the Head Offices of the donors, Bristol and West, founded in 1850 when Brunel – 'adventurous, arrogant and astounding', as described in a booklet on *Famous Bristolians* – was at the height of his career. (*Note* nearby the drinking fountain to George V, 1936, with reliefs of labourers present and past.)

On College Green is J.E. Boehm's 50th Jubilee marble of Queen Victoria, mouth turned down, diminished by removal of its steps, railings and shady tree in College Green alterations of 1950. Outside the west front of St Mark's, just north, is a smooth bronze form, 'Refugee 1980, to the victims of all racial persecutions', by Naomi Blake.

The water garden in the curve of the New Council House, overlooking the Green, has Charles Wheeler's large white stone statue of a Tudor sailor, supposedly John Cabot, pensively tugging his beard and holding a charter from Henry VII; behind the building are hippocampi – fish-tailed horses – ridden by infants.

Walking from Broad Quay along Colston Avenue, one meets bronzes of Edmund Burke (d. 1795), MP for Bristol, writer, orator and political philosopher, by the Bristolian John Harvard Thomas, and of the Bristol philanthropist Edward Colston (d. 1721) by John Cassidy. They were erected after the gardens were laid over part of the Floating Harbour in 1893. Bristolian J. Havard Thomas also carved an uninspiring High Street marble of the philanthropist Samuel Morley in 1887, the year following the MP's death; it was moved to the Haymarket Roundabout in 1921.

In Broad Mead, not too far north of the Rysbrack, is A.G. Walker's lovely bronze statue of John Wesley the incorrigible wayfarer. This simple study of horse and rider, given by a Mr Lamplugh in 1932, occupies the courtyard of England's oldest Methodist chapel, the New Room, built by Wesley 1739 and restored in 1930. On the chapel's Horse Fair side is a full-

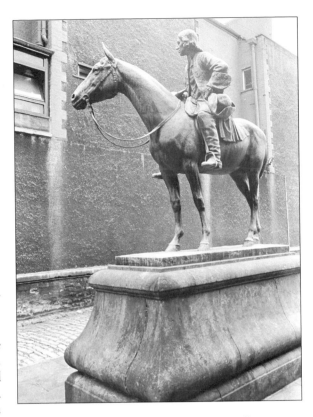

John Wesley (1703–1791). Sculptor: A. G. Walker (1932). Location: Wesleyan Chapel, Broad Mead.

length bronze of Charles Wesley, by Brook Hitch, unveiled 1939.

Lesser works include the Edward VII statue-fountain in Queen's Road by Henry Poole, 1913, described by the *Clifton Chronicle* as a 'perfect casting', and a marble tablet carving of 'MISS EMMA SAUNDERS The Railwaymen's Friend' (d.1927) in fur tippet and hat, dispensing a late-Victorian version of Meals on Wheels, erected by rail workers at Temple Meads after 50 years of 'devoted Christian service'.

Crowning the town on Brandon Hill is the magnificent Cabot Tower by W.V. Gough, a 'Tudor Gothic' belvedere of rugged red sandstone carrying a white statue of an angel, its viewing balconies liberally embellished with inscriptions – some identifying sights in the dizzying views. One lists Cabot monuments in Nova Scotia and Newfoundland; another records the tower's erection by public subscription, 1897–8, to the navigator John Cabot (1483–1557) and his sons Lewis, Sebastian and Sanctus. Henry VII paid John Cabot £10 for discovering Newfoundland (which Cabot thought to be Asia); the Cabot Tower in Brandon Gardens cost £3,300. The city and its monuments lie far below.

Somerset

Pen Hill

Roadside Feature:

Romulus and Remus and the she-wolf
('Lupa Capitolina')
Concrete statue supported on pillars
Sculptor Gaetano Celestra
Location A39 (east side), between Chewton
Mendip and Wells

Facing Pen Hill across a dangerous stretch of the A39, the sculpture's four square-cut cement pillars, patterned with chiselled crescent shapes, stand on a farm wall built flush with the road. This part is the work of stonemason Gaetano Celestra, one of 1,000 Italian prisoners interned at Penleigh Camp near Wells in the Second World War. Over the pillared arches stands his she-wolf with pricked ears, ugly teeth and glaring eyes, scanning the gentle Mendip contours as the infants Romulus and Remus urgently reach up to suck milk. Celestra's signature is scratched into the concrete base of this raw work of art.

*'Lupa Capitolina'. Sculptor: Gaetano Celestra (copy, c. 1943).
Location: A39 above Wells.*

Copied from a 50-lire bank note, his famous symbol of Rome showing the city's founders and their surrogate mother is taken from a bronze Etruscan sculpture of a wolf, dating from *c.* 500 BC. The children were added later, probably in the 15th century. Cellestra, working in a farm outhouse, used plaster with concrete over a wire frame to create the group which he said would remind him of Italy (although he had grown up in North Africa).

A local newspaper feature reported that the hollow figures had attracted a swarm of bees, but more commonly were used by nesting birds, the parents with their offerings entering through the wolf's gaping jaws. After the war, Celestra received a 'Dear John' letter from his wife in Tunis and decided, with other PoWs, to stay in Somerset.

He worked on the farm and later with the Wells builder Androsini, but after taking other jobs Celestra emigrated to Rhodesia, and eventually lost touch with his adopted home. His rough but tender image of Romulus and Remus and the wolf remains a local landmark, a surprise for Italian visitors, and a reminder of Rome in the Somerset hills.

Devon

Exeter

City Feature:

General Sir Henry Redvers Buller (1839–1908)
Bronze equestrian statue, large stone pedestal
Sculptor Adrian Jones
Location New North Road

A past master at portraying military men and their horses, Capt. Adrian Jones, one-time army veterinary officer, shows the plumed-helmeted general astride a fine horse. The statue occupies an island on the Crediton road, also leading to his birthplace, Downes. In the style of military monuments, the big pedestal catalogues his campaigns, far-off yet familiar names in the days when Britain policed the world from India and China to Canada, across Egypt and 'Soudan', and South and West Africa. One inscription proclaims 'HE SAVED NATAL'.

Buller's golden career in these theatres brought mentions in dispatches; orders, decorations and the honour of a V.C. in the Zulu wars (1879). As Lord

General Sir Henry Redvers Buller (1839–1908). Sculptor: Adrian Jones (1905). Location: New North Road, Exeter.

Wolseley's chief of staff at the relief of Khartoum in 1885, he distinguished himself in a skilled retreat, and Wolseley observed his 'rare instinct for war'. He earned distinction in organisation and administration as well as in battle, but after ten years in desk posts (including an uncomfortable term as Lord Salisbury's under-secretary for Ireland, too sympathetic with the Irish peasantry), Buller's indecision and caution helped delay the relief of Ladysmith in 1900.

Despite sharing official credit for winning the Boer War, Buller's popular image suffered, and at a public luncheon he made a speech of self-defence which led to removal of his command in 1901. His statue, erected in 1905 'by his countrymen at home and beyond the seas', was to have been unveiled by Lord Wolseley, but ill health prevented this. Three years later, Buller died and was buried at Crediton. His pedestal records the motto of his regiment the King's Royal Rifle Corps: CELER ET AUDAX.

Exeter Selection

Near General Buller's statue at the top of Queen Street is a superb clock tower and drinking trough of red sandstone, warm limestone and grey granite, all Devon stone, signed by the architect T.A. Andrews, and the builders J. Easton & Son (1897). It is festooned with inscriptions and sculpture: family

arms, sea horses and serpents, a brass griffon resting its paws on a water basin, biblical texts; a pair of bullocks with locked horns. Erected to William Miles at Queen Victoria's 60th Jubilee 'from his widow, on behalf of the animal creation', it is itself in need of care and affection.

Apart from the general's statue, a marble statue by Alfred Drury of 'Hooker the Judicious' seated on Cathedral Green (1907), and J.E. Boehm's white marble statue of Lord Northcote, Exeter has a collection of conventional commemorative works by the home-grown sculptor Edward Bowring Stephens, most of them assembled in the Northernhay gardens (first laid out in 1612) which form a plateau above the 18th-century portico of the largely Victorian county prison. An exception is the gardens' centrepiece, the county monument to the First World War, comprising a broad stone column topped by a graceful, half-draped bronze, raising her clenched fist and triumphantly trampling a scaly dragon. At the base are lifesize idealised bronze figures, the uniformed nurse carrying the signature 'John Angel Sc. 1923'. A prisoner in chains bears the founder's name, 'Morris'. The dedication is to 'men and women of Exeter and Devon'.

Another exception is signed by Harry Hems, also Exeter born, who gives us a roundel portrait (1895)

Richard Hooker (1554–1600). Sculptor: Alfred Drury, RA (1907). Location: Cathedral Green, Exeter.

at the base of a fancy column of Dartmoor granite and Portland stone, the worn marble high relief showing Sir John Bucknill (bald-headed, long-bearded and kindly looking), whose knighthood conferred in 1894, and services to the Volunteer movement, are recalled in the inscription. Boehm's lichened marble of Stafford Henry Northcote, 1st Earl of Iddesleigh (1818–1887), seems about to make a sombre announcement; secretary to Gladstone in 1842 and later Disraeli's Chancellor, he helped found the Royal Albert Memorial Museum with its entrance hall statue by E.B. Stephens of Albert, Prince Consort (1870) in Caen stone.

Also in the hall is a memorial tablet to Sir Thomas Dyke Ackland, whose pensive, youngish figure in marble was unveiled in the gardens by the Earl of Devon, 1861, almost 40 years before Ackland's death aged 89. Carved letters commend his 'private worth and public integrity'; his 'generous heart and open hand'. Gale damage from 1930 severely mars his image, carved by E.B. Stephens. Another local benefactor, the gentle-looking John Dinham (1790–1864), is shown seated in a long coat, his marble statue signed 'E.B. Stephens ARA, London 1865'. Dinham, here honoured for 'his piety, integrity and charity', is portrayed in the Royal Albert Museum by a local painter, Thomas Mogford (d.1868).

The Exeter sculptor E.B. Stephens (1815–82), who assisted in Edward Hodges Baily's London studio, is commemorated at Northernhay's North Road/High Street entrance with his own work 'The Deer Stalker', which apart from the war memorial is the sole bronze casting amongst this unusual outdoor group of marble memorial statues. Its presentation 'to his native city by a number of friends and admirers', at Bedford Circus in 1878, was followed by a public dinner given in Stephens's honour. In common with others, the sculptor seems less at ease in working on an idealised piece than in creating representational images. His hunter, clad in a loin cloth and attended by a hungry hound, conspicuously scans the horizon whilst shading his eyes with a hand. The exaggerated pose is relieved by a homely touch – the Deer Stalker has the plump features of a country lad reared on Devon dumplings and cream. The group was resited here in 1880.

Stephens's marble statue of the 2nd Earl of Fortescue MP unveiled, 1865, in the Castle Yard, wears the collar and cuffs of the Lord Lieutenant of Devon (1839–41); the sculptor made a bronze statue of the 11th Earl of Devon, wearing a bow tie and a creased forehead, about to speak from his low pedestal which now stands in a paved area – part of a city land-scaping scheme at the corner of Bedford and High Street. Fifty thousand subscribers contributed to his statue in 1879; it was 'rescued' from Tan Lane and re-erected on the site of Bedford Circus, destroyed in the Blitz, in 1981. Note the fine additional decoration with an art nouveau flavour.

Exeter has a lovely series of façade statues, some – lions and full-breasted ladies – carved on dark timber-framed buildings, some painted, like the small, regal Queen Victoria on a Queen Street shop near High Street, her niche platform supported by a powerful lion. She wears an aubergine jacket and purple skirt, with matching purple crown. Almost opposite, on the parapet over Marks & Spencer, is a white-painted statue of Victoria raised by the former shop's owner, Mr Ferris, on the young queen's birthday in 1848. In High Street on the turn-of-century half-timbered Abbey National building, a sickly, saintly Leofric (first Bishop of Exeter) is labelled 10Leofric50 in Gothic script – his niche has a space for the ubiquitous pigeon.

Other examples of street furniture, some recently designed, enrich the centre; a little way beyond, opposite Exeter Central station in New North Road, a small building with a custard-yellow pediment has a beautiful stone, full-breasted sphinx – 'PURITAS VIRESQUE'.

At the corner of Denmark and Barnfield Road, on the Martyrs' Memorial obelisk unveiled 1909, are bronze plaques showing 'Thomas Benet nailing his protest against the Cathedral door AD 1531', and – on the back – Agnes Prest chained to the stake, with the wood bundles and the flames, and a horrid old monk shaking his fist: 'burnt upon Southernhay AD 1555'. Harry Hems Fecit.

Plymouth

City Feature:

Sir Francis Drake (c.1540–1596)
Full-length bronze statue on polished pink granite pedestal
Sculptor (Sir) Joseph Edgar Boehm, Bt., RA
Location The Hoe

The Devon Sea Dog, Vice-Admiral at the defeat of the Armada, Drake is shown swaggeringly handsome and confident as befitted the popular image of the Elizabethan buccaneer. The image was strengthened by Newbolt's patriotic poem *Drake's Drum*, published in 1897, but a painting in the National

Portrait Gallery shows a wide-eyed, bullet-headed, gingery individual. The Spanish reckoned their dreaded adversary courteous and humane, something of a braggart, ambitious, and piratical without being too cruel. His sword at his side, he is shown resting his callipers proprietorially on the globe which he circumnavigated, the first English sea-captain to do so, from 1577–80. The globe is supported by mermaids.

The pedestal lacks the epic *bas*-reliefs which adorn the original bronze, erected at Tavistock one year before Plymouth's, in 1884. Scenes from Drake's legendary career show Elizabeth I knighting her premier sea captain on *The Golden Hind* at Deptford, after his world voyage; bowls on the Hoe, when his fleet should have been guarding the Channel entrance against the approaching Armada, and the sea burial off Portobello, after Drake's death from dysentery on the failed last venture to the Spanish Main. His men are lowering him over the side, naked and stiff, in a sling.

Drake's drum, by which the captain signalled his crew, was returned to England, and can be seen at Buckland Abbey (NT) which Drake, rich and famous from the world voyage and its plunder, acquired in 1581 from Sir Richard Grenville. He became Mayor of Plymouth in the same year.

Born on a farm near Tavistock, Drake trained at Chatham before his first command in 1567 introduced years of privateering on the Spanish Main where Elizabeth's Protestant English challenged the Papal backing of the Spanish and Portuguese claim to the riches of the southern oceans. When Drake arrived home from Nombre de Dios in Panama one Sunday morning, with booty worth £40,000, Plymouth churches were emptied as their congregations hastened to greet him.

When war eventually and inevitably came after the execution of Mary Queen of Scots, Drake spoiled the Spanish invasion fleet at Cadiz whilst, as he put it, 'singeing the King of Spain's beard', an action considered unduly reckless by the Queen.

Even so, England's first great sea victory, commanded by Lord Howard, established Drake as hero of the Armada then and for future generations, whilst country people credited him with supernatural powers. It was said that 'the old warrior', on completing his game of kales, chopped a great timber into blocks which were cast from the Hoe into the Sound, and arose as unquenchable fire ships.

More prosaically, Drake brought water from Dartmoor to Plymouth in a feat of engineering unsurpassed at that time. A stretch thought to be

Sir Francis Drake (c.1540–1596). Sculptor: Sir J. E. Boehm Bt., RA (1885). Location: Plymouth Hoe.

Drake's Leat, revealed during a drought, runs through Drake's Square Gardens in Tavistock Road.

Locally or nationwide, mariner or superman, pirate or Admiral, Drake has remained a household name from Elizabeth I's reign to our own.

Plymouth Hoe Selection

Backed by the rebuilt, post-war city, this blustery promenading ground still has its bowls pitch, municipally manicured and signposted with a small painted relief figure of the arch-bowlsman Sir Francis Drake. It was 'researched, designed and fabricated by T. Arrol McKinnes, 1981'. Other monuments here have military or seafaring dedications (except for the earliest, a rocket-like Victorian-Gothic drinking fountain surmounted by a lady with an urn, erected to Marianne Norrington by her husband in 1881).

All are grouped around Smeaton's Tower (next door to Drake's statue), the original Eddystone Light

Drake at Bowls; statue pedestal panel. Sculptor: Sir J. E. Boehm Bt., RA (1885). Location: Plymouth Hoe.

re-erected here in 1882. The steep stairway climbs to the glass dome and lamp, and low-railed platform overlooking town and Sound. Biblical inscriptions and explanatory dedications appear at every turn.

Most are to John Smeaton, first man to be classed Civil Engineer, 'whom God hath empowered with the most extraordinary abilities'. Smeaton built the Eddystone lighthouse of Cornish granite blocks, with Portland stone dressing, in 1756–9. His bust, one floor below, is in a glass case. All is shipshape with polish, varnish and paint, giving vivid reminders of former lighthousemen's lives on 'the notorious Eddystone Reef', 14 miles seaward.

Directly landward (and northward) is the Armada column by Gribble and W.C. May, its foundation stone laid 300 years after the first sighting from here in 1588. Baring-Gould thought it 'ridiculously bad', but note Britannia; cannon balls; sculptured lions and elephants' heads; crude reliefs of Elizabethan seadogs; armorial shields recalling Devon ports that sent ships, and evoking West Country families Rashleigh, Stugley, Grenville, Prowse; and inscriptions that include the Armada victory echo: 'He blew with his winds and they were scattered'.

Between this and Drake's statue is the Naval Memorial obelisk erected 1920–4 to commemorate the Great War, and amended to include the Second War. It is identical with those in the other Manning Ports, Chatham and Portsmouth, except for lacking the pavilions, but still humbling in its white, Portland-stone spaciousness. The stone figures of sailors are repeated, and at the entrance is McMillan's fer-

ocious stone Neptune, with bucking seahorses (1953). The designer was Sir Robert Lorimer.

All the monuments on the Hoe are sumptuously decorated. Worth noting on the Boer War obelisk are bronze, Art Nouveau, do-or-die battle scenes; also 'General White's despatch' of 1900. Outside the Smeaton Tower entrance, on the Royal Marines' World Wars Memorial (topped with an angel), note the stone-carved Tommy's elderly face. Artists' signatures appear on all monuments. Unluckily, their bronze work (including McMillan's) has been painted Great Western Railway brown.

Away from the Hoe, seek out Sir John Rennie's massively grand Royal Victualling Yard, his only important architectural work bar bridges. Note William IV's 13ft stone figure over the gateway: also the great bulls' heads carved from the stone blocks. Rennie's first diving bell was used when constructing the sea walls – almost half the acreage is reclaimed.

On Mount Wise is Albert Hodge's big, elaborate monument to Scott of the Antarctic (1868–1912), a Devonport boy whose former Oatlands house was fatally damaged in the Blitz. Local street names recall members of the fated expedition, who also appear on the monument: 'they died For King, Country, Brotherly Love, and Knowledge'. The monument went up the following year.

Further west is a touching reminder of pre-Blitz town scenery, the old Guildhall of 1821–3, best viewed up Monument Street. Its Coade-stone armorial figures are painted jolly primary colours, Britannia with rude red lips, the lion with fierce black teeth. Nearby is the 101ft Doric column designed by the same architect, John Foulston (1824), to mark the renaming of Plymouth Dock as Devonport.

Cornwall

Penzance

Town Feature:

Sir Humphry Davy (1778–1829)
Full-length marble statue on granite pedestal
Sculptors T. & W. Wills
Location Market Jew Street

Cornwall's two conventional commemorative statues are L.S. Merrifield's striking bronze to Richard

Trevithick, carrying a model of his steam locomotive at his birthplace in Camborne, and this carved
figure of Trevithick's equally illustrious contemporary. One of the Wills brothers' better efforts, it is
as pleasingly sited as any statue in England.

Based on the portrait painted by Sir Thomas
Lawrence for the Royal Society, it shows the great
chemist with a hand on his famous 'Davy' lamp, his
commanding stance fully complementing the granite
portico and dome of the old Market House that
closes the long rise of Market Jew Street.

A nearby plaque marks the site of Davy's birthplace where he spent early childhood, the eldest of
a wood carver's family. The career which brought
eminence – and a knighthood – some time before
Davy's invention of the miners' lamp, for which
he is popularly remembered, is summarised in a
bicentenary panel beside his statue:

'Davy's major work was in the field of electro-
chemistry, through which 6 new elements, including
sodium and potassium, were discovered. In his lifetime, Davy initiated important work on nitrous oxide
(laughing gas); presented a major treatise on the
chemistry of agriculture; refuted the myth that
oxygen was found in all gases; discovered and fostered the talents of Michael Faraday; popularised
science education and assisted the development of
both the Royal Institution and the Royal Society, of
which he was President for 7 years.'

The lamp was invented in 1815, after a terrible
pit disaster prompted Sunderland coal owners to
seek help against the threat of methane gas (fire

*Sir Humphrey Davy (1778–1829). Sculptor: T & W Wills.
Location: top of Market Jew Street, Penzance.*

damp), which without warning would ignite the
naked flame of miners' lights to cause devastating
explosions. Going below ground to observe conditions, Davy confounded the mining engineer by
promising a result; he contrived to encase the flame
in wire gauze (which dissipated the heat before it
could ignite the gas), and added a metal sheath to
partly encase the gauze mantle in a draught.

Once developed, the lamp was an immediate
success throughout Europe. The impetuous and
amiable Davy would not take out a patent, but was
incensed at counter-claims for George Stephenson
as the inventor. At an honorary dinner given by
Tyne and Wear colliery owners, the 1st Earl of
Durham presented Davy with a fine service of plate,
and the following year (1818) he became a baronet.

The Davy lamp added popular acclaim to Sir
Humphry's *éclat* in scientific and social circles as a
brilliant scientist lecturer and scientific writer. He
saw himself as a 'chemical philosopher'. Napoleon
had granted him freedom of travel in France, with
his elegant wife and his assistant Faraday, even
during the wars. In Naples, Davy studied volcanoes
and worked with the foremost classical sculptor
Antonio Canova on the pigmentation of colours
used by the ancients.

English friends included the poets Wordsworth,
Coleridge and Byron. Southey encouraged him in
his poetry when Davy was superintendant of the
Pneumatic Institute at Clifton in Bristol, where they
sampled the pleasures of nitrous oxide.

Davy lived 'abroad' (in Bristol and London), but
never forgot West Cornwall's 'rocks and sea, dead
hills and living hills covered with verdure'. His early
life at Penzance and later Ludgvan, as his biographer
Anne Treneer noted, was 'as intensely and vividly
local as his later life was cosmopolitan'. Puddling in
Penzance gutters kindled a later passion, angling; the
infant observed the curing process in tan pits lower
down Market Jew Street, and watched mules passing
from the St Just copper mines to Penzance Quay.

He later found learning 'a pleasure, but in most
schools it is made a pain'. With an elderly Quaker
saddler, Robert Dunkin, Davy practised crude
electro-chemical experiments. However, leisure time
in a makeshift attic laboratory, whilst apprenticed to
a Penzance apothecary and surgeon, alarmed his
gentle master – 'he will blow us all up!'

Davy's wish for a monument at Gulval Carn,
then wild moorland overlooking the Mount near
Ludgvan, never came to fruition, although verses
were written to carve in the rock. Instead, his statue
serves to enhance the charm of Market Jew Street.

Llywelyn the Great (1167–1240). Sculptor: E. O. Griffiths (1898). Location: Lancaster Square, Conway.

Wales

'Land of My Fathers'

*The multitude sang Cymric hymns
and 'The Land of My Fathers'*

(Part of the inscription carved on the
'Gladstone Slab' on Walker's Path above Nant
Gwynant, on the slopes of Snowdon)

*T*he Gladstone Slab, cemented to its rocky outcrop, marked the opening of a new pathway on the slopes of Snowdon. More gloriously, it recalls a typical Welsh occasion of massed song and national pride.

The statues and stones by which this small, mountainous land typically celebrates its forebears mirror the continuing history of its rich and separate culture. Throughout the principality, carved inscriptions in Welsh and English proclaim the worth of warrior princes, poets and firebrand preachers, politicians and educators, whose exertions were rooted in the perpetuation of the national identity.

The monuments of the mountainous north, and parts of mid-Wales, most commonly recall the literary, Calvinistic and Liberal figures whose causes fostered Welsh language and culture. Those found in Mid Wales and the south commemorate the 19th-century industrialists whose mines and railways brought monoglot Welsh speakers from the north and west in the great migrations of the Industrial Revolution — the ensuing common parlance helping to reinforce the Welsh language and culture in English-speaking Wales.

In the southwest and on the coasts and Marches, English influence is evident in columns, clocks or Gothic 'crosses' erected to honour British royalty, military heroes, establishment worthies and landed gentry. Some, indeed, demonstrate active English enthusiasm for the Welsh national cause.

Throughout Wales, even in the remote villages, a single cause fought under the Union Jack is acknowledged in the staggering losses of the two World Wars, and is commonly measured in luxuriantly-dressed stone emblazoned with names, and accompanied by figures in bronze or stone. While there are interesting variations, such as clock towers in villages like Dinorwic, and Gwalchmai on Anglesey, like all Welsh monuments the war memorials are broadly better-sited, better-finished and better-kept than their English counterparts.

A peculiarly Welsh monument (that does have its counterparts in Cornwall) is the ritual Gorsedd circle of inscribed stones, planted by JCBs in meadows outside towns such as Bala and in Llandudno's Happy Valley Gardens on a steep hillside overlooking the resort. These stones mark the proud occasion of a National Eisteddfod – the annual Welsh contest of excellence in poetry, music, crafts and other disciplines. As national arbiters of standards in the arts, particularly with regard to classical Welsh poetry, the eisteddfodau play a vital role in nurturing language and literature, and thus the presence of a town's stone circle signifies a persisting nationalism.

Successive periods of nationalistic revival can be identified in many of Wales's individual monuments, notably the rare and atmospheric 9th-century Pillar of Eliseg near Valle Crucis Abbey, just north of Llangollen. Its weathered inscription, last renewed in 1696, records the descendants and deeds of Eliseg 'who united the inheritance of Powys (laid waste for nine years) out of the hand of the English with fire and the sword'. Similarly, the Alleluia Stone outside Mold, set up in 1736 to mark a Celtic triumph over heathen hordes, marks an early enthusiasm for antiquarianism, for delving into people's Celtic origins and for studying the lives of the saints.

By the beginning of the 19th century, a romantic revival, combined with the craze for scenic tours, led a local landlord to 'discover' the grave of Prince Llywelyn's misjudged hound, near Beddgellert; the 'memorial stone' attracted even the King, and *The Goat Inn* subsequently became *The Royal Goat*.

A more recent revival is evident in the image of Llywelyn the Great at Conway; E.O. Griffiths's bronze statue, naturalistically painted, shows Wales's unifying Prince standing erect with large sword and dashing moustache on a small, fluted Corinthian column over a stone drinking-fountain. It was presented by Albert Wood in 1898 to mark the installation of a water supply. The carved octagonal basin proclaims 'Llewellyn ab Iorworth, Founder of Conwy Abbey AD 1184'.

A profoundly-influential nationalist movement is recalled in monuments to Calvinist Methodist figures such as Thomas Charles and the Rev. Lewis Edwards, whose statues make ensembles with their respective chapel and theological college at Bala in Gwynedd. A founder of this great movement, Lewis

Evans (1719–1792) is commemorated at Adfa in a small, white-washed pillar outside the Gerazim Chapel which he also founded. Deep in the companionable Powys hills, its Gothic script reminds us 'He had trial of cruel mockings and scourgings, yea, moreover of bonds and imprisonment', whilst the chapel and pillar are broader indicators of the movement's vital work in spreading Welsh language and literacy through denominational tracts, Sunday school and the thunderous oratory of preachers.

A handsome, church-like, roadside column (1905) stands beneath Dolwyddelen Castle between Blaenau Ffestiniog and Betws-y-Coed. Carved from the polished granite is a dedication to 'four eminent brothers, John, William, David and Richard Jones, three preachers and one elder'.

A nearby track leads to the farmhouse, Tan-y-Castell, the gable of which displays an earlier monument of Bethesda slate. It is the birthplace of John (1796–1857), a celebrated and powerful preacher who wrote: 'Do not expect anything great or magnificent from me, I only speak Welsh, and was bred at the foot of Snowdon. I have nothing for you except what is in the Welsh bible'. New slate walling marks the local quarrying tradition which provided work for John as an unschooled, fatherless boy.

The stoneworking industry is represented in Welsh monuments everywhere, in polished granite pedestals, in the solid finish of stone copings and dressings, and in the megalithic memorials themselves. Impressive examples include one to Llywelyn the Last, 'Our Prince', at Cilmeri, and one to the writer Daniel Owen, whose rugged boulder dominates a row of council houses which superseded his mean birthplace in Mold, Clwyd. At Blaenau Ffestiniog, where glinting slate heaps dwarf the town, a big, roughly-shaped slate slab makes a civic fountain for the town square (1983). And on the Betws-y-Coed approach, the First World War tribute set up by the Oakley Quarry owner to his workers consists of their names engraved on a great slate slab with a stonework surround; it is signed by the designer and engraver, O.O. Roberts (1919).

Further north, at Trawsfynydd, a rough-hewn plinth makes a foil for L.S. Merrifield's clean-cut bronze figure of Hedd Wynn, the 'Shepherd Poet', striding out from houses, gateposts and the nearby chapel, all made of the same sombre stone slabs. Tenby's National Monument to 'Albert Dda' (1863), showing the Prince Consort in Field Marshal's uniform, was carved from Sicilian marble by John Evan Thomas but is complimented by a broad flight of steps and an 18ft pedestal with carved marble panels and big, scrolled side-wings, all in local fossiliferous limestone. This dazzling landmark on its rocky promontory perfects the High Street panorama of seaside villas, harbour, cliffs and sands.

At Bedwelty Park in Tredegar, a millstone is preserved to recall early hill farming, while the skills and pride of the coal industry are nakedly displayed in a single, 15-ton block of coal won by John Jones in 1851. Other industrial relics in this silvan setting include a pit cage and a stone sleeper from the Rassau tramroad. More gracious, however, is the domed, cast-iron fountain erected at the south end of Merthyr Tydfil High Street to commemorate Robert and Lucy Thomas, 'pioneers in 1828 of the South Wales Steam Coal Trade' on which the South Wales Coalfield built its prosperity. At the far end of the town, in contrast, Richard Trevithick's memorial stone incorporates sleeper stones and tram rails.

Monuments often reflect everyday lives dominated by the landscape, especially a rugged terrain such as that around Merthyr Tydfil, which is entered from the moorland Brecon road across a cattle grid. The age-old association of mining and hill farming is contained in a sad little obelisk near Corn Dhu on the Brecon Beacons, where five-year-old Tommy Jones got lost in his Sunday sailor suit whilst walking from Brecon station to his grandparents' farmhouse, Cwm-llwch, in a deep valley north of the Brecons.

After 'an anxious search of 26 days', as told in the inscription, Tommy's body was found 1,300 ft above the place where he had separated from his father, a Rhondda miner. The spot was revealed to a Brecknockshire woman in a dream. Jurors' fees from the inquest, which found 'death by exposure and exhaustion', formed the basis of the voluntary fund for the memorial stone, dragged on horse sled to the ridge in July 1901.

Tommy's small rugged obelisk now makes a wayfarer's mark for ramblers, but the graves of school children buried under a sliding coal tip at Aberfan in October 1966 have become a place of pilgrimage for visitors to the Valleys. The individual memorials are linked by a row of small white arches – rich, elaborate stone monuments overlooking the grey mining valley and somewhat at odds with the corporate negligence of the coal industry which impoverished the lives of the Aberfan villagers.

At Llwynypia Miners' Institute, near Tonypandy, Walker Merritt's statue of the Scottish mine owner Archibald Hood (1823–1902) is very much part of its landscape, which Hood developed from a secluded valley to a scene of smoking industrial activity. A director of the new Barry Dock, and a partner in the

1st Duke of Wellington (1769–1852). Sculptor: John Evan Thomas (1858). Location: the Bulwark, Brecon.

Glamorgan Coal Company, Archibald leans on his cane, pointing rigidly across the valley at the Glamorgan Colliery, formerly the 'Scotch' colliery.

The local passion for colour-washing iron railings and gates, window frames and front doors all along this long, deep, mining valley has swept over this dignified bronze, which is exuberantly painted in the same shell-shades, giving Mr Hood a grey morning coat with black tail buttons, primrose trousers, a pink pate and coal-black eyes. The Institute also carries a restrained marble relief of a past president, John Hopla, an executive member of the South Wales Miners' Federation, and a member of the strike committee in the Cambrian Colliery Dispute of 1910–11.

Whether they show coal owners, bishops or bards, statues in Wales display the handiwork of Welsh sculptors, the most popular and gifted being the Cardiff-born artist Sir William Goscombe John, whose work is represented from Glamorgan to Clwyd. Next in popularity is John Evan Thomas, who modelled the hawk-like Duke of Wellington, among others, from life. Thomas presented the bronze statue to his home town Brecon in 1858, as is explained on the front of the pedestal. The back, inexplicably, is marked 'PICTON'.

A confusion with J.E. Thomas's work provided Brecon with another sculpture, a bronze casting of Boadicea and her handmaidens (1855), which was removed from Birmingham during redevelopment. At first, Boadicea found herself incongruously positioned over the Elan Valley Dam, the source of Birmingham's water supply. Later she languished in a local storage depot, until some workmen noticed the signature 'John Thomas'.

Alice's *White Rabbit. Sculptor: Mr Forester* (1933). *Location: North Shore, Llandudno.*

In 1981, after the group was attributed to Brecon's John Evan, it was salvaged to fill a gap caused by the demolition of a public convenience, and Boadicea now brightens a shady courtyard behind the Brecknock Museum. Another inscription scratched on the bronze explains the work's origin: 'From the marble group in the possession of Sir Morton Peto, Bart'. John Thomas received much patronage from Peto, and further evidence confirms Brecon's work as that of John, rather than John Evan, Thomas.

Other, genuinely-Welsh works include Edward Davis's statue of General Nott at Carmarthen (where there is also a monument to General Picton), and at Wrexham, a fine bronze casting of Queen Victoria aged 42, queenly and solemn, the gift of Henry Price to his home town (1905) on the Powys-Cheshire border. Victoria, 'Queen and Empress', is rarely commemorated in Wales.

At Llandudno is a delightful marble figure of *Alice in Wonderland's* hurrying White Rabbit, carved by a local stonemason, Mr Forester. It was unveiled in 1933 by David Lloyd George under the cold hills of Llandudno's North Shore, where 'Alice' spent childhood holidays. Sadly, repeated vandalism is threatening this much-loved but vulnerable work.

Works by modern sculptors include statues by Jonah Jones at Llansannan, and his 'Princes of Aberffraw' on Anglesey; at Harlech Castle, Ivor Roberts-Jones's 'Two Kings' is based on a tale from the *Mabinogion*. In Whiteland, Dyfed, a series of memorial gardens with carvings and mosaic illustrations was devised in 1984 by Peter Lord on the site of Hywel Dda's White House and of the old cattle market. It recalls the meeting convened by the king, at which new Celtic laws were codified into a legalistic framework that endured from the 10th century until Union with England in 1536.

This *pièce de resistance* of participation art employed many artists working in Wales, but has also attracted brick-bats and vandalism, perhaps because local appreciation of Hywel the Good's unifying influence has receded with time.

Other sculptures by artists such as Hideo Futura and Alain Ayers, commemorating native writers, feature on the admirable Powys Sculpture Trail, which was set up by the Welsh Sculpture Trust and the county council in 1984 from an idea by a local sculptor, Ben Jones. At Fishguard, in Dyfed, a small but appealing relief-carving shows a bespectacled, peppery-looking individual, D.J. Williams (1885–1970), 'Man of literature and nation lover', a local grammar school teacher who was a founder member of Plaid Cymri. He stares out from a part-submerged in 1859, on whose property the king first set foot 'to continued acclamations and shouts of welcome' in 1821. Farther north, at Machynllyth in Powys, a massive gothic clock tower of variegated stone was erected to mark the coming of age of Viscount Castlereagh, eldest son of the 5th Marquis of Londonderry, in 1873.

At Denbigh in Clwyd, a marble statue of Dr Evan Pierce, county coroner, J.P. and five-years' mayor, is elevated on a 72ft Doric column (1872); melodramatic bronze reliefs by Mario Raggi represent, among other charitable acts, the doctor's heroic efforts in the cholera epidemic of 1832. Dr Pierce, who would have preferred a Grammar School Memorial Fellowship, provided the Jubilee Garden, in which he placed a pair of triffid-like cast-iron fountains (since painted bathroom green) bearing the names and titles of Queen Victoria's royal children.

Memorial stone; to D. J. Williams (1885–1970). Sculptor: Vicki Craven (1885). Location: West Street, Fishguard.

boulder (formerly a gate post), its face rubbed silky-smooth, in West Street. The sculptor, Birmingham-born Vicki Craven, was commissioned to carve an inscription, but felt inspired to create in the likeness of 'D.J.' her first portrait carving.

Here at the edge of Wales the monuments are more diverse and international, both in dedication and form. A clifftop stone at Carreg Wastad recalls the 'last invasion of Britain' (1797) by the Black Legion, when 1200 French convicts, under the command of the American Colonel Tate and sailing on half rations to heighten their ferocity, aroused local fury by falling on the householders' casks of wine salvaged from a shipwreck. A plaque on Goodwick Beach marks their unconditional surrender to the 1st Baron Cawdor of Castlemartin, whose force of 600 yeomanry was attended by housewives armed with pitchforks. A gravestone in Fishguard churchyard commemorates the 'Welsh Heroine' Jemima Nicholas, who took several French prisoners.

At Milford Haven, the 'memorable and interesting event' of George IV's refuge 'from violent and succeeding tempests' is lauded in a long, effusive inscription on a richly-decorative marble tablet at the east end of Victoria Bridge. It was installed by Robert Fulk Greville, builder of the first timber toll bridge

Bridge tablet (to mark George IV landing, 1821). Location: Victoria Bridge, Milford Haven.

Across Vale Street, a 1980s Food Market has overtaken Dr Pierce's hospital and his home, where as a widower of 79 he took to wife one of his maidenly patients. At his death in 1895 he was propped up for public view in his coffin, wearing black bow tie and pork-pie hat: the monument recalls 'A PHILANTHROPIST, A PATRIOT, AND A CHRISTIAN'.

Just north of Denbigh off the Nantglyn road, a track and path lead to 'THIS SPOT' by the secluded river, 'often dignified by the prefence of Dr Johnson LLD' and marked by a pretty stone pillar with an urn. Apparently, upon hearing of a Mr Myddleton's intention to erect this graceful tribute (c.1775), the doctor grumbled of 'an intention to bury me alive'.

Robert Owen (1771–1858). Sculptor: Gilbert Bayes, completed by W. C. H. King (1954). Location: Short Bridge Street, Newton.

Wales has its share of individualists, its eccentrics and its libertarians whose 'alternative' approach brought commendable results. Dr Price of Llantrisant is perhaps most notorious; his actions established cremation as a legitimate option, and his statue shows his fox-skin hat and cloak which he wore at Llangollen's definitive National Eistedfodd, master-minded by himself and two other countrymen in 1858.

The Co-operative pioneer Robert Owen (1771–1858) was refused commemoration in his birthplace, Newtown, because of his free-thinking religious and social philosophy. However, a stock image – but a touching one – was finally commissioned by the co-operative societies from Gilbert Bayes, who signed the bronze which was completed after Bayes's death in 1954. Behind the figures of Owen and a clinging waif are more-stylised wall panels, pleasingly modelled in relief by the completing sculptor W.C.H. King; they show milkmaids, carpenters and other inhabitants of an ideal Owen community.

Most of Wales's immortalised heroes lived and worked in the land of their fathers, their monuments set up in towns or villages often only superficially changed since their time. At Corris in Gwynedd, high on the village bypass (A487), a 'Celtic' cross commemorates Alfred W. Hughes who, like Robert Owen, made his mark away from home. Professor of Anatomy at King's College in London, Hughes died of fever in 1900 while superintending the Welsh Hospital during the South African war, but he 'began his life's work among these hills'.

As on Pontypridd's greater monument to Evan and James James, creators of the national anthem *Land of my Fathers*, the cross by Goscombe John bears a small bronze cameo portrait of the dedictee. A young man matured by a wing collar and waxed moustache, Hughes looks out over towering slopes of slate slack that recall the industry dominant when he was born at Fronwen in 1861. Far below, the village church contains family monuments including his father's memorial window, recently saved by villagers' fund-raising efforts. One of the donors was Professor Hughes's nephew, whose father continued his dead brother's work in South Africa.

From Hughes's decorative cross, the view beyond the village is of a lonely road in its river valley winding north to 'these hills'. And that is entirely appropriate because, whether statue, slab or cross – set among hill villages, industrial valleys or stone-built towns – Welsh monuments honour not only the Fathers, but also their Land.

North and Mid Wales Gazetteer

Note: The counties of Wales, which in 1974 were reduced in number to correspond with the ancient demarcations, appear in loosely topographical order. Within each county, monuments are listed under their locations, which appear in alphabetical order. The old counties of North and Mid-Wales contained within the present three, Clwyd, Gwynedd and Powys, are indicated after a location by the letters (F) Flintshire; (D) Denbighshire; (Mr) Merionethshire; (Cv) Caernarvonshire; (R) Radnorshire; (Mg) Montgomeryshire, and (B) Brecknockshire.

Clwyd

Llansannan (D)

Village Feature:

'The Girl' – a monument to five Welsh writers:
Tudor Aled (fl.1480–1526)
William Salesbury (c.1520–c.1584)
Henry Rees (1797–1867)
Gwilym Hiraethog (William Rees, 1802–1883)
Iorwerth Glan Aled (1819–1867)
Gilded bronze statue of seated child, plain stone obelisk.
Sculptor (Sir) William Goscombe John.
Location Village Street

The idea may seem incongruous, the long-haired, cross-ankled child a sentimental figure, but the textures of matt-painted statue and granite obelisk compliment the plain house fronts of concrete, pebbledash and stone, patched with colour from window boxes along Llansannan's main street. The monument was first proposed by the Liberal MP for Merioneth, Thomas Ellis, when staying at Gwylfa Hiraethog on the parish boundary. And 'The Girl' was unveiled by the MP in 1899, the year of Ellis's death.

The monument celebrates achievements most frequently lauded in the northern part of the principality: those of poets, writers, preachers and

'The Girl' monument; to five writers (fl. between 1480 & 1867). Sculptor: Sir W. Goscombe John, RA (1899). Location: village street, Llansannan.

patriots. It is said that these five distinguished names, born in the parish between the 15th and 19th centuries, could have been augmented by a dozen other literary figures from the same locality.

The earliest commemorated is the poet and bard Tudor Aled, influential during the richest flowering of medieval Welsh lyric poetry. His death (*c.1526*) makes him just contemporary with the next commemorated, the patriotic writer, classical scholar and linguist William Salesbury, who was born in Llansannan *c.1520*. Assisting Richard Davies, Bishop of St David's, Salesbury translated the Prayer Book and most of the New Testament, the first ever expression of either work in Welsh.

The three remaining belong to 19th-century Calvanistic Methodist families. Henry Rees and his brother William were born on a farm beneath Mynydd Hiraethog, and Edward Roberts (Iorwerth Glan Aled) at Llansannan. Roberts, who trained at the theological college in Bala, is honoured as poet, writer and preacher, and Henry Rees (ordained at Bala in 1827) as one of the great Calvanistic leaders of his day. William became a minister of the Independent Church, and founded the first successful Welsh newspaper as a vehicle for his political essays; written in local dialect, *'Letters of an Old Farmer'* emanated from Rees's adopted home in Liverpool along with poems, hymns, prose, plays and sermons.

The selection of names, and the monument's form, remain an enigma. Some say that the child with her garland was from the village, others that she belonged to a wealthy local family, or that she represents Wales mourning past glories. According to a Llansannan historian she is not in national dress, since she has 'escaped the crowning nonsense of the steeple-hat' (Welsh national costume is regarded, in some parts, as an English, late-Victorian fancy).

Today, village people take pride in the statue, and some still feel sore at the efforts of a local builder who, unasked, obscured the bronze patina with gold paint. Care is vested in the village's Community Council, owners of this distinctive work.

Mold/Yr Wyddgrug (F).

Town Feature:

Daniel Owen (1836–1895)
Full-length bronze statue on stone pedestal
Sculptor (Sir) William Goscombe John
Location Daniel Owen Precinct

Daniel Owen (1836–1895). Sculptor: Sir W. Goscombe John, RA (1901, resited 1976). Location: Mold.

The literary tailor, in top coat and stiff-brimmed hat, is portrayed as a sternly-purposeful individual, yet good-humoured and shrewd. He holds a copy of his most popular novel, *Rhys Lewis*, at a new location outside the lately-built library, where the Daniel Owen Memorial Room has been furnished to resemble the New Street tailor's workshop at which Owen made his livelihood. The first Welsh novelist, Owen is scarcely known outside the principality.

The resiting of the statue, from its 1901 location in County Hall Field to the Daniel Owen Precinct of 1976, forged links between the changing town and the 19th-century, Welsh-speaking Mold which appears mirrored in Owen's work. Spectator and player, Owen based his writing on the school, the chapel, the shop, the inn and the workhouse, and — commanding the fortunes of a God-fearing community — the then-declining colliery trade.

Brought up by his impoverished and widowed mother, Owen's early schooling was supplemented by attendance at Sunday school in the Calvanistic Bethesda Chapel, and by his apprenticeship at the age of 12 in the tailor's workshop, where he learned his trade in an atmosphere of discussion and debate about Welsh and English literature. His early efforts at writing were rewarded by prizes in local literary competitions.

Owen's two years away from Mold were spent at the Calvanistic college in Bala, but in 1867 he ended his course early and returned to care for his mother and her younger family, later opening his tailor's and draper's shop. Ill-health cut short his preaching and he began to write sermons and then to serialise domestic stories which appeared in book form as *Y Dreflan*, which the town council translates as 'our village'.

Fiction was then considered unsuitable for Non-conformist Wales, and chapel-goers' reading was confined to biographies of ministers and preachers. Owen subtitled his next serialisation *Minister of Bethel*. The resulting book, the popular *Hanangofiant Rhys Lewis* ('Memoirs of Rhys Lewis'), is said to be the first modern novel in the Welsh language. Followed by novels about local industrial and rural life, *Rhys Lewis* introduced characters that were cherished by Owen's fellow townsmen as people akin to themselves – if not themselves.

At today's Memorial Room, his robust and humorous prose is displayed in his letters and advertisements. The writer's philosophy is recorded on his statue's pedestal in Latin, English and Welsh: *Not for the wise and learned have I written, but for the common people.*

Mold (and locality) selection:

From the Gwernaffield road can be seen the Alleluia Monument, a monolith set up in Maesgarmon Field in 1736 by Nehemiah Griffith to celebrate the rout of Pictish and Saxon hordes by Bishop Germanus in 429 AD.

Overlooking the A494 to Ruthin, Moel Famma (1820ft) has George III's 50th Jubilee Tower. Designed by Thomas Harrison and erected 1810–12, it was blown down in 1862, but the top of the obelisk on its battered podium was restored in 1970.

Gwynedd

Bala (Mr)

Town Feature:

Thomas Edward Ellis (1859–1899)
Full-length bronze statue on stone pedestal with carved relief panels.
Sculptor (Sir) William Goscombe John
Location The High Street

Thomas Edward Ellis (1859–1899).
Sculptor: Sir W. Goscombe John, RA (1902).
Location: High Street, Bala.

Tom Ellis's statue, which dates from 1902, stands at the north end of Bala's wide High Street. The sculptor has portrayed him in his ceremonial gown, fierce-browed, one arm upraised as if haranguing the town. Occasionally the town responds, and the former Liberal Member for Merioneth and leading member of the Welsh Language Society appears with a handbag slung over the declaiming arm.

Ellis's birthplace, Cynlas, stands north of Bala on the A494 Chester road, and the statue's prominent site in Bala High Street reflects Ellis's vigorous promotion of Welsh causes both in and outside the Principality. An eroded relief on the statue's pedestal shows the Old College at the University College of Wales, Aberystwyth, where he studied before going up to New College, Oxford. (A casting of this bronze stands in the Old College Quadrangle.)

Later on, Ellis became private secretary to the industrialist John Brunner, Liberal MP for Northwich, before entering Parliament in 1886. At a speech in Bala (perhaps recalled in this rather histrionic figure), Ellis propounded as his prime political objective a separate Welsh legislature, but his popularity did not sway his countrymen to accept this radical plan. As Chief Whip from 1894 under Gladstone, he remained the vigorous champion of Welsh politics, religion, literature and education, but his career was cut short by his death in Cannes at the age of 40.

Bala (and locality) Selection

Ellis's town at the north end of Bala lake, now a sailing and holiday haven, has various monuments to its former importance as a religious centre. The Calvinist Methodist College flourished under the directorship of its founder, the teacher and theologian Lewis Edwards (d.1887), whose bronze seated image by Goscombe John now contemplates the town from the front lawn overlooked by the castellated central tower. This building (1870), on the A4212, is now a Youth Training Centre.

Outside the Calvinist Methodist Church in Tegid Street, a marble statue by William Davies (1875) commemorates one of the movement's great leaders, Thomas Charles (1755–1814), grandfather of Lewis Edwards's wife Jane and of Edwards's brother-in-law, David Charles who, with Edwards, founded the theological college. The fine pedestal panel shows the Reverend Charles holding audience, finger raised. On his house in High Street, a round plaque recalls Charles as 'one of the founders of the British and Foreign Bible Society'.

Among other plaques is one to Mari Jones (1784–1866) whose 'example inspired the foundation of the Bible Society in 1804'. (At Llanfihangel-y-Pennant, near Abergynolwen, a small obelisk of pink polished granite stands in the tree-shrouded ruin of the cottage whence 16-year-old Mari, carrying her six years' savings, set out barefoot on a 40-mile walk over the saddle of Cader Idris, and northward to Bala to buy a Welsh bible from the Reverend Charles. Not having a spare he gave her his own. Mari's monument was erected 'by the Sunday Schools of Merioneth', and her bible is at the Society's London headquarters.)

At the eastern edge of town, a Gorsedd stone circle marks the National Eisteddfod of 1967. And further north, off the A4212, a small pillar near Bwthyn Tai'r Felin has a slate relief portrait of farmer-folk singer Bob Robert, looking like a scout master:

'BOB TAI'R FELIN (1870–1951), CANWR CERDDI'. This charming piece is by Jonah Jones.

Also by Jonah Jones at the Llanuwchllyn village cross roads south of the lake, is a rather stiff bronze group of the venerated educationalist and conservator of the Welsh language, Syr Owen Morgan Edwards (1858–1920), and his son Syr Ifan ab Owen Edwards (1895–1970). Their *cylfach*, or arbour, of handsome slate pavings was designed by architect Quentin Hughes; the stone relief shows figures tending the Welsh language in the form of a tree.

These statues supersede Jones's bronze head and torso of 'O.M.', made in 1959. The 'man on the pillar' (so-called by village children) is now at the Meirionnydd College, Dolgellau. The group, in its remote setting, was installed in 1972 by the *Urdd Gobaith Cymru* (Welsh League of Youth), which Syr Ifan founded in 1922.

Caernarvon/Caernarfon (Cv)

Town Feature:

David Lloyd George MP (1863–1945)
Full-length bronze statue on Caernarvonshire granite pedestal, featuring bronze relief panels.
Sculptor (Sir) William Goscombe John
Location Castle Square

Fist raised in the heat of debate, the figure of David Lloyd George occupies a corner beneath the battlements in Castle Square. This statue, and the national memorial in Cardiff, portray him as the compelling platform speaker who could sway minds and hearts; he is still esteemed as the Welsh-speaking, Nonconformist country boy whose family savings went towards his schooling and solicitor's training before he embarked on his political career in 1890. Lloyd George represented Caernarvon boroughs as Liberal MP for 55 years, and the pedestal also reminds us that he was Constable of Caernarvon Castle.

Beyond this arresting study spreads a backdrop of fields and trees on the opposite bank of the River Seiont, the entrance of which into the Menai Strait is guarded by the castle and the town's ancient walls. The present Prince of Wales was invested in Castle Square in 1969. The first investiture of modern times, in 1911, honoured HRH Prince Edward, the future Duke of Windsor. This splendid ceremony, brainchild of the Bishop of Asaph, was sanctioned by George V — at the persuasion of the charismatic David Lloyd George, Chancellor of the Exchequer.

David Lloyd George (1863–1945). Sculptor: Sir. W. Goscombe John, RA (1921). Location: Castle Square, Caernarvon.

The village school of Llanystumdwy, where Lloyd George spent a humble boyhood, is shown in finely-detailed bronze relief on his statue's pedestal. On the other side we see the British Prime Minister at the Paris Peace Conference of 'Allied and Associated Powers' (1919–20). Perhaps with tongue in cheek, the sculptor depicts the great orator holding forth before an audience which exhibits all stages of interest from politely attentive to fast asleep.

Lloyd George's statue was presented by the mayor of Caernarfon in 1921, a preparatory bust having been exhibited at the Royal Academy. A year later, his coalition government fell and he resigned office. At the outbreak of the Second World War, he retired to Llanystumdwy (where a bust by Lady Scott now stands outside his Memorial Musuem). He was created Lloyd George of Dwyfor, after Llanystumdwy's river, three months before his death.

Caernarfon Selection

Nearer the centre of the square stands J. Milo Griffith's more formal bronze of Anglesey-born educationist Sir Hugh Owen (1804–1881), prime mover

in founding the University College of Wales, Aberystwyth (1872). The statue, 'erected by a grateful nation', was unveiled in 1888. Outside the church at the far end of the square stands the 'Caernarvon Heroes' War Memorial, unveiled in 1922. And over the King's Gateway at Caernarfon Castle is a dilapidated stone figure of the first Prince of Wales, Edward II.

Llanfair P.G. (Anglesey/Mon)

Village Feature:

Henry William Paget, 1st Marquis of Anglesey
(1768–1854)
Full-length bronze statue on 100ft grey marble
Doric column.
Sculptor Matthew Noble
Designer of column Thomas Harrison
Location A5 approach to village from Menai Strait

Paget Monument: column & statue to 1st Marquis of Anglesey (1768–1854). Architect: Thomas Harrison (1817). Sculptor: Matthew Noble (1860). Location: Llanfair P. G., Anglesey.

Llanfairpwllgwyngyllgogerychwyrndrobwllllantysi-
liogogogoch (Llanfair P.G.), the village with the
world's longest and most outlandish name, can also
boast two of Wales's tallest and most outlandish
statues, one to Nelson and one to the Marquis
of Anglesey, cavalry commander at Waterloo. The
Marquis's statue was hoisted on to its Doric column
in 1860, 43 years after the column was completed.
Like the village's name (which was invented by a
local tailor), both statues are a 19th-century conceit.

The Marquis's fine column on its rock-fort knoll
is approached through a field just outside the village.
Over £860 was raised within a week of the 'numerous and respectable meeting', as reported by the
North Wales Gazette, which opened a subscription
for an 'eligible memorial': its long inscription recalls
the Marquis's distinguished military achievements
in the Peninsula war and 'at the memorable Battle
of Waterloo'.

The viewing platform and drum are crowned by
the 12ft bronze of the Marquis as colonel of the
7th Hussars, with Order of the Bath and Waterloo
Medal. The plume of his shako reaches some 360 ft
above the Menai Strait. Building stone came by
water from Moelfre, on Anglesey's east coast, and
the statue, weighing between two and three tons,
was hoisted and positioned through an intricate
system of scaffolding and pulleys devised by a Mr
Haslam of Carreg Bran, Anglesey. This feat is illustrated on a copper engraving fixed to the statue's
pedestal.

The statue does not, as is claimed locally, show
the Marquis complete with his 'Anglesey Leg', the
first-ever articulated wooden limb. The original was
shattered by a cannon ball as Paget and Wellington
were riding off the battlefield at Waterloo, the Duke
observing the French retreat through his spy-glass.
The painful episode is handed down to fable through
the Marquis's observation 'by God sir, I've lost my
leg!' and Wellington's celebrated response (slightly
lowering the glass): 'by God sir, so you have!'

The leg was salvaged and buried under a small
monument in a garden at Waterloo; George Canning
is said to have written its epitaph. The shapely
'Anglesey Leg' is displayed, still in working order,
in the cavalry museum at Plas Newydd (NT), the
Paget family's historic home on the shore of the
Menai Strait.

The 'Anglesey Column' (115 wooden steps)
reveals one of the finest panoramas from any belvedere in England or Wales. The Menai Strait gleams
to the east and south, the lush fields of Anglesey
spread to the north and west. Bridges by Telford

and Stephenson, and the BBC Llanddona and the
IBA Arfon transmitters, can also be seen. Electricity
pylons stalk the Menai shore above the colossal
statue of Nelson, which stands near 'St Mary's
Church in a hollow by the white hazel close to the
rapid whirlpool by the red cave of St Tysilio' – or
'Llanfair P.G'.

Nelson's formidable figure, staring stonily across
the strait, can be contemplated at low tide from a
wrackish shoreline west of Britannia Bridge. This
striking statue, accessible from a path through St
Mary's churchyard, was created as a landmark by
Admiral Lord Clarence Paget in 1873. A churchyard
obelisk commemorates construction workers who
died in the building of Britannia Bridge between
1846–1850, and during reconstruction in the 1970s.

Anglesey Selection

Other large-scale monuments on Anglesey include
an obelisk to Sir Richard Bulkeley (d.1827) on
Cremlyn Hill, a landmark above Beaumaris. The
family owned Beaumaris Castle until 1925.

At the other end of the island in Holyhead, along
Turkey Shore Road, a silvery column overlooks the
ferry terminal and town. It was erected as a landmark
and with affection by 'his very numerous friends to
the memory of John Macgregor Skinner, R.N., for
33 years captain of one of the post office packets on
this station'. Like Nelson, Skinner lost an arm and
an eye in various battles; his years in Holyhead were
shared by a tame raven, who would fly out to the
paddle steamer *Escape* and perch on his shoulder.

Near Marine Square in 1824, Thomas Harrison
designed a granite Doric arch on Old Harbour to
mark the landing of George IV in August 1821;
detained by the weather, the king was entertained
at Plas Newydd where he received news of Queen
Caroline's death. He continued his journey to Ireland,
leaving ahead of his escort on one of Holyhead's
new-fangled paddle steamers commanded by
Captain Skinner. Nearby, a handsome plaque on
Mackenzie Pier 'expresses the pride of the people of
Holyhead' at the landing of Elizabeth II and family
on a visit in 1958.

Apart from lauding old soldiers, sea dogs and
landed gentry, Anglesey has smaller monuments
(mostly of this century) to lifeboatmen and shipwrecked mariners, at Rhoscolyn and Red Wharf Bay;
to the Welsh Princes, at Aberffraw, the capital of
Gwynedd in the days of Llywelyn the Great; to the
country poet, Mathew Williams (Mathew Bach of
Caergeiliog, 1876–1964), in a roadside monument

of inscribed slate; and to 'patriotic brothers of the Cymric race' Lewis, Richard and William Morris, poets and scholars who held public office in the 18th century. A Celtic cross of 1910 overlooks Dulas Bay, their birthplace, from Penrhos Lligwy.

On the lovely, turfy high-tide 'island' of Llanddwyn, a cement-rendered 'White Cross' marks the site of the island's 5th-century abbey church; a Celtic cross erected on the next hillock the following year (1904) commemorates the church's dedicatee, Dwynwen, daughter of the prolific Irish king of Brycheiniog (Brecon), and patroness of true lovers. Llanddwyn is reached through Forestry Commission land from the village of Newborough (Niwbwrch).

Nantgwynant, Snowdonia (Cv)

Mountainside Feature:

'The Gladstone Slab'
W.E. Gladstone (1809–1898)
Inscribed, polished-granite slab affixed to rock face.
Stone mason Not known
Location The Walker Path, Nantgwynant

SEP 13th 1892 – UPON THIS ROCK
THE RIGHT HONOURABLE W.E. GLADSTONE MP
WHEN PRIME MINISTER FOR THE FOURTH TIME AND 83 YEARS OLD
ADDRESSED THE PEOPLE OF ERYRI UPON JUSTICE TO WALES
THE MULTITUDE SANG CYMRIC HYMNS AND "LAND OF MY FATHERS"

The plain-cut letters stare out from the polished granite slab rudely cemented into a 100ft granite outcrop on the Watkin path, which ascends the southeast flank of Y Wyddfa (Snowdon) towards the summit, the highest point in England and Wales. The occasion was the path's official opening by W.E. Gladstone in the presence of its creator, Sir Edward Watkin (1819–1901), the Mancunian Railway King, whose mountain retreat — a well-appointed corrugated-iron chalet where W.E. and Mrs Gladstone were staying as guests — overlooked the track.

The full account of the G.O.M.'s oratory, and the crowds and the choirs, should lighten the step of anyone contemplating 'this rock' in the grassy bowl of the Welsh mountains, a mile above the path's

Gladstone Slab: affixed to rock after opening of Walker Path (1893) by W. E. Gladstone (1809–1898). Stone cutter not known. Location: Nantgwynant, Snowdon.

starting point from the lovely valley of Nantgwynant.

The indomitable old Gladstones had already made an excursion (in an open carriage and a downpour) to Aberglaslyn, a local beauty spot. By the time they and their entourage had hiked up to the rock, the afternoon sun was beating down on the spectators, whom Gladstone rewarded with a powerful speech on the 'Land Question in Wales'.

The crowds in their turn transported the old man with their singing, as described by a local writer D.E. Jenkins, in 1899: 'he was loath to do anything except listen to the music; but an address from the Liberal Association of Festiniog, and another from the quarrymen of Llanberis, had to be read in the vernacular, before the second hymn was given'. Speeches were made by David Lloyd George, future Prime Minister, and by Thomas Edward Ellis, whose statues now ornament their former constituency towns, Caernarvon and Bala.

In the mutual veneration and delectation of things Welsh, Sir Edward's path was forgotten and went unmentioned throughout the proceedings. The path was opened the following day when the Gladstones, together with their hosts, rode up to the path, he in a carriage, she on a donkey. The occasion was marked in 1893 by Sir Edward, who had this tablet cemented into the rock face. It is considered a good exercise in rock climbing for beginners.

Nantgwynant locality selection

Near the church at Beddgelert, a stone marking 'Gelert's grave' has been acquired by the National Trust. Prince Llywelyn's faithful guard dog, Gelert, discovered with blood on his jaws near the over-turned cradle of Llywelyn's infant son, was killed by the grief-stricken father who then discovered the live baby and remains of a wolf nearby.

The dog's grave, with the stone supposedly raised by the remorseful Llywelyn, was 'discovered' centuries later by a village innkeeper, after he had procured a suitable boulder from Nantgwynant. As one historian put it, 'tourists agog, shekels pour in'. Even so, the roots of the story go deeper than 19th-century melodrama, being at least as old as the name Bedd Gelert ('Gelert's Grave').

The Trust is restoring dignity to the tree-shaded site by removing barbed wire and a concrete path. An intrusive 1950s inscribed slate, replacing the vandalised original, will be replaced by a smaller slate inscribed in Welsh. The gentle hay field compliments the grandeur of its surrounding craggy hills, Craig-y-Llan, Moel Hebog and Aberglaslyr (NT), the scene of the Gladstones' outing.

Trawsfynydd (Mr)

Village Feature:

Ellis Humphrey Evans (1887–1917)
Full-length bronze statue on rough-cut granite base.
Sculptor L.S. Merrifield
Location Village street

*E. H. Evans (1887–1917). Sculptor: L. S. Merrifield (1923)
Location: village street, Trawsfynydd.*

The shepherd poet is shown with cloak and gaiters, striding forward with his crook from a plinth of the same dense grey stone as the chapel and houses in this long, sloping street. Despite the rustic dress, his clean-cut features and upright stance recall the idealised soldiers portrayed in First World War war monuments, and the statue has been rightly described as a poignant representation of a lost generation. Villagers can still see the likeness in other members of Evans's family.

Known by his bardic name, Hedd Wyn, the poet is remembered as the winner of the Chair at the 1917 National Eisteddfod in Birkenhead. When Evans's *nom-de-plume* was announced in the Chairing Ceremony, it was revealed that he had died some weeks earlier at the battle for Pilkem Ridge, and the chair was then draped in black – this became the Eisteddfod of the Black Chair. The chair (specially made, according to custom) is kept at Hedd Wyn's birthplace, *Yr Ysgwrn*, a local farm now occupied by a nephew of the poet.

A collection of Hedd Wyn's work was published in 1918, under the title *Cerddi'r Bugail* (The Shepherd's Poems). They reveal inspiration from nature and from the Bible, ready influences for an eldest son who left the village school at 14 to work on the family farm. Evans's early promise, recognised by his headmaster, was also encouraged by regular attendance at Sunday School, a traditional training in Welsh literacy for ordinary people. Welsh newspapers and denominational magazines, and informal teaching, would have furthered Evans's mastery in the complex art of composing to eisteddfod standards and rules.

Although his early commitment to the farm disappointed his headmaster, it allowed Evans to feed his imagination and dreams through close involvement with the natural world, and to develop his passion for poetry at his own pace. He won his first Chair at the Bala Eisteddfod of 1907, and his winning ode at the 1917 eisteddfod, *The Hero*, relates the myth of Prometheus to Christian symbolism. It is judged his best poem.

The bronze memorial, which cost £600, was unveiled by the poet's mother in 1923. Beneath the statue is inscribed the rather warlike *englyn* (a single two- or four-line verse in strict Welsh metre) written by Hedd Wyn in memory of Dio Evans from neighbouring Blaenau Ffestiniog (nine miles north), who was killed in action in 1916. He shares a memorial stone near the town's memorial hospital with his father R.D. Evans (d.1924), for 50 years a practising physician in Ffestiniog.

Powys
Cilmery/Cilmeri (B)

Roadside Feature:

Llywelyn ap Gruffydd (the Last, d.1282)
15ft monolith of 'Trefor Grey Granite' from the Penmaenmawr quarries, Caernarfon.
Designer Prince Llywelyn Joint Committee
Location South of A483, west end of village

A big standing stone on a grassed mound stands in a field off a layby on the village bypass. Under a spreading oak, rugged stone steps lead up between slate slabs carved in English and Welsh:
NEAR THIS SPOT
WAS KILLED
OUR PRINCE
LLYWELYN
1282
The steps incorporate the trimmed stones and inscription of the 1905 obelisk which originated as Wales's national monument to the warrior who united her people under their own brief rule. The unveiling speeches, in 1956, honoured this great achievement and mourned the 'dark cloud of

Llywelyn's death' whilst urging vigilance over Wales's nationhood: 'Are we to be submerged under the flood of alien forces and deadened by apathy, or shall we rise to the occasion as Welshmen proud of our great heritage?'

Llywelyn was the first and last native Welshman to be recognised by the English as Prince of Wales, and he built on the legacy of his grandfather, Llywelyn the Great, to revive and hold Gwynedd against Henry III and the Lords Marcher. The robust policy towards the Scots of Henry's successor, Edward I, was perhaps misread by Llywelyn, whose power and prestige could not withstand Edward's

Llywelyn Monument: monolith commemorating Llywellyn the Last (d.1282). Designer: Prince Llywelyn Joint Committee (1956). Location: just W. of Cilmeri.

fury after the Welsh Prince had refused to acknowledge English supremacy through the act of homage.

After a series of disastrous defeats, Llywelyn was obliged to join a final uprising of other Welsh leaders. Whilst preparing a raid on an English garrison at Builth Castle, in an attempt to take Powys, he was separated from his troops and killed on December 11th by one of Edward's knights. Llywelyn's head was severed and washed, and delivered to the King's Anglesey barracks before being displayed in London – a grim termination of all hopes for Welsh independence.

Since then Wales has embarked on successive periods of national revival. Over 600 years after Llywelyn's death, the question of a suitable site for a national memorial was decided by an English landowner, S.P.M. Bligh, who erected a small obelisk near the site of Llywelyn's demise. After Bligh's death in 1949, the local authority acquired obelisk and field; a more substantial memorial was proposed by a council member, and a design was agreed and an appeal launched for costs of £1,750.

The 'far from enthusiastic' response (as judged by the Society's magazine in 1956) was offset by the gift from Llywellyn's home county, Caernarvonshire, of the great granite stone. The unveiling under the flag of the Red Dragon, presided over by the Archdruid and assisted by schoolchildren in national dress, attracted patriots from all corners of the principality.

Today, the field and stone are well-tended, the design and construction handsome and well-finished – with a look of permanence typical of Welsh monuments, large and small – and contrasting with the general tackiness of their English counterparts of latter years. There are no Heritage Information Boards, so the dignity and intimacy of Llywelyn's death site is preserved. Even so, some local people rate it as 'just a stone in a field', although the scale, solidity and careful landscaping make it a fitting national monument.

Llandinam (Mg)

Town Feature:

David Davies (1818–1890)
Full-length bronze statue on stone pedestal, casting of the original at Barry Dock.
Sculptor Alfred Gilbert, RA
Location West of the A470, overlooking the bridge over the Severn

David Davies (1818–1890). Sculptor: Alfred Gilbert, RA (1894). Location: Llandinam bridge.

Gilbert portrays a thickset, forthright industrialist, feet planted wide, scrutinising a plan of Barry Dock, which Davies founded near Cardiff as an alternative outlet for his company 'Ocean Coal' in the rapidly-expanding Rhondda between 1884 and 1889. The statue has presence enough to hold its own in two striking locations; the Llandinam bronze being set on the bridgehead beneath a deep, wooded hillside near Davies's birthplace; the Barry Docks original is prominent on vast lawns fronting the Victorian opulence of the dock offices, overlooking the rusting and underworked harbour.

Both settings are appropriate. Davies's first public contract was to construct the approach road to the graceful Llandinam bridge (designed by Thomas Penson). It was offered in 1846 soon after the broad-backed, go-ahead young farmer had inherited the family smallholding, where he had served as farm-hand and assistant sawyer since leaving school at the age of 11. Barry Dock, on the other hand, was the last of Davies's works, founded in his later years after a struggle against powerful opposing interests. By then his name was venerated throughout the principality, perhaps because, amongst the powerful captains of industrial Wales, Davies was one of the few native Welsh.

Vowing always to be 'top sawyer' (on the two-man saw) after his father's death, Davies instead achieved wealth and national repute as landowner, railway contractor and colliery proprietor. Liberal MP for Cardigan district from 1874–1877, he also served as a Governor and first Treasurer to the University College of Wales after it opened at Aberystwyth in 1872.

The Llandinam statue was raised at a cost of £1,200, soon after the unveiling of its original close to the site where the first sod was cut for Barry Dock just over ten years earlier. As noted in Ivor Thomas's biography *Top Sawyer*, it has Davies's 'powerful, stocky frame and forceful manner well displayed'; the Railway King affected a workaday appearance and bluff manner, using colloquial speech but recommending English as the money-making language.

Devout, teetotal, a tough but respected employer and dutiful family man, 'Davies yr Ocean' of the Rhondda never left Llandinam, serving weekly as Sunday School teacher and as deacon at the Calvinist Methodist chapel. The new chapel (1873) and a school were his gifts, his annual distribution of coal and his Sunday school outings continue, and the Davies family preserves its association with the university college which Davies served and endowed.

Overlooked by the statue, the road from Wales's first iron bridge winds west to the fine family house, 'Broneiron', built in 1864 by Davies and now owned by the Girl Guide Association. The selection of the location characterises the man in his prime: it was close to his birthplace, his chapel, and Llandinam railway station.

Powis Castle (NT), near Welshpool (Mg)

Castle Feature:

Fame
Lead equestrian group on Grinshill stone pedestal.
Signed Andries Carpentière (Andrew Carpenter)
Location The Castle Courtyard

Semi-draped and sounding a trumpet, Fame abandons herself to the wings of her prancing stallion,

*'Fame'. Sculptor: Andrew Carpenter (early C18).
Location: Courtyard, Powis Castle (NT).*

Pegasus, whilst dominating the small forecourt at Powis Castle's twin-towered west entrance.

The castle's south front spreads along the edge of red sandstone cliffs with views of the Breidden Hills across gardens and woods. The rocky hillside descends in hanging terraces, ornamented with urns and clipped yews. Along the balustrade on the second terrace, the views are set off by a series of 18th-century lead figures, rustic youths and maidens, playing pipes or dancing. Outside the Orangery below is a lead statue of the Piping Faun (after the antique), whilst other statues await discovery in the gardens. Powis seems the most enchanting of enchanted castles, and the *pièce de résistance* is Fame.

Like the garden statues, Fame is thought to have come from the workshop of John van Nost (d.1729); the composition is signed by one of van Nost's craftsmen, Andrew Carpenter, and the quality of workmanship accords with this. The shepherds and shepherdesses are likely to be stock figures, and it is thought that some of the lead may have come from the productive mine worked by the Marquises of Powys in the first half of the 18th century. This goes for parts of the cascade which once dominated the Powis water gardens, removed and grassed over in the late 18th century.

Powis is a fortress rooted in Welsh history. In 1286, four years after Llywelyn's death, the last hereditary Prince of Powys, Owain ap Gruffydd ap Gwenwnwyn, renounced his Welsh title and paid homage to Edward I as Baron de la Pole (or of Pool, or Powis Castle).

The fortress, then *Castell Coch* (or 'Red Castle'), had been destroyed by Llywelyn, and today's building dates largely from the early 14th century, when Owain's rebuilding was completed by his daughter. It has been occupied by members of the same family since a descendant sold it to Sir Edward Herbert, second son of the Earl of Pembroke, in 1587.

Fame and Pegasus have succumbed to almost as many changes as the medieval castle and its park. Originally the centrepiece of a fountain in the water gardens, the group was salvaged early in the 19th century and placed above an arch in the inner court, then removed to the centre of the courtyard. Towards the end of the century, the architect G.F Bodley turned Fame into a fountain, with water dribbling out of her trumpet into a red stone basin — 'not a success', according to the incumbent Countess, who complained that the horse looked as if it was failing to jump out of a footbath. She dismissed the fountain — 'Peace be to its ashes' — and had its basin and works removed.

In 1952 the fourth Earl bequeathed the castle to the National Trust, who have continued the family's policy of maintenance and improvement by restoring 'Fame', as well as the lead figures on the terraces.

The lead equestrian ensemble signed by Andrew Carpenter is derived from the marble group of Fame by Antoine Coysevox, made for Louis XIV's palace at Marly and later displayed at the gardens of the Tuileries in Paris. (The Tuileries now have a reconstituted stone group; the Coysevox original is installed inside the Louvre.)

The Powis Fame and Pegasus disport themselves over a lead trophy of arms created in 1986 by the conservator sculptor Andrew Naylor, from the Louvre original. The trophy was first rough-carved in polystyrene, and the fine detail then modelled in Polyfilla. The pedestal, by a local stone-mason, is a copy of the Marly Gardens original by Coysevox.

Severe but familiar problems were corrected by Naylor Conservation. Corrosion of iron supports inside the horse had caused the iron to swell, and the lead to burst and distort; a core of concrete had been poured into the horse's fore- and hind-quarters, in an earlier misguided attempt at preservation; and the horse's hollow underbelly had collapsed inward over an inadequate base.

The group is now supported on an armature of stainless steel, packed with polyurethane foam to take up slight thermal movement that occurs naturally in metal works. Final painting undertaken by the National Trust shows, not the original stone-coloured paint, but a silvery sheen which may mellow with weathering.

The red glow of the castle stonework compliments the vitality of Fame's welcome to visitors approaching the splendid castle interior, in which there is an admirable collection of furniture and pictures, and also sculpture (much of it acquired by Clive of India, whose son married Lord Powis's daughter, Lady Henrietta Herbert, in 1784).

Outside the forecourt walls, a children's garden trail identifies Hedgehog Holly, 300-year-old topiary yews, a statue of Hercules killing the hydra, and a distant volcano (extinct). From the classical marble busts in the Orangery, the trail invites a drawing of the Roman Emperor most resembling a father or school teacher. It explains that the wyverns on the Marquess Gate each has a hand in its mouth to mark a divided inheritance, while at the Great Lawn where Fame and Pegasus once romped over water gardens, the leaflet imagines an enemy faced with the red cliffs, natural ramparts for this beautiful Powys fortress of medieval princes.

West and South Wales Gazetteer

Note: The counties of Wales, which in 1974 were reduced in number to correspond with the ancient demarcations, appear in loosely topographical order. Within each county, monuments are listed under their locations, which appear in alphabetical order. The old West and South Wales counties contained within the present five, Dyfed, West, South and Mid Glamorgan and Gwent are indicated after a location by letters (Cd) Cardiganshire; (Cm) Carmarthenshire; (P) Pembrokeshire; (G) Glamorgan, and (Mn) Monmouthshire.

Dyfed

Aberystwyth/Yr Wyddgrug (Cd)

Town Feature:

HRH Edward Albert, Prince of Wales, future Edward VIII, later Duke of Windsor (1894–1972).
Full-length bronze statue on stone pedestal.
Sculptor Mario Rutelli
Location New Promenade, Old College, University College of Wales

The only known full-length statue of the Duke of Windsor, then Prince of Wales, bears scant resemblance to its subject, apart from a pleasantly-youthful demeanour and the richly-embroidered robes of the College's fourth Chancellor. He carries a tassled mortar board under one arm.

Nearby stands a bronze figure of the University's first Principal from 1872 to 1891, Dr Thomas Charles Edwards, portrayed by the past-master of this singular art, Sir William Goscombe John. Edwards's statue was unveiled in 1922, the same year as Rutelli's Prince of Wales.

Both bronzes, painted matt brown, look out from the narrow forecourt of the original College building, a grandly-Gothic pile on Aberystwyth's sea front in the crescent of Cardigan Bay. The Old College belongs to a grand seaside panorama of cliffs, amuse-

Edward Albert, Prince of Wales, future Edward VIII & later Duke of Windsor (1894–1972). Sculptor: Mario Rutelli (1922). Location: Old College, Aberystwyth.

ments, and the cliff-top castle ruin fronted by Rutelli's *pièce de résistance*, the extraordinary First World War monument featuring a colossal bronze nude Amazon in front of a big, stepped obelisk crowned with a winged 'Victory'. The castle ruin's Gorsedd circle is from the National Eisteddfod of 1916.

Distant on the southern skyline of Pen Dinas is the pencil-like silhouette of the Wellington column, erected in 1852. (A crowning equestrian statue of the Iron Duke, planned to scare off the French, lingered for years in the stableyard of Nanteos Mansion, and is now unaccounted for.)

Perhaps because this is a seaside town, vandalism is of the energetic variety and Rutelli's bronze of Prince Edward, as reported in *The Cambrian News* of April 1987, has 'been white-washed, painted green and had its head sliced off' – 15 months after this last insult the head was soldered back, in time for the Duke of Windsor's great-nephew, Charles, Prince of Wales, to be installed as seventh Chancellor of the University of Wales (July 1977).

College history involves many of the names attached to statues in various corners of Wales. After years of campaigning led by Hugh Owen, the college was founded at Aberystwyth through the unfortunate bankruptcy of David Davies' former partner, Thomas Savin; his exotic, speculative hotel building by J.P. Seddon was bought unfinished at a cutprice £10,000, and the college opened with T.C. Edwards as principal in 1872.

Early days saw severe money worries which neither Liberal nor Conservative governments would reduce, and the college depended on aid from industrialists such as David Davies. Essentially a working-class college, it also received the penny contributions of quarrymen and miners, and other working homes. An allowance from Gladstone was used up by the Great Fire of 1885, after which Seddon rebuilt the north wing and added the mosaic to the south wing tower turret. The Royal Charter was granted in 1889.

The College by the Sea has been largely replaced by the College on the Hill, its 1950s and 60s university buildings with their carved reliefs dominating the town skyline. The Quadrangle of Old College has a cast of a bronze made by Goscombe John of an early student, T.E. Ellis, for his native town Bala.

Prince Edward's statue is a proud possession, its singularity confirmed through energetic research in 1984 by an Aberystwyth man. He discovered the only other known figures to be statuettes, one showing the prince as golfer and one – by C.S. Jagger – as tennis player. (A full-length statue, once

carved in butter for the Wembley Exhibition, was not built to last. A pity – it must have been a better likeness.)

Aberystwyth (and locality) Selection

Rutelli's 'Humanity' and her 80ft obelisk (1933) add the finishing touch to Aberystwyth's seafront panorama. They were were rebronzed at a cost of £1,000 in 1970, only to be struck by lightning and then daubed with paint. However, the scars do not show and the memorial, in detail, composition and prime siting, is most striking and rare. The First World War memorial at the Tabernacle Chapel in Powell Street is also the work of Rutelli, and his bust of Sir John Williams stands in the National Library.

The town's most charming street statuary includes a figurehead of Queen Victoria in coronation regalia, at the corner of Baker Street and Eastgate, formerly the Victoria Inn. It was salvaged from the ship *Victoria* at the breakers' yard. An equally appealing statue of Edward VII (first chancellor of the University College) appears over the Museum parapet in Terrace Road.

Five miles north at Borth, on the cliff path to Clarach, a small, rugged First World War memorial incorporates a cross and pillar on a high base in a handsome mix of polished granite, slate and beach stone. It was 'damaged by a thunderbolt on 21st March 1983 and re-erected by public subscription 1984'. Ten miles east, near Devil's Bridge, a rustic Jubilee Arch straddling the B4974 to Cwmystwyth was constructed for Thomas Johnes of Hafod, one of Wales's most eminent patrons of the arts, on the 1810 anniversary of George III's accession.

Carmarthen/Caerfyrddin (Cm)

Town Feature:

General Sir William Nott (1782–1845)
Full-length bronze statue on large granite pedestal.
Sculptor Edward Davis
Location Nott Square

There is a military flavour to all the principal monuments in this agreeable market town. Most prominent is that of General Sir William Nott shown as a handsome soldier in full uniform, his statue dominating the narrow square which has his name. The bronze casting was given by the East India Company

Albert, Prince Consort (1819-1861). Sculptor: Charles Bacon (1874). Location: Holborn Circus, London.

Daniel Rowlands (1713-1790). Sculptor: not known. Location: Llangeitho, Dyfed.

Ariadne - copy of the sleeping Ariadne at the Belvedere garden of the Vatican.
Location: the Grotto at Stourhead (NT), Wiltshire.

Queen Victoria (1819-1901). Sculptor: Alfred Turner (1902). Location: Victoria Park, Huntingdon Place, Tynemouth. **Note:** *The statue is due to be cleaned and repaired.*

*The Albert Memorial to Albert, Prince Consort (1819-1861). Sculptor: John Foley, RA (1867-75).
Designer: Sir G.G. Scott (1862-72). Location: Kensington Gardens, London.*

*Welsh national monument,
to the First World War.
Sculptor: A.B. Pegram (1928).
Designer: J.E. Comper.
Location: Alexandra Gardens,
Cardiff.*

The Haldon Tower – monument to Major-General Stringer Lawrence. Erected: 1788.
Location: near Exeter, Devon.

Sir Thomas More (1478-1535). Sculptor: L. Cubitt Bevis (1969). Location: Chelsea Old Church, London.

'Achilles' – commemorating Arthur Wellesley, 1st Duke of Wellington (1769-1852). Sculptor: Sir Richard Westmacott, RA (1822). Location: Hyde Park, London.

Augustus John, OM, RA (1878-1961). Sculptor: Ivor Roberts Jones (1965). Location: Fordingbridge, Hants.

Time – part of sundial dated 1725. Sculptor: C. G. Cibber. Location: Belton House (NT), Lincs.

Charles Bradlaugh (1833-1891). Sculptor: George Tinworth of Doulton.
Location: Abington Square, Northampton.

Monument to the Titanic 'Engine Room Heroes' – later (1916) dedicated as a First World War monument. Sculptor: Sir W. Goscombe John. Location: Pierhead, Liverpool.

'Split Spiral Spin.' Sculptor: Lillian Lijn (1982). Location: Birchwood Science Park, Warrington.

Victoria Jubilee Clock. Location: Weymouth Esplanade.

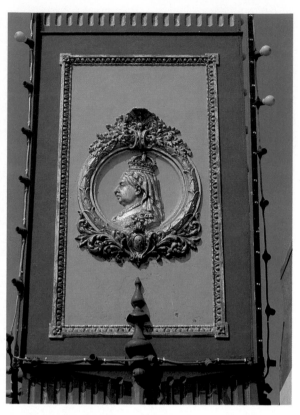

Detail of Victoria Jubilee Clock (see left)

*George III (1738-1820). Sculptor: Coade & Sealy
(1804); plinth by James Hamilton (1809).
Location: Weymouth Esplanade.*

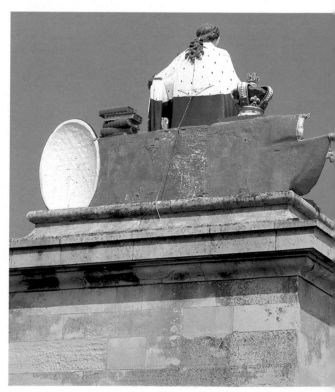

Rear view of George III (see left).

'The Bugler' – commemorating soldiers of the Royal Sussex Regiment who fought in the South African War (1900-02). Sculptor: Charles L. Hartwell (1904). Location: Regency Square, Brighton.

Ceres. Sculptor: F. Franchi (1850). Location: Belton House (NT), Lincolnshire.

'Commerce' & 'Agriculture' (formerly decorating the Corn Exchange). Location: entrance to multi-storey car-park, Balkerne Way, Colchester.

Lion (regilded 1990). Location: gateway to Victoria Park, Bath.

*Burrow Mump (NT) – hill and ruin dedicated as Second World War monument (1946).
Location: near Burrow Bridge, Somerset.*

*Lansdown Monument (NT) – on site of Oldbury Castle (Iron Age fort), – and Cherhill White Horse.
Location: Cherhill Down, Wiltshire.*

Lion – commemorating James Long, builder of Devizes-Urchmont road (1768).
Location: near Etchilhampton Hill (on A343). **Note:** *restored in 1990.*

Annie, Lady Jerningham (d. 1902). Sculptor: O. P. Penchine (1906) from sketches by Walter Ingram (1904).
Designer: Sir Hubert Jerningham (1903). Location: Bank Hill, Berwick-upon-Tweed.

from cannon captured at the battle of Maharajpur. Set on a granite pedestal in the shadow of the castle remains, the statue occupies the site of the market cross, dismantled when the market was resited, and Nott Square created in 1846.

The pedestal was erected in January 1851, and the statue arrived by sea later that month. On hand to help supervise was the sculptor, a Carmarthen man trained at the Royal Academy Schools, whose father David Daniel Davies had achieved prominence in London as a physician. The inauguration ceremony had to be postponed because the monument was incomplete but at last, on October 18, Mayor and Corporation led a procession to Nott Square. Unfortunately, the committee representative arrived so late that the crowd, tired of waiting, had gone home.

Soldier or statue, General Nott was prone to pick the short straw. Son of the landlord at the popular Ivy Bush Inn, formerly in King Street, Nott enrolled in the Carmarthen volunteer corps formed after the French invasion alarm at Fishguard; two years later, as an 18-year-old Bengal cadet of the East India Company, Nott began his arduous and frustrating Far Eastern military career.

Promoted to Brigadier Officer in the first Afghan war (1838), the outspoken Nott was unable to contain his impatience at 'the silly scions of the aristocracy' (as he described them) whose petty intriguing undermined the hard-won professionalism of Company officers under their command. Other clashes with superiors cost promotion, but 'the foresight, judgement and courage' shown during Nott's command at Kandahar, and his 'brilliant and successful march to Ghazni and Kabul' on retreat from Afghanistan, earned him these acknowledgements and a grateful annuity from the East India Company in 1844.

By now a sick man, the general on his retirement received a hero's home-coming at Carmarthen, but died four months later. A memorial subscription fund was augmented by a gift of 200 guineas from Queen Victoria; the square was renamed the following year, and the statue assembled five years after.

Carmarthen (and locality) Selection

Inside the statue's cast-iron railings, a decorative bronze tablet proclaims: 'Near this spot suffered for the truth, on Saturday March 20th 1555, Dr Robert Ferrar, Bishop of St Davids'. It was erected 'by a Protestant of this Town' in 1902. (From this period

General Sir William Nott (1782–1845). Sculptor: Edward Davis (1851). Location: Nott Square, Carmarthen.

in Haverfordwest High Street, 28 miles west, a handsome red granite column with urn honours William Nichol, 'burnt at the stake for the truth' in 1558.)

Other noteworthy monuments include the Boer War Memorial (1906) in front of the Guildhall – although the stone statue does not deserve the richness of its inscribed red granite pedestal. In Lammas Street stands the pretty Fusiliers' Crimea Monument, recently refurbished but damaged by a lorry immediately afterwards, and originally erected in 1859 by Colonel Lysons and brother officers. Note the originality of the cast iron railings. (Its designer, Edward Richardson, was often asked to do Crimean memorials.)

Outside the railings, until the Second World War, a Russian gun carriage served as a 'bar' for the local landlord's flagons of ale left for policemen on the beat. At Priory Street Hospital, Goscombe John's sombre bronze shows a bandaged soldier battle-scarred from the Great War.

On the western approach to the town, Picton Terrace hosts a 60ft obelisk to General Sir Thomas Picton (1758–1815), killed at Waterloo after a brilliant career marked by reckless heroism. The monument of 1847 was struck by lightning in 1854, and completely rebuilt in 1988. The bold, brief inscription, now in phosphor bronze letters, cost £3,000 alone, but should last indefinitely – or at least longer than an earlier grandiose monument, designed by John Nash between 1825–7. It was made of inferior stone and removed 18 years later 'inelegant and dilapidated', as the local newspapers put it.

Edward Hodges Baily's statue of Picton (1826), made for the original and lost, is the subject of a local poem; the County Museum at Abergwili holds his *bas*-relief of a battle scene, found in a nearby garden and restored at Dyfed College of Art. Edward Davis served his apprenticeship in the sculptor's workshop. Portraits of Picton and Nott hang in the Guildhall, which also holds Edward Davis's bust of Nott (1851).

South of the of B3400 near Llanarthney village, Paxton's Tower (NT) looks out to Dryslwyn Castle and Dinefwr, Carreg Cennen and gentle wooded hills along the Tywyi valley. Thought to honour Nelson, its three towers on a triangular base were designed by S.P. Cockerell (*c*.1815), who also built Middleton Hall for the free-spending Sir William Paxton, London banker, Mayor of Carmarthen (1793–5) and developer of the resort at Tenby. The hall was gutted by fire in 1931, and demolished in 1951. The plaques in the tower make a good read; the hill is called *Golwg y Byd* – 'Sight of the World'.

Tregaron (Cd)

Town Feature:

Henry Richard, MP (1812–1888)
Full-length bronze statue on Aberdeen
granite pedestal.
Sculptor Albert Toft
Location Tregaron Square

The frock-coated gentleman personified in bronze belongs to Victorian market-square art, but the stone-built river town belongs to the wild Welsh

Henry Richard (1812–1888). Sculptor: Albert Toft. Location: Tregaron Square.

uplands which once made the square a centre for sheep and cattle trading, and for country fairs. The statue stands near the Tourist Information Centre, which helps augment Tregaron's agricultural tradition with craftwork and pony trekking, and promotes interest in the nature reserve at Tregaron Bog at the head of the Teifi Valley.

Meanwhile the portly and bewhiskered figure of Henry Richard, MP for Merthyr Tydfil and 'Apostle of Peace', presses a point with his *pince-nez*, holding in his other hand a paper inscribed PEACE.

The one-time draper's assistant, son of a Tregaron classical scholar and Methodist divine, was ordained in London in 1835. The base of his statue's high pedestal records in English and Welsh other landmarks in a career following Welsh traditions of Nonconformity and Liberal politics, espoused in such causes as Welsh education and language, and mine workers' rights. Indeed, 'such was his concern for Welsh affairs that he became known as "the member for Wales"'. Richard also achieved world-wide recognition as an advocate of international arbitration, secretary of the Peace Union and organiser of the Peace Congress at Paris presided over by Victor Hugo in 1849.

However, there are one or two small anomalies: some have argued that he was not a Welsh speaker (although his promise not to forget 'the language of my country' is inscribed on his monument), and it is said that Richard had good sight, and would never have used spectacles. In a 1988 centenary year school questionnaire, the question 'Who was Henry Richard?' elicited the reply from Tregaron house-holders: 'The chap whose statue is in the square'.

The statue looks well cared-for. During the centenary year it was washed down with hot water and finished with a coat of silicone wax oil, at a cost of £12 plus labour; innocuous as well as cheap, the treatment achieves a natural effect while preserving the statue from various dangers, notably, acid rain. This no-nonsense approach matches the grey solidity of the town.

Tregaron locality Selection

Four miles west in Llangeitho, outside the Calvanist Methodist Chapel, a small, funereal marble portrays Daniel Rowland (1713–1790), renowned preacher of the Great Awakening, with his fist raised in the heat of saving souls. The chapel of 1806 retained its outside staircase to the pulpit, which permitted the appearance of the preacher as if from on high. Chapel and statue occupy the site of the former meeting house, scene of Rowland's early hell-and-damnation

sermons. The village square with its shady tree is completed by the statue of a World War One soldier on a richly-dressed, polished granite pedestal.

At Cardigan on the Teifi estuary, a fine bronze figure of a Teifi Valley otter was unveiled on Prince Charles Quay by David Bellamy at Dyfed's Wildlife Trust Jubilee in 1988. It was made by local sculptor Geoff Powell, and cast by Fiorini of London.

West Glamorgan

Swansea/Abertawe (G)

Town Feature:

Dylan Thomas (1914–1953)
Seated bronze statue on granite plinth
Sculptor John Doubleday
Location Dylan Thomas Square, South Dock Marina

Dylan Thomas leans forward from a chair on the tiled waterfront concourse, with a view of masts and speed-boats surrounded by marina buildings in post-modernist brick. The rough-modelled, rather doll-

Dylan Thomas (1914–1953). Sculptor: John Doubleday (1984). Location: Swansea Marina.

like statue is recognisable as a work in the sculptor's distinctive style rather than as a portrait of the poet, either as a 'young dog' or as the legendary figure who was to become one of the most widely-read English language poets.

Slightly elevated, the portrait conveys Thomas's small stature but not his 'wren's-bone' frame, nor the broad brow and baleful eyes, delicate bridge to a clumsy nose, pouting mouth over small, receding chins, and dishevelled bow tie. These inimitable features may be difficult to project without resorting to caricature.

On a plaque, raised lettering quotes the last line of *Fern Hill*: 'Though I sang in chains like the sea'. Behind, the flaking façade of the Dylan Thomas Theatre stands out bluntly against its modish surroundings, much as the poet once did.

Perhaps a truer monument to Thomas, and to pre-war, pre-blitzed Swansea, is the stone carved by Ronald Cour quoting the same lines and installed in 1963 by the poet Vernon Watkins, Thomas's lifelong friend, at Cwmdonkin Park.

Nearby at his home in the Uplands, 'a lowland collection of crossroads and shops', Thomas's mother coddled and indulged her unhealthy child whilst his father, D.J. Thomas, read Shakespeare to Dylan from infancy, encouraged his writing, and allowed him the pick of his extensive and eclectic library. A pupil at Swansea Grammar School, where his father was a feared and respected English teacher, Dylan left at 16 with a prodigious reputation for English, having failed in every other subject, and found work as a cub reporter on the local newspaper.

From work accumulated in his adolescence and late teens at Cwmdonkin Drive, Thomas published his first volume *Eighteen Poems* (1934), a few weeks before leaving this 'ugly, lovely town' to make his way in London, as Constantine Fitzgibbon records in his biography, 'with a pullover, a few shirts, a red tie, some poems and some stories'.

Thomas was a convivial, or uproarious, companion as the occasion demanded, but the schoolboy who 'threw pebbles at windows, scuffled and boasted', the not very industrious reporter, the penurious artist who frequented London's Soho pubs and clubs, and even the hard-up family man, devoted long, sober hours to crafting his poems. Film work as a scriptwriter brought a wartime living, but frightened off 'the lovely gift of the gab'; the post-war years brought fame and following but never fortune, although some earnings came from journalism and broadcasts, and lecture tours in the United States.

During these last years Thomas's *Collected Poems* (1952) won him widespread acclaim, and his work on *Under Milkwood* brought to production – though never completion – a rare and endearing masterpiece in English radio drama. Meanwhile, living up to the press image of the outrageous and dissolute genius, Thomas disaffected his friends, disappointed his patrons, wrecked his marriage, and fulfilled his own lifelong forebodings of an early death. He is buried in the churchyard at Laugharne.

Over 30 years after Thomas's death in America, the marina statue was unveiled by Lady Wilson, herself a poet and wife of the former premier: 'I wonder what he would have made of the proceedings today', she remarked. The plinth is part of a granite coping stone from the old South Dock. The cost of £16,000 was met by Swansea City Council, aided by a retired London businessman, an admirer of the poet.

The town has produced a leaflet, *Uplands Trail*, giving a more realistic portrait of Thomas and including excerpts from his prose in which he recalls his Swansea 'crawling, sprawling, slummed, unplanned, jerry-villa'd, smug-suburbed by the side of a long and splendid curving shore'. One wonders what Thomas would have made of Swansea's post-modernist Marina.

Swansea (and locality) Selection

Other late 20th-century sculpture includes sturdy, decorative marina building reliefs and portraits by Philip Chatfield. Earlier statues include a formula bronze by John Evan Thomas (1857) of John Henry Vivian MP, 'universally lamented', now in the Maritime Village; also a grimy bronze statue of mayor William Thomas, 'pioneer-champion of open spaces', unveiled in his presence (1906) and haunting Patti Pavilion in Victoria Park. The most compelling image, a medallion profile by the same sculptor, Ivor Thomas, enhances a forgotten fountain outside the park toilets. It shows the dispeptic-looking Henry Evan Charles who ' went about doing good'.

Mario Raggi has a bronze of Vivian's son, the 1st Baron Swansea, unveiled (1886) in Victoria Park and now in St David's shopping precinct; also a substantial bronze statue of Howell Gwyn MP in Victoria Gardens at Neath. At Clydach, in the mountainous setting of the Swansea Valley, Lantéri's bronze of the industrial chemist Ludwig Mond broods outside 'The Mond', the nickel works which he founded in 1902. (The original, or a cast, of the same formidable figure stands outside the first Brunner-Mond works at Winnington in Cheshire.)

South Glamorgan

Cardiff

City Feature:

Godfrey Charles Morgan, 1st Viscount Tredegar
(1831–1913)
Bronze equestrian statue on pedestal of Darley
Dale stone.
Sculptor (Sir) William Goscombe John
Location Boulevard de Nantes, Cathays Park

The bristling image of a 19th-century officer and gentleman, Lord Tredegar, in the flamboyant uniform of the 17th Lancers, glares down from astride his war horse 'Sir Briggs'. This was Goscombe

1st Viscount Tredegar (1831–1913).
Sculptor: Sir W. Goscombe John, RA (1909).
Location: Cathays Park, Cardiff.

John's first equestrian work, won in competition with Adrian Jones, a specialist in military and equestrian figures. On the side of the high pedestal, carved letters recall horse and rider's youthful glory: 'Unveiled on the 55th anniversary of the day on which Lord Tredegar then Captain Godfrey Charles Morgan led a troop of XVII Lancers in the Charge of the Light Brigade at Balaclava'.

Above the inscription, the ghastly debacle of October 25th 1854 is enacted in heroic bronze relief. Beneath a matching panel on the other side are the words, 'Erected by the county of Glamorgan as a tribute of respect and affection', and on the back is carved the family emblem, with the motto *Deus Nobiscum Qvis Contra Nos*. The bow front has a stone-carved portrait head of Lord Tredegar in profile – a Glamorgan gentleman in his later years.

As a 23-year-old cavalry officer, Morgan was one of few who survived against impossible odds in the infamous charge against Russian heavy artillery at Balaclava. His graphic account from the battlefield in a letter to his father is thought to have inspired Tennyson's epic poem *The Charge of the Light Brigade*. On his return, Morgan entered Parliament, serving as MP for Brecknock from 1858 until 1875 when he succeeded his father as 2nd Baron Tredegar. He was created 1st Viscount in 1905.

Morgan's charger, Sir Briggs, was wounded at Balaclava by a sabre cut over the right eye. A suggestion that the horse might have been 'knighted' for gallantry came in a recent *Western Mail* article, which noted that in some accounts the charger was styled 'Mr Briggs'. A successful steeplechaser before the Crimea, Sir Briggs is buried in the Cedar Garden at the family home, Tredegar House near Newport, where his headstone records action at the Alma, Inkerman and Balaclava.

In Newport, a seated statue of Earl Tredegar's grandfather, Sir Charles Morgan (1760–1846), is known locally as 'the Old Man', whilst Park Gardens, where the statue was installed, is referred to locally as 'the Old Man's Park'. The statue by the Brecon-born sculptor John Evan Thomas was erected in 1851.

Cardiff (and locality) Selection

Apart from Goscombe John and Alfred Toft, whose Winged Victory marks the Boer War Memorial near the Law Courts, the only other sculptor represented in Cathays Park is Michael Rizzello with his forceful figure of a clench-fisted David Lloyd George in heated debate. The statue is the national monument to Lloyd George, and was funded from 'the pence of pensioners as well as the pounds of the better off', according to the inauguration programme. The ceremony was performed outside the Civic Hall by Harold Macmillan, then Prime Minister, in 1960.

Outside the Law Courts, good-humoured and portly in his court dress, is the Welsh-speaking County Judge, Gwilym Williams of Miskin (1839–1906), county squire and coal owner, and once described as 'a terror to malefactors'; his bronze, a masterly show of self-esteem, was unveiled in 1910. At the south end of the Gardens, Goscombe John's 'speaking likeness', so called, of the philanthropic coal-exporting magnate John Cory (1828–1910), fiercely moustached and carrying his top hat, also shows booming self-confidence. The statue was erected in 1906.

Between them stands Lord Ninian Edward Crichton Stuart (1883–1915), who fell 'fighting bravely',

Archdeacon Buckley (1849–1924). Sculptor: Sir W. Goscombe John, RA (1927). Location: outside Llandaff Cathedral.

at Loos, in 1915. Unveiled in 1919, the work commends Crichton Stuart to posterity as a Lieutenant Colonel in the Welsh Regiment, smartly lowering a pair of field glasses.

It is to posterity's good fortune that the Cardiff-born sculptor William Goscombe John was active when demand for, and creativity in, public sculpture were at their peak. Since the sculptor had no Welsh equal, his work was popular with memorial committees: in towns and villages from south to north, Wales can now boast a rich collection by the master of this particular art. His portraits are animated characterisations rather than formal studies, his subjects' foibles are stated with affection, and their virtues with respect – it seems certain that each had personal acquaintance with the sculptor, so approachable is his work.

A leading exponent of the New Sculpture, Goscombe John is represented in collections at the Civic Hall and National Museum. One of his finest public portraits can be seen in the bronze of Archdeacon James Rice Buckley, erected outside Llandaff Cathedral in 1927. The man of God appears in flat hat and gaiters, pudgy-faced and with a faintly mutinous smile. The pedestal is inscribed, 'Man he was to all the country dear'.

In Alexandra Gardens a formula bronze of Lord Aberdare, by Herbert Hampton (1898), has a grand view of Cardiff's civic buildings. Nearby is the beautiful Welsh national World War Monument, a domed, colonnaded fountain designed by J.E. Comper with ideal sculptures by A. B. Pegram. It was unveiled by Edward, Prince of Wales in 1928.

Cardiff's other statues enliven streets as well as parks; most memorable is a bronze of International scrum-half Gareth Edwards making a pass from the base of scrum. Modelled by Bonar Dunlop and unveiled by the Welsh rugby hero himself in April 1982, it brings artistry and vitality to St David's shopping arcade, built by the Heron Corporation who commissioned the statue.

A stiff and shiny bronze of Aneurin Bevan, by Robert Thomas of Barry, stands at the top of Queen Street. It was unveiled (inevitably) by Michael Foot in 1987, and berated (predictably) by the Conservative MP for Cardiff North, Gwilym Jones, as a wrong image of a forward-looking city, and a waste of public money. It cost £16,000.

Similarly, just over 100 years earlier a bronze of 'The Friend of Freedom' John Batchelor, by J. Milo Griffith, attracted tar and paint, a mock epitaph by political rivals in the *Western Mail*, and a 1200-signature petition for its removal. Raised by his fellow Liberals in The Hayes, and now a Grade II Listed monument, Batchelor's figure still attracts traffic cones and other such unstatesmanlike ornamentation.

Cardiff's earliest public statue, erected late in 1851 after display at the Great Exhibition, has a fine prospect of city architecture at the south end of St Mary Street. John Evan Thomas's bronze of John Crichton Stuart, 2nd Marquis of Bute (1793–1848), commemorates the man who built up Cardiff as the world's principal coal-exporting port; his son the 3rd Marquis (1847–1900), enormously rich and philanthropic, rebuilder of Cardiff Castle and fantastical folly Castell Coch, stands in Friary Gardens between the castle and City Hall. His bronze is by P. Macgillivray (1930).

The Castle should be noted for its 'Animal Wall', ornamented with exotic glass-eyed beasts energetically escaping from captivity. Nine were carved by the Lambeth sculptor Thomas Nicholls in the 1890s, as originally planned by William Burges (architect of Castle Coch) for Lord Bute; in 1931, the Edinburgh sculptor Alexander Carrick carved six more, including a pair of racoons. No longer naturalistically painted, they remain as agreeable as any statue or building sculpture in this agreeable city.

Mid Glamorgan

Aberdare/Aberdâr (G)

Town Feature:

Griffith Rhys Jones ('Caradog', 1834–1897)
Full-length bronze statue on plain stone pedestal.
Sculptor (Sir) William Goscombe John
Location Victoria Square

Bronze baton raised outside the Black Lion Hotel, Caradog conducts the town, his energies directed down the slope from his pedestal at the top of Victoria Square to the Caradog Arms and the cenotaph in Cardiff Street. At his feet, a violin rests against a fringed piano stool.

Unconcerned, Aberdare continues its business; the largest town in the Cynon Valley, with new industries replacing old, it has seen much change since Griffith Rhys Jones, leader of the prize-winning Aberdare Choral Union, was chosen as conductor of

Griffith Rhys Jones (1834–1897). Sculptor: Sir W. Goscombe John, RA (1920). Location: Victoria Square, Aberdare.

'the renowned South Wales Choral Union' in 1872. The Canon Street Temperance Hall, where the appointment was made, is now a Bingo Hall. The Nonconformist chapels, publishing houses and meeting places, and the dominating hardship of the coal and iron trade, remain as echoes from his day.

So does Rhys Jones's *Côr Mawr* ('Great Choir'), which 'won the chief choral prize valued at one thousand pounds in open competition at the Crystal Palace, London in July 1872 and 1873', as recorded on the statue's plain pedestal. This boost for Welsh pride and working class morale was marked by the *Côr Mawr* Centenary Festival in Aberdare, in 1973.

The triumphant choir, praised for its 'fresh and vigorous voices' (*The Times* music critic complained of 'rawness and shouting') twice brought home the sumptuous silver-gilt trophy, to be met by cheering multitudes, bands, bells, cannon fire and fog signals — marred only by the absence of the choir's conductor, who had gone home to Treorchy. Thereafter the ambitious Class One competition was abandoned, causing much bitterness, since any thrice-victorious choir was to have won the Crystal Palace trophy in perpetuity. The trophy was deposited in Cardiff's Welsh Folk Museum in 1986, only after the disbanding of London's GLC.

Caradog – 'Griff o'r Crown' to his intimates – has been described as a shy man, who could be moved to tears at Roubiliac's monument to Handel in Westminster Abbey; blacksmith son of a Trecynon iron-works engineer, he followed his father's later occupation as a publican. A noted violinist, he formed his first choir at the age of 19 and after a prize-winning competition, himself acquired its title, 'Caradog' – the Welsh name for the Romano-British general Caratacus. The name's other meaning, 'amiable', may be more appropriate to the musician than the general. Mourned at his death as Cambria's 'noble leader', his statue was unveiled in 1920 by Lord Aberdare. Amongst the large crowd which had assembled in a downpour were 120 members of Caradog's *Côr Mawr*.

Aberdare Selection

In Aberdare Park, Trecynon, a bronze casting of local coal owner Lord Merthyr (1837–1914) stands at the centre of an ornamental pond. Inscribed *Hirbahad* ('Everlasting'), it was unveiled in 1913. Sir Thomas Brock's original stands in Merthyr Tydfil.

Llantrisant/Llantrisaint (G)

Town Feature:

Dr William Price (1800–1893)
Full length statue cast in glass-reinforced plastic with stone aggregate, on a convex base of engineering brick.
Sculptor Peter Nicholas
Location The Bull Ring

Immortalised in his fox-skin hat, the wild man of 19th-century Llantrisant dominates the town's small Bull Ring. A slate tablet pronounces 'Surgeon, chartist and self-styled druid', whilst the tablet's carved border incorporates the words 'Innovator of modern cremation'. The doctor's Druidical cloak with sword, crescent and torch motifs, indicates a life of bizarre action fired by fantasy and delusion.

Dr William Price (1800–1893). Sculptor: Peter Nicholas (1982). Location: the Bull Ring, Llantrisant.

The statue is a symbol of continuing change in this old hill town with its post-modernist craft centre, new saddlery, Indian take-away and other new ventures. Tourism is the mainspring of a local authority attempt to preserve Llantrisant's way of life as well as its steep, huddled streets.

By reincarnating the colourful Dr Price as a sculptural centrepiece, today's town planners challenge dull cultural uniformity just as Price, a qualified doctor, rebuffed 19th-century, God-fearing, small-town conformity. Anticipating many of today's popular causes, Price performed various outrages against respectability, mischievously (and brilliantly) upholding his behaviour in the local courts.

Antiquarian, revolutionary and atheist, Price thundered against local iron and coal owners ('the blood-sucking Pharaohs of Wales'), promoted nature healing, opposed vaccination, practised vegetarianism and espoused free love, living with a series of local maidens and fathering his last child after the age of 90.

His weird figure stares out at the neighbouring hilltop, East Caerlan, where he achieved national notoriety by attempting to cremate his baby son, Iesu Grist (Jesus Christ). Forcibly prevented by local residents, the doctor was apprehended and brought to court in a test case recalled on a Cremation Society tablet outside the Zoar Chapel; he was indicted but aquitted by Mr Justice Stephen 'who adjudged that cremation was a legal act'. The chapel occupies the site of the cottage where the doctor died. His own cremation attracted a crowd of thousands.

Artistically, the work reflects its sculptor's own assessment, explained in a Borough Planning booklet: 'I enjoy the design/drawing process the most, my enthusiasm waxing and waning as the clay work or full size stage work progresses'. The statue may lack technical brilliance, but it has prolonged Dr Price's notoriety, which even now arouses indignation among the townspeople.

Llantrisant (and locality) Selection

North of Llantrisant near Pontypridd (on the A470), *Y Carreg Siglo* (the Rocking Stone), taken by Dr Price to be the Temple of Ceridwen, was used by Price and others in an attempted Druid revival.

Pontypridd's *Ynysangharad* War Memorial Park (named after Angharad, a virtuous princess) has a hilltop obelisk to the Great War, overlooking a sumptuous monument to Evan James and James James who 'united poetry to song and gave to Wales her national anthem, *Hen Wlad Fy NHADAU*', in 1856. The first verse of 'Land of my Fathers', was written by Evan James at his home and woollen factory in Mill Street; his son, an accomplished harpist, had previously composed the tune during a Sunday afternoon walk.

Their small, engaging double-relief portrait brings a touch of humanity to Goscombe John's ensemble of stock bronzes symbolising Poetry and Music (with harp).

In 1973 the remains of Evan James were transferred from the neglected Carmel Baptist chapel graveyard, and ceremonially reinterred at the foot of the monument which stands on a flight of steps. James James is buried at nearby Aberdare.

Merthyr Tydfil (Gm)

Town Selection:

Robert Thomas (1770–1829) and Lucy Thomas (1781– 1847)
Domed, canopied, cast-iron fountain.
Supplier Saracen Foundry, Glasgow
Location St Tydfil's Parish Church

This sumptuous, traceried fountain was installed as a landmark at the south end of Merthyr Tydfil High Street to commemorate Robert and Lucy Thomas of Waunwyllt, 'the pioneers in 1828 of the South Wales Steam Coal Trade', who opened up the prosperity of the South Wales valleys from the mid-19th century.

At this time the iron industry which had built the fortunes of Merthyr Tydfil was on the wane, and with it demand for the surface coal tapped from the upper Taff Valley to feed the iron forges. The

The Thomas Memorial Fountain: to Robert (1770–1829) & Lucy Thomas (1781–1847). Design: not known (1906). Location: outside St Tydfil's Church, Merthyr Tydfil.

Thomases sank deep shafts south of Merthyr Tydfil, which yielded highly-superior coal. Their success lay in recognising and marketing the deep-seam coal's potential for driving the new boilers and engines of the rapidly-expanding steam-powered industries in Wales and England.

Geological variation and faulting presented great difficulties which the Thomases overcame, securing a monopoly which the astute Lucy Thomas exploited to build a flourishing concern – first persuading the powerful railway and steamship companies of the coal's exceptional properties. Others who eventually followed in sinking deep shafts sold their coal on the name 'Merthyr', which they considered synonymous with superior quality steam coal. These mines were productive until the mid-20th century.

The black and brown fountain recalls Merthyr Tydfil's traditional industries in a spectacular fusion of delicacy and power. A statuette of Samson crowns the open scroll-work dome, which is supported on ornamental cast-iron columns. Decorative shields in the spandrel arches show figures of miners, and symbols of coal. Beneath, the fountain with its water spouts, vase and gun-metal drinking cups is ornamented with storks, swans and reeds. Installed c.1900, the ensemble was restored and repainted in 1966 at the Ivor Steel works in Dowlais before being resited outside St Tydfyl's Parish Church.

The inauguration was performed in 1906 to mark the granting of the town's charter. The mayor was able to appear ceremonially-robed in public for the first time; the mayoress turned on the water with a silver key, and later the company partook of a sumptuous banquet.

Among the speech makers at the inauguration was Sir William Lewis, coal, docks and railway developer, co-donor of the fountain and husband of the Thomas's granddaughter. His bronze statue by Thomas Brock stands outside St Tydfil's Hospital, and a long citation on the back of the pedestal records Lewis's industrial contribution and his contribution to improving worker-owner relations.

Merthyr Tydfil Selection

Merthyr Tydfil's monuments pay homage to iron and coal, but not to the most illustrious ironmasters, the dynastic Crawshays, Guests, Homfrays and Hills, who built a village into Wales's foremost industrial centre over the last half of the 18th century. Nor do they reflect the working conditions through which iron or coal workers died old and exhausted before reaching their twenties. However, a plaque on the library wall (1977) commemorates Dic Penderyn, 'Martyr of the Welsh Working Class', hanged after the Merthyr Riots of 1831. And the town's history is told in the Museum and Art Gallery at Cyfarthfa Castle, a turreted pile built in 1825 for William Crawshay II opposite his ironworks.

Among other monuments, the most striking is the First World War cenotaph (1931), standing on a bank overlooking the road north of High Street. The sculptor L.S. Merrifield presents bronzes of a miner and a hollow-eyed mother, with her baby swaddled in her shawl. They stand to right and left of a hooded St Tydfil with arms raised at the centre of the Portland stone apsidal screen. Merrifield used an architect's wife from Neath as a model for the female figures, which he expressed with particular intensity.

Across Pen-y-Darren Road is a sombre block to Richard Trevithick (1771–1833), 'Pioneer of high-pressure steam'. In 1804 his steam locomotive, the first to run on rails, 'Traversed the spot on which this monument stands'.

A statue of Trevithick was commissioned by Lord Rhondda, who died before L.S. Merrifield could start work. The rugged memorial, designed by I.S. Williams of Cardiff, incorporates sleeper stones and rails of the old tramroad, and was unveiled in 1934. The dressed-stone paving has been replaced by cheap-looking concrete and gravel chips, not often used in Welsh monuments. Treacly, coal-black paint covers Goscombe John's bronze statue of mine owner Henry Berry Seymour, 1st Lord Buckland of Bwlch, standing outside the library. Committed to the care of the Corporation 'in perpetuity' after appearing at the Royal Academy (1933), it does not take to paint as handsomely as the Thomas's cast-iron fountain.

Gwent

Ebbw Vale/Glynebwy (Mn)

Town Feature:

Aneurin Bevan (1897–1960)
Four inscribed limestone blocks
Mason Albert C. Janes
Location Waun-y-Pound, off the A4047

Four huge white rough-hewn boulders stand on the moorland overlooking Aneurin Bevan's former parliamentary constituency of Ebbw Vale; on the centre stone, greater in size and elevation, is the carved message:

It was here that Aneurin Bevan spoke
to the people of his constituency
and the world.

The lesser boulders represent each of the three former mining towns served by Bevan, Labour party rebel and architect of the National Health Service, relentless agitator in the causes of mine workers and the unemployed, and a leading campaigner for the revival of the Ebbw Vale steel-works (1938).

The name of each town, Rhymney, Tredegar and Ebbw Vale, is cut into the limestone face of its boulder, and the view from that craggy face reaches across ragged moorland and new industrial estates to the town in its valley. The stones, standing 1200ft above sea-level, were won from the British Steel Corporation's Trefil quarries north-west of Tredegar. The nearby hills reach 1800ft, and on the northern skyline lie the Llangynidr and Llangattwg Moors at the southern edge of Brecon National Park.

The monument forms the starting point of the Sirhowy Valley Walk, where thousands gathered at the unveiling ceremony of 1972, attended by Bevan's widow, Baroness Lee, and his successor and biographer, Michael Foot. The *Western Mail*, bitter critic of Bevan in his early political career, noted the parking problem and compared this impressive affluence with the decades of gloom when 'crowds of pinched and angry men' massed here to 'share Aneurin Bevan's gift of brilliant wrath'.

In his speech, Michael Foot recalled the time he first heard Bevan speak, in Whitehall, to the Pontypool hunger-marchers. Foot's biography graphically portrays the pre-War, pre-Social Services Tredegar of Bevan's boyhood, and the harsh working and living conditions which fired Bevan's eve-of-poll speeches at rallies on Waun-y-Pound hillside where the stones now stand.

It was in these surroundings that Bevan formed his political loyalties and began his lifelong succession of protest: against an overbearing headmaster at elementary school; against pit managers; against the Tredegar Iron and Coal company; against the appalling privations suffered by South Wales mine-working families, the poor, and the unemployed. A self-taught graduate of Tredegar Public Library, Bevan later displayed his encyclopædic knowledge in brilliant parliamentary speeches and in articles for *Tribune*, which he edited from 1942–1945.

Bevan cut his political teeth as a union and local government activist before taking his seat as Labour

Standing stones to Aneurin Bevan (1897–1960). Mason: Albert Janes (1972). Location: Waun-y-Pound, A4047 Tredegar-Ebbw Vale.

member for Ebbw Vale from 1929. On the opposition back benches he could employ his 'savage and seductive tongue' to challenge his own party policies as robustly as those of the Government. Bevan's goal was social change, and the only means available, in his terms, was a parliamentary Labour Party that held an unswerving prime commitment to social justice for the working classes. As Minister for Health in Attlee's post-war government, Bevan fought successfully for the realisation of these principles in his National Health Service Act of 1946.

These tenets were reiterated at the unveiling in a bitter wind as Michael Foot declared 'we dedicate ourselves afresh to the political aims which he gave the Labour movement'. Local memories came from Jennie Lee: 'This is the spot where Nye raised his standards, collected his armies and prepared for battle: battle not with guns but with ideas'. She recalled the stammering Tredegar schoolboy whose knuckles were rapped for being left-handed, who went down the pit before he was 14 and who surprised her, the university graduate, with his superior breadth of self-acquired knowledge; 'Aneurin got nothing in life easily – not even me'.

The stones have no lengthy inscription recalling

landmarks in Bevan's career, relived so vividly under the flapping Red Dragon flag. The monument was devised by Michael Foot and his wife Jill Craigie, together with organisers Ron Evans (agent of both Bevan and Foot) and Eugene Cross, a founder of the Ebbw Vale Labour Party. It is seen as a fitting memorial, although local opinion is not all favourable: 'We don't need a mini Stonehenge at Sirhowy-top to tell us what Nye accomplished'. Necessary or no, the great white stones on Bevan's local rallying ground respect a Welsh political hero of the working classes whose audacity, passion and powerful logic must have offered rock-like comfort during the days of despair.

Ebbw Vale locality Selection

In Tredegar, Aneurin Bevan's Charles Street birthplace has made way for redevelopment. The town Circle's cast-iron town clock, painted apricot-and-cream and dedicated to 'England's Hero' Wellington, features a small relief-figure of the Iron Duke on two sides. It was presented in 1858 'from the proceeds of a bazaar mounted by the late Mrs R.P. Davies', wife of the Tredegar Ironworks manager; centenary celebrations included a speech by Aneurin Bevan from the base of the 72ft column.

In Bedwelty Park, a pit cage holds a single 15—ton lump of coal too huge for transportation to the Great Exhibition of 1851. It was cut from Tredegar Iron & Coal Co's yard seam by John Jones, *Collier Mawr* — the Great Collier.

Monmouth/Trefynwy (Mn)

Town feature:

The Hon. Charles Stewart Rolls (1877–1910)
Full-length bronze statue on polished
granite pedestal.
Sculptor (Sir) William Goscombe John
Pedestal Sir Aston Webb
Location Agincourt Square

The pioneer aviator C.S. Rolls is shown contemplating a model of the plane in which he died. Kitted for flight, he has clean-cut features and an airman's moustache, and the piercing gaze of the zealot. His Wright biplane is shown with the specially-fitted tailplane that caused the fatal crash during a flying competition at Bournemouth. Just

over a year later, on October 19th 1911, Rolls's statue was unveiled by Lord Raglan outside Monmouth's classical Shire Hall in Agincourt Square.

Present at the ceremony was Sir Aston Webb, designer of the Victoria and Albert Museum on which Goscombe John worked. Webb's pale pink granite pedestal carries a lengthy inscription recording Rolls's 'great achievements in motoring, ballooning and aviation'. Decorative *bas*-reliefs depict quaint scenes that might just be remembered by older citizens of Monmouth, since the lanes, fields and hills around his home — the Hendre — provided testing grounds for the third son of the 1st Baron Llangattock, and his new-fangled machines.

It was here that Monmouth, after a two-day wait, saw its — and his — first car when Rolls arrived in a $3\frac{3}{4}$ horsepower Peugeot at midnight in December 1896. Later, Rolls took the Duke and Duchess of York motoring, and launched ballooning parties from the local gasworks which served as a filling station. The 'hare' in an annual balloon chase, Rolls used a specially-equipped *Silver Ghost* Rolls-Royce to retrieve his small balloon, the 'Imp'.

Rolls was too practical and fanatical to use his mechanical genius merely as a rich man's fancy. With a Cambridge degree in Mechanics and applied Science, he set up a London car sales and repair firm, proving his engines through arduous but prize-winning performances at international rallies. He also helped popularise motoring through his writing and lectures, and his work with motoring organisations.

Finally, Rolls interlocked his name with the concept of prestige motoring after his search for a reliable manufacturer introduced him to the self-made engineer Frederick Henry Royce. The renowned Rolls-Royce partnership was formed, and two years later it began production of the fabulous *Silver Ghost* (1906).

Once car travel had been tamed, Rolls turned to more exciting transport. Writing for *The London Magazine* in May 1908, he described flight in an airship: 'The engine roared; the ship trembled from stem to stern; the wind brushed past our faces. This was something worth living for. It was the conquest of the air'. In a booklet published by the Monmouth Historical and Educational Trust, Rolls is photographed sitting stiffly on a biplane with the pioneer American aviator Wilbur Wright. Later, he entertained the first Channel-flyer Louis Blériot, and soon after taught himself to fly.

In June 1910, Rolls made his famous double Channel crossing, starting from Dover at 6.30pm and returning within 45 minutes of circling the San-

The Hon. C. S. Rolls (1877–1910).
Sculptor: Sir W. Goscombe John (1911).
Location: Agincourt Square, Monmouth.

gatte tunnel works at 7.15pm. However, on his last flight just over a month later, Rolls's flimsy machine came to grief at a Bournemouth tournament during a second attempt to land. The gear connecting the rudder snapped, and in the too-cramped space the plane nose-dived to the ground. Nationally mourned, the first British aviator ever to be killed in flight was buried at the church of Llangattock Vibon Avel, northwest of Monmouth.

Monmouth (and locality) Selection

Witness to the early motoring forays from Agincourt Square is a large painted figure of Henry V, occupying a niche on Shire Hall. His decidedly-bad statue by a Monmouth sculptor, Charles Peart, London-based modeller of portrait busts for Wedgwood, was installed in 1792 at a time when the Wye Tour was popular and river towns were vying for visitors. 'Harry of Monmouth' was born at Monmouth Castle in 1387, but unlike the Hon C.S. Rolls, did not stay to leave his imprint on the town.

In St Thomas Square near Monnow Bridge, a Victorian Jubilee fountain with a robustly-carved chevron arch emulates the church's Norman arch and its rich, pinkish stone. Over the Wye Bridge, off the Forest of Dean road, a steep lane climbs the 850ft Kymin Hill (NT), where a pleasure ground was made after the Round House was built in 1794 as a meeting place for 'the first gentlemen in Monmouth'.

In 1800, two years after the Battle of the Nile, a Naval Temple was built in honour of Nelson and other admirals, dedicated to the Duchess of Beaufort, and crowned by a figure of Britannia seated on a rock. Restoration was completed in 1989. One of the admirals, Somerset-born Sir George Brydges Rodney, has a memorial column on the slatey Breidden Hills between Shropshire and Montgomeryshire, marking his victory over the French off the West Indies in 1782.

The Burton Cooper'. Sculptor: James Butler, RA (1977). Location: Central Shopping Precinct, Burton-on-Trent.

Central Counties

'Everyman'

*Every man has a lurking wish
to appear considerable in
his native place*

(The inscription on Dr Johnson's statue in
Lichfield Market Place)

Dr Johnson cogitating outside his Lichfield birthplace, Stanley Matthews dribbling a football through Hanley and the Burton Cooper hammering wooden trussing hoops to a cask may have little in common, but they all appear considerable in their native county, Staffordshire. The Central Counties' palette is bound to be broad, since the region stretches from the lush Thames and Chilterns to the Derbyshire Peaks, and contains the Heart of England, the East and West Midlands, the Black Country and the Potteries.

Characters commemorated are as various in achievement as Alfred the Great, George Palmer the Biscuit King, and the Ape God Thoth, who inhabits the Cheshire Cottage near 'Egypt' at the renovated exotic gardens of Biddulph Grange (NT) in Staffordshire. Thoth and other stone beings are the work of Waterhouse Hawkins, creator of the famous Crystal Palace dinosaurs.

The sculptors are equally and appropriately diverse, numbering Alfred the Great's creator in marble, Count Gleichen of Hohenlohe, whose cousin Edward VII, as Prince of Wales, performed the unveiling at Wantage (1877); George Blackall

Simonds, later Chairman of Simonds Brewers, who, whilst at Reading in 1889, made a realistic bronze portrait of his fellow townsman George Palmer with hat and umbrella in Palmer's Park; and the eminent 19th-century sculptor Sir Richard Westmacott, who carved a luxuriantly-robed figure of Mary Queen of Scots for the 6th Duke of Devonshire — misgivings over 'the open air, and the playful public', causing the removal of the statue to Hardwick Hall from Queen Mary's Bower at Chatsworth, one of Mary's various places of confinement in the Derbyshire wilds whilst captive of her cousin, Elizabeth I.

This rich region also shows a proportionately generous number of works by women, among them Count Gleichen's daughter Feodora (Florence Nightingale, Derby) and Doris Lindner, whose bronze of the legendary Arkle, thrice winner of the Cheltenham

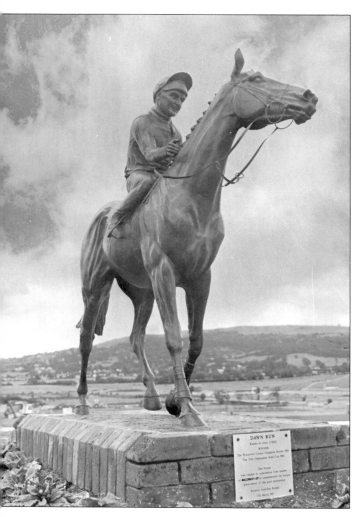

Dawn Run (d.1986), ridden by JonJo O'Neill. Sculptor: Jonathan Knight. Location: Parade Ring, Cheltenham Racecourse.

Gold Cup, was the first of three race horses sculptured for the Cheltenham Parade Ring.

Besides the Ape God and Arkle, other heroic figures from legend or history include Robin Hood in Nottingham, Lady Godiva in Coventry and, well-known locally, Guy of Warwick with the Boar, who guards the entrance to the Guy's Cross Park housing estate on the Coventry Road, Warwick. Recalling knightly love, a princess, a dragon and the Dun Cow, the pair were wrought by Keith Godwin in typical '60s 'Slim Jim' style from cold cast bronze (fibreglass and resin mixed with bronze powder). The plinth is of cast concrete containing grey granite aggregate, wire-brushed for texture. By way of contrast at Hoddesdon in Hertfordshire, a gentle 17th-century stone statue of the Samarian Woman pouring water once marked the High Street water supply.

This kaleidoscopic region does have its particularities, one of which is its firm claim to the centre of England, 'by tradition' marked on a restored medieval cross at Meriden near Coventry. Also on the green, a large obelisk honours cyclists who died in the Great War. Much further south, near Stretton-on-Dunsmore, a crowned obelisk on a roundabout marks the spot where George V reviewed his Gallipoli troops 'Here in the centre of England, Where Telford's coaching road from London to Holyhead is crossed by the Fosse Way'.

In its disparate collection this is a region of firsts and prototypes, the most venerable being the medieval crosses raised by Edward I to mark the stages of Queen Eleanor's funeral cortège (1291). Two survive in Northamptonshire, and one at Waltham, as England's earliest prominent public memorials. Victorian Gothic stone spires, intricately carved, emulate the Eleanor Crosses in almost every English county, notably in Oxford, where George Gilbert Scott's version stands as the Martyrs' Memorial.

At Marlow in Buckinghamshire, one of the first non-royal commemorative public monuments is now kept in the porch of All Saints' Church. It was erected by public subscription, in 1686, to Sir Miles Hobart MP, who went to the Tower for locking the door of the Commons against Charles I. Outside the church, a nude marble maiden occupies a decorative pedestal: 'For it is not right that in a house the muses haunt, mourning should dwell..'. This pretty monument salutes the theatrical impresario Charles Frohman, who went down with the *Lusitania* in 1915.

Landlocked Birmingham claims England's earliest surviving Nelson monument (October 1809) — Hereford commemorated England's hero in the same year – and Walsall's stately figure of Nurse Dora Pattison can claim to be cast from the first conventional public statue erected to any woman not of royal blood (1886).

Queen Eleanor and Sister Dora are two among many determined women celebrated in the Central Counties, their stories expressed in their images. Florence Nightingale lifts her lamp in Derby, long-haired Godiva rides naked in Coventry and Catherine Mumford, Salvation Army Mother, appears comely but resolute in her bonnet and bow, her bronze bust overlooking a park at her native Ashbourne, Gateway to the Peaks.

Cliveden in Buckinghamshire, ever exclusive and now an hotel, shows in its gardens (NT) Roman and classical sculptures – an extra pleasure, in the Ilex Grove, is a bronze of Joan of Arc, strong and soulful in armour, her visor and gauntlets at her side. Intended for the interior of the house, it was modelled by Princess Marie d'Orléans, a visitor of the Duke and Duchess of Sutherland. (Nearby, Prince Albert in Highland dress, by the younger William Theed, was the gift of another visitor to Cliveden, Queen Victoria.)

Nuneaton's bronze statue of the novelist George Eliot shows her in a gown which is displayed at the town's museum. Born here as Mary Anne Evans, she shocked small-town England by living with G.H. Lewes, whose first name she chose for her *nom de plume*, and whose great-great grandson unveiled the statue in 1986.

The sculptor, John Letts, portrayed a woman with powerful features in a pose designed to be decorative rather than controversial. (Letts opens his studio to visitors at Church Lane, Astley, where a field footpath leads from across the lane to a cairn marking the spot where Lady Jane Grey's father, the Duke of Suffolk, was 'betrayed by his Keeper' whilst hiding in a hollow oak.)

Other 1980s statues in this area can be seen at Rugby, where the work of Ivor Roberts-Brown can be recognised in a contorted bronze of Rupert Brooke, and at Worcester and Bromsgrove, which have bronze statues of Elgar and A.E. Housman by Kenneth Potts.

Subject or sculptor, Everywoman is well represented in the Central Counties' many new towns, developed since the 1920s, in which sculpture is planned as part of the townscape. Worth finding are Franta Belsky's 'Joy Ride' in Stevenage town centre in Hertfordshire, or 'Dawn', by David Evans, nakedly awakening from the central reservation of Welwyn Garden's Parkway, with 'Ad Astra' by Lady Scott on

Martyrs' Memorial: 'Eleanor Cross' to Thomas Cranmer (d.1556), Hugh Latimer & Nicholas Ridley, (d.1555). Architect: Sir G. G. Scott (1841). Sculptor: H. Weekes. Location: St Giles, Oxford.

the Campus. Wendy Taylor's stainless steel 'Octo' is part of an expanding modern sculpture collection visible from the wide white boulevards of Milton Keynes, Buckinghamshire. The famous cows realistically occupy a meadow; outside the library, most entertaining, is a bronze edition of a sculpture by André Wallace: 'The Whisper' shows two hefty girls delicately swapping office gossip whilst perched on the railings.

André Wallace also shows a successful and striking ensemble incorporating a figure of Thomas

Thomas Telford (1757–1834). Sculptor: André Wallace (1987). Location: Telford New Town.

Telford at Telford New Town, Shropshire, which has a vigorous programme of sculpture, street art and 'art as landmark' to help travellers from one urban centre to the next.

The Kodak company's policy of acquiring gallery works, in the 1970s, gave us Auguste Rodin's extraordinary, unrestrained rendering of Balzac (1897) – Britain's only bronze cast of the 12 made before the mould was broken – standing outside the Kodak Headquarters block at the edge of Hemel Hempstead, Hertfordshire. It was purchased by the then Managing Director Norman Brick, art connoisseur and friend of Lillian Browes whose gallery had acquired the cast. She invited Henry Moore to help site the figure, acclaimed as one of Rodin's greatest works and his most controversial.

Central Counties have most of England's new towns but none of its coast, yet there are monuments to seafarers and explorers in all corners. A medallion portrait of the first Channel swimmer Captain Matthew Webb occupies a market place obelisk at his birthplace, Dawley, now in Telford. Webb learned to swim in the River Severn, at the bottom of his garden. Derbyshire has a small gritstone obelisk to Nelson, raised on Baslow Edge by John Brightman of Baslow. Behind, three huge grizzled outcrops are each incised *Victory*, *Defiant*, or *Royal 'Soverin'*, in strong letters on the 'bows'. And Crich Stand has a 'lighthouse' tower, with a beacon, to honour the Sherwood Foresters Regiment.

At Arcadian Shugborough (NT) in Staffordshire,

portrait busts of Admiral and Lady Anson are elevated over the park on Hadrian's triumphal arch, raised to mark Anson's circumnavigation of 1740–4 by Anson's elder brother, Thomas, whose squire's income was augmented by the Admiral for the beautifying of Shugborough. James 'Athenian' Stuart designed the arch and other classical garden monuments. The Ansons' sculptor, Peter Scheemakers, also made the fine marble relief after Poussin, *'Et in Arcadia Ego'* (1765) in a frame of bizarre rusticated pillars at the other end of the park.

Most rewarding, in a copse across the cast-iron Chinese Bridge (1813), is the lofty pillar and urn surmounted by the scowling stone image of the Admiral's cat, a companion in his global expedition. Amongst the treasures in the house is the Wedgwood Queen's Ware sauce tureen decorated with the Shugborough acres' Triumphal Arch.

Near Chalfont St Giles, a small moated flint and brick tower stands in a cattle-grazed pasture near Vache Park, former home of Captain Cook's mentor Sir Hugh Palliser, Comptroller of the Navy. Marble panels chiselled with long, flowery inscriptions report the adventures of the great navigator, 'unnfortunately killed by the Savages of the island Owyhee' in 1779. A footpath leads the intrepid sightseer through Buckinghamshire woodland to this quintessentially English scene. The Vache is owned by the Coal Board, appropriately perhaps, since Cook made his epic voyages in a refitted Whitby collier.

Some of the region's best statuary enriches the

surroundings of country houses, notably in Buckinghamshire. Waddesdon and the grounds of Stowe School (both NT) are prime examples, Stowe having England's richest collection of 18th-century commemorative and architectural garden monuments, and one of the finest examples of William Kent's landscaped gardens. (There is a pedestal bearing JACOBO COOK's pudgy, smiling profile, Grecian style, sited near Captain Thomas Grenville's rostral column – decorated with beak-like prows of ships.)

The house was altered and the grounds embellished for the Whig politician Sir Richard Temple, 4th Baronet, who employed leading sculptors and artists to work at Stowe. The lead equestrian statue of George I, outside Vanbrugh's remodelled north front, is thought to be by John Nost, executed in the 1720s and inspired by the Roman statue of Marcus Aurelius. Like most of Stowe's monuments, stone busts by Rysbrack and Scheemakers, made for the Temple of British Worthies, survive as symbols of Whig politicking and power. The family name and motto *Templa Quam Dilecta* ('How Pleasing are Thy Temples') survive in the monuments.

Hartwell House, now a country hotel, has resited its statues, including the lead equestrian figure of Frederick, Prince of Wales. The columnar statue carrying a full-length statue was dedicated to William III *c*.1730, but in 1757 a mason was paid to carve the name still visible on the pedestal: George II. This, and other lead garden sculptures of the 1730s, can be viewed by arrangement. Just over the Hertfordshire border, on the Ashridge Estate (NT), is a granite belvedere to the coal-owning 'Navigation Duke', the 3rd Earl of Bridgewater.

Southward at Stoke Poges Golf Club (ninth hole), a Doric column carries Rossi's gilded, artificial stone statue of Edward Coke, county sheriff and celebrated Chief Justice. (Elizabeth I visited him at his manor house, but he retired here, as he lamented, 'alone on earth'.) James Wyatt designed his monument, erected 1800, and also, in a meadow adjoining the churchyard of St Giles's, the great raised sarcophagus to Thomas Gray. Lines from the *Elegy* speak out from the stone. Erected 1799, it is cared for by the National Trust.

Buckinghamshire, with its country seats and columns, also has the biggest and most bizarre of the region's monuments in the great roofless hexagonal hilltop mausoleum of flint and stone, and the nearby church with a golden globe, that recall the bawdy and outlandish rituals of Sir Francis Dashwood's Hellfire Club. Memorial urns and busts of Sir Francis's family, or club members from high echelons of

English society, can be seen through the arches of the monument, erected 1764–5 to the designs of John Bastard. Alterations at West Wycombe Park (NT), effected by Sir Francis in the 1760s, reveal the more cultivated aspect of England's Chancellor of the Exchequer (in his own opinion, 'the worst').

Considerable persons in the Central Counties are honoured chiefly with statues or busts, but monuments in general are unevenly spread. Counties with particularly rich collections are Staffordshire and the West Midlands, Derbyshire and Buckinghamshire, the last two having a higher proportion of minor, or non-sculptural, memorials.

Derbyshire's crop of individualistic landmarks suits its sombre, wind-scored moors such as those above the Derwent Reservoir Dam, where a stone recalls Dam Buster pilots who died on practice runs, leaving fragments of their Lancaster bombers still on the surrounding hills. By the water a few yards away is a sorrowful stone to 'TIP, THE SHEEPDOG WHO STAYED BY THE BODY OF HER DEAD MASTER' through the cruel winter of 1953–4.

The towns do not follow the county pattern. Half of Oxfordshire's free-standing statues belonged to Berkshire (at Wantage and Abingdon) until the county boundary changes; but Oxford college

Rostral column to Captain Thomas Grenville (1719–1747). Raised 1748; moved to Elysian Fields, and 'Hercules' replaced by the 'Muse of Heroic Poetry' by Van Nost (1763). Location: Stowe School grounds (NT).

statues, as well as Blenheim's Victory Column and the Elysian charm of the classical statuary at William Kent's Rousham garden, make up for this dearth.

Gloucestershire's dearth is cured by interesting concentrations in Gloucester, and in Cheltenham where Lady Scott's bronze portrait of Edward Wilson, who died with her husband Captain Scott on the North Pole Expedition of 1912, recalls Scott's final letter home: 'He died as he lived, a brave true man'. The statue was unveiled in 1914 in the presence of Dr Wilson's parents, in the tree-lined Promenade, not far from the family home.

Other Cheltenham monuments have the local touch, most being provided by the founders, R. Boulton and Sons, who cast the statue of Dr Wilson. A florid contrast to Dr Wilson's is the supine Neptune in a version of Salvi's Trevi fountain (Rome, 1731–62), at the top of the Promenade. In Montpellier Walk, the Boultons' drinking fountain, given in 1914, has a rare statue of Edward VII in mufti, with an anonymous child, by Ambrose Neale who modelled the Boar War soldier in the Promenade.

In Montpellier Gardens, a rare and oddly-proportioned figure of William IV marks the coronation of 1830 and not the Reform Bill, as was inscribed. It was 'wholly and solely designed and executed by Mr William Gardner (fl.1812–1843), sculptor and engraver of this town', according to the contemporary *Cheltenham Journal*.

Rural Gloucestershire has a marble statue of the river god Thames, one of a series made for the Crystal Palace by Rafaelle Monti, and bought by the Water Conservancy Board in Crystal Palace's Great Sculpture Sale of 1957. It was set up at the rivers' remote source beyond Chicklade and consistently maltreated until removal over the river boundary to St John's Lock, on Berkshire-Oxfordshire border, where Thames now surveys Lechlade across the meadows.

Northamptonshire, apart from the precious Eleanor crosses, mostly keeps its statues in the county town. The Triangular Lodge at Rushton, northwest of Kettering, is not strictly a free-standing monument, but an architectural symbol of the Trinity created in 1574 by the recusant Sir Thomas Tresham, whose family held Geddington Manor. South of Kettering, at the children's park created by the renowned makers of swings, slides and rides, there are monuments to the firm's founder Charles Wicksteed and to

Jerry
Constant companion of
Charles Wicksteed
1920–1928

This refers to a bronze statue of a soppy dog sitting up and begging on a tasselled cushion. There is a heartrending dedication. Bring a hanky.

Leicestershire and Nottinghamshire have grand selections of street sculptures and statues to animate their county towns, but otherwise little for the monument fancier apart from some handsome war memorials. An exception is the 'Boy with a Thorn' in Loughbrough, and – minor but memorable, on the roadside at Welbeck Park in Nottinghamshire – a stone screen with urn and watering trough carrying the bronze profile of Lord George Frederick Cavendish, a younger son of the Duke of Portland, near the spot where he died in a hunting accident in 1848. The sculptor A. Hood presents an image combining classical nobility with Victorian propriety; according to Disraeli's inscribed tribute, Lord Cavendish 'valued life only as a means of fulfilling duty'. Behind him spread his family's gentle, landscaped acres.

Dutiful or constant, or 'alone on earth', every man, woman, God or dog celebrated in Central Counties' monuments leaves a persistent and pleasing image of one who appeared considerable – if only in his native place.

2nd Earl of Dudley (1817–1885). Sculptor: C. B. Birch (1888). Location: Castle Gate, Dudley.

Central Western Counties Gazetteer

(**Note:** The Central Western Counties appear in roughly topographical order. Within each county, monuments are listed under their locations, which appear in alphabetical order. Letters after a location indicate its county of origin – ie. (W) Worcestershire; (S) Staffordshire, and (Wk) Warwickshire.)

Gloucestershire

Gloucester

City Feature:

John Hooper (c.1495–1555)
Full-length statue in Portland stone under crocketed
and pinnacled canopy
Sculptor Edward W. Thornhill
Canopy Medland & Maberley
Location St Mary's Square

*Bishop Hooper (c.1495–1555). Sculptor: E. W. Thornhill (1862).
Location: St Mary's Square, Gloucester.*

Bishop Hooper 'was burnt to ashes on this spot'. His statue faces the cathedral's west gate from which, passers-by will relate, his martyrdom was watched by Bishop Bonner, a supporter of Mary Tudor, through a window over the arch. The bishop wears the Geneva cap and gown recognised by Calvin's followers, including Bollinger whose views he embraced whilst chaplain to Sir Thomas Arundel. Arousing the hostility of the Bishop of Winchester, Hooper fled to the Continent, married, and settled in Zurich where Bollinger was pastor. One of the Somerset-born cleric's books written and printed in exile bears his inscription: 'John Hooper, in heart and by right an Englishman'.

In 1549, Hooper returned to join the revived English Reformation, preaching to large crowds at St Paul's Cathedral and giving the Lent sermons attended by the recently-crowned boy king Edward

VI. In 1550 he was nominated Bishop of Gloucester; against Cranmer's objections he was allowed to make revisions in the consecration ritual, but agreed in return to wear the traditional vestments associated with Rome's doctrine of transubstantiation in which, during mass, the bread and wine become, rather than symbolise, the flesh and blood of Christ. The bishop's newly-emblazoned crest – a lamb in a flaming bush – prompted his prediction of death, as had his farewell to his friend Bollinger: 'you shall hear that I was burned to ashes'.

Finding ignorance and apathy among the clergy in his diocese, Hooper revised the system of state appointments. Strict but not repressive, he won the affection of town and country parishioners through his industrious zeal. With Protestant persecution refuelled at Mary Tudor's accession in 1553, he stood his ground, and was imprisoned on a false pretext; after two grim years in the Fleet he was brought before Bishop Gardiner.

Condemned, Hooper was returned to Gloucester on horseback, and on the eve of his burning is said to have slept and prayed at a house in Westgate. As Victorian unveilings would, so Marian burnings made public spectacle, and thousands came to watch the St Mary's Gate martyrdom.

'This spot', site of many burnings, was marked by a modest 19th-century stone, removed in 1862 for the present powerful and decorative tribute, the sculptor of which was commissioned through competition. The foundation stone was laid with Masonic rites, after a solemn procession. On the 350th anniversary of the martyrdom, after restoration, the statue and canopy were unveiled by the mayor of Gloucester, with the costs again met by public subscription. It is the most beautiful and best-sited of the city's public monuments and features in Town Trail no. 2, 'Sculpture in the City of Gloucester' (available from the tourist centre).

Gloucester Selection

The Town Trail includes statues and war memorials, and building sculpture such as Medland & Maberley's market portico in Eastgate, featuring carvings of fish and fowl between arches. In the pediment is a foliage-festooned clock flanked by figures of Pomona, goddess of fruit trees, and Father Time carrying hour glass and scythe – THE EARTH IS THE LORD'S, AND THE FULNESS THEREOF – by Henry Frith (1856). Modern relief murals decorate Sainsbury's, British Home Stores and Boots.

Amongst the town's oldest sculptures is Charles II in crown and Roman tunic, eerily wasted, stone-carved by Stephen Baldwyn for the wheat market in 1662, found in pieces in a garden three centuries later and resited near St Mary's Square. (Baldwyn's jollier carving of the King can be seen on Worcester Guildhall). Off Westgate Street in the cement-rendered Fountain Inn's courtyard, a small pediment relief shows GVLIEMVS III's legendary ride upstairs on his white horse.

The park has Thomas Brock's bronze of Robert Raikes, editor of the Gloucester Journal and a founder of England's Sunday School movement. Gloucester still has dwellings similar to those opened for Raikes's schools to help workshop children. The statue, a cast of London Embankment's centenary marble, was unveiled on the Movement's 3rd Jubilee in 1930. Across Spa Field stands the pale form of Queen Anne, originally erected in Southgate, carved by John Ricketts the Elder (d.1734) whose petition in 1710 for freedom of the city was granted in return. At the Park's east corner, the Gloucestershire Regiment cenotaph carries a bronze sphinx.

In the cathedral close, a large stone cross to the Royal Gloucestershire Hussars has Adrian Jones's bronze reliefs of battle in foreign fields, also – unusually – reliefs of Second World War scenes. East of the town centre, off London Road in a corner of Hillfield Gardens, robust carvings adorn the 17th-century conduit, and biblical scenes enliven the 'King's Board' nearby.

Berkshire

Reading

Town Feature:

The Maiwand Lion
Cast-iron statue of lion with commemorative panels mounted on pedestal clad in Portland stone
Sculptor George Simonds
Location Forbury Gardens

Created as a symbol of courage, this snarling muscular beast stands over 13ft high, and measures 31ft from its wrinkled nose to the tip of its tail. It was erected by Berkshire residents, comrades and friends to 11 officers and 317 NCOs and men of the 66th Berkshire regiment. Their names are listed on the

The Maiwand Lion, memorial to soldiers of the Berkshire Regiment and the Battle of Maiwand, 1880. Sculptor: George Simonds (1886). Location: Forbury Gardens, Reading.

pedestal panels, one of which also bears the commendation made in Lord Primrose's dispatch:

> History does not afford any grander or finer instances of gallantry and devotion to Queen and Country than that displayed by the 66th Regiment at the battle of Maiwand on the 27th June, 1880

The battle was fought in a rearguard action which averted the annihilation of the entire force. A single column of the 66th retreated in the face of 40,000 Afghan warriors until 100 remaining men were trapped in a walled garden, passing on their colours as they fell. Finally, the two remaining officers and nine men formed up and made their final charge. This naked heroism was worthy of the VC, but it could not be awarded since no one was left to make the recommendation. The custom of carrying colours to be defended to the last in battle, however, was dropped after this.

The only survivor was a dog named Bobby, who was returned to England and decorated by Queen Victoria, but soon after suffered the ignominious fate of being knocked down in the road, stuffed, and displayed at the Regimental Museum in Salisbury.

At the monument's unveiling ceremony in December 1886, George Simonds's statue was said to be the largest in the world of a standing lion. The lifesize model was exhibited at the Royal Academy before being enlarged threefold and cast in nine sections, not without difficulty, by the same Pimlico founders that made the sphinxes for Cleopatra's Needle in London. The sculptor had observed London Zoo lions before committing himself to clay,

but was still criticised (rightly) for giving the lion an unnatural stance.

Almost 100 years after the unveiling of the Forbury Lion, a 'bold and imaginative' plan to reposition it over the inner ring road caused uproar and 'hurt', and the idea was dropped. For many, the monument has become the symbol of the town itself.

Reading Selection

The sculptor George Simonds belonged to the brewing family which helped build Reading's name for 'beer, biscuits and bulbs' — consumables all represented in Reading monuments. Simonds's marble statue of Queen Victoria looking like an imperious fishwife stands outside the old town hall, whilst his bronze of the Biscuit King George Palmer walks out with top hat and umbrella in Palmer Park.

Palmer received the freedom of the city at the unveiling in Broad Street (1891), and later that day day attended the ceremonious opening of the park, his gift to the town. His statue has been called 'inartistic', but is candidly assessed in a *History of Huntley and Palmers* (1967): '..it depicts the large Palmer nose and the slightly stooping posture, and authentically conveys an impression of dignity and power'.

Representing the 'bulbs', Palmer's friend Martin John Sutton, of Sutton's Seeds, gave the imposing coronation bronze of Edward VII, sculptured by George Wade, outside Reading Station. Edward gave several sittings, clad in Field Marshal's uniform as for the state opening of Parliament. (A replica was sent out to Madras, and a similar bronze stands in

Bootle). The pedestal of shaped polished granite carries a mouth-watering record 'of the commemorative celebrations and public rejoicings' held in Reading on coronation day in 1902.

Unwanted in New Delhi after Indian Independence (1948), C.S. Jagger's marble statue of Rufus Isaacs, 1st Lord Reading (1860–1935) was unveiled in George V Memorial Gardens in 1971. A Spitalfields fruiterer's son, Isaacs was variously cabin boy, fruiterer and Stock Exchange 'jobber' before qualifying for the Bar. He became Liberal MP in Reading's 1904 by-election (after George Palmer sought the Chiltern Hundreds), retiring on his appointment as Chief Justice. Subsequently, he was made Viceroy of India in 1921.

Windsor

Park Feature:

George III (1738–1820)
'The Copper Horse'
Large-scale bronze equestrian statue with copper coating, on granite 'rustic' pedestal
Sculptor (Sir) Richard Westmacott RA
Architect Sir Jeffry Wyatville
Location Snow Hill, Windsor Great Park

George III rides out on Snow Hill, robed as a Roman emperor and pointing the way back to Windsor Castle, his favourite home. His statue was designed to be as effective in distant silhouette as on approach, and makes a grand landmark at the focal point of the Long Walk, three miles from George IV's Gateway. (The double row of trees, planted by Charles II, was replanted in 1945 after succumbing to elm disease.)

Born and bred in England (unlike his predecessors), George III adored riding and stag hunting in Windsor Great Park, which he drained and farmed. As Britain's ruler he was inept, but as a royal 'squire', simple and inquisitive, he visited and quizzed his subjects in their homes, and wrote agricultural papers under the pen name Ralph Robinson. When he returned to Windsor after treatment for the disease which brought about his insanity, he was met by cheering crowds.

George's blameless but dull domesticity was rejected by his son the Prince Regent, later George IV, whose profligate ways caused much family discord. Despite this, the new king commissioned

George III (1738–1820). Architect: Sir Jeffry Wyatville. Sculptor: Sir Richard Westmacott, RA (1829). Location: Snow Hill, Windsor Great Park.

the statue the year after his father's death, whereupon the Duke of Wellington issued 25 tons of old brass ordnance to be used by Westmacott, who received £18,712 for the work. Ten-foot foundations were dug for the 30ft base, built up in massive stone blocks at a cost of £5000 and said to resemble Peter the Great's statue by Falconet in St Petersburg. The base was designed by Sir Jeffry Wyatville who was George IV's architect at the castle.

Designer and sculptor were present at the unveiling of the base in 1829. George IV performed the ceremony with the words 'Now, Westmacott, we depend on you for the remainder'; but he did not live to see delivery in 1831. The horse alone was so heavy that its wagon overturned on the Snow Hill, breaking off a leg which was soldered back *in situ*. Three weeks later, George III's plump form was placed astride 'the Copper Horse'. His son William IV, the new king, did not attend the unveiling.

In 1961, when the statue was cleaned, recoated with copper and filled with plastic compound preservative, several starlings and a wood pigeon were found to be nesting within the Farmer King's laurel crown.

Windsor Selection

Windsor's outdoor statues are all royal and all well-placed. Queen Victoria's bronze statue by Sir J.E. Boehm majestically crests the hill to the castle; her features are impassive, although her life at Windsor was eventful. Here she asked her cousin Albert Saxe-Coburg's hand in marriage, and here 22 years later, his cold hand in hers, became the 'Widow of Windsor'. As is common, Boehm's statue shows the queen in her later years. His equestrian statue of the Prince Consort, standing near Cumberland Lodge in Windsor Great Park, was given by the 'Women of England' for the Jubilee of 1887.

The former Court House, designed by Thomas Fitch, has a graceful niche statue of Queen Anne dated 1707. That of her consort, Prince George of Denmark, was given in 1713 by Christopher Wren, whose eminent father had supervised building after Fitch's death in 1688. Carved into the façade beneath Anne's are lines in Latin translated in a Windsor *Guide* of the 1800s: '*Sculptor thy art is vain, it cannot match the semblance of the matchless Anne's grace: thou mayest as soon to high Olympus fly, and carve the model of some deity*'. But Prince George, in Roman toga and periwig, has the handsomer image.

Beneath the castle's Round Tower, an equestrian statue carries the slight, bowed, Romanised form of Charles II towards his Quadrangle and State Apartments. A bronze cast from a wood carving by Grinling Gibbon, the horse is signed 'Josias Ibach Stadti Blarensis 1679 fundit'. The massive pedestal has four marble panels by Gibbon who, with Verrio, worked on the sumptuous interiors for Charles and his queen, Catherine of Braganza.

At the curve of Thames Street under the castle walls is W. Goscombe John's bronze of the domed-headed, dutiful soldier, Prince Christian Victor of Schleswig-Holstein, standing in an arched stone cubicle. A grandson of Victoria, he died at Pretoria in 1900. Replicas of his medals edge the bronze plaque, recording 'admiration of his qualities as a man and a soldier'. Near his statue, at the very end of Thames street, is the Lutyens monument in pale stone to King George V, 'first sovereign of the House of Windsor'.

Victoria's son-in-law (Christian's father, the Steward of Windsor,) officiated at the unveiling of her statue on the day after her 50th Jubilee. After the ceremony, as Victoria noted in her diary, 'amidst cheering, the ringing of bells, and bands playing, we drove up to the Castle. This completed the pretty and gratifying welcome to good old Windsor'.

Oxfordshire

Blenheim Palace

Park Feature:

John Churchill, 1st Duke of Marlborough
(1650–1722)
134ft Doric column surmounted by full-length lead statue of Duke with winged Victory
Sculptor Robert Pit
Architect Henry Herbert
Location Grand Avenue

Palace, park and column mark the triumphs of 'that glorious man' the Duke of Marlborough. The former

Column of Victory: raised to 1st Duke of Marlborough (1650–1722). Architect: Henry Herbert. Sculptor: Robert Pit (1730). Location: Grand Avenue, Blenheim Palace.

was an appreciative gift from Queen Anne, whilst the Column of Victory was raised by Marlborough's adoring and manipulative widow Sarah, one-time confidante of the queen. The superb Baroque mansion, built to the designs of Vanbrugh, was named after the Battle of Blenheim (1704), Marlborough's most resounding victory in the wars of the Spanish succession. The Marlboroughs with their designers planned the house and landscaped acres through subsequent political vicissitudes, proposing an obelisk to mark the demise of Woodstock Manor, which Vanbrugh had wanted to restore.

Marlborough's death intervened, but in 1730 Sarah's column was raised not to Woodstock and its romance of Henry II and Sweet Rosamond, but to the Duke himself. It satisfies every requirement for a large-scale monument, elevating the Duke's image over the Oxfordshire countryside whilst the enquiring traveller encounters, at the base, marble tablets chronicling Marlborough's brilliant campaigns.

Another tablet records, at no less length, the minutiae of laws passed to secure Blenheim for future Marlborough generations through the female line: 'The ACTS OF PARLIAMENT infcribed on this Pillar Shall stand as long as the BRITISH Name and Language laft'. The chronicler was an earlier admirer, Lord Bolingbroke: he later plotted Marlborough's downfall but here extolled his victories, declaring him 'The Hero not only of his Nation, but his Age'.

The hero's plans for an obelisk, originally designed by Nicholas Hawksmoor with lines by Pope (c.1727), can be studied in the Blenheim archives with Hawksmoor's *Explanation of an Obelisk*, and a drawing of Trajan's Column in Rome. The elevated statue retains its rich detail: the silhouette of Victory, winging from his hand; the muscles in the torso, and pleats in the toga; folds in the cloak; and at the corners of the pedestal, feathers of war eagles.

From the column's base the eye is drawn north along the Grand Avenue planted in battle formation, replaced by the 9th Duke in the 1920s but since decimated by Dutch Elm disease. Lime saplings now give an idea of early Blenheim. Southward across the bridge and 'Capability' Brown's spreading lake is the exuberant skyline of Vanbrugh's palace, begun the year after Blenheim.

Garden sculptures include the Bernini fountain on the Duchêne Water Terraces, created for the 9th Duke from 'Capability' Brown's grassing-over. Here amid fountains and classical figures, Visseau's Sphinxes bear the perplexed features of the Duchess. The same sculptor persuaded an assistant gardener, working on the rock garden, to model for the north-

the northernmost of a fine row of water-bathed caryatids and atlantes.

But it is the Column which dominates the park. 'It is extraordinarily moving and successful' declares the official *Guide* and, passing over the splendours of the house, 'There is nothing finer at Blenheim'.

Outside the walls, on the park's east boundary, lie the village of Woodstock and its church. From the village, visitors enter through the Triumphal Arch designed by Hawksmoor, completed the year after Marlborough's death and inscribed in Latin and English: '... The services of this great man to his country the pillar will tell you which the Duchess has erected for a lasting monument of his glory and her affection for him'.

Oxford

City Feature:

William Herbert, 3rd Earl of Pembroke (1580–1630)
Full-length bronze statue on stone pedestal
Sculptor Hubert Le Sueur
Location Old Schools Quad, Radliffe Square

Full of charm and self assurance, the earl stands at the entrance to the Bodleian Library. He has a pointed Elizabethan moustache and beard, and wears a sash over half-armour, with a lace collar and bucket-top boots; one hand rests on his hip, fingers curled.

As University Chancellor (1617–30) he gave his name to Pembroke college, and helped draw up its statutes, while to the Bodleian he gave the greater part of the Barocci collection of Greek manuscripts, stating that the MS should be borrowed by students if need be. The Bodleian, however, has always refused to loan material, even to Charles I and to Cromwell (who later bought and donated the rest of the collection).

The Earl's persona has something of the Elizabethan gallant, and it was from the queen's court that Pembroke was banished, when younger, for fathering the child of a lady-in-waiting. He regained influence as a courtier of James I, whose stone image now faces Pembroke's bronze across Old Schools Quad from 'a frontispiece', says Pevsner, 'prouder than any in England'. This is the tower of five orders, each stage showing a different classical architectural style. The fourth carries a sculpture of the University kneeling before James, attended by Fame; in the lacy pinnacled parapet are the Stuart Arms.

3rd Earl of Pembroke (1580–1630).
Sculptor: Hubert Le Sueur (resited 1950).
Location: Radcliffe Square, Oxford.

Oxford (and locality) Selection

Oxfordshire's commemorative statues are nearly all to be found in the city of spires and classical college gateways. The statues portray college founders, or benefactors of the University, each stone-carved character occupying a niche in the appropriate gate or porch. Like the stately but domestic architecture, their original purpose remains unchanged; the munificence they represent is still at work: decorative and intimate, they watch over the bicycle-busy streets, dark passages, stairways and quad lawns.

An early Oxford gateway can be seen in the remains of St Bernard's College (begun by Archbishop Chichele in 1437). Its St Giles entrance bears the original statue of the saint flanked by figures of the archbishop and of Thomas White, who founded St John's College (1557) on the site of St Bernard's.

From the inner gateway Eric Gill's statue of St John, carved in 1936, seems to have mellowed as pleasantly as Front Quad's late medieval buildings which it overlooks. A bronze statue of Charles I faces Queen Henrietta Maria across Archbishop Laud's Canterbury Quad from its west gateway – both are by Le Sueur. (Note in the royal arms the lion with lolling tongue, tired from the chase.)

Man and wife, Somerset landowners, ornament Wadham College's Front Quad. Nicholas Wadham appears in knightly armour, his wife Dorothy in a

Perhaps true to form, if not in fact, the earl's debonair head, separately cast, is supposed to have been rotated to suit the light from a window of Wilton House, Wiltshire, seat of the earls of Pembroke. In 1723 the head was given to visiting undergraduates, and carried for safe transport on horseback, followed by the body which the 7th Earl sent on by carrier.

After two centuries in the Upper Reading Room, the fully-assembled statue was resited (1950); a receptacle for rainwater, it is at risk from weathering but gives pleasure to many. Intended for indoor display, it now represents one of our earliest public freestanding bronze statues, and one of the few Oxford statues which is a movable ornament, rather than an element in the grand design.

Charles I (1600–1649). Sculptor: not known. Location: Gateway to Botanic Gardens, Oxford.

wimple. He holds the college building which she built to his plan after his death in 1609. The fine four-tier gate tower is a contemporary of Old Schools Quad's five-tier, and James I also figures here, hand on hip, above the more sober Wadhams.

Restrained grace haunts the narrow lane on New College gate tower, where founder William of Wykeham and the Angel Gabriel kneel before the Virgin. The same weathered group recurs inside the gateway with its 14th-century doors, and on the Muniment Tower across Great Quad.

For contrast, note the Madonna and babe with genial angels on St Mary's Church south porch in High Street. Baroque with a hint of the pagan, the group shows Flemish influence and is ascribed to Nicholas Stone. Commissioned by Laud's chaplain Dr Morgan Owen, its carvings were named in the indictment at Laud's trial. Later still, the Civil War brewing, it was fired on by an incensed Parliamentarian.

Oriel College's High Street entrance has a grey statue of Cecil Rhodes in a suit, accompanied by Edward VII and George V. Front Quad porch, above the words REGNANTE CAROLO forming the parapet in big stone letters, has large stone crowned figures of Edward II and Charles looking like Tweedledum and Tweedledee. A rare James II wearing a Roman toga ornaments the High's University College Upper Gateway, facing inward. Outside is a florid Queen Anne. Queen Mary and Dr Radcliffe on the Lower Gateway may be by Francis Bird, 1720 and 1717.

Among the statues of Tom Quad, Christ Church, is one of H.G. Liddell, father of Lewis Carroll's 'Alice'; his companion on Fell Tower is the educational reformer Dean Fell. Other rich sculptural ornament in Oxford takes the form of heraldic badges or allegorical set pieces, whilst gargoyle or corbel heads make early and modern caricatures of college characters. (See Magdalen College and two brothers' winged heads, carved for Christ Church in 1986 after life service as 'Scouts'.)

The most marvellous oddities (twice restored) are the 'Emperor' heads, unidentified Roman venerables raised on plinths around the curved frontage of Wren's Sheldonian Theatre in Broad Street. They are the work of William Bird of Oxford and John Dener (1666–7).

Quite extraordinary is a late-Victorian marble rendering of Percy Bysshe Shelley's drowned body, lying behind a grille under a domed canopy off Front Quad in University College. Like the poet, who was sent down in 1811, Onslow Ford's sculpture has

raised some eyebrows. A modern statue that attracts criticism is John Doubleday's bronze ('frighteningly legless' according to a recent Oxford Guide) of the classical scholar Sir Maurice Bowra (1898–1971) to be seen in Front Quad, Wadham College, where Bowra was 30 years warden.

The best known monument of town as opposed to gown is the Martyrs' Memorial, commemorating the Protestants Thomas Cranmer, Hugh Latimer and Nicholas Ridley, burned for heresy in Broad Street (1555–6). Their Caen stone statues were made by Henry Weekes in Chantrey's studio. A scholarly emulation of the Waltham Eleanor Cross by George Gilbert Scott (1841), its true purpose was to demonstrate anti-Tractarianism. It stands outside the church of St Mary Magdalen (restored as part of the scheme) and closes the southward view as St Giles Street approaches the heart of Oxford.

A copy at Banbury – long famed for its cross and cakes – commemorates the wedding of Queen Victoria's eldest daughter Vicky to the Crown Prince of Prussia; statues of Victoria, her eldest son and her grandson, were added in 1914.

Outside Oxford, at Port Meadow bridge, Wolvercote, a tablet shows a Bristol-Coanda monoplane which crashed here *en route* to Flying Corps manoeuvres in 1911. Locally carved in glittering, coloured polished granites it is a minor monument, but very rich.

Warwickshire

Coventry

City Feature:

'Self Sacrifice'
Lady Godiva (d. 1067)
Bronze equestrian statue on stone pedestal
Sculptor (Sir) William Reid Dick RA
Pedestal attrib. (Sir) Edwin Lutyens
Location Broadgate

Reid Dick's resourceful Godiva rides with bare bosom and bare haunches; the work, which has been called corny, is unremarkable but is not prudish or coy, nor even demure. From the 16th century onwards, visual images of Lady Godiva's ride through the streets of Coventry have revealed the

Lady Godiva (d.1067). Sculptor: Sir W. Reid Dick, RA (1949). Location: Broadgate, Coventry.

Saxon countess nude or semi-nude. The first known account given near the end of the 12th century, by the chronicler Roger of Wendover in his *Flores Historiarum*, preserves the lady's modesty beneath her mass of long hair.

A translation of the *Flores* from the Latin describes Godiva's incessant pleas for her husband Leofric to relax the taxes on the people of Coventry, and his exasperated challenge to 'Mount your horse naked' and ride through the town; but Godiva 'loosened her hair from its bands, and her whole body was veiled except her fair white legs'. After his lady's ride, modesty and honour secured, Leofric duly revoked Coventry's taxes and fixed Godiva's name as self-sacrificing founder of the city's liberties.

Not one version of this compelling tale tallies with Coventry's entry in *Domesday* as a rural settlement, largely in ownership of the countess, developing around the Benedictine abbey founded by her husband Leofric, Earl of Mercia. Godiva's ride belongs to legend rather than history.

The legend evolved to include a respectful citizenry shutting itself behind blank windows as its naked countess rode past – all but for one who looked, and was struck blind. He is first noted by a traveller in the margin of Camden's *Brittanica* as a town statue with a story (1659); Defoe, on his *Tour*, saw him 'looking out of a garret in the High Street'.

The original statue, probably depicting St George and altered during the Reformation, now stands in the Hotel Leofric, Broadgate. The household name first appears in O'Keefe's comic opera, *Peeping Tom of Coventry*; Tennyson's romantic poem *Godiva*, which established the popular Victorian legend, described his eyes 'shrivell'd into darkness in his head'.

Lines from Tennyson's work are carved in ornamental letters on the pedestal of Reid Dick's £20,000 statue unveiled at noon in 1949 by the wife of the American ambassador, on the ninth centenary (to the hour) of Godiva's ride. It was Coventry's first civic function to be televised.

The 80 year-old donor, W.H. Bassett Green, called

his statue 'a thing of beauty'; Mrs June Mills, who had appeared as Lady Godiva 'demurely draped in chiffon' at the town's George V Coronation Procession, was not present on this occasion but had visited the sculptor at work. She found the figure 'lovely, although perhaps a little too alert'. It is probably the country's only outdoor free-standing commemorative statue to show its subject nude. (Nelson's in Liverpool forms part of an ensemble.)

If not the most eminent of works, Reid Dick's 'Godiva' is Coventry's most popular free-standing sculpture. Commissioned before, completed during, and unveiled after the 1940s air raids, it has come to symbolise not only Self Sacrifice as inscribed on the pedestal, but also Coventry's regeneration from the ashes.

Coventry Selection

Amenity art featured strongly in Sir Donald Gibson's post-war rebuilding, with wall sculpture and murals, and later free-standing sculptures, specially commissioned. A 1980s' redevelopment staged a street display, resitings and restorations, including Alma Ramsey's war relief 'Guy and the Dun Cow', resited near Bull Yard.

The city's most prized public sculpture is the bronze composition of St Michael and the Devil by Sir Jacob Epstein (1958). The figures are spreadeagled above the steps of the inspired new cathedral, designed 1950–52 by Sir Basil Spence to rise from the rubble of the original blitzed cathedral.

Against the south wall of the ruin is Epstein's 'Ecce Homo', of Subiaco marble, made in 1935 and sited in 1969; the totem-like figure stares across to the new cathedral's doors of engraved glass, with handles derived from Epstein bronzes of children's heads. Near the old altar lies mitred Bishop Yeatman Biggs, clasping the original spired cathedral church, a bronze church monument made by Sir Hamo Thornycroft in 1925, and now open to the sky.

Other pre-war sculptures include images of Lady Godiva and Leofric amongst a profusion of painted statues that makes the Council House of 1913–20 a sight for sore eyes. The oak-carved figure of 'Peeping Tom' in the Hotel Leofric is dated from its medieval armour at c.1500, and an undated sandstone figure of Peeping Tom leers down from a modern footbridge across Hertford Street.

It leered down on, and was spruced up for, the town's 1877 Godiva procession, in which the leading lady was 'decently attired, a fine-looking woman, of light complexion and hair, and a good set of teeth'.

Coventry's few Victorian monuments all survived the Blitz, and two now stand in Greyfriars Green. The Wills Brothers' marble figure of Sir Thomas White (1883) looks down at a real bible, open in a case; nearby, James Starley's luxuriantly-bearded features are carved in marble on an elaborate monument by Whitehead of London.

The inventor, pioneer of Britain's bicycle industry, also founded the Coventry Sewing Machine Company. With its marble 'Fame', its rich granite columns and its appliquéd tricycle silhouettes – the 'Coventry Rotary' and 'Royal Salvo' – his bruised and battered memorial (c.1882), a relic of earlier city regeneration, deserves proper care.

Stratford-upon-Avon

Town Feature:

The Gower Memorial
William Shakespeare (1564–1616)
Seated bronze statue on high drum pedestal of Bath stone; figure on plinth (now detached) at each corner
Sculptor Rt. Hon. Lord Ronald Sutherland Gower
Architects Peigniet & Marnet, Paris
Location Bancroft Gardens

The bard holds court high above four of his own creations, a triumphant Prince Hal and a corpulant Falstaff, Hamlet with the skull and Lady Macbeth in her madness. At the pedestal's base, a Tragic or Comic bronze mask holds in its teeth a garland of flowers and fruits appropriate to the scene of History, Comedy, Philosophy or Tragedy enacted by each principal.

To modern eyes this may be hamming, but the elders of Victorian Stratford were proud to accept the work presented by Lord Gower, patron and practitioner of the arts, after 12 years' labour assisted by the sculptor M. Madrassi. Among other names inscribed on the pedestal are those of the three Paris foundries; Gower's was added later, against his wishes. The bronzes have been recently lacquered.

The original site by the Memorial Theatre (later burned down) was chosen by Lord Gower. The 1888 unveiling, with its civic ceremonial and verbal back-slapping, was attended by Gower's friend Oscar Wilde; he observed that whilst London had been the scene of Shakespeare's labours, 'you in Stratford have the hearth and ashes'. There was ironic comment on

The Gower Memorial: statue and ensemble to William Shakespeare (1564–1616). Architects: Peigniet & Marnet.
Sculptor: Rt. Hon. Lord R. S. Gower (1888). Location: Bencroft Gardens, Stratford on Avon.

the irritating Bacon theory, since thought to be based on disbelief that writing like Shakespeare's could belong to a glove maker's son.

Shakespeare's work is drawn from historical sources, or from existing dramas; basic facts about his own family and life in Stratford come from sparse public records. John Shakespeare's Henley Street house, much restored, survives as William's supposed birthplace, and the grammar school is his likely source of education. The Shakespeare Trust occupies New Place, bought in 1597 for his older wife Anne who was already pregnant at their marriage when Shakespeare was 18. Here she cared for their two daughters and son, Hamnet, who died in youth; her husband's London period as leading player and poet is reckoned from his mid 20s.

Other records and hearsay involve family friends, business associates or neighbours such as Sir Thomas Lucy from whom Shakespeare is surmised to have poached Charlecote deer, an episode mirrored perhaps in *The Merry Wives of Windsor*, written towards the end of Shakespeare's London career. Affable and easy in company, shrewd and careful in business, Shakespeare of the 'honeyed tongue' was a celebrated writer by the 1600s, when he seems increasingly associated with his provincial home.

The histories, some comedies, and *Romeo and Juliet* were already written; later years yielded such dark tragedies as *Hamlet*, *Othello*, *King Lear* and *Macbeth*. *The Winter's Tale* and *The Tempest* (c.1611) just preceded Shakespeare's retirement to Stratford.

He died, it is said, 'after a merry meeting' with Ben Jonson (for whom he was 'Sweet Swan of Avon') and Michael Drayton, and is buried at Stratford in Holy Trinity Church, where his monument is a painted alabaster bust, holding a quill, by Gerard

Janson. The prosaic features may not accord with people's concept of genius, but are believed to derive from a death mask prepared by Shakespeare's son-in-law, a Stratford physician.

The Bard brings continuing fame and income to his town, the streets of which are furnished with carved or mosaic Shakespearean images, or quotations from the works. Prettiest are the lead statue by John Cheere (1769), a gift of David Garrick, on the Town Hall; the Shakespearean scenes in terracotta on the Midland Bank, across the street; and hidden at the end of New Place Garden, a sweet stone fancy by Thomas Banks depicting Shakespeare between the Dramatic Muse and the Genius of Painting, and made for Alderman Boydell's Gallery in Pall Mall London, 1789. (Note Drama's headpiece.)

The latest, at time of writing, is John Blakeley's bronze of Sir Laurence Olivier in full armour, brandishing his sword as Henry V in his best-loved Shakespearean role. Described by a city publicist as 'mightily imposing', the £40,000 statue was unveiled in April 1990, within a year of Lord Olivier's death, and a week after the inauguration of the Maybird shopping centre (off the Birmingham road) where the statue stands. Both belong to the Bird Group, a local family firm.

The pedestal of Hornton stone carries the famous rallying call: 'Cry God for Harry, England and St George!' – and it is the Memorial Theatre (designed by Elizabeth Scott, 1928, with sculptures by Eric Kennington) that nurtures Shakespeare's true monuments, his works, which spread the wealth of his language and imagery far beyond Stratford to other countries and tongues. In Ben Jonson's words, Shakespeare's talent was 'not of an age, but for all time'.

Sir Edward Elgar OM (1857–1934). Sculptor: Kenneth Potts (1981). Location: High Street, Worcester.

Hereford & Worcester

Worcester (W)

City Feature:

Sir Edward Elgar OM (1857–1934)
Full-length bronze statue on pedestal (by Ben Davis)
from Forest of Dean limestone
Sculptor Kenneth Potts
Location High Street

Widely regarded as the greatest English composer since Purcell, the creator of 'Pomp and Circumstance'

is shown wearing his Cambridge Doctorate of Music gown and the Order of Merit, on a well proportioned pedestal close to the site of the family's High Street music shop.

Here Elgar augmented a mean living as a local musician talented enough to take first violin at the prestigious Three Choirs Festival, and as a music teacher whose mind was always too much on his own compositions. The slightly tense bronze figure with the familiar luxuriant moustache, one silhouetted hand held tightly behind his back, evokes the restless but engaging personality encountered on first hearing one of his compositions.

Across a noisy new road is the Cathedral, where the choirmaster's son would hurry from the earlier service at his Catholic church to hear the last Voluntary. By this and other means he taught himself, in his words, 'harmony, counterpoint, form, and, in short, the whole of the mystery of music'.

His career accelerated after marriage at 32 to one of his pupils, older and 'better' than he, who encouraged him to seek recognition in London. Within 15 years Elgar had achieved international repute as the composer of *The Enigma Variations* (1899), his portrait sequence of Worcestershire friends, and *The Dream of Gerontius*, from John Henry Newman's poem in a volume given as a gift at Elgar's wedding.

Alice Elgar nurtured her husband's brilliance as he sought inspiration in various homes, living for a time in the Malvern Hills, which were an important creative influence. In 1905, the year after his knighthood, Elgar returned to Worcester as England's foremost composer to receive the Freedom of the City from the mayor, his boyhood friend Hubert Leicester. Almost 20 years later, he was appointed Master of the King's Musick.

Later, in a book by Hubert Leicester, Elgar wrote of his 'undimmed affection' for the city where he was raised and educated, but he never erased the hurt of his too-humble beginnings; his speech maintained a Worcestershire ring, while his dress and bearing emulated that of a country gentleman. Even so, Worcestershire's quintessential Englishness echoes in such works as the *Variations*, and the much loved *Pomp and Circumstance* marches.

The Elgar family's music shop and much else has been cleared to accommodate new roads, and to create the 1980s pedestrianisation for which the statue was commissioned after the requisite £25,000 was raised by public subscription. The idea for the statue came from owners of a music shop near the cathedral, and the sculptor, then working at the Royal Worcester Porcelain Company, offered a maquette to the committee of local Elgarians, whose approval was confirmed by the Royal Academy. After the unveiling, performed by H.R.H. the Prince of Wales, a celebratory concert at Worcester Cathedral rang out Elgar's legacy.

The bronze cast of Potts's original maquette, the gown in which Elgar is portrayed, other sculptures of the composer and much memorabilia can be seen at Elgar's birthplace, a cottage in Broadheath three miles west of Worcester. The town's tourist office in the Guildhall provides an Elgar Trail leaflet to follow through city and county.

Worcester (and locality) Selection

A call at the Tourist Office is recommended, if only to marvel at the 18th-century Guildhall's façade featuring exuberant painted statuary by Stephen Baldwyn, a rich avowal of the Royalist stance taken by 'the faithful city' in the Civil War. Outside the Shire Hall, a battered marble Queen Victoria shows the work of the fashionable sculptor Thomas Brock (born in Worcester 1847), another beginner at the Royal Worcester Porcelain Factory. Birmingham has a bronze copy.

Two of Brock's early statues stand in Kidderminster (15 miles northwest of the town). The first, of the great divine Richard Baxter (1615–1691), was unveiled in Kidderminster Bull Ring in 1875. The Dean of Westminster officiated, as he had a year earlier at Bedford's unveiling of its statue by Boehm to John Bunyan, a contemporary of Baxter.

Gaunt in Sicilian marble, the author of *The Saints' Everlasting Rest*, and the hymn 'For all the Saints' — favourites in this locality — now sermonizes over the Ring Road, outside the church 'which had the chiefest of my labours, and yielded me the greatest fruits of comfort'. (Nearby *see* Drury's fine bronze war memorial, a feeling variation on the Winged Victory theme). Brock's other marble figure portrays Sir Rowland Hill, originator of the Penny Post in 1840, outside Kidderminster Town Hall. Erected by '200,000 SUBSCRIBERS THROUGHOUT THE THREE KINGDOMS, THE COLONIES AND THE CONTINENTS OF EUROPE AND AMERICA', it was commissioned one year after the unveiling of Baxter's statue, and is the essence of Victorian public statuary. Time-capsule items buried beneath it in 1881 include a set of British stamps, and a mite (half-farthing).

East of Kidderminster in Bromsgrove, Elgar's sculptor Kenneth Potts has since made a bronze of the classicist and poet A.E. Housman, a native of the town. Elgar's contemporary is shown striding with cap and walking stick into the landscape that permeates poems like *In Summertime on Bredon*, or his best-loved work *A Shropshire Lad*.

Nearby in pedestrianised High Street *see* the cast of 'Dryad and Boar' modelled by Louis Weingarten of the Bromsgrove Guild (founded *c*.1900 and disbanded 1966). The mould of 1892 was restored by Terry Simons. And at Whitley Court (English Heritage), where Elgar accompanied his father on piano tuning trips, a huge fountain displays Perseus's Rescue of Andromeda, sumptuous in Portland stone, by James Forsyth.

West Midlands

Birmingham (Wk)

City Feature:

Horatio Nelson, 1st Viscount Nelson, Duke of
Brontë (1758–1805)
Bronze full-length statue in ensemble of symbolic
objects, on marble cylindrical pedestal
Sculptor (Sir) Richard Westmacott RA
Location Bull Ring

This considerable tribute, inaugurated on October 25th, 1809, is claimed as the earliest public memorial erected to Nelson's memory. Hereford, too, records completion of its grand memorial column in 1809, but with no definite unveiling date – it was begun in 1806 to the design (later modified) of Thomas Hardwick. Both are amongst the earliest public memorials dedicated to a deserving citizen, rather than a

Admiral Lord Nelson (1758–1805). Sculptor: Sir Richard Westmacott (1809). Location: formerly Bull Ring, Birmingham.

member of royalty, and they mark the unprecedented depth of feeling that Nelson inspired after his glorious victory and death at the Battle of Trafalgar in October 1805. Like Liverpool's (partly by Westmacott, unveiled in October 1813), both were subscribed within weeks of Nelson's death.

Following petitions whilst on his Midlands tour of 1802, Nelson had visited Hereford in August and Birmingham in September, to a welcome of crowds, banners and speeches. His carriage was unyoked and pulled by the populace; he toured Birmingham factories and foundries, including the famed Soho works where special medals were struck; his party attended a dinner at which Lady Hamilton sang, and at his dismay that an old seaman had not received a service medal, the ageing Matthew Boulton (visited on his sickbed by Nelson) offered his own.

Just over a fortnight after the city received news, in November 1805, of the tragic victory, a meeting was called to decide on a memorial 'monument, statue or pillar'. Perhaps aware of its novelty, the sculptor Westmacott left a long account of Birmingham's tribute in which he depicted Nelson 'invested with the insignia of those honours by which his sovereign and distant princes distinguished him'. The hero appears bare-headed and brooding, his right sleeve empty but both eyes intact (the right eye was blinded, but not lost, at Santa Cruz). His arm rests on an anchor, and next to him is a ship, its figurehead 'Victory' holding aloft a wreath.

Some years after the inauguration, a local trader bequeathed to the city council sixpence a week for keeping the statue clean; this it seems to have done.

At time of writing, the ensemble overlooks the market stalls of Birmingham's Bull Ring, itself a period piece. Flashy, tacky and dilapidated, overlooked by high-rise and ring-road, it is soon to be rebuilt. Its tenant traders hold it dear, it is an unusually intact example of planning philosophy, but it resembles a period style that has lost favour, even with the theorists.

Meanwhile the ensemble's sculptured drum pedestal showing Birmingham 'in a dejected attitude, murally crowned, mourning her loss . . .' and the 'iron palisadoes, in the form of boarding pikes, connected by a twisted cable' – precursors of Victorian solidity – make contrasts with much of modern Birmingham.

Birmingham Selection

Successive city revamps have done some rum things to Birmingham statues. They have been resited, put

'Conversation Piece': group comprising bronzes of Matthew Boulton (d.1809), James Watt (d.1819) & William Murdoch (d.1839). Sculptor: William Bloye (1956). Location: formerly Broad Street, Birmingham.

into store, revived as bronze casts from the marble, truncated to make busts, or dispatched to parks.

Striking examples include William Bloye's bronze *Conversazione* between Boulton, Watt and Murdoch of the Soho Foundry, gilded at its 1956 unveiling in Broad Street, later painted yellow ochre and now to be repatinated (and resited). The bronze statue of Sir Robert Peel by Peter Hollins, erected in 1868 outside the Exchange, was railed off against 'Tories and Protectionists', later resited, knocked down by a lorry in 1926, and has finally come to rest outside the Police Training Headquarters in Pershore Road. A stint outside Birmingham Town Hall brought forth a joke, 'Why is the town hall like an orange . . .?' This piece of Victoriana has lost its pedestal but acquired a jazzy black-and-white tiled plinth.

A journey through this changing city introduces some memorable images in unexpected places. Near Chamberlain Square, Thomas Woolner's full-length statue (1880) of the blameless looking George Dawson emerges from a shrubbery with a beautiful railed surround. It was rated 'ludicrously bad', and stored; a replacement by F.J. Williamson survived until 1959, later to reappear cast as a bronze bust, showing Dawson with foaming forked beard staring angrily across Small Heath Park, on the Coventry Road. The reconstituted Woolner is part of a 1980s development.

Chamberlain Square has two Victorian statues from storage, a marble figure of James Watt by Alexander Munro (1866) and a bronze cast from J.F. Williamson's graceful marble of Joseph Priestley. Both were members of Birmingham's Lunar Society, which met at full moon (an aid to travel) to discuss science and industry. Priestley's statue was unveiled on the 1874 centenary of his unwitting discovery of oxygen as 'dephlogisticated air', and it shows him with his mercuric oxide and lens.

Other persistent images include the square's luxuriant Gothic clock tower and fountain of 1880 with a marble medallion of Joseph Chamberlain, 'during whose mayorality many great public works were notably advanced'. Woolner has not spared his long, sharp nose. Outside St Philip's Cathedral, a small but personable bronze of Bishop Gore (1852-1932), by T. Stirling Lee, was unveiled by the Archbishop of Canterbury in 1914; bare headed, in convocation robes and with pastoral staff, it was, according to the subject, 'horribly like me'.

Also in this big public churchyard, find the pedestal to John Heap and William Badger, killed while building the Town Hall (1833), and, in high relief on a soot-encrusted obelisk, the powerful features of a moustached military man, one Thomas Unett, who 'met death in the calm and undaunted spirit of a Christian soldier'.

Off Five Ways Roundabout in Auchinleck Square shopping centre, a statue of Field Marshal Sir Claude Auchinleck, arms folded, in desert boots and shorts, is the work of American sculptress Fiore de Henriques (1965). It marks construction of the centre by Auchinleck's company in 1965. Over the roundabout presides John Sturge, carved in Portland stone by John Thomas, who died before its completion (1862). Sturge, Quaker corn merchant, 'laboured to bring freedom to the negro slave, the vote to the British workman and the promise of peace to a war worn world'. He and his hand maidens Peace and Charity (with Temperance behind) hold their own against the latest skyline of office towers.

The city ring road and roundabouts have huge mural or mosaic memorials to individuals representing all aspects of Birmingham, as well as world heroes such as J.F. Kennedy, whose memorial mural is in St Chad's Circus. Holloway Circus has a bronze nude, 'Hebe' (daughter of Zeus and Hera, and cup bearer to the gods), draped across an ornamental fountain 'placed here to mark the commencement of the inner ring road'. She looks vulnerable, but not out of place. Birmingham is a city of incongruities.

Birmingham's oddest (and wittiest) work is the 'Wattilisk', worth seeing outside the new red-brick Crown Court, Newton Street. Of black Indian granite, about 12ft high, it features a series of heads diminishing in size but gaining in detail with height. The top one has James Watt's sardonic, half-smiling features, reputedly after Chantrey's marble bust of 1835, but each one becomes less defined down to the plain block-base. By Vincent Woropay (1988), the work was inspired by Watt's 'polyglyptic' machines used in copying sculptures.

Walsall (S)

Town Feature:

Dorothy Wyndlow Pattison (1832–1878)
Full-length bronze statue on polished Peterhead granite pedestal with bronze relief panels
Sculptor F.J. Williamson
Location The Bridge

A metal plaque summarising Sister Dora's story claims, not entirely accurately, that she 'became the country's first woman, other than members of the royal family, to be commemorated by a statue'. The sculptor has given her a queenly presence in her full-skirted uniform, with surgical scissors hanging at the waist, and a bandage in her hand. Her work in Victorian working Walsall is harshly but movingly shown on the pedestal reliefs, added after the original Sicilian marble statue was unveiled with feasting and fireworks in 1886. A lifetime later, in 1956, the townspeople paid for a bronze cast of the weathered original to be erected in its place.

Dorothy's repressive father forbade her to follow Florence Nightingale to the Crimea, but after her mother's death she left the family's Yorkshire home to join an Anglican sisterhood for nursing training, adopting the title 'Sister Dora'. Soon after, a scarlet fever epidemic sent her to the cottage hospital at Walsall. When larger premises were opened, with Sister Dora in charge of domestic services, her ideals of thrift and hard work built the new hospital into a national model of economic efficiency. Until her

Dorothy Wyndlow Pattison, 'Sister Dora' (1832–1878). Sculptor: F. J. Williamson (1886, bronze cast 1956). Location: The Bridge, Walsall.

death 13 years later, she 'worked ceaselessly to establish a professional medical service in the town'.

A hard task master, but hardest on herself, Sister Dora was sustained by a deep religious conviction which was never imposed on staff or patients. Her medical knowledge impressed the hospital surgeon who urged her to train as a doctor, but she rejected the years of study for practical nursing. In the same cause, despite offers, she consistently denied herself the warmth and affections of marriage. Working tirelessly through Walsall's epidemics or industrial disasters, sometimes single-handed, her courage and devotion became legendary.

A relief panel shows Dora comforting relatives of victims at the Pelsall Hall pithead disaster of 1872, in which 22 men were entombed; although she was not at the grim scene of the 1875 boiler explosion, this is also shown. Nursing the dying she met one of the foundry owners, with whom she conducted a secret love affair through official meetings and correspondence between 'Sister Dora' and 'Mr Jones'. Her final letter, written in the final stages of cancer (which she also kept secret), addresses Mr Jones by his first name.

Dorothy's letters are printed in a booklet, *Sister Dora* (Walsall Local History Centre, 1988). They give vivid glimpses of her daily round. Other accounts show that the affection of patients, staff and doctors derived not only from Sister Dora's technical abilities but from her 'bright, sunshiny way ... medicine of the best kind'.

The cast for her statue's bronze replica, originally kept in the General (Sister Dora) Hospital, can now be seen in the Council House foyer. The statue itself was cleaned in 1988, by a team of Walsall Manor Hospital porters using toothbrushes, as part of an appeal for a new hospital.

Walsall Selection

Further south in Hurst Hill, Coseley, a neatly bearded bust on a small column commends I. J. Baker, a family doctor who 'endeared himself to all' and remained long in local memory, especially of poor families whom he visited without payment, sometimes leaving money for food or coal, or kneeling to pray at their death beds. His bust was tended regularly by a local resident for years after it was erected in 1914.

Shropshire

Shrewsbury

Town Feature:

Charles Darwin (1809–1882)
Seated bronze statue on polished granite pedestal
with stepped base
Sculptor Horace Montford
Location Castlegates Library

His eyes deep-set beneath bushy brows, Charles Darwin looks up from a sheaf of papers, marking his place with a finger. Sitting with his knees crossed outside the library, the former school of which he

was an illustrious old boy, the domed-headed, full-bearded figure is immediately recognisable; with other 19th-century figures like Tennyson and Disraeli, Darwin projects an image which remains fresh in the public eye.

Perhaps this is because no serious challenge has ever been made to Darwin's revolutionary theory of the evolution of species by means of natural selection, propounded at a time when the biblical account of Creation was not popularly questioned. Subsequent knowledge has elaborated Darwin's theory of evolution, but not challenged it.

Charles Darwin was not a diligent scholar at school or at Edinburgh University where he studied medicine, his father's calling. In 1828 he went to Cambridge to prepare for the Church, there meeting botanists, and the self-taught geologist Adam Sedgwick, who encouraged and influenced him. After

Charles Darwin (1809–1882). Sculptor: Horace Montford (1896). Location: Castlegates Library, Shrewsbury.

gaining a 'pass' BA, Darwin was recommended by his tutor and mentor, the great botanist Ralph Henslow, as ship's naturalist on board the survey ship HMS *Beagle*, and in December of that year (1831), he set sail on an exploratory circumnavigation of the world.

Having observed the teeming wildlife and the rich fossil remains in South America, the Galapagos Islands, Australia and other Pacific lands, Darwin returned a convinced Evolutionist. He now completely accepted Lyell's *Principles of Geology*, which he had begun to read at Cambridge, and the 'blasphemous' evolutionary concepts of the French naturalists Buffon and Lamarck, as well as the ideas of his own grandfather Erasmus (lifelong friend of Darwin's other grandfather, Josiah Wedgwood).

During the 20 years in which he continued his studies and his classification of the collection from his *Beagle* trip, Darwin worked on his book explaining his unique contribution, the process of natural selection by which evolution could credibly have occurred. 'The Origin of Species', a hasty outline of the intended book, was urged on Darwin by friends aware of the similar theory of the zoologist Alfred Wallace, with whom Darwin was to read a joint paper at a meeting of the Linnean Society in London (1858). *The Origin* appeared the following year.

The ensuing furious debate did nothing to dissuade Darwin from producing a further remarkable range of pioneering works which themselves would have established an enduring scientific reputation. Meanwhile this gentle and timid personality, dogged by lifelong ill health (probably hypochondrical), was shielded from the rage and derision of the Victorian establishment by his wife Emma, also a Wedgwood, and by friends and fellow scientists.

His frowning and powerful statue does credit to its position on the old school forecourt, at a lofty corner overlooking the gates of Shrewsbury's red sandstone castle. The site outside the Free Library was selected by the Shrewsbury sculptor Horace Montford, commissioned in 1896 after testimonials were received from Hamo Thornycroft and Onslow Ford.

An oval plaque at the library door gives a brief history of the stone buildings which went up between 1594–1630 and were occupied until 1882 (the year of Darwin's death) by the school, founded by Edward VI in 1592. Other famous pupils were Sir Philip Sidney and Judge Jeffreys. The buildings were reopened as a library in 1983 after a complete renovation.

The statue's bow-fronted pedestal of beautiful dark, polished granite carries a single word in upraised letters: DARWIN. His chair, ornamented with scallop shells, carries a small inscription at the back: 'Erected by the Shropshire Horticultural Society'. Records reveal that the public subscription fund for a county memorial having failed its target, the Society stepped in and covered costs of at least £1000 in sculptor's fees.

As is usual, there seems to be no formal maintenance programme for the statue, now owned by the Borough, but one feels that help will be forthcoming from other quarters should the need arise in the future.

Shrewsbury Selection

Looking out on High Street in the narrow Market Square is Marochetti's imposing bronze statue of Robert Clive, 1st Baron Clive of India, with sword, ruffles and tricorn hat. A native of Shrewsbury, Clive was the town's mayor for 1772 and its MP from 1761–74. The statue was erected c.1860. A wall tablet on St Mary's Church, St Mary's Street recalls Robert Cadman (1711–1739)

'who by'n attempt to fly from this tall spire
Across the Sabrine stream he did acquire
His fatal end. 'Twas not for want of skill
Or courage to perform the task he fell.
No, no, a faulty cord being drawn too tight
Hurried his Soul on high to take her flight
Which bid the Body here good Night
Febry 2nd 1739 aged 28'.

On London Road at the eastern approach to the town, by the ugly mass of the Shire Hall (1967) a 133ft column carries the Coade stone statue of the Peninsula veteran 1st Viscount Hill, modelled by Joseph Panzetta in 1817. At the column's base are four lions of Grinshill stone.

At the southwest corner of the river loop, the Dingle in the Quarry Park is ornamented with various statues. The lead copy of the Farnese Hercules, thought to be by John Nost, was made for Condover Hall. 'Sabrina', on her shell-moulded stone plinth, was carved for the Earl of Bradford by the Birmingham sculptor Peter Hollins in 1846, and presented to Shrewsbury in 1879. And the Victorian figure of an eagle erected by the Shoemakers' Guild in Kingsland, southwest of the Quarry across the river, was re-erected here in 1887.

Also across the Kingsland Bridge is the later Shrewsbury School by Sir Arthur Blomfield, opened in 1882; a war memorial of 1923 carries A.G. Walker's bronze statue of Sir Philip Sidney in armour, his helmet under his arm. His friend and biographer Fulke Greville entered Shrewsbury School on the same day as Sidney in 1564. Greville recounted Sir Philip's chivalry in an incident where, mortally wounded in battle against the Spanish at Zutphen (1586), and thirsting from loss of blood, he passed on his water bottle to another soldier.

Staffordshire

Lichfield

City Feature:

Samuel Johnson (1709–1784)
Seated statue in Yorkshire limestone on stone pedestal with carved relief panels
Sculptor Richard Cockle Lucas
Location Market Place

Dr Johnson's large and melancholy form broods outside his market square birthplace in 'a ponderosity of stone', as described by the visiting American Consol, the writer Nathanial Hawthorne, almost 20 years after the statue was given to Lichfield by the diocesan chancellor in 1838. The admirable pedestal carvings of scenes from Johnson's life show influence, says Pevsner, of Donatello's *schiacciato* work (very light, low relief).

According to the sculptor, the relief of Johnson's Penance was carved not by an assistant, but 'direct from the mind to the stone'. The intensely-worked statue shows Dr Johnson in the robes of his Oxford LL.D., conferred in 1755, years after poverty cut short his studies at Pembroke.

In contrast across the square is Percy Fitzgerald's bronze of Boswell (1908) natty in a tricorn hat, cane behind back, sword at side and notebook under arm, ever alert to the main chance. Small pedestal medallions portray Johnson's London circle, among them Garrick, student of Johnson the inept local schoolmaster, and Reynolds, whose portraits provided models for the Lichfield statues' heads.

Other reliefs (repeated on Fitzgerald's statue of Johnson in London) show the friends at Johnson's London Club, and on their *Journey to the Western Islands of Scotland*. (Johnson's version came out in 1775.) Johnson, literary lion and pioneering compiler of the English *Dictionary*, set out as an unknown for

Samuel Johnson (1709–1784). Sculptor: R. C. Lucas (1838). Location: Market Place, Lichfield.

London with Garrick in 1737. Another scene shows his stay with Boswell at the *Three Crowns* Inn, next to his birthplace, 40 years on.

In 1855, Nathanial Hawthorne, visiting Uttoxeter about 30 miles north, protested at the local people's ignorance of Dr Johnson's Penance for his youthful refusal to man his sick father's bookstall in Uttoxeter. This act had preyed on Dr Johnson's mind until one market day in his old age, he kept lone vigil in the wind and rain amongst the shoppers and stallholders. The story is told in Boswell's celebrated *Life* of Johnson (1791). The town met Hawthorne's complaint with a copy of the *Penance* carved by Lucas, installing it on the new market place conduit.

The Uttoxeter Heritage Centre has material on the *Penance*, and about the annual ceremonial wreath-laying followed by coffee and rum at the White Hart

Hotel. The small pedimented conduit now serves as a newspaper stand. The Lichfield Birthplace Museum holds memorabilia, and information about the monuments and the eccentric R.C. Lucas. He retouched his 'literal, matter-of-fact' sculpture 21 years after the unveiling, having won few commissions since; better known for his wax portraits, his *forté* is perhaps reflected in the Lichfield reliefs.

Lichfield Selection

On Lichfield Cathedral (south face) Dr Johnson, reading a book, appears amongst a pantheon of sovereigns, saints and deities that include amongst their number five medieval statues. Vigorous 19th-century carving is signed 'W.R. Ingram'. (In the south transept, *see* busts of Johnson and Garrick by Richard Westmacott, 1793.) Westward in the War Memorial gardens, St George and the Dragon tussle under a pedimented arch.

Across the road by the library is a locally-carved sailor with a rifle, rejected for York's 1914–18 memorial as too warlike. In the park, a stone statue of Edward VII was a gift of the sculptor, Robert Bridgeman, then city Sheriff (1908). As Mayor Bridgeman, his stone masonry firm installed Lady Scott's bronze of Captain Smith of the Titanic (*Note* the dedication, ending with Commander Smith's reputed words: "BE BRITISH".) The statue, accepted grudgingly by the city after rejection by Smith's native Hanley, was unveiled in July 1914.

Stoke-on-Trent

City Feature:

Josiah Wedgwood (1709–1784)
Full-length bronze statue on stone pedestal
Sculptor Edward Davis
Location Wilton Square

Josiah Wedgwood I is commemorated by this well-known bronze, centred on the forecourt of the North Stafford Hotel and facing Stoke station. It was shown at the International Exhibition of 1862 and unveiled in 1863, attended by processions from each of the six towns; 'God Save the Queen' was sung, cannon were fired and dignitaries dining at the hotel were served *Crème de Bouzy* Champagne at every sumptuous course. The hotel and station, with their graceful Jacobean gables, were just over ten years old.

Josiah Wedgwood (1709–1784). Sculptor: Edward Davis (1862). Location: Wilton Square, Stoke-on-Trent.

'The Father of the Potteries' is shown buckled and bewigged, one thumb firmly wrapped round a handle of his famous copy of the Portland Vase. The sculptor features the ornamental reliefs and the special seal of the Portland Vase, *tour de force* of the Potter's art, copied in black and white jasper ware from the Roman original of glass. Wedgwood's 50 reproductions of 1790 marked the peak of a career dating from his father's death, when nine-year-old Josiah left school to work for his brother Thomas.

At 14 Josiah was apprenticed to learn 'the Art, Mistery, Occupation or Imployment of Throwing and Handleing', being the fourth generation in a family of Potteries craftsmen. He showed skill in all aspects of the craft, although incapacitated by smallpox; his illness gave the embryo designer time for study and thought.

Wedgwood's name and fortunes were established by his creamware, cheap table crockery developed at his Burslem works which opened in 1759. Its popularity ended the Delft monopoly in 'useful' wares, guaranteeing Wedgwood's home and export trade. By 1766 the creamware was called 'Queen's ware', after delivery of a 1,000-piece tea set for Queen Charlotte; that year Wedgwood cut the first sod in Brindley's Trent and Mersey Canal, opened his London showrooms, and began to build his model factory, village and mansion in Stoke.

The pottery was named 'Etruria' after the mistaken belief that Greek vases (most of which had at that time been found in Italy) were of Etruscan origin. Etruria produced ornamental ware, notably black basaltes, carrying the Wedgwood mark; the famous thousand-piece 'Frog' service was delivered to Catherine the Great's marshland palace ('La Grenouillère') near St Petersburg, and by the the mid-1770s Josiah had developed his jasper ware, the most important ceramic innovation since the Chinese discovery of porcelain. John Flaxman and other young artists produced neo-classical designs for this new medium.

After production of the Portland Vase, semi-retirement brought membership of the Royal Society (1783), and varied work such as collaboration on researches with Joseph Priestley. Josiah died on his daughter Sukey's birthday, and soon after she married the son of his friend Erasmus Darwin. In 1809 Sukey became mother of Charles, whose name, like Wedgwood's, was to become a household word.

In 1957 a bronze cast of the statue was erected outside Wedgwood's Barlaston factory, where the family continued in ownership until the mid-'70s. It was made from the original plaster cast which was discovered in a storage depot by a corporation worker, and subsequently repaired by Wedgwood's chief modeller, Eric Owen (d.1975).

Wedgwood's *Experiments Book*, and examples of his art, are on show in Barlaston's Wedgwood Museum, which also holds the firm's archives. In Stoke Church, John Flaxman's relief portrait of 1803 bears the essential tribute to Josiah, 'Who converted a rude and inconsiderable Manufactory into an elegant Art and An important part of the National Commerce'.

Stoke-on-Trent Selection

Outside the 1950s Minton Factory, in the London Road, is Thomas Brock's bronze of Herbert Minton's nephew, Colin Minton Campbell (1827–1885), 'A successful manufacturer, A leading townsman, and generous friend'. Props include a model of the Minton 'Stork' pedestal that was made in majolica for conservatories, supporting a tazza (a shallow ornamental bowl with handles). The Duchess of Sutherland unveiled the statue in 1877.

On the Stone road south of Stoke, past the grim Sutherland Mausoleum at Trentham Park, a statue and column dominate the skyline; this is the 1st Lord of Sutherland (d.1833), supposedly presented by Francis Chantrey as the Shepherd of his People. (The first cast, 1834, stands on Ben Vraggie in Sutherland.) Charles Winks designed the column (1836) and C.H. Tatham the mausoleum, 1807–8.

Humbler monuments include the small obelisk (by R. & W. Burt) at the south end of London Road by the infilled canal, in 'grateful memory' of Timothy Trow, still recalled locally as 'the lad that jumped into the cut'. In April 1894 the tram conductor, a non-swimmer, saved the life of a drowning child, but lost his own life. His father received a black-edged certificate, and Stoke, in October, this publicly-subscribed tribute.

Near Burslem's blackened town hall — featuring a bulgy clock tower and lofty caryatids in a forest of muscular elbows — a brick screen bears a bronze relief profile of Enoch Arnold Bennett (1867–1931), a modest piece of memorial art, vulnerable and unloved. On the Wedgwood Memorial Institute façade, Josiah inspects his Portland vase amongst rich terracotta reliefs of the months of the year; his agreeable image was unveiled in 1873 by Sir Smith Child, himself honoured 20 years on by 'the Ladies of Tunstall' with a market place clock tower.

Perhaps as an antidote to pomposity, the city council is bravely erecting new works (see in Gilmore Place, Hanley, 'My Head' by Dhruva Mistry; also 'Man Can't Fly' by Ondré Nowakowski for the new road near Stoke Station). Stiff commemorative statues by Colin Melbourne include the visored 'Steel Man' outside Hanley City Museum, marking the struggle against the works closure (1974) and repeating in mirror-polished stainless steel the 'Vic' Theatre's original gladiatorial logo for its documentary 'Fight, Fight, Fight for Shelton Bar'. Hanley's new centre has a bronze of footballer Stanley Matthews, a townsman, unveiled by himself: 'A magical player, by the people, for the people'.

The people, faced with their new sculptures, are prone to cry 'monstrosity', whilst others argue that this reaction confirms the works as art. Meanwhile Stoke's true monuments — working buildings rich in brick and terracotta and tile — conceal hard-graft history beneath decades of city grime. A good clean up would bring justifiable pride to a city whose face mirrors its continuing traditional industry, as few other English cities can.

Central Eastern Counties Gazetteer

(Note: The Central Eastern Counties appear in loosely topographical order. Within each county, monuments are listed under their locations, which appear in alphabetical order.)

Derbyshire

Clay Cross

Town Feature:

'Weeping Angel'
Full-length marble statue with cluster column on pedestal base.
Sculptor John Holden
Stonemason E Tinkler
Design Rollinson & Son
Location Danesmoor Cemetery

Grief stands straight and tall but with downcast head, an eye obscured by one hand. From her other hand hangs a palm frond, whilst the uncovered eye gives a stare of blank sorrow. This beautiful and well-loved monument, which faces the street, commemorates 45 colliery workers, fathers and sons, lost in the disastrous Park House Pit explosion of November 1882.

The pedestal carrying the names of the dead is signed by the stone mason, a Clay Cross man. The architects were from Chesterfield, the sculptor from Sheffield. Half the cost of £160 was paid by fellow workers and public subscription, the rest from the disaster fund. After the unveiling in 1884, *The Derbyshire Courier* reported: 'the design is chaste, free from any frivolity of ornamentation, and is of a solemn character'.

In the disaster centenary year, the monument was

'The Weeping Angel'. Design: Rollinson & Son. Sculptor: John Holden (1884). Location: Danesmoor Cemetery.

refurbished by the Parish Council and costs met by the Biwater Company, formerly the Clay Cross Company who sank the Park House Pit in June 1866 close to the village of Danesmoor. Colliers' houses built by the company at this time, and known as the 'Blocks', were demolished late in the 1960s, soon after the National Coal Board closed the pit and levelled the tip. All the company's other pits in the area are closed, and the Weeping Angel serves as a reminder of a vanished era.

The inquest found naked candle flame to be the cause of the firedamp explosion at Park House Pit (also known as 'Clay Cross No 7', and sometimes as 'Catty'). Thereafter, safety lamps took over from candles, and fan ventilation replaced the furnace at the bottom of the upcast shaft. No blame was accorded to the company, who contributed £500 to the disaster fund. Naturally, in those days of establishment interests, no mine worker served on the inquest jury, and

> ... The owner, he great honour paid:
> Flowers on their coffin he did throw
> As one by one was laid below.

Two years later, 'Grief' was unveiled by an old colliery worker in the presence of a large assembly, which included the company manager. At the request of the workforce, the pits stood idle throughout the day.

Sir F. H. Royce (1863–1933). Sculptor: F. D. Wood (1923, resited 1990). Location: Rolls-Royce Moor Lane Offices, Derby.

Derby

City Feature:

Sir Frederick Henry Royce (1863–1933)
Full-length bronze statue on stone pedestal
Sculptor Francis Derwent Wood
Location Rolls-Royce Offices, Moor Lane

The creator of the world's most prestigious and successful motor car is shown in his later years, informally posed with hands in pockets and head bowed in thought. His statue was completely restored by the company in 1989, and was reinstated with due ceremony at the junction of Moor Lane and Victory Road in September 1990.

Both month and year mark the crucial role of Sir Henry's engineering advancements in winning British air superiority during both World Wars. September 1990 was the 75th anniversary of Rolls-Royce's first aero engine, the Eagle, developed to match German air power; and it was also 50 years since the turning point in the Battle of Britain, fought and won in the Hurricane and Spitfire. Both were powered by the Merlin, the last engine specified by Sir Henry before his death in 1933. The 60th anniversary of his Baronetcy, recognising his work on the Schneider Trophy engine, fell in the same year.

Rolls-Royce became a public company and opened its purpose-built Derby car factory in 1906, two years after the momentous first meeting between the wealthy automobile entrepreneur, the Hon. Charles Rolls, and the unknown but gifted engineer Henry Royce. The Manchester firm Royce Ltd. was already producing 10hp cars and Rolls was seeking the perfect machine for his prestigious London car firm. Within two years of its formation and the move to Derby, Rolls-Royce had perfected the six-cylinder, silver-plated *Silver Ghost*. Silent, opulent and powerful, it was the rich man's dream.

Derby's original Nightingale Road works, which Royce himself designed, still preserves his first cramped, white-tiled office close to the assembly line. Perhaps fired by childhood privations, Royce was hard on himself and his workforce, and this led to domestic difficulties and persistent ill health.

The successful new company was run by C.S. Rolls and his partner Claude Johnson, whilst Royce concentrated on design and technical innovation under the official title 'Engineer in Chief'. After Rolls's untimely death in 1910, and Royce's serious illness of the following year, Johnson as the company's General Managing Director brilliantly eased the burden on the work-centred genius.

For the company's contribution in the First World War, Claude Johnson was awarded a knighthood; proposing in his place Royce, who had been offered the OBE, he was told that knighthoods were 'not awarded to Chief Engineers'. The company commissioned the statue forthwith and in 1923, despite Royce's embarrassment and his absence, it was unveiled in the Arboretum, the provinces' first public park. (*Note* the stone image of donor Joseph Strutt over the entrance arch in Arboretum Street. The park was opened in 1840, arch and statue added in 1853.) In 1987, after an unsuccessful relocation to deter vandalism, Derby citizens voted the Rolls Royce offices to be Sir Henry's natural home.

Derby Selection

Derby's marble statue of Florence Nightingale with her lamp (1820–1910) is appropriately placed outside the Royal Infirmary, but exposed to the London Road. She is accompanied by her pet owl, and is obviously a good sort. The statue by Countess Feodora Gleichen was unveiled in 1914. The Nightingale family were landowners near Cromford, and Florence lived long in local memory as a neighbourhood, rather than a legendary, figure.

Across the road in Trinity Street, her prim niche statue marks the Florence Nightingale Home. Facing the main road, outside the Infirmary, a matriarchal bronze of Queen Victoria was unveiled by Edward VII in 1906. It was the last work of C.B. Birch.

In the Wardwick outside the library a bronze statue of the library's donor MP Michael Thomas Bass (1799–1884) shows a careworn gentleman, head bent over a mini-pedestal with library plans. 'J.E. Boehm Fecit' in 1885, with formal Victorian dress but an informal pose, perhaps showing influence of the New Sculpture movement which adopted a more naturalistic approach after the French style. The shopping centre civic sculpture by Wilfred Dudeney, 'Boy and Ram' (1963), a fine bronze on a

Derbyshire granite base, is hard to appreciate in its tawdry, but brash surroundings.

Derby notables appearing on a 19th-century half-timbered building in St Peter's Street (an original Boot's store) include the Lady with the Lamp, Joseph Strutt, and silk mill pioneer John Lombe. On Exeter Bridge are bronze medallion portraits of Lombe, philosopher Herbert Spencer, historian William Hutton, and Erasmus Darwin, poet and philosopher, grandfather of Charles.

In Midland Street near the station, a stately War Memorial to Midland Railway employees takes characteristic Lutyens form – a stone catafalque elevated on a monumental pedestal (1921). Outside the Guildhall (with reliefs, *'Scientia'* and *'Industria'* by John Bell), the county War Memorial in bronze, by William Walker (1924), makes a striking variation on the mother and child theme.

Nottinghamshire

Hucknall

Town Feature:

Zachariah Green (1817–1897)
Victorian-Gothic drinking fountain of polished granite with bronze medallion portrait and additional dedications
Designer Whitehead & Sons, Westminster
Location Titchfield Park

This handsome memorial once stood in Hucknall's market place, a tribute to

ZACHARIAH GREEN,
A NATIVE OF THIS TOWN
WHO WAS GIFTED IN THE ART OF HEALING
AND SPENT HIS LIFE IN ALLEVIATING THE
SUFFERINGS OF HIS FELLOW MEN.

On the front of the fountain in a columned, arched recess, a bronze relief depicts a plain and resolute man, his neckerchief tied in a half-bow. Below are gilded Gothic letters of dedication. The richly-coloured granites have patterns of foliage and *fleur-de-lys* carved into their polished surface.

In 1927, endangered by market traffic, Zachariah's fountain was moved but not forgotten. Since its completion in 1898, tributes have been added to his son Samuel, Samuel's son Zachariah Albert, and to

Memorial fountain to Zachariah Green (1817–1897). Design: Whitehead & Sons (1898, resited 1927). Location: Titchfield Park, Hucknall.

Mary's gifts, enhanced by an early spell at Great Ormonde Street Hospital for Children. Although married she used her maiden name, working from the family house until her brother set up as GP, and moving back after 'Dr Zac's' early death. In her 90s, consultations were reduced to three a week. In today's hectic world, Mary's declaration, inscribed on the fountain, echoes older values: '"NOT ME ... BUT GOD WORKING THROUGH ME"'

Hucknall Selection

Hucknall's cream-painted statue of Byron, languid in a market place niche, was built up in cement in 1903, the 'gift of Elias Lacey of this town'. In 1974, the 150th anniversary of the poet's death, this town was outraged at the statue's repainting in technicolor. Most offensive were the blonded locks claimed to result from research. In fact, townspeople could recall a 1938 investigation of Byron's family tomb at Hucknall church, where the embalmed poet was reported still to have grey-brown curls.

Byron wished for burial beneath the monument to his Newfoundland dog Bo'sun, probably the only dog with an epitaph composed by a major poet, to be

Inscription to Botswain (1803–1808), Byron's dog.
Designer: not known. Location: Newstead Abbey.

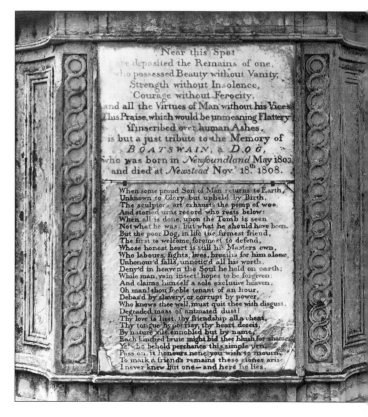

Dr Zac's sister Mary 'who with the same skill and devotion continued for 65 years the healing ministry of her family'. Their work, undertaken for basic costs of medicaments, is recorded in a manuscript kept at Hucknall library. *'The Green Family of Hucknall: A Story of Healing'* was written by a former county councillor and completed in 1982, the year in which local stonemason John Scott carved Mary's tribute.

The family workshop in Beardall Street is preserved as it was when Mary's grandfather Zachariah made stockings, and his son Samuel silk underwear for such customers as the Prince of Wales and the German Emperor. 'Zachy' learnt his trade and healing by helping his father, who settled here after serving as a medical orderly in the Antwerp hospital where he was treated for wounds in the Napoleonic wars. Zachariah extended the family's practise and reputation, continued by his son Samuel who served the town's collieries; injured underground, the miners were carried to his surgery 'in their pit dirt'. Samuel's daughter Mary assisted in healing from her teens.

Almost all Hucknall's population benefitted from

seen at Newstead Abbey off the A611 northbound. Byron's heart is buried beneath his crowned statue at Missolonghi in Greece.

Nottingham

City Feature:

Captain Albert Ball, VC (1897–1917)
Full-length bronze statue with allegorical figure ('Air'), on bow-fronted granite & Portland stone pedestal with stone relief panels & ornamental inscription tablets on stepped base
Sculptor Henry Poole
Architects Brewill & Baily
Location Castle Grounds

Captain Ball's straight-backed figure and his tip-toed attendant, hair and drapery billowing, are perhaps most visually satisfying in silhouette; close-to it is the details that please. The bronze of the figures,

and the pedestal's symbolic torch, feather and wreaths, have been painted chocolate brown. The richness of the stone pedestal remains, with reliefs flying motifs, and letters carved in cartouche frames:
CAPTAIN
ALBERT BALL VC
7th *Robin Hood* Battalion Sherwood
Foresters attached Royal Flying Corps
D.S.O. *Two Bars* M.C.
Croix de Chevalier Legion d'Honneur
Order of St George *Russia*
Hon Freeman of the City of
Nottingham
His dates appear on the reverse: '. . . killed in action, fighting gloriously, May 7th, 1917. Aged 20 years'.

Proudest of the city centre monuments in subject, site and design, the statue of this Nottingham-born ace fighter pilot is a period piece crafted with as much care and generosity as many town and county memorials of the First World War. (The sculptor also worked on the Royal Naval monuments for the War Graves Commission.) Stone pedestal reliefs show the 'stick-and-string' aircraft in which Captain Ball

Monument to Captain Albert Ball, VC (1897–1917). Architects: Brewill & Baily. Sculptor: Henry Poole (1921). Location: Nottingham Castle.

and his fellows duelled, killed and died while protecting reconnaissance planes behind enemy lines.

The sculptor has faithfully recreated the airman's bulky flying coat, boots and gauntlets, but he made the figure bareheaded, without goggles, as Captain Ball habitually faced the enemy. Sometimes flying in shirt sleeves, he favoured single combat ('they call me John the Lonely One'), establishing the lethal tactic of piloting his plane at the enemy, who would veer away exposing the craft's under-carriage.

A trainee engineer, Ball enlisted and gained his commission with the Sherwood Foresters; in training at Luton, he motor-cycled to Hendon and back for flying lessons, returning before the 0645 parade. He subsequently joined the Royal Flying Corps, and was posted to France in 1916. In early 1917 he was a Flight Commander in a new S.E.5 120mph, two-machine gun bi-plane, and by April was averaging a victory a day. The military potential of air combat was still unrecognised, and Ball's startling successes gave strong encouragement to Britain's under-valued, underfunded and embryonic airforce.

Still in his teens, Britain's Red Baron was decorated and adulated, but he wrote home: 'am beginning to feel like a murderer. Shall be so pleased when I am finished'. This last letter, written shortly before his plane disappeared over France, is preserved with many others in the city archives. In all, as recorded on his posthumous VC citation, Ball accounted for 43 enemy aeroplanes and one raiding 'Zeppelin' balloon. Fighter pilots on both sides had a life expectancy of a few months; Albert's skill and single-minded dedication singled him out as exceptional.

He was buried with full military honours by his adversaries, who dropped news of his fate two weeks later – 'killed by a pilot of equal skill'. The pilot was claimed to be Lothar Von Richthofen, cousin of Germany's notorious Red Baron. French eye-witnesses held that Ball had fallen foul not of a well-matched adversary but of anti-aircraft fire.

Later, Albert's father, Alderman Albert Ball, erected a cross at his grave, and a stone on the spot where his son had died in the arms of a village woman. Medals, and other memorabilia, can be seen at the Castle Museum. A memorial service is held annually near the statue at the time of Captain Ball's death 'in the fading light'.

Nottingham Selection

Lining the colonnaded, curved museum entrance in Nottingham Castle are bronze busts of local litterati by eminent turn-of-century sculptors, commissioned from the bequest of William Stephenson Holbrook (1826–1900). He was Secretary at the castle when it opened in 1878 as the first municipal museum of art in England. The best known subject is Byron, here shown youthful and improbably clean-living by Alfred Drury.

The elderly poets William and Mary Howitt make a harmonious centrepiece, decorated with a Frampton frieze of trees. Alfred Toft's bust of Philip James Bailey is the epitome of the venerable bearded bard (an image which irritated the bard's contemporaries). Extracts from his interminable life-work, *Festus*, appear on the pedestal. Another bust by Toft, on the path to the museum, shows an adjutant of the Robin Hood Rifles, Major Jonathan White (1804–1889), a keen-eyed old soldier remembered for his 'simple manliness'.

On Castle Road, Nottingham's folk hero Robin Hood appears as anti-hero, squat and muscular. The bronze was unveiled in 1952 shortly before Richard Green swashbuckled his way to our hearts on early TV. James Woodford's work has been deemed 'a constant source of irritation' to archery lovers, but attracts arrow fanciers. The ensemble has setpieces of Robin's men assembled by Horace Deane of Lambeth. The rockface is hung with bronze reliefs of Robin's exploits, marriage and death.

Also near the town centre, in Wilford Road, the Arboretum features a bust of reformer Samuel Morley (1809–1886), an opportune replacement of a pompous full-length marble replica, carelessly smashed in transit from Theatre Square (1927). Joseph Else, principal of Nottingham School of Art, worked the likeness from photographs. (The original, by Bristolian sculptor J.H. Thomas, stands in Bristol where Morley was Liberal MP.)

The top of the Arboretum harbours a marble image of MP Feargus O'Connor by J.B. Robinson, Derby monumental mason and energetic author. 'Erected by his admirers' in 1859, 'This vile statue', as it was also judged, attracted brickbat poem, tar and feathers. Irish lawyer and Chartist agitator, O'Connor fired passions with his politics; after he died insane in 1855, his funeral drew 50,000.

Out of the centre, another maverick MP, Tory Robert Juckes Clifton (1826–1869), was moved to Wilford Bridge in 1903. His image appears hewn from pitted sandstone and his big, square hand rests on a massive lump of coal. The statue, by stonemason William Philip Smith, was unveiled in Queen's Drive in 1883.

On the Victoria Embankment is Toft's stately marble statue of Queen Victoria, given by Jesse Boot

Jesse Boot, Lord Trent (1850–1931). Sculptor: C. L. J. Doman (1934). Location: University Boulevarde, Nottingham.

and unveiled in the old market square in 1905, but since 1953 forming an ensemble with the county war memorial's triumphal arch and gates by T. Wallis Gordon (1927).

University gates frame a bronze bust of Jesse Boot, Lord Trent, by former Art School student C. Doman. Boot has the look of a Wild West sheriff, no doubt suited to the reformer of the patent medicine trade. He stares shrewd-eyed across University Boulevard at his Beeston factories, built up from the family herbalists' in Goose Gate: 'Before him lies the monument of his industry; behind, an everlasting monument of his benevolence'.

Further east, in Sneinton, the Bendigo Arms (1957) has a statue of legendary pugilist-turned-preacher, William 'Abednego' Thompson (1811–1880). 'Half of him was whalebone, half of him was steel', and this half is fibrous cement with steel reinforcement from a model by Jack Mann. Bendy is buried under a superb marble lion in St Mary's Rest Garden, Bath Street: 'tranquil in Zion'.

In the old market square, Nottingham city centre, a new bronze sculpture, 'Quartet' by Richard Perry, shows 1980s Nottingham citizens hurrying on their common round. Lifesize, and set at eye-level, their High Street clothing and tense expressions belong to their period no less than Toft's Queen Victoria of 1905. Outside the Theatre Royal is Hillary Cartwell's 'Carmen' (1988), a figure made in wire.

Leicestershire

Leicester

City Feature:

John Henry Manners, 5th Duke of Rutland (1778–1857)
Full-length bronze statue on stone pedestal
Sculptor Edward Davis
Location Corn Exchange, Market Place

Leicester has omitted to make its market place into a car park, the centre still vibrates to the clamour of stall holders, and a 1972 facelift reinstated the bronze statue of the 5th Duke of Rutland (formerly relegated to Castle Gardens) beside the handsome Venetian-style stairway of the Corn Exchange. The statue, a work of engaging ineptness, was erected 'during the 50th anniversary of his high office' in 1852. It is said to portray the Lord Lieutenant of Leicestershire in the act of making an address but *The Builder* in 1851 complained, 'His Grace is made to look positively intoxicated'.

It was the 5th duke (son of the famed Marquis of Granby) whose bride employed James Wyatt, between 1801–13, to remodel the family seat as a medieval castle. Sculptures in Belvoir Castle grounds include garden statues by Cibber (1680), and the beautiful marble monument by Matthew Cotes Wyatt to the duchess (d.1825), with her four dead children, in the Mausoleum.

Charles Greville in his *Memoirs* observed that the duke 'never does what he does not like, and spends his whole life in a round of such pleasures as suit his taste'; but he also described the servants' hall where 145 ' had just done dinner' and were drinking the Duke's health, 'singing and speechifying with vociferous applause'.

The duke's statue was first resited in 1872, from its position over the town conduit. A prominent townsman (one 'J. B'), proposing the move in a letter to the *Leicestershire Journal*, suggested that if the statue were then gilded ('do not be startled! – it is right'), this would 'excite the wonder of many by the immensity of the improvement thus effected'. The gilding has since worn off. The Lord Lieutenant was certainly not afforded an elevated or noble position, but perhaps there is a measure of affection in his positioning in the hubbub of the market place.

The same letter from John Burton praised other town improvements, giving three examples of 'ornamental erections and statuary' but forbearing to mention that he himself was the driving force behind their creation. The two statues and a Gothic clock tower today form part of the sculptural mélange animating the city streets.

Leicester Selection

In the town centre, 'Burton's Hobby' (1868), the 80ft Gothic town clock, commemorates earlier Leicester luminaries (including Simon de Montfort, the Earl of Leicester, in armour, and William Wigston in Tudor ruff). Lifesize statues at the corners were carved from Portland stone by Samuel Bardfield. The sculptor, designer Joseph Goddard, and civic functionaries, including J. Burton, are immortalised on the south panel inscription. Their 'ornamental erection' is something to wonder at, spotlit on a winter's afternoon.

In De Montfort Square, in Sicilian marble, a fearsome-looking ox of a man, Baptist minister Robert Hall, was unveiled by the sculptor J. Birnie Philip in 1871. Eccentric to the point of insanity, but kindly remembered by contemporaries, Hall's oratory and writings brought him a following in Leicester from 1807–25. At Welford Place, on a fine drum pedestal, a statue of MP John Biggs, thrice mayor – 'that large-hearted, open-handed man', wrote Burton – was unveiled by the sculptor, G. A. Lawson (sculptor

of the Scott Memorial in Edinburgh), after which tea and speeches were delivered at the Temperance Hall (1863). Today's bronze was cast from the original marble by J.H. Morcomb in 1930.

Leicester has other statues, notably that of Cardinal Wolsey in Abbey Gardens, and in Castle Gardens James Butler's anguished bronze of Richard III 'killed at Bosworth ... buried at Leicester', given by members of the Richard III Society in 1980. Organisers listed on the rugged pedestal include the 'Patron of the appeal fund His Grace the Duke of Rutland'. The work bears the hallmarks of the artist whilst projecting the powerful individuality of its

5th Duke of Rutland (1778–1857). Sculptor: Edward Davis (1851). Location: Corn Exchange, Market Place.

subject. A ceramic tablet near West Bridge approximates to the spot where lie the remains of the 'last of the Plantagenets'.

Abbey Gardens also are part of England's ancient history, but Cardinal Wolsey in textured concrete owes more to Leicester's hosiery industry, being DONATED TO THE CITY BY WOLSEY THE INTERNATIONAL KNITWEAR FIRM. Wolsey died at the abbey in 1530, and is buried in the grounds. His statue is wonderfully bad, but well-sited at the approach to a rustic bridge.

Other appealing images decorate city buildings, adding to a sense of ease gained through walking in Leicester. Particularly fine are figures of the Comic & Lyric Muses, also Music and Dancing, by Rossi with J. Bingley; they occupy niches on the County Rooms in Hotel Street. Instructive and charming friezes over Thomas Cook's original building in Gallowtree Gate have bronze reliefs of Cook's first package tour, to a Loughborough Temperance rally, and later more exotic locations, including the Nile with paddle steamer, pyramids and palms.

There are also some rich curios. In Humberstone Street on the Secular Building, pink terracotta busts by Vago of Robert Owen, Thomas Paine, Voltaire, a formula 'Jesus' and Socrates; the next-door pub's Old Black Lion looms large on panels in raised Delft tiles; down by Castle Gardens, a Peacock Lane hostelry has big, domed, staring Shakespeare's Heads at either side of the corner entrance – pub art, 1950s, and worth looking after; and on the corners of West Bridge, there are small turrets studded with Chaucerian heads.

On the bridge approach, Art Nouveau reliefs of mermaids in terracotta, salvaged from the Wholesale Market and mounted on brick, are signed W.J. Neatby, April 11th 1900. The seats have shell motifs. South of the town on Walnut Street, the parapet of the former Liberty Shoe Factory bears Leicester's very own (concrete) Statue of Liberty.

Loughborough

Town Feature:

Pineau ('The Boy with the Thorn')
3ft bronze replica statue (seated) on Clipsham stone pedestal. A copy of C17th bronze in Epinal, France and moulded from 460BC Greek bronze *Spinario* held in the Vatican, Rome.
Location Granby Street, outside Library

'Pineau', a copy of a C17th bronze in Epinal, France, and moulded from the 460BC Greek 'Spinario'. Location: Granby Street, Loughborough.

The pedestal plaque explains:
THE BOY WITH THE THORN
HAS STOOD IN THE OLD TOWN OF EPINAL
SINCE
THE XVIIth CENTURY, SUFFERING MANY
VICISSITUDES
AND WITNESS OF MANY WARS. THE STATUE
AND ITS
SUCCESSIVE REPLICAS SYMBOLISE THE
TOWN'S NAME
IN THE MINDS OF ITS INHABITANTS.

The small figure of a naked boy, seated on a rock, intently examines one foot which is supported on his knee. Wars and vicissitudes will have passed him unnoticed, which in itself may have brought some solace to generations of Epinal inhabitants.

The Epinal bronze, bomb damaged in the 1940s, is kept in its town hall, whilst another copy stands in the street. The Loughborough figure, presented in 1957 to mark its twinning with the French town, has seen no wars but has already made up for this in vicissitudes.

This generous gift was first announced at a Loughborough Twinning Committee meeting in November 1956, together with the French town's expectation 'that in return the town of Loughborough will present to Epinal a bell'. The minutes note that 'at no time has any promise of such a gift been made'. Embarrassment was overcome by energetic fund-raising which accumulated over £400, and an order went to Loughborough's world-famous bell makers, John Taylor & Sons. Meanwhile 'the Boy with the Thorn', then valued at £2,000, was unveiled by the Mayor of Epinal in the garden of Island House; the following year, Loughborough's bell was installed close to the French statue in Epinal.

Island House Garden has since been replaced by the new library extension, with the Boy placed outside; surviving this change, the statue was stolen in December 1980, and all hope of recovery lost. In February 1983 a Loughborough citizen cleaning his shoes on the *Howdenshire Gazette* (left by his visiting son) lit on a picture of a mysterious statue found in the mud of the River Ouse, near Goole. The report rang a bell, the town council was alerted, and the Boy was returned with a forearm missing. Local newspapers reported saw-marks on the body, and an attempt at 'castration by chisel'.

A restoration was carried out by David Tarver, Head of Sculpture at Loughborough College of Art and Design. He assessed the work as a beautiful piece of sculpture, one that 'works from every direction'. In February 1984 the repaired, repatinated figure was reinstated and, as the *Loughborough & Coalville Trader* put it, left in peace to 'get that thorn out of his foot'.

Loughborough Selection

Near the library, and dominating a small park, the 151ft War Memorial Tower contains the 'Loughborough Carillion' of 47 bells, unveiled in 1923. Designed by Sir Walter Tapper, its cost of almost £22,000 was met by public subscription; individual bells are inscribed with names of firms and families who 'bought' their bell for the cause. Sir Edward Elgar composed 'Memorial Chimes' for the opening recital, given by maestro Chevalier Jef Denyn of Malines, Belgium, home country of carillon. The largest bell commemorates three sons of John Taylor (then owner of the Loughborough bell foundry), all killed in action. The public gallery looks out over Taylor's bell foundry to the Charnwood Hills.

Northamptonshire

Geddington (& Hardingstone near Northampton)

Village Feature:

Eleanor of Castile (1245–1290)
13th century 'Eleanor Cross' of local limestone.
A triagonal shaft in three stages with diaper work on the lower stage and fine-grained limestone statues under gabled canopies, on an hexagonal plinth with stepped base (replaced 1800)
Sculptor Not known
Location Village Square

Triangular in plan and slender, worked to a lacy patina of floral shapes, this is the most beautiful and

Hardingstone Cross: one of the original monuments to Eleanor of Castile (1245–1290). Sculptor: not known, C13th. Location: A508 S. of Northampton.

complete of the three surviving crosses to immortalise Eleanor, queen and consort of Edward I. Canopied niches on the second stage of the shaft hold stone statues of the Queen in travelling veil and mantle; below are her armorial shields of Castile and Léon, Pointlieu, and England. The cross stands within sight of Geddington's 13th-century bridge, in the shadow of the medieval church spire.

Eleanor died in 1290 at Harby, Nottinghamshire having fallen behind, fevered, as Edward's entourage pressed north to deal with the Scots. The grieving king accompanied the queen's body to its burial place at Westminster Abbey (her heart rests at Lincoln Cathedral).

Soon after, using his best artists and craftsmen, the king raised stone crosses at all the halting points of the funeral cortège on the 155-mile journey to London. Architecturally, the three remaining crosses are amongst the first examples of the rich English Decorated style. Widely emulated in Victorian times, the crosses form a basis for any study of England's public commemorative monuments.

The idea came from memorials set up along the funeral route of Louis IX in France, in 1271. Two years earlier Edward, accompanied by Eleanor, had joined Louis on the fifth Crusade, in the course of which they received news of Edward's succession to the English throne (1272), and learned of the death of their two eldest sons. On this expedition, too, Eleanor gave birth to two children. When Edward's life was threatened by a Saracen arrow, she sucked the poison out, a story that furthered the romance and legend of their marriage, arranged and solemnised when the prince was 15 years old and his bride a girl of nine.

The memorials stood at 12 halting points, from Lincoln to Charing Cross (*Chère Reine* Cross, supposedly) in London. Geddington's vanished royal hunting lodge was the fourth, and Delapré Abbey at Hardingstone near Northampton, where another cross survives, the next. The third remaining, much altered, cross was built near Waltham Abbey and gave its name to the Hertfordshire town.

Hardingstone cross has also suffered early alteration, notably in honour of Queen Anne THE GLORY OF MIGHTY BRITAIN, who *PACEM RESTITUIT* through the Treaty of Utrecht (1713). Its heavily-restored statues survive *in situ*, unlike Waltham's Victorian copies; Waltham's (showing traces of original paint) are in the British Museum.

Waltham's octagonal and Hardingstone's hexagonal crosses were begun in 1291, Geddington's three years later. No cross, it seems, was the same,

but they are all thought to have supported crucifixes. Most others, ancient by Cromwell's time, were destroyed in the Civil War (as Louis' fell in the French Revolution). Hardingstone's cross is separated from its village by the Northampton ring road; in a 1984 restoration, citizens were invited to climb the scaffolding for a close look at Queen Eleanor. Geddington's was first repaired in the 1920s, 50 years before conservation by English Heritage.

Ancient or half-ancient the crosses are monuments to journeying, for as Eleanor died so she lived, often at the rear of her husband's contingent, always *en voyage*. Edward left these sculptured spires as reminders of their last journey, and of a king's human impulse to preserve the soul of the departed, to acknowledge worth, and to formalise grief. Writing to the Abbot of Clugny, he was to declare:

Living I loved her tenderly
and I shall never cease to love her dead.

(Note: Detailed accounts of the Northamptonshire crosses' history and of their protagonists appear in the periodical *Northamptonshire Life* (March and May, 1981), whilst historical and technical details appear in an English Heritage Bulletin on the 1987 conservation of the remarkably-intact Geddington cross.

Northampton Selection

In Northampton, Eleanor features in vigorous scenes from the town's history carved by T. Nicholls in the darkened stone of the Gothic revival Town Hall, St Giles Square, showing influence of Ruskin's *Stones of Venice* on the architect Edward Godwin (1861–4). She also appears with others on the library in pedestrianised Abington Street, whilst statuettes (by R.L. Boulton of Cheltenham) said to represent Queen Eleanor and Edward I, appear on No 11 next to Peacock Place.

On All Saints' Church near the Town Hall, a small, haughty figure of CAROLUS II by John Hunt stands above the portico. Given in return for Freedom of the Town, *c*.1712, the King wears Roman dress, and a luxuriant Restoration wig. Big letters record Charles's gift of A THOUSAND TUN OF TIMBER TOWARDS THE REBUILDING OF THIS CHURCH ... to a town who had supplied shoes to Cromwell's troops.

Also in Abington Street on the site of a cast iron fountain, destroyed for rebuilding, a bronze sculpture of an enormous shoe last, upside down, carries figures of running children. It symbolises the town's traditional industry, and is by the Barnsley

Lieut-Col Edgar R. Mobbs DSP (1870–1917). Sculptor: Alfred Turner (1921, resited 1938). Location: Abington Square, Northampton.

sculptor Graham Ibbeson. Largely paid for with grants from East Midlands Arts, the controversial £16,000 ensemble was disowned in 1986 by the mayor who refused to unveil it, but suggested it should be installed without fuss 'like a traffic light'.

Further north in Abington Square is a white-painted terracotta statue of free-thinker Charles Bradlaugh, 'four times elected to one Party in vindication of the rights of constituencies' (and seven times expelled from the House), 'MP for Northampton 1880–1891'. The pedestal is covered with lines after McGonagall by a local shoe worker; on the front is Bradlaugh's motto: THOROUGH. The statue is by George Timworth of Doulton at Lambeth, and was unveiled 1894.

At the north end of the square is a head and shoulders of Lieut-Col Edgar R. Mobbs DSO (1870–1917), a local rugby hero who 'founded Mobbs Company, joined as a Private, and rose to command the Battalion to which it belonged' (7th Northamptonshire Regiment). Alfred Turner's monument carries reliefs of 'Sport' and 'War', and is surmounted by a heroic female figure. The clean-cut, boyish portrait bust brings the human touch to this period piece, best viewed gloriously wreathed after the March ceremony marking the Mobbs Memorial Rugby Match between East Midlands and the Barbarians.

Bedfordshire

Bedford

Town Feature:

John Bunyan (1628–1688)
Full-length bronze statue on stone pedestal with bronze relief panels
Sculptor (Sir) Joseph Edgar Boehm Bt RA
Location St Peter's Green

The most conspicuous statue in Bedford is that of the prison reformer John Howard (d.1790), standing with chin in hand, wearing tricorn hat and pigtail; 'more a representative effigy than an attempt to produce a faithful likeness' according to the sculptor,

John Bunyan (1628–1688) Sculptor: Sir J. E. Boehm, Bt RA (1874). Location: St Peter's Green, Bedford.

Alfred Gilbert. The Lord High Sheriff of Bedfordshire's statue was erected in 1894 outside St Paul's Church, on the town side of the Georgian bridge. His shapely stone pedestal carries Gilbert's intricate, faintly decadent decoration of fish-tailed, helmeted infants brilliantly modelled and cast.

Blunter symbolism attends Boehm's work erected in 1874 at the far end of the High Street, but the broken fetter round Bunyan's calf also recalls Howard's reforms, which he began after investigating Bedford gaols.

Unlike Howard, Bunyan was a local man, a tinker's son from the village of Elstow, whose life and works are rooted in the history of Nonconformist Bedford. His statue's pose mirrors the quote inscribed on the pedestal:

'... EYES LIFTED UP TO HEAVEN
THE BEST OF BOOKS IN HIS HAND ...'

Bunyan's own use of deep symbolism is recalled on the pedestal's panels, bronze relief scenes from his *The Pilgrim's Progress*, begun towards the end of his

12-year prison term in Bedford Gaol for 'devilishly and perniciously' preaching without a license.

Other books written in gaol included *Grace Abounding to the Chief of Sinners* (1666), Bunyan's vivid account of his alarming conversion after a humble childhood and youthful ways of blasphemy and innocence.

Bunyan served with Cromwell's Army, returned to tinkering, and was encouraged in religious reading by his first wife; after joining an Independent Congregation at St John's Church in Bedford, they moved to town. He began to practise his gift for preaching a few years before the Restoration.

At his arrest in 1660, his eloquence was established: 'If I were out of prison today, I would preach the gospel again tomorrow, by the help of God'. Instead, he wrote the first part of *The Pilgrim's Progress*, an allegorical work derived not from the classics but from Bunyan's deep familiarity with the Bible and with the tongue of ordinary people.

Thought to have been completed during his shorter gaol term (1676–77), the book was first published in 1678, and again with Part Two six years later. By then 'Bishop Bunyan' was a familiar figure between London and Bedfordshire, like his character Christian a traveller, seeking God through making his faith accessible to every man.

His statue's busy High Street corner was a quiet site outside St Peter's when Boehm selected it shortly before the unveiling in 1874. The proceedings were attended by the Dean of Westminster and a crowd of thousands, with unpuritanical feasting and fireworks. The statue, given by the 9th Duke of Bedford, was cast from Chinese cannon and bells. The site of Bunyan's first meeting house, a converted barn, is occupied by the Bunyan Meeting, now a museum. (Note the bronze reliefs by Frederick Thrupp of scenes from *The Pilgrim's Progress* on the doors, also given by the 9th Duke.)

Bunyan's allegory appears in almost 200 translations, many held in the museum. Bedford County Reference Library has a collection of his works, and the St Paul's Square Tourist Centre provides a town and country trail leaflet.

Bedford (and locality) Selection

In Harpur Street behind St Paul's, the Town Hall – former School House (1756) – carries Benjamin Palmer's charming statue of Sir William Harpur, Bedford-born Lord Mayor of London, who founded Bedford Grammar School. (Note the inscription: 'Ecce Viator! ...')

Pedestal detail, Howard Monument. Sculptor: Alfred Gilbert, RA (1894). Location: outside St Paul's Church.

Beyond Bedford, on the Northampton road, two ghostly grey stone figures stand below the mill race at Turvey (view from the trafficky bridge): 'Jonah' with a dolphin, a 17th-century statue said to be from Ashridge House, and his bearded 'wife', assembled in 1953, 99 years after Jonah's arrival, from a body and assorted heads found by the mill owner in a nearby barn.

Buckinghamshire

Aylesbury

Town Feature:

John Hampden (1594–1643)
Full-length bronze statue on stone pedestal with
bronze relief panels
Sculptor Henry C. Fehr
Location High Street

County memories are long: H.C. Fehr's striking bronze of the Patriot was given by 'the rep-

resentative of an old Buckinghamshire family', James Griffin, who laid the foundation stone on Coronation Day in 1911. A festivities programme and other mementoes were laid beneath, while local school children sang *Land of Hope and Glory*, led by the Aylesbury Printing Works Band. The vote of thanks to the donor expressed belief that the new king, George V, would govern according to the traditions of the Constitution; 'if this had been done in Hampden's time there would be no occasion for the memorial today'.

In 1638, Hampden made his famous stand against Charles I's Ship Money tax on landowners, imposed during the period of rule without Parliament. The court found for the king, but by a small enough margin to give 'Ship Money Hampden' a moral victory. Himself a member of an old county family, and a cousin of Oliver Cromwell, Hampden as MP

John Hampden (1594–1643). Sculptor: H. C. Fehr (1912, resited 1989). Location: High Street, Aylesbury.

for Buckinghamshire played a decisive role in the Long Parliament's measures against the king.

He was amongst the five MPs accused of High Treason whose arrest Charles sought in his ill-judged personal appearance at the House of Commons in 1642. This brought from Bucks a 4000-strong deputation, carrying at the ends of their pikes copies of the Grand Remonstrance, Parliament's final call for further constitutional and military change.

During the Civil War of 1642–1649, in which Cromwell's troops were garrisoned at Aylesbury, Hampden commanded a Bucks regiment, the Green Coats, under the inadequate leadership of Robert, Earl of Essex. Fatally wounded at Chalgrove Field, he died at the Greyhound Inn, Thame, on June 24 1643. He was sadly mourned in Bucks. His philosophy, engraved on the Hampden Jewel, is restated on his statue's pedestal:

"AGAINST MY KING I DO NOT FIGHT
BUT FOR MY KING AND KINGDOM'S RIGHT".
The battle scene, and his burial at Great Hampden Church, are shown in bronze relief panels on his statue's pedestal. The bronze figure above appears in battle dress, rather self-consciously heroic, pointing towards his village; his story is contained in crested bronze panels. The words of Richard Baxter, Protestant divine, affirm:

"MR JOHN HAMPDEN WAS ONE THAT
FRIENDS AND
ENEMIES ACKNOWLEDGED TO BE MOST
EMINENT,
FOR PRUDENCE, PIETY, AND PEACEABLE
COUNSELS,
HAVING THE MOST UNIVERSAL PRAISE OF
ANY
GENTLEMAN THAT I REMEMBER OF THAT
AGE."
The statue stood on the spot where it is said Hampden passed with his troops after the Battle of Holman's Bridge in 1642. During a late 1980s pedestrianisation it was moved to the top of the High Street, safe from passing lorries.

Aylesbury (and locality) Selection

Near Hampden's statue at the top of the market square is Fehr's bronze figure of Disraeli, richly robed as Chancellor, erected in 1923. The Pedestal carries Disraeli's promise of PEACE WITH HONOUR, made at the peak of his political career and quoted by Neville Chamberlain after Munich.

Robert Gibbs's *Worthies of Bucks* (1888) describes the young, ambitious Disraeli with 'his ringlets of silken black hair, his flashing eyes, his effeminite and lisping voice, his coat of black velvet . . . his ivory cane'. He was popular locally, with an admiring tenantry and devoted friends. His south Bucks home, Hughenden Manor (NT), acquired in 1848, has relics of his domestic and political life. West of the grounds, a fine ornamental Bath stone obelisk to his father Isaac D'Israeli (d.1848) was a home-coming surprise from Benjamin's wife in 1862.

At the lower end of the market square, outside the County Hall, stands a bronze statue of a trim, uniformed soldier, holding a hunting crop. It is a restrained portrayal by John Tweed of the 3rd Baron Chesham KCB, Commander of the Bucks Yeomanry in the Boer War, a popular and respected member of a county family, and Master of the Bicester Hounds.

He is attended by a pair of great black cast iron lions, hauled by means of a steam roller in 1888 from Waddesdon Manor (NT), built for the Rothschild family whilst Disraeli was arranging the £4 million Rothschild loan to buy shares in the Suez Canal (1875). Like Waddesdon's flamboyant architecture (*see* also its splendid garden statuary), the lions are from France. Lord Rothschild attended the unveiling of the statue in 1907, the year of Chesham's death following a hunting accident.

On the village green of Latimer, near Chesham, a small stone mound marks the grave of the warhorse Villebois, brought here in 1900 by Lord Chesham, whose life was saved by its rider General de Villebois Mareuil, on active service in the Boer War. Latimer soldiers remembered on a modest obelisk nearby include Chesham's eldest son John. Further north on Coombe Hill (NT), the highest point of the Chilterns, a tall obelisk with gold-painted torch stands as the county's Boer War memorial whilst making a landmark across the beautiful Bucks ridges and plains.

Hertfordshire

Hatfield

Town Feature:

Robert Arthur Talbot Gascoyne-Cecil, 3rd Marquis of Salisbury (1830–1903)
Seated bronze statue on stone pedestal
Sculptor (Sir) George Frampton RA
Location Station entrance, Hatfield House

Stately wrought-iron portals, and the drive winding towards one of England's finest Jacobean houses, make the frame for Lord Salisbury's statue on its lofty pedestal. He appears deep in thought, robed as Chancellor of Oxford University with the collar of the Order of the Garter, facing Hatfield Station across the soulless new dual carriageway. When the station was built in 1877, this approach was upgraded as the main entrance. The carved terracotta gate piers show damage from tourist buses.

Hatfield, built between 1607–1611 for Robert Cecil, 1st Earl of Salisbury, still belongs to the family. Cecil lions adorn the gate piers, the big coat of arms on the statue's pedestal and the family crest on the back of its Elizabethan chair. The 3rd Marquis suffered a lonely and aristocratic boyhood here, redeemed by rearing his own family of seven children with a closeness, respect and freedom unusual at that or any period, and amusingly described in Lord Salisbury's biography by his grandson Lord David Cecil.

As MP, Secretary for India and thrice Prime Minister, Lord Salisbury entertained a great diversity of notables at Hatfield, including Gladstone and Disraeli, Lewis Carroll, and the Shah of Persia. He attended meals, but left the entertaining of guests to his wife, and to their children whose interests ranged from fierce debates, reading Homer, trying out the guns or 'riding recklessly round the park'.

The estate was also overseen by Lady Salisbury, whose husband claimed uncertainty of the difference between a cow and a horse. He preferred to experiment, testing an early intercom by intoning nursery rhymes; visitors were even more alarmed at his inflammable electric wiring, doused by cushions tossed against the ornate ceiling whilst talk flowed unabated. The 3rd Marquis also redecorated much of Hatfield, including the chapel in which optional daily prayers were held.

In public life Lord Salisbury's aristocratic aloofness and indifference to democratic rule isolated him from his fellow-conservatives, but he was favoured with the affection of Queen Victoria, who loved to be amused and even called him 'my greatest prime minister'. His statue, signed 'G.Frampton, 1806', was erected by HIS HERTFORDSHIRE FRIENDS AND NEIGHBOURS, IN RECOGNITION OF A GREAT LIFE DEVOTED TO THE WELFARE OF HIS COUNTRY.

3rd Marquis of Salisbury (1830–1903). Sculptor: Sir George Frampton, RA (1806). Location: station entrance, Hatfield.

Beyond the gates in the grounds, the West Garden has statuary recently brought from a Palladian villa at Vicenza. The Lime Walk has a lifesize frieze in artificial stone of statues from London's Royal Exchange of 1825. It shows Elizabeth I opening the new building with an entourage including Burleigh, Gresham and the Bishop of London. Here, too, from the same building, a large head of the Queen by the same sculptor J.G. Bubb recalls the early illustrious days of the Cecils.

Thomas Paine (1737–1809). Sculptor: Sir Charles Wheeler, RA (1964). Location: Outside Council Offices (the King's House), King Street, Thetford.

Eastern Counties

'All Creatures Great and Small'

Flower in the crannied wall,
I pluck you out of the crannies,
I hold you here, root and all, in my hand,
Little flower — but if I could understand
What you are, root and all, and all in all,
I should know what God and man is

(Lines from Alfred Lord Tennyson's poem *Flower in the Crannied Wall* inscribed on a panel beneath the poet's statue in the precinct of Lincoln Cathedral)

The craggy bronze persona of Alfred Lord Tennyson turns away from the medieval majesty of Lincoln Cathedral to study a sprig of ivy-leaved toadflax. The sculptor G.F. Watts was interpreting the Lincolnshire born poet's work, but he also speaks for the Eastern Counties, where God roots man in the soil while skies and crop fields dominate.

Close preoccupations and large gestures share a place in the region's commemorative monuments, which range from stone waymarks in Norfolk and Suffolk and village pumps in Sussex villages, to celebratory obelisks such as that erected by the people of Derry to their bishop the 4th Earl of Bristol (d. 1803), near his fabulous mansion Ickworth in Suffolk, in 1817. This jolly and eccentric character built his palace, with its rotunda, to contain '... pictures, statues, busts, and marbles without end ...', but the collection was confiscated in Italy by the invading French in 1798; the Earl died on his travels and was shipped home, his coffin disguised as the packaging for an antique statue, to circumvent the sailors' superstitions.

Eastern Counties' statues appear in other out-of-the-way places such as Braintree in Essex, where Faith Winter's new bronze figure of John Ray, father of natural history, stands near the market place; Babraham in Cambridgeshire, where the 'Southdown Improver', Jonas Webb, appears by the road in a bronze masterpiece of shrewd-eyed native hauteur by Marochetti; or Kirton, in Lincolnshire, where the 'Potato King' William Dennis (1841–1924) was immortalised in bronze by P. Lindsey Clark in 1930.

The international agricultural company which Dennis built from one field still flourishes. He sits patiently, back bowed, his walking stick between his knees, outside the town hall which he gave to his fellow citizens. Memories of a true son of the soil are expressed in carved stone reliefs of fenland scenes.

In fens, in woods, in Gainsborough's pastoral Suffolk, the landscape's theme is produce; fields of root vegetables, beans or fruit, plantations of trees, and endless corn crops rolling from road to horizon under big, open skies. No wonder that grand monumental gestures repeat the theme by focussing on small things such as a small dog carried by 'Peace' on an elaborate fountain at Bury St Edmunds, birthplace of the Victorian romantic novelist 'Ouida' (Marie Louise de la Ramée). Even the agrarian reformer 'Coke of Norfolk's' prodigious column with its wheatsheaf crown, erected at Holkham Hall (1845–50), is enriched at the capital with kneeling bulls, in foliage of turnips and mangel wurzel.

Far south at Great Yarmouth, Nelson's 'Norfolk Pillar' is surmounted by Britannia, but she turns her back to the sea, the mighty medium of her hero's triumph, and offers her laurel wreath inland perhaps to Burnham Thorpe, Nelson's birthplace where he expected and wished to be buried. Local hearsay has it that the sculptor was French, and the positioning of Britannia provocative.

Small towns are as likely to have imposing works as the county capitals, only three of which possess free-standing statues. Of the other three, a park in Ipswich has its Martyrs' Memorial, still 'cherished locally' according to a Suffolk historian. Huntingdon turned down the chance to buy a statue of its most famous son, Oliver Cromwell, on the 300th anniversary of his birth in 1899.

Cambridge has no 'market square' statue, but the streets and quads show college-gateway niche statues, not as rich or extensive a collection as Oxford's, but with the same animating effect. A statue of Henry VIII, over Trinity's Great Gate, has long since lost his sceptre to a chair leg. St John's painted gateway has the saint carrying the poisoned drink that turned into a snake; said to have been hidden during the Commonwealth, it is also recorded in the Audit Book of 1662–3 as costing £11. The gate itself, and that of Christ's, are the most beautiful in either city, carrying Margaret of Beaufort's faunal and floral emblems in vibrant pastel-coloured relief.

Column to Admiral Lord Nelson (1758–1805). Design: William Wilkins (1819). Location: South Promenade, Yarmouth.

Two 19th-century statues of great charm adorn Tree Quad at Gonville and Caius College (known as 'Keys'). Conspicuous over the corner doorway (and trapped behind an energetic vine) is the stone-carved figure of Dr Stephen Perse, holding a model of the college and fingering a goatee beard; hidden behind the staff bicycle shed is the Reverend Bartholomew Wortley, who modelled his provision for fellowships and lodgings on the will of Dr Perse.

In replacing the old, elegant Tree Court, the architect Alfred Waterhouse promised statues of the original benefactors, but unaccountably omitted the third: perhaps Dr Perse's friend and successor Thomas Legge, who also bestowed a building, lurks stonily in some dim recess waiting to be affixed.

Present in force, lined up on the Trinity Street façade, are famous former members and college benefactors. The small, blackened heads, with period headgear, are individually named. Cambridge has many other oddities and treasures, including an Eric Gill crocodile engraved in brickwork on the Cavendish Laboratory, and Michael Ayrton's dark, contorted *Talos* in Guildhall Street. On a Market Square shop a relief head of the poet C.S. Calverley appears over his *Ode to Tobacco* (1862): '... they who use fusees, All grow by slow degrees, Brainless as chimpanzees ...'

On another plane, opposite Wordsworth's Trinity College lodgings, the ante-chapel has Roubiliac's timeless marble statue of Newton (1755) '..with his prism and his silent face'. Symbolic figures made by Cibber in 1681 (Mathematics counting on her fingers, noted the author Norman Scarfe) line the top of Trinity's columned Library façade. The Library's statues include Thorwaldsen's 'Byron' (1829), forbidden a site in Westminster Abbey. Other university buildings contain fine sculptures, with works by masters such as Rysbrack and Nollekens.

Town or country, small or sweeping, the more personal the tributes, in this individualistic and landed region, the more particular the charm; where else other than in Lincolnshire might one find in a field (near Somerby), raised 'in gratitude', a pretty column and urn with entwined serpents, celebrating 'anno felicis conuigit XXIX'. Ironically, Edward and Ann Weston's 'happy conjugal union of 28' years ended in Edward's death that same year (1770).

The early death of Lord Yarborough's wife, Sophia Aufrere, was marked by a plantation on the Brocklesby Estate, and in 1840 their son laid the foundations of a belvedere in Pillar Wood, near Caistor, to celebrate the planting of 12 million trees (1787–1828). Designed by E.J. Willson, the tower is guarded by two great lions (one asleep) by W.D. Keyworth, and can be climbed on application for the key at the gamekeeper's cottage nearby. At Great Limber, Sophia's cedar-ringed mausoleum, with her lovely statue by Nollekens, is open by arrangement. It was designed by James Wyatt (1787–94).

A smaller wood, near Woodhall Spa, was 'RAISED' by Colonel Richard Elmhirst 'FROM ACORNS SEEDED IMMEDIATELY AFTER THE MEMORABLE BATTLE OF WATERLOO'. The narrow meadow between the trees and the road sprouts an octagonal column with a bust of 'THAT GREAT CAPTAIN OF HIS AGE, HIS GRACE THE DUKE OF WELLINGTON' staring hawk-like towards Elmhirst's home at West Ashby.

This personal salutation is one of many roadside monuments in the Eastern Counties, another haunting memorial being the Holme Fen Post on a lonely road at Whittlesey Mere Nature Reserve. Brought from the Crystal Palace Exhibition in 1851, the cast-iron post was driven 22ft into the peat until its top was flush with the ground. Since then, *c.*15ft has been revealed as the peat has shrunk through erosion.

More conspicuous, on the A1 at Norman Cross, was a bronze wild eagle alighting on a column above cultivated Cambridgeshire, raised by the Entente Cordiale Society to honour 1,770 Napoleonic prisoners who died near this spot. Two weeks after the grand unveiling, England entered the 1914–18 war. Mean-spirited thieves removed the eagle in 1990.

In Essex, on the west side of Woodford High Road (A11), flowers are still laid at Sylvia Pankhurst's small, stone, bomb-shaped 'protest against war in the air', erected in 1935.

Entente Cordiale Society Monument to Napoleonic prisoners. Architect: H. P. Cart de la Fontaine. Sculptor: J. A. Stevenson (1914). Location: Norman Cross, (A1) near Peterborough. (Note the column was toppled and the original bronze of the eagle stolen, October 1990).

Wayside monuments, especially Norfolk's small ones, are intrinsically parochial. On the A10 near Ryston Hall, a parish boundary cross commemorates L.H. Pratt of the Hall, and C.D. Prangley of the next parish, Bexwell: 'All that we had we gave'. The friends were killed on the same day, one year apart (1915/16) during the Great War. An earlier medieval cross may have marked the spot where John de Bekyswell was killed by an arrow. The site's developer remembers his father tending a wild garden here, for the then landowner.

Wayside monuments also stand in Attleborough, where the Connaught Pillar marks the end of the Crimean War whilst giving mileages; on the old A11 to Wymondham, where the Dial Stone (long without sundial) vows GRATEFULL REMEMBRANCE to Sir Edwin Rich for road repairs (1675); at Holt, listing mileages to Norfolk country seats; and near Raveningham Hall, where a handsome cast-iron mileage pillar known locally as 'the Monument' was restored in 1988.

The National Trust keeps a small patch of wilderness on the B1149 (west side, south of the B1145) for the Duelling Stone, a pillar and urn mutely marking the mortal wounding in 1698 of Henry Hobart, 4th Baronet, for whom Robert Lyminge designed Blickling Hall. More accessible is the vigorous sculptural decoration of Blickling's Jacobean architecture, small stone figures enlivening the east façade, and the Hobart Bull on Doric columns at the grand entrance.

Garden sculpture includes the hairy 'Dog of Alcibiades' (Austin & Seeley, 1877), and a Hercules in the Orangery, perhaps by Nicholas Stone (c.1640), a very early example of English garden sculpture after the Antique. The Bull and a greyhound, from the family coat of arms, adorn the family mausoleum (1793), a sombre pyramid by Joseph Bonomi occupying a yew-edged clearing on the woodland Weaver's Way. The inscription reads like a genealogical conundrum.

Country estates usually give extra pleasure in their ornamental sculpture, often emblematic and personal, as at Blickling. Audley End in Essex is entered by a stately lion gate which was 'REST.ET.ORN' by Lord Howard, formerly Sir John Griffin Griffin, for George III's visit in 1786. Unfortunately the king's illness intervened, but his recovery was celebrated by the most prominent of Audley End's fine architectural memorials, a Corinthian temple erected in 1792.

Sir John was nephew and heir of the Countess of Portsmouth (d.1762), and on Windmill Hill north of the park, Robert Adam's Doric column with vase was erected 'in gratitude' in 1774. The Billingbear Bulls' heads at the Cambridge exit, vigorously modelled of Roman cement, date from the last century. Similar gates on the Neville family's Billingbear Estate in Berkshire appear in a painting at Audley End, inherited from Sir John by Richard Neville. (Three-quarters-of-a-mile west in Saffron Waldon market place, the marble-columned porches of this Jacobean house are recalled in a foolish Gothic memorial fountain with much coloured stone, and carved religious scenes. The architect, J.F. Bentley, designed Westminster Cathedral.)

In Lincolnshire at Belton House (NT), the formal gardens were renewed, after the 1880s, by Adelbert Wellington Brownlow Cust, 3rd Earl Brownlow, and the Countess Adelaide. Based on the original plans, the garden's centrepiece is a lichened limestone figure of Time, with cherub, carved by C.G. Cibber and probably contemporary with the house (1685). Time's bronze sundial is dated 1725.

Unexpected pleasures include a marble Ceres holding up the box hedge, and inscribed urns to Lady Brownlow's favourite dogs, but best is the bronze bust of Adelbert in a shubbery near the Orangery, his titles and official posts listed on the inscription. 'Nina Cust Fecit': she was Emmeline Welby (d.1955), wife of the earl's cousin, Harry Cust. A marble head and shoulders of the 3rd Earl in uniform lines up with classically-styled marble busts of unknown figures, and some family portraits, in the Orangery. The family's funerary monuments in the church are of surpassing interest.

Marble or bronze, statue or bust, the Eastern Counties portraits amount to a portrait of the Eastern Counties: scarcely one dedicatee comes from beyond his county border; even the great Nelson, as his Yarmouth Column proclaims, NORFOLK PROUDLY BOASTS HER OWN. An exception, at Woodbridge, Suffolk, is a bronze group of two boy soldier-heroes, based on a Rudyard Kipling tale of Afghan hordes; but this unusual subject is the work of a Norfolk sculptor, an accomplished amateur, the 8th Earl of Albemarle. Standing outside the council offices, it was presented in 1980 in memory of the 9th Earl by his widow Diana, Countess of Albemarle.

Also Norfolk's own is Frederick Savage the 'Showmen's Friend', a Hevingham crow scarer turned agricultural engineer, entrepreneurial mayor of King's Lynn in 1889. Lifesize stone portraits of Charles II and his father grace King's Lynn Street Custom House (formerly the Exchange) and the Bank House in King Staithe Square, but Savage's Portland stone statue was erected 'by his friends' on a fine pedestal at the South Gate entrance to the town.

The better known Thomas Paine has a gilded statue, the work of Charles Wheeler, outside the council offices in his native Thetford, Suffolk. Paine is shown theatrically brandishing book and quill pen, an exotic ornament for a small town. Presentation by the Thomas Paine Society of New York caused a local storm in 1964: the radical ideas in *The Rights of Man* can still inflame, 173 years on. The pedestal's fine-carved and lengthy pronouncements are typical of American monuments in England.

Famous sons of Lincolnshire are personified in their native towns. Charles Bacon's marble of Sir John Franklin with anchor, rope and telescope stands in the thick of Spilsby market, whilst a dull marble of Herbert Ingram by Alexander Munro stands in the shadow of the Boston Stump; Ingram's contribution to his town's water supply is recalled by a bronze maiden, with her flagon, on the pedestal. Ingram founded the *Illustrated London News*, which announced his sudden death by drowning in 1860, '... with a trembling hand and sorrowing heart'.

Isaac Newton at Grantham, gowned as Master of Arts, points with ruffled sleeve at a diagram from *The Principia*; his formal bronze by the younger Theed is backed by the satisfying bulges and curves of the Town Hall. Also on St Peter's Hill is George Simmond's more animated bronze of Frederick Tollemache MP, with hat and staff, erected in 1891 by 'friends who revered his memory, irrespective of political opinions'. One morning in 1897 the citizens of Grantham, at pains to find a willing mayor, awoke to see a mayoral chain round Tollemache's neck, and a card attached: THE PROBLEM SOLVED.

Sleaford's MP for South Lincolnshire, Henry Hanley (d.1846), is locally — and erroniously — said to have donated his own rocket-like Gothic monument, designed by William Boyle in 1850. It is now a traffic island at Southgate's northern end, the carved angels carrying an inscribed scroll obscured by traffic signs. Restoration funds in 1982 could not stretch to replacing the right arm on the statue by John Thomas.

Among Southgate's rarities is a stone-carved sign over the Black Bull Inn, depicting a bull-baiting with dog and handler (1689); outside the new Law Courts a columned drinking fountain, embellished with lovely carvings of fruit and birds, is dedicated to the Marquis of Bristol 'from a few of his Lincolnshire tenants' (1847).

In a region of monumental rarities, Lincolnshire has some prime examples ranging from the venerable Scrivlesby Lion (with crown; Passant Guardant over

'The Drums of the Fore and Aft'. Sculptor: 8th Earl of Albermarle (cast c. 1900, resited 1980). Location: Council Offices, Woodbridge.

the greenstone arch entering the estate of the Dymoke family, and of the Queen's Champion) to the bizarre stone carvings of Thomas Lovely, a church stonemason, adorning the garden wall of his self-built Victorian villa at Branston, north of Sleaford. Family portraits mingle with monkeys erected to rebuff local tongue-wagging about a mortgage ('monkey money'). At Holton le Moore near Market Raisen, the 'Moot House' lauds local and English heroes, including Wellington and General Gordon, in wall reliefs faintly reminiscent of Essex pargetting.

Sculptural and architectural specialities, like the pargetting that enriches timber-framed houses, help preserve fast-eroding county identity: go to Market Hill in Saffron Waldon for exuberant plasterwork showing 'Thomas Hickathrift and the Wisbech Giant'; to Blakeney in north Norfolk, where a small-arched war memorial is faced with knapped flint (locally called 'cobbles') after the vernacular architecture; to Swaffham, where the legendary Pedlar appears with dog and crock of gold on the painted village sign of seasoned oak, carved by Harry Carter of Swaffham, then the most celebrated practitioner of this short-lived, thematic, Norfolk craft introduced by George V.

Among the building figures that stand out in small as well as larger towns, is a rare 'Justice' without blindfold, lead-covered, set up in 1754 on the octagonal Buttercross (1689) in traffic-rattled Bungay. Still a local meeting place the cross once contained a cage for wrong-doers waiting to appear in court, too poor for bed-and-foot- or hand-irons at the Swan Inn. Pevsner nominates Henry Cheere as sculptor.

The crowning glory of Colchester Town Hall is St Helena, patron saint, reputed daughter of Old King Cole. She began as the Virgin Mary, but was modified when funds ran out, and now holds aloft the 'true cross' from the Victoria Tower.

Other varied regional treasures include a 13th-century statue in Crowland; and in neighbouring

Wisbech (Cambridgeshire), a worn red sandstone relief of a slave in chains, The Suppliant was 'created by Josiah Wedgwood' after James Hackwood's cameo, as a side panel on the Gothic monument to the anti-slaver Thomas Clarkson of Wisbech (1760–1846). John Oldrid completed the canopy at the death of his father Sir George Gilbert Scott, brother of the then vicar.

Present day East Anglian speech has echoes in an inscription stone beneath a 1950s obelisk near Hadleigh, in a field off the Sudbury Ipswich bypass (Lady Lane). That marks the site of Dr Rowland Taylor's martyrdom in 1555, having as its base the original stone: 'D. TAYLER . IN . DEFENDING . THAT . WAS . GOOD . AT . THIS . PLACE. LEFT . HIS . BLODE'.

Also in Suffolk on Lowestoft's sea front, which has something for everyone, Royal Plain displays a pair of rather flabby Bath stone Tritons – sons of Neptune – bearing cornucopias. Restored by A.J. Woods of Norwich in 1983, they were set up by Sir Samuel Morton Peto for whom the architect-sculptor John Thomas worked at the rebuilding and setting of Somerleyton Hall (1844–57), five miles northwest.

At the edge of the Lincolnshire Wolds, a roadside memorial preserves the names of Dalderby village's entire male population, bar three, who went to the Great War. The accolade, fine-cut in slate, was no less hard-won – even though they all came home.

This, in essence, is Lincolnshire, and this is the Eastern Counties: large gestures, respect for fine detail, and a particular pride.

(*Note*: Two interesting bronze compositions in the Eastern Counties can be viewed by arrangement. One is a high relief head and shoulders of Dr Thomas Barnardo (1845–1905), at Barnardo's Home in Barkingside, Essex, created *gratis* by Sir George Frampton in 1908. In the late 1980s, the widowed husband of one of the attendant bronze orphans was still occupying the residential home opposite the memorial – Barnardo's really does care 'from the cradle to the grave'.

The other is at King's Lynn, where King Edward VII School has a magnificent figure of Edward in academic robes uneasily seated in a sumptuous chair whilst two pudgy-buttocked putti hover with the crown. The work of W.R. Colton, it was unveiled by Queen Alexandra in 1906.

Also privately owned, but visible from the road at Sandringham Stud, is Adrian Jones's lifesize blue metal statue of Persimmon, 1896 Derby-winner and one of the greats. It was presented to the Prince of Wales by the Jockey Club.)

Edward VII (1841–1910). Sculptor: W. R. Colton (1906). Location: King Edward VII School, King's Lynn (view by arrangement).

Eastern Counties Gazetteer

Note: The Eastern Counties appear in loosely topographical order. Within each county, monuments are listed under their locations, which appear in alphabetical order. Letters (Hn) after a location indicate its county of origin, Huntingdonshire.

Essex

Chelmsford

Town Feature:

Sir Nicholas Conyngham Tindal, Lord Chief Justice
(1776–1846)
Seated bronze statue on stone pedestal
Sculptor Edward Hodges Baily
Location Tindal Square

The judge sits in Tindal Square near the magistrates' court in the old Shire Hall. He has been given a fine judge's slouch, but his features match the testament of the inscription: 'directed by serene wisdom, animated by purest love of justice, endeared by unwearied kindness and graced by the most lucid style'. Sir Nicholas was not considered eloquent or persuasive as an advocate, but he was respected for his wisdom, clarity and dry wit, and for a familiarity with the obscurer points of law.

Sir Nicholas was born at Moulsham Street, son of a Chelmsford solicitor. He attended the Grammar School and later Trinity College, Cambridge, then studied at Lincoln's Inn Fields, and quickly established a reputation as a practising lawyer on the Northern Circuit. He was associated with some of the *causes célèbres* of the day and lost an appointment as Crown representative through serving as an advocate for Queen Caroline with Brougham and Denman. He was elected MP for Wigtown District in 1824, and in 1826 was appointed Solicitor General, receiving a knighthood at the same time.

Judge Tindal's refusal to accept the post of

Sir Nicholas Conyngham Tindal (1776–1846). Sculptor: Edward Hodges Baily (1850). Location: Tindal Square, Chelmsford. (Note this was restored 1989).

Attorney General was put down to his 'characteristic modesty', but his talents better suited his later appointment as Lord Chief Justice of the Common Pleas (1829).

His statue was executed and exhibited in 1847, and erected in 1850. In 1867 the Art Journal claimed it to be a rehash of John Bacon the Elder's Sir William Blackstone (All Souls Oxford, 1784); it was 'open to criticism' according to the *Essex Review* of 1901. John Bacon's Coade stone reliefs of Justice, Wisdom and Mercy enrich the pediment of the stately Shire Hall, and in the Hall foyer stands a Coade stone lifesize statue of Hygeia, goddess of health, that topped a domed conduit now standing in the Tower Gardens.

The conduit's original site in Tindal Square is now occupied by the judge's statue, which received a much-needed 1980s restoration, tardily reviving the inscription's avowal of 'undying remembrance'. Memorable or forgotten, or a 're-con', the judge in his wig and robes brings a touch of humanity to the modern surroundings of banks, estate agents and building societies.

Town Selection

All public works are 'open to criticism', and a honey coloured ferro-cement grouping by Sioban Coppinger, 'Bringing Home the Bacon', caused an uproar when proposed in 1989 as part of the borough centenary celebration. Featuring a grinning pig in a bronze shopping trolley pushed by a Farmer Giles figure, it was presented by Countryside Properties plc as a joint symbol of the market town's agricultural tradition and its present commercial boom. Conceived as an 'event' in the landscaping of a High Street motorbike parking reservation which replaced the motorbikes with seats, plants, marketeer and pig, it drew cries of 'revolting' and 'meretricious' during a period of brisk and sometimes heated public debate over its 'suitability'.

East Tilbury

Town Selection:

Tomas Bata (1876–1932)
Full length bronze statue on polished
granite pedestal
Sculptor Hermon Cawthra
Foundry John Galizia & Son, London
Location St Margaret's Road

Tomas Bata (1876–1932). Sculptor: Hermon Cawthra (1932). Location: St Margaret's Road, East Tilbury.

The Czechoslovakian shoemaker Tomas Bata stands beneath his shoe factory, set up near Tilbury marshes and the industrial Thames two years before Bata died in a plane crash at the height of his astonishing career. Designed by Bata architects, the factory, with its workers' accommodation and shopping and recreational facilities, was modelled on those overlooking Bata's birthplace, Zlin. Here he began as an impoverished shoemaker, and with relentless drive created the Bata organisation in a modernistic industrial complex and 'garden city' on the pine clad slopes overlooking the small Moravian town.

Dedicated to making good-quality shoes for the masses, Bata made his own machinery, built tanneries, paper and dye mills, and pioneered mass-production techniques. After the First World War his factories used 'the Bata System', based on decen-

trification, open accounting and worker participation. Bata averted a bankruptcy crisis by price-
slashing, set up retail chains with pedicure services
and taught his store managers other entrepreneurial
techniques. His buyers scoured the globe in search
of materials – 'If you can't use a truck, use a camel';
posters, bearing similar, 3ft, slogans instructed the
workplace.

Incensed at Zlin's new tax-funded town hall (with
a huge statue of a blacksmith signifying industry),
Bata espoused politics and was voted mayor in
return for a town modernisation programme on a
benevolent business agreement. (Philanthropy, he
believed, curbed people's instinct for self-help).

At his death, Bata factories were producing shoes
the world over, and today the family is still associated with the organisation, which operates an
updated version of the original Bata System.

Tomas Bata's sculptor has made a true character
study of his cropped-haired subject, recording his
prominent ears as well as his hawk-eyed smile. The
texture of the suit with its turn-ups, and the creases
in the shoes, are part of the careful detailing in an
informal work of great charm. It was unveiled in
1955, on the 23rd anniversary of Bata's death,
together with the company's cenotaph by Cawthra.
The bronze urn and flame powerfully recall Bata
employees who fell in the Second World War.

Suffolk

Aldeburgh

Town Feature:

Snooks
Dr P.M. (Robin) Acheson (d.1959)
and Dr. Nora Acheson (d.1981)
Small bronze statue of dog on stone pedestal
Sculptor Gwynneth Holt
Location Crabbe Street, Model Yacht Pond

Sitting alert and watchful, his attention on children
and fathers with their model boats, the figure of this
little terrier guards the water whilst the plinth carries
a tribute from 'the people of the borough to Dr.
Robin P.M. Acheson, who cared for them from 1931
to 1959, and to Dr Nora his wife, who died 1981
whilst still caring'.

The second part of the tribute was added in 1981,
twenty years after the unveiling of Snooks by the
Achesons' small granddaughters. The statue was a
contribution from their mother and Dr Nora and
was added to Dr Robin's memorial from the town,
the model boat pond enlarged from a Second World
War water tank. This aptly recalls Dr Robin's love
of children and of sailing and, as a borough councillor
from 1945, his interest in improving the town's
amenities. This particular town amenity was a recognition of his skill, prudence and humanity.

Dr Robin served with the army in the Second
World War, whilst his wife cared for the local community, being one of the first women doctors to go
out with the lifeboat. Local people remember her
driving on missions during air raids with a loaded
revolver in her bag, and restoring the cottage hospital within 24 hours of its being bombed – 'she
could turn her hand to most things, and would
remove fish hooks from fingers in seconds, with a
pair of wire cutters'.

Also first-aid instructor for the St John's Ambu-
lance Brigade and the Aldeburgh Lifeboat, in her

'Snooks', monument to Dr Robin (d.1959) and later dedicated
also to Dr Nora Acheson (d.1981). Sculptor: Gwynneth Holt
(1961). Location: Crabbe Street, Aldeburgh.

81st year Dr Nora, still treating patients, received an illuminated scroll naming her as an Honoured Citizen in a ceremony near Snooks's statue. Aldeburgh had lost borough status under the 1970s local government reforms, and the scroll symbolised Freedom of the Borough.

Snooks was a familiar figure in the neighbourhood, roaming his 'patch' with a written exhortation on his collar, *'Please do not throw stones at this dog'*, and leaping into his master's car at his call as it was passing. His statue fits in well with the town's fishy shingle shore and the grand old sea-front cottages of brick or flint, showing the odd Dutch gable.

Only a few yards along the front, past the War Memorial cross, the Moot Hall recalls Aldeburgh's days as a flourishing port, before the sea washed half of it away and left the Moot Hall not in the centre, but on the sea-edge of the town. The hall now contains the local museum. Dr Nora's scroll can be seen here, and the shops sell a reprint of her children's book, *Up the Steps*: it is a smugglers' tale based on true stories told to Dr Nora by her patients from fishing families. The statue she gave, inevitably known as 'Snoopy', will live in future childhood memories of Aldeburgh.

Town Selection

In St Peter and St Paul Churchyard is a big, rocky marble memorial to seven lifeboatmen, drowned after capsizing 'in the teeth of an easterly gale and a heavy rolling sea' on December 7th, 1899. The church has a memorial window to Benjamin Britten (1913–1976), whose opera *Peter Grimes* was inspired by a tale from George Crabbe's *The Borough* (1810), Aldeburgh local history contained in a long poem. George Crabbe's monument by T. Thurlow is in the church. Both writers are buried here.

Sudbury

Town Feature:

Thomas Gainsborough (1727–1788)
Full-length bronze statue on Portland stone pedestal
Sculptor (Sir) Bertram Mackennal, RA
Location Market Hill

This is Suffolk's only conventional commemorative statue, and it occupies a prime position at the top of Market Hill, outside the stately west front of St

Panel from statue of Thomas Gainsborough (1727–1788). Sculptor: Sir Bertram Mackennal, RA (date). Location: Market Hill, Sudbury.

Peter's Church. The painter is poised as if in the studio, bareheaded, with ruffles at wrist and throat, holding palette and brush. A relief panel on the shaped pedestal shows a Gainsborough lady, and a panel on the back has a pretty arrangement of viol, mandolin and paint brushes after Gainsborough's love of music and musical instruments.

His lifelong preoccupation, however, was with landscape painting, combined with matchless effect in the portraits of friends, high society and royalty that brought his living and his reputation.

His statue was unveiled by Queen Victoria's daughter Princess Louise, patroness of the monument and herself a painter and sculptor. It was earlier exhibited at the Royal Academy, of which Gainsborough was the only provincial founder-member — though not the most dutiful or compliant.

Gainsborough's birthplace, an early 18th-century town house, is open for view near the bottom of Market Hill. He lived here with his brothers and sisters, the family of a Sudbury cloth trader, and is said to have developed his early talent for landscape work through sketching trips on truant from his uncle's grammar school. At 13 he went to London to study art, and earned his keep as an assistant engraver and illustrator.

After his marriage to Margaret Burr, Gainsborough settled in Ipswich, seeking work in the genre of portrait figures in landscapes which he largely popularised. In some scenes his work shows the influence of Dutch masters; others are more formal, with lakes and temples. One of the most successful is his marriage portrait of Mr and Mrs Andrews of Ballington Hall, he with gun and dog, she on a pretty park seat, the scene completed with thunder clouds and sheaves, in a Suffolk wheatfield. Another lovely portrait, of Gainsborough's daughters chasing a butterfly, was painted just before Gainsborough moved to fashionable Bath in 1759.

His success was sealed with a series of full-length portraits of society figures. Many were exhibited in London, and in 1774 Gainsborough moved to the capital where he received commissions from royalty. Famous and prosperous, he enjoyed home life but avoided high society or London litterati; he was highly respected by fellow painters, but happiest amongst actors and musicians.

Impetuous, generous and quarrelsome, he broke with the Royal Academy, temperamentally at odds with his rival, Sir Joshua Reynolds. However, he made amends on his deathbed, and Reynolds was among the Academy members who acted as a pall bearer at his funeral. Soon after, Reynolds devoted his 14th Discourse to the work of Gainsborough, whom he had described 'the first landscape painter in Europe'.

Norfolk

Cromer

Town Feature:

Henry Blogg, GC BEM (1876–1954)
Bronze bust on granite pedestal
Sculptor James Woodford, RA
Location North Lodge Park, East Cliff

Lifeboatman Henry Blogg's bronze memorial bust shows Cromer's greatest son in oilskins and life

Henry Blogg, GC BEM (1876–1954).
Sculptor: James Woodford, RA (1962).
Location: East Cliff, Cromer.

jacket. Under the sou'wester, his leathery but homely features are creased against the weather, and his shrewd eyes search the North Sea, which is the friend and foe of this seafaring town.

The bust in its paved, seated recess makes a gossiping point for day trippers and locals. Behind are the Council Offices in a house faced with flint cobbles, as are most buildings in these parts. Nearby is the bowling green, and further on, the town's tiled roofs crowd round the church tower. Beneath the sea-bitten cliffs the crab boats make a line of colour along the shore.

The inscription is tersely eloquent:

... 'COXWAIN OF CROMER LIFEBOATS 1909–1947, WINNER OF THE RNLI GOLD MEDAL FOR CONSPICUOUS GALLANTRY 3 TIMES, OF ITS SILVER MEDAL 4 TIMES; WITH THE HELP OF ITS GALLANT CREW RESCUED 873 LIVES DURING 53 YEARS OF SERVICE. ONE OF THE BRAVEST MEN THAT EVER LIVED'.

The bust was given by Miss E.M. Scales, who remained anonymous until her death some years after the unveiling in 1962. She and her sister were disappointed, on visiting Cromer, to find no better tribute to Blogg than a public memorial shelter by the church. Her gift was unveiled by Commodore the Right Honourable Earl Howe, then chief of the RNLI.

To the staying-power, courage and sea skills demanded of all lifeboatmen, who are unpaid volunteers, Coxwain Blogg added an ingenuity and panache that made his exploits famous and himself a living legend. He took over as Cromer coxwain in a pulling and sailing lifeboat, the 'Louisa Heartwell', in which he won his first Gold Medal (1917); his last voyage was made in 1948 at the age of 71, in a new lifeboat, the 'Henry Blogg'. His coxwain and successor, Henry 'Shrimp' Davies, later laid a wreath at the unveiling of Bloggs's memorial bust. The sculptor's artistry makes a fitting tribute.

Cromer locality Selection

Down the coast at Great Yarmouth, the Norfolk Pillar exalts '..*The terror of the world, That Nelson, by birth, lineage and education, By mind, by manners, and by disposition, Norfolk proudly boasts her own ...'*. The architect, William Wilkins, was also Norfolk-born. His 144ft Greek Doric column is surmounted by a cupola carrying fibreglass Victories, replacements of Coade stone originals; they support a fibreglass 'Britannia' who rules the waves with her back to the sea, facing northwest towards Nelson's native

village, Burnham Thorpe. Completed in 1819, and predating Trafalgar Square's by 20 years, the fluted Pillar is prolifically inscribed. On certain days, a 117–step climb admits views of industrial, fishing and Kiss-me-Quick Yarmouth, invigorating in climate and in style.

Norwich

City Feature:

Sir Thomas Browne (1605–1682)
Seated bronze statue on granite pedestal
Sculptor Henry Alfred Pegram
Location South side St Peter Mancroft Church,
Hay Hill

This distinctive bronze shows Sir Thomas Browne, physician and writer, sitting in deep contemplation outside the church where he lies buried, opposite his former home in the old Hay Hill. London-born, Browne studied at Winchester and Pembroke College, Oxford, then travelled in Ireland and in Europe before settling in Norwich, where he practised as a physician. His statue now makes a focal point in a modern development of seats and fountains which attract, among others, graffiti-artists and church-roosting pigeons. Unchanged is the daily clamour round the market stalls.

Browne's statue shows him pondering a fragment of urn which, with the urn-shape of his pedestal, is a reference to his work *Hydriotaphia*, or *Urn Burial*. Written in the 1650s, this was occasioned by archæological discoveries in Walsingham and other parts of Norfolk. It is recognised as a reflective work of rare eloquence and power, but it was Browne's first work, the private treatise *Religio Medici*, inspired by his travels and published in 1642, that established his fame as a scholar and writer.

Browne's encyclopædic interests in the antique and natural worlds, the metaphysical and the fantastic, brought many visitors and correspondents, among them the botanist John Ray, and John Evelyn; Evelyn's diary records his admiration for Browne's collections of the rarities and natural finds. Browne supported the Royalist cause in the Civil War, and in 1671 was knighted in Norwich by Charles II.

The closing thoughts in Browne's *Urn Burial* ponder the inefficacy of monuments: 'There is no antidote against the opium of time ... Pyramids, arches, obelisks, were but the irregularities of vain-

Sir Thomas Browne (1605–1682).
Sculptor: H. A. Pegram (1905). Location:
Hay Hill, Norwich.

glory, and wild enormities of ancient magnanimity'. His statue was erected in 1905. His skull, dug up by workmen in the 19th century, preserved in the museum at Norwich Hospital and since reinterred, can be seen in plaster copy at the Post Graduate Library of Norfolk and Norwich Hospital.

Norwich Selection

In Tombland, outside the Cathedral Close where she is buried, stands a bronze portrait bust of Edith Cavell, 'NURSE, PATRIOT AND MARTYR'. H. A. Pegram presents a steadfast, sensible British nurse set on a tall pedestal, with a stone figure of a soldier reaching up a wreath (1918).

At Swardeston, Cavell's birthplace, where her father was rector, the village church has the shaft of a wooden cross erected over her first burial place near Brussels, where she was shot for helping British soldiers escape during the German Occupation. The church has a memorial window, and holds a service on the Saturday nearest the anniversary of her death. Her national monument in London overlooks Trafalgar Square.

The richly-carved Erpingham Gate (1420), entrance to the Close, has a niche statue of its builder, Sir Thomas Erpingham, in plate armour with surcoat. The upper close has an algae-greened marble of a dandified Nelson by Thomas Milnes, and on the north side is a bronze statue of the Duke of Wellington by George Adams, who took the death mask of Wellington. Both statues were unveiled in the Market Place in 1854 but later resited, Wellington's in 1936 to rumblings of a 'pacifist plot'.

Opposite the close and Nurse Cavell's memorial are nicely incongruous figures of Samson and Hercules, Christian and pagan figures of fortitude. They support the porch of a four-gabled house said to date from 1657, lately venue of the Samson and Hercules Club. (*See* also majestic City Hall lions and, on Agricultural Plain, the Boer War memorial with winged Victory.)

Cambridgeshire (& Huntingdonshire)

Harston/Little Shelford

Countryside Feature:

Gregory Wale (1669–1739)
Tapering limestone obelisk with fluted globe finial
on large, cement-rendered truncated pyramidal base
Designer Charles Bottomley
Location St Margaret's Mount (near Little Shelford)

The slim obelisk with its globular flame and pyramidal skirt is revealed to the walker only after negotiation of country roads, a rusting gate and a rough fieldpath ascending through crops to the boundary of skyline trees. Past the trees the view opens out, the path ascending to the right to the top of the field, and a limestone obelisk the colour of ripe corn.

London-Cambridge trains rattle past within view, whilst the M11 flyover crosses the lane which gives on to the crop field, but the land may be little changed since the 1730s when 'Maggot's Mount' was a Sunday meeting place for James Church of Harston and Gregory Wale of Shelford, who each pledged that the last one to die would raise a monument to his friend. Both names are incised in the stone. A slate records the monument's restoration by Rattee & Kett in 1985.

It was Gregory Wale, JP and Conservator of the River Cam, who died first, 'universally lamented' — some say he was the victim of a highwayman, others of a fall from his horse. He held no high national office and performed no far-famed deeds, but his surviving friend records attributes that would fit most people's aspirations:

HE LIVED
AN ADVOCATE FOR LIBERTY,
A GOOD SUBJECT,
AN AGREEABLE COMPANION,
A FAITHFUL FRIEND,
AN HOSPITABLE NEIGHBOUR,
AND IN ALL PARTS OF LIFE
AN USEFUL MEMBER OF SOCIETY.

He was buried as he had wished, within sight of Little Shelford Church and the manor house, in the family vault opposite the church. A house called 'Gregory's Close' was built there in the 1950s, after the vault was moved, and was occupied by descendants until the 1970s. Relatives still live in the village.

By the 1980s the monument had succumbed to frost damage and general weathering, but was by no means forgotten. Villagers who feared further deterioration were finally spurred to action by a letter to the parish council from a motorway traveller who had become concerned about this 'delightful little monument'.

Proceeds from village fêtes and coffee mornings were augmented by contributions from county conservation groups and societies, neighbouring parish councils and Wale family relatives and well-wishers. Amongst them was an octogenarian who sent a drawing of the original brick base, looking like a hoop skirt — the cement was applied in the correspondent's schooldays.

Funds mounted close to £3,000, enough for a thorough restoration including replacement of the stone finial and the inscription panels, recutting of

Wale Monument: obelisk to Gregory Wale (1669–1739).
Designer: C. Bottomley (restored 1985). Location: St
Margaret's Mount, near Little Shelford.

the stone mason's name, making good stone and brickwork, re-rendering, repointing, cleaning and weatherproofing. The original inscription's spelling has been straightened, but Gregory Wale's obelisk is once again worthy of 'so worthy a gentleman'.

Gregory Wale remains a shadowy figure, a gentleman of leisure whose ancestors of Norman blood had estates at Shelford and Harston Hall. His second wife was the daughter of a preacher, Captain Hitch, and their granddaughter Margaret is recorded as 'the toast of Cambridge'. A descendant, Blennie Powell, sold some land to the council at a favourable price, and since the 1970s these local allotments have been known as 'Blennie's Patch'.

However, more meaningful than these and other fragments of his story is Gregory's Obelisk, a 'publick testimony of friendship', a friendly waymark for travellers, and a sign of continuity in this locality made up of satellite villages, lonely lanes and rich cultivated fields.

(*Note:* Visitors should keep to the specially-maintained footpath.)

Hilton (Hn)

Village Feature:

William Sparrow (1641–1729)
Turf maze; stone pier with cornice and ball filial at centre, commemorating cutting of maze by William Sparrow in 1660
Location The Green (north approach to Hilton on the B1040)

'SIC TRANSIT
GLORIA MVNDI
GVLIELMVS SPARROW
GENNATVS AN: 1641 . . .'.

William Sparrow's monument, with old letters biting deep into lichened stone, tells in Latin and English the rudimentary history of man and maze. The inscribed pillar with its globe occupies the centre of the turf-cut maze, under some trees, and at the edge a framed printed council notice gives a brief historical account.

Maze, & pillar to William Sparrow (1641–1729). Location: the Green, Hilton.

A circular, carved medallion contains the Sparrow family arms, featuring three roses and a unicorn.

This bit of old England is approached between big, cultivated fields ending at the spacious irregular green, the common land at the edge of the village. William Sparrow lived on the site of Park Farm opposite, where a painting of the arms of James I was found. This is now kept in Hilton parish church.

'HOS GYROS FORMAVIT 1660', the year of Charles II's Restoration, and it perhaps marks the end of the Cromwellian regime. Its intricate geometric pattern is thought to have been recut rather than originated by Sparrow, possibly from a maze in Comberton (since destroyed) where his brother-in-law, Baron Brittaine, lived.

Turf mazes were once a feature of the village green, being used in fertility rites or to deter the Devil, who is reputed only to travel a straight path. Few survive. The Parish Council returved the paths of the Hilton maze in 1988, the grass is now cut regularly in summer, and in this way the maze is perpetuated.

To follow William Sparrow's maze is to experience, briefly, the power that ritual and superstition held over medieval minds. Like Hilton's, and the remaining mazes in England, these phenomena have not entirely died away.

Potto Brown (1797–1871). Sculptor: not known. Location: the Green, Houghton.

Houghton (Hn)

Village Feature:

Potto Brown (1797–1871)
Bronze bust on polished pink granite pedestal
Sculptor Not known
Location The Green

This unsigned work reflects all the glowering authority of a bronze or marble statue raised for some Victorian City Father, but Potto Brown's leonine head and shoulders face the village clock under its thatched shelter, the cast-iron pump, and the surrounding timbered, gabled houses.

The only unsightly feature is the Green's tarmac, where grass grew when the Miller of Houghton '... spent his life devoting himself to the best interests of those around him'. He was born and bred, thrice married, twice widowed, and died in a red brick house on the St Ives road. His mill on a tributary of the Ouse, a well-loved local building, is now preserved by the National Trust.

The pedestal's fine-carved, forceful biblical texts recall Potto Brown's work as 'Village Philanthropist', and his missionary work as a dissenter. Born to the Quaker faith, he took over his father's mill partnered by his friend Joseph Goodman, with whom the unschooled Brown later set up a parish school in Houghton; an astute businessman, he diverted his not inconsiderable profits to establishing a free church and parish schools.

After Goodman's lamented early death, Potto Brown continued his work, opening a missionary church at Houghton, and holding his breakfast time meetings to plan religious and educational operations prompt at 7am. He conducted Sunday School, and took up preaching, despite his discomfort at public speaking. He set up the popular High Temperance Festival with preachers and games (but excluding 'Kiss in the Ring') to coincide with the Houghton Feast, which had brought dancing and strong drink to the village green. And he was evicted from his tenant farm by the squire's wife, Lady Olivia

Sparrow, who disapproved of Brown's success at the expense of the local Established Church and schools. Subsequently acquiring his own farm, he apportioned 10% of the annual profits to charity.

Brown was a great Houghton character, purposeful, devout and droll. His portrait manages to reflect these qualities and his exploits are recounted in his biography, *Potto Brown: the Village Philanthropist*, by Albert Goodman (1878).

Lincolnshire

Crowland

Town Feature:

Trinity Bridge statue
14th century triangular stone bridge with 13th-century seated statue
Sculptor Not known
Location Centre of town

The 14th-century bridge is a rare survival and itself a monument to the past. Its three arches meet at an apex, and just below, on the southerly rise, is the seated statue. It gives little hint of its provenance, since the centuries have weathered its features away to the hollowed eyes, and the outline of long hair, robes and, perhaps, a beard. The 13th-century crowned figure holds a worn object in the manner of a king with his orb, but probably represents Christ with the globe.

The statue is six feet high and has a forward projection of only ten inches, perhaps indicating that it was carved for the front view. This supports the theory that until 1720 it occupied the west gable of Crowland's ruined abbey (c.1260-80), which stands on the east side of the town. The abbey was founded in 716 by King Ethelbald of Mercia near the swampy site of the cell built by his kinsman, St Guthlac, whose life appears in relief with tiers of figures representing saints, apostles and kings on the abbey's surviving west front.

Ethelbald has been suggested as a possible subject for the crowned statue. Other unlikely historical figures include Our Lady of Walsingham, or Oliver Cromwell holding a penny loaf. A member of the Spalding Gentleman's Society has refuted the idea of Cromwell — 'not after what he did to Crowland'.

Trinity Bridge statue. Sculptor: not known. Location: Crowland.

A notice mounted by the society gives historical details of the statue and bridge.

The bridge once provided a foot-crossing over a divergence of the River Welland, the waters of which still flow beneath North and West Streets. It is now parked at the four-ways cross with South and North Streets, forming the centre of a conservation area for this quiet fenland town.

Now the town's meeting point, the ancient bridge is thought formerly to have supported a canopied cross, providing a station for devotions and preaching at the pilgrims' approach to the medieval abbey. Recent restorations were carried out only after years of deliberation on the part of the Department of the Environment; yet with its mysterious statue, the Triangular Bridge is part of fenlands history, and one of England's treasures.

Lincoln

City Feature:

Alfred Tennyson, 1st Baron Tennyson (1809–1892)
Full-length bronze statue on Polyphant marble
inscribed base
Sculptor George Frederic Watts, RA, OM
Base designer Christopher Turnor
Location Outside Chapter House, Lincoln
Cathedral

The massive rough-textured figure, wearing a cloak and holding a wide-brimmed hat, broods over a small plant held up to his short-sighted gaze in the other hand. He is watched by his rugged companion Karenina, a Siberian Wolfhound. The plant is a sprig of ivy-leaved toadflax, thought to have been introduced to England entwined round classical statues brought from the Continent in the 18th century. It is the *Flower in the Crannied Wall* contemplated in Tennyson's 'compactly miniature and glinting

Alfred Lord Tennyson (1809–1892). Sculptor: G. F. Watts, RA, OM (1905). Location: Lincoln Cathedral.

philosophical poem' – so described in a biography of 1972 by Christopher Ricks. The single verse, written in 1869, appears on bronze Art-Nouveau-lettered panels affixed to the flaking stone of the statue's base.

Tennyson is most admired for his great lyrical powers, but other works reflect a sombre melancholy (probably nurtured in a troubled childhood home), and anxieties typical of an age struggling to come to terms with unprecedented technological and scientific advance. Even so, Tennyson was the most popular and revered of the Victorian poets: works like *Morte d'Arthur* and *The Charge of the Light Brigade*, and the line 'Come into the garden Maude', are still part of the popular literary reference.

Tennyson's friend and admirer G.F. Watts recalls in the statue 'the wonder and reverence with which Alfred always cared for the least marvel of the natural world'. One of 12 children of a village rector, he was home-educated (after a miserable period at a boarding school in Louth) in the remote Lincolnshire village of Somersby. His elder brothers Charles and Frederick were minor poets.

Tennyson's illustrious years as poet and sage were passed at Freshwater on the Isle of Wight, and later also at a second house in Haslemere, about ten miles from F.W. Watts's Surrey home. The move south came three years after Tennyson was appointed Poet Laureate in November, 1850; publication of his long poem *In Memoriam A.H.H.*, in May of that year, had been followed by a June marriage to Emily Sellwood, sister-in-law of his brother Charles.

The Epilogue of *In Memoriam* celebrates Charles's marriage of 1836, at which Tennyson fell for Emily, the bridesmaid. The series of elegies was composed over 17 years in response to Tennyson's grief at the early death of his Cambridge friend and prospective brother-in-law, Arthur Hallam in 1833. It was on reading the manuscript in 1850 that Emily was persuaded finally to marry Tennyson, some eight years after he had broken their engagement for lack of means and through unease (shared by Emily's family) at his family background and the bluff gloom of his personality.

Watts's bronze portrait gives an impression of the dark-featured figure who would stride across the countryside, cloak billowing, declaiming his works to children and admirers. The poet also enjoyed regaling more formal and distinguished gatherings. He was made a peer in 1884; like Watts, his friend of 50 years, he was still working in his 80s.

One of Watts's paintings of Tennyson is in the National Portrait Gallery, and the Lincoln statue's original plaster cast is preserved at the Watts Picture Gallery in Compton, Surrey. The figure was modelled in Watts's last years, but its force and power belie the arthritic twinges of the octogenarian. The sculptor used *gesso* instead of clay, even though it set too fast for him to 'look, and alter, with finger and thumb' – so he confided to Canon Rawnsley, whose parish at Crosthwaite was familiar to Tennyson, a friend of James Spedding of Mirehouse.

Watts created the model as a gift, but did not live to see the casting. The base was a gift of its designer, Christopher Turnor of Stoke Rochford, architect of the Watts Picture Gallery. Canon Rawnsley composed a poem for the statue's unveiling, performed in 1905 by the Countess Brownlow of Belton who, with her husband the 3rd Earl, Lord Lieutenant of Lincoln, initiated and organised creation of this county memorial to Tennyson. (An engaging bust of the bewhiskered and uniformed 3rd Earl, by his cousin-in-law Nina Cust, occupies a shubbery at Belton House.)

The question of siting strenuously occupied the indefatigable Mrs Watts, who travelled frequently to Lincoln on her husband's behalf; eventually the statue stayed more or less where it was delivered. Watts himself favoured the cathedral location. The handsome base carries a plaque recording the statue's 1970 restoration, commissioned by Mrs Maud Scorer and Mrs Edyth Cowan, in memory of their late husbands.

The restoration followed denials of ownership, and thereby responsibility, from all quarters, despite the pleas of the then newly-formed Tennyson Society. Lincoln Corporation has since assumed care of this impressive piece, which in 1905 was a triumph of modernism combined with popular appeal – a rare combination.

Lincoln Selection

On the Castle lawn stands the head and shoulders of George III, from a 15ft full-length statue cast by Eleanor Coade after a model by Joseph Panzetta. It was hoisted up on to the 'Dunstan Pillar' lantern for the Duke of Buckingham at the King's 1810 Jubilee, but itself removed as a hazard to aircraft in 1941. The pillar, set up in 1751 on wild heathland by Sir Francis Dashwood as an inland lighthouse, is now a ruin between two maisonettes on the A15.

Stored in the Museum of Lincolnshire Life, in the segments of which it was originally formed, the statue was later part-reassembled and restored by a Lincoln stone mason, John Ivory. (Note the fore-

George III (1738–1820). Sculptor: Joseph Panzetta for Coade (1810, resited 1974). Location: Lincoln Castle.

man's initials 'J.P., August 1974' under the left shoulder.) One can now out-stare 'George the one-third' eyeball to protruding eyeball, and savour the crisp detail of crown, fur trim, tassel and badge, coated with nature's green algae over Ivory's protective layers of waterproofing and epoxy resin. George's remaining bits are reckoned past assembly.

On the corner of Union and Carline Roads, outside the former Lawn Hospital, a marble statue of Edward Parker Charlesworth was put up in the year of his death, 1853, to commemorate his 'pioneer work in the field of mental health' as Vice President and Physician at the hospital. 'The White Doctor' was the work of Thomas Milnes, sculptor of Nelson's statue at Norwich.

In the Arboretum on Monks Road stands a large and hungry lion 'Presented by F.J.Clarke', Mayor of Lincoln in 1872. Made from moulds of Austin & Seeley, London, its mix of Portland cement, broken stone, pounded marble and coarse sand was also widely used for ornamental fountains and church tablets, among other items. A fountain nearby marks the opening of bore-holes at Elkesley, Nottinghamshire, in the 1900s; the fountain pillars are constructed of cores from the borings. This wondrous contraption, one of the county's many engaging monumental oddities, has recently been restored to working order.

John Bright (1811–1889). Sculptor: Sir W. H. Thornycroft (1891, later resited).
Location: Broadfield Park, Rochdale.

Northern Counties

'High Causes'

... it is the duty of every man according to his ability
and opportunity to do something in the town,
in the neighbourhood and the nation
to promote the wellbeing of its inhabitants.

(James Stuart (1830–1929), 'A citizen of Hull': inscribed under his statue in
Holderness Road, 1906)

In my early days
there were few schools to help us
in the pursuit of learning
If we wanted to climb we had
first to make our own ladders.

[The weaver and dialect writer Ben Brierley (1825–1896), inscribed on the
pedestal of his statue (statue since partially destroyed) in
Queen's Park, Manchester, 1898].

R esounding from a front garden in Hull, and an empty pedestal in a Manchester park, these stone-cut sentiments set the theme for monuments on either side of the industrial Pennines where working conditions in factories, mills and mines inspired the 19th-century crusades for self improvement and social reform.

From this period almost every northern working town has a prestige-boosting town hall, flamboyant or stately, carrying symbolic and thematic decorative sculpture; 'improving' libraries and institutes rich in terracotta moulding, or carving; and at least one statue immortalising, in formula bronze, a self-made founding father or a tub-thumping reformer. Many

Sir Titus Salt (1803–1876). Sculptor: F. Derwent Wood (1903). Location: Roberts Park, Saltaire.

works show the hand of leading Victorian sculptors; others are home-grown.

John Foley modelled Honest John Fielden, hero of the Ten Hour Bill, at Todmorden. Richard Oastler the 'Factory King', ranting champion of factory children and the Ten Hour Bill, is sentimentally portrayed in Bradford by J. Birnie Philip, who died whilst completing his plainer statue of Colonel Ackroyd. This was completed by Philip's pupil C.E. Fucina outside All Saints Church, designed for Ackroyd by George Gilbert Scott close to the model village built for his cloth workers in 1861. Ackroyd looks out on the Halifax mills from a narrow sloping green, where children from the stone terraced dwellings play football and tag.

The teetotal cotton master Hugh Mason crosses bronze arms in Henry Square, Ashton-under-Lyne; model mill owner and patriarchal employer, his powerful persona perpetuated by J. W. Swynnerton was unveiled in 1887 to wholesale rejoicing and beerswilling. The statue has been thrice resited; it was tactless, some say, to place him outside the Anglican church, and facing the pub.

A contrasting monument to a similar figure, the Leverhulme Memorial to William Hesketh Lever, 1st Viscount Leverhulme, makes its mark outside the domed Art Gallery dedicated to Lever's wife, at the first garden village, Port Sunlight. This was planned for his workers by Lever and the Warrington architect William Owen in 1888.

Fusing representationalism with stark modernism, J. Lomax Simpson's columnar memorial (1930, sculpture by Sir William Reid Dick) gives no visual image of 'the Chief', his nonconformist principles of hard graft and clean living, or his entrepreneurial and innovative flair which created the household names Persil, Lux, and Sunlight Soap. (Early customers insisted on 'that stinking soap'). On Lever's Warrington residence of 1886–88, a bull-headed, smiling but tight-lipped bronze profile gives a hint.

The famous model township Saltaire, near Bradford, has F. Derwent Wood's statue of its founder Sir Titus Salt in Roberts Park, erected in 1903 on the centenary of his birth to mark the golden jubilee of his alpaca mill. Salt and the pioneering Samuel Cunliffe Lister, inventor of the world's first reliable wool combing machine, both appear as marble patriarchal presences in Lister Park, Bradford, the fortunes of which were built on their lucrative innovations.

Other captains of industry are commemorated in old industrial ports like Barrow–in–Furness, the first mayor of which, James Ramsden, founded the town's iron-based industries, as H.W.F. Bolckow had in Middlesborough. Hartlepool's statue of the railway developer Ralph Ward-Jackson by E. Onslow Ford was privately presented as a tribute to the 'enterprise and perserverence of its founder' in 1897, jubilee year of the town's first harbour and dock. Most railway kings, founding fathers or factory barons were self-made men, whilst the powerful landowners exploited iron, and built sumptuous mansions on profits from coal.

Some left blackened landmarks like Lord Durham's hilltop temple of 1844 near Penshaw, or the eye-catchers and belvederes of the coal-owning Earls of Strafford, punctuating the coal-scarred farm land between Barnsley and Sheffield. The best known is Hoober Stand, a blackened triangular tower marking the defeat of the 1745 Rebellion and the Peace of Aix-la-Chapelle (1748). Its designer was Henry Flitcroft, whose East Front at Wentworth Wood-house stretches to some 600ft, the longest frontage in England.

At Wallington Hall (NT), the row of grimacing Griffin heads on the east lawn once formed sup-porters for the arms of the Bishop and the City of London on Bishopsgate. They were brought up as ballast with other stone statuary, according to tradition, on William Blackett's coal ships.

The workers' monuments, more modest and obscure, are all too often stark reminders of the price of coal, cotton or wool. A bronze Athene records the country's then worst coal disaster, the Oaks Explosion near Barnsley in 1866; children's names listed on a churchyard memorial mark 'a sudden irruption of water into the Coalpits of R.C. Clarke Esqr' on July 4th 1838, at Silkstone near Barnsley, and churchyard monuments record deaths by fire at Kirkharle of factory children, and at Huddersfield of women textile workers – this in 1941 – trapped on the fifth floor without a fire escape.

In Church Lane at Otley, a stone copy of the castellated Bramhope Tunnel entrance com-memorates construction workers killed whilst build-ing the Leeds-Thirsk Railway (1845–1849). This, and all the older monuments are covered with thundering biblical texts.

Near Rochdale art gallery the earthy, God-fearing sentiments of the four Rochdale Dialect Writers, reverberating from their monument, are also mir-rored in their relief portraits. Their writings bolstered the morale and expressed the privations of working people, through their dour Lancastrian humour, in their own vivid and fast-eroding speech. Nearby stands Sir Hamo Thornycroft's bronze of the orator and Corn Law reformer John Bright (1891), a friend of one of the group.

The repeal of the hated Corn Laws is celebrated by statues of Cobden and Bright in Stockport and Manchester, whilst Sir Robert Peel's image is repeated in bronze on either side of the Pennine divide, including his native town Bury, near Man-chester (by E.H. Baily, 1852). Preston, on the other hand, claims the earliest statue, stone-carved in 1851 by Thomas Duckett of Preston and castigated for 'closeness of the nether garments' at the unveiling in May, 1852. (Lancastrian statues' artistic worth does not accord with the subjects' fame, nor is sculptural expertise the *sine qua non* of a statue's charm.) Near Bury, the 128ft Holcombe Tower was also erected within two years of Peel's death.

The Corn Law Rhymer Ebenezer Elliot, crusading poet, has a bronze statue by Nevile Northey Burnard (1854) in Sheffield's Weston Park, but personal cam-paigns are honoured mostly away from the towns in remote localities where the landowner held sway, in the depths of the Yorkshire Wolds or green and pleasant Cheshire, or the Cumbrian fells and wildernesses stretching to Scotland. Shepherds, clim-bers, airmen and Dales stalwarts like 'Wonderful Walker' are lauded in the small monuments isolated among the Cumbrian waters and fells. Rugged local sentiment commends a Master of the Hounds who died after a fall in 1952, the spot marked by a small boulder facing the Screes across Wast Water: "HE'S AWAY MY LADS AWAY".

Perhaps most rare are the moorland crosses and carved stones that make waymarks, such as those along the packhorse, ironstone and jet miners' routes, and smugglers' trods on the North York Moors. One such, near the Lyke Wake Walk, Lilla's Howe,

'Lord Dacre's Cross' (Battle of Towton, 1461). Location: B1217, Towton Lane.

is reputedly the grave of a servant who died for his master, Edwin of Northumbria, in 626 AD.

In the remote Northumbrian villages, the later cause of clean water left numerous wells or 'pants', many now dry, carved and inscribed with the provider's name. The poet W.W. Gibson of Hexham (b.1878) wrote the verses inscribed in bronze on the town's red stone fountain, installed 'for the common good' in 1901, and at Whittingham, a small statue of a slightly-bowed man in shooting dress tops the column of a fountain – one of three – for people and animals. Carved by H. Brownlee from dense grey stone, the 3rd Earl of Ravensworth with his dog at his feet was commemorated 'by his dear wife Caroline ...' and unveiled in 1905. The 'waters of comfort' have dried, the Ravensworth estate is sold, but villagers still tend the fountain with flowers.

Personal monuments are not always modest, as shown in the Tenantry Column or 'Farmers' Folly' (1816) at Alnwick, where David Stephenson elevated the Percy Lion on a fluted column, accompanied on its massive circular platform by four large recumbent Coade stone lions, two roaring and two silent. It was raised in gratitude for reduction of rents during the Napoleonic Wars, but according to the story ('best known and least true' according to a town guide), the Duke raised the rents again soon after.

Another big gesture – 'the grandest monument in England', says Pevsner – is the Taj Mahal of the North at Lancaster (by John Belcher, 1907–09), a neo-Baroque temple commemorating the second – but not last – wife of Lord Ashton, Lino King; and in Wigton near the Solway Firth, the work of the Pre-Raphaelite sculptor Thomas Woolner commemorates the first Mrs George Moore (d.1858) on a big, decorative spired fountain signed by J.T. Knowles. With reliefs of the four Acts of Mercy and bronze gilt busts of Eliza Moore, it takes up much of the town's small market centre. Near the Northumbrian border and in other remote locations, small stone monuments ring out the cause of war: Percy against Douglas, Scots against English, Lancastrian against Yorkist. On Towton Lane south of York (B1217), Lord Dacre's Cross overlooks the 'Bloody Meadows' in which Wakefield was avenged by the House of York in a Palm Sunday snowstorm of 1461. The lonely, leaning cross, honouring 36,000 dead, was 'Repaired 1986. F. HERTINGTALL. WEST AUSTRALIA, PERTH'. We should salute this unobtrusive beneficience which leaves the cross, its holly tree and the flat muddy fields to tell us everything.

Northward at Marston Moor, a Cromwellian Association obelisk of 1939 handsomely proclaims 'here in his native country Sir Thomas Fairfax, the famous Yorkshire soldier, fought for Parliament with brilliance and success', while on the Preston road, Wigan, a stone pier honours the Royalist Sir Thomas Tyldesley, who 'was here slain' in the last Civil War battle fought on Lancastrian soil (1651).

Between Churton and Farndon in Cheshire, four big, sorrowing lions guard a roadside obelisk to Roger Barnston of Crewe Hall, who died of wounds received at the Relief of Lucknow. Other personal war memorials include studies of local soldiers, by Alfred Drury in Warrington, 1907, and at Hexham in Northumberland by John Tweed, veteran of military sculptures (1904).

Hilltop monuments include Stoodley Pike, subject of legend and epic verse, overlooking Todmorden, and the 'White Nancy' Waterloo monument, a beehive-shaped landmark overlooking the Cheshire mill town of Bollington.

Near Oldham the 'Pots and Pans' landmark, named after its rocky outcrop on Saddleworth Moor, commemorates the First World War. This conflict inspired, at Canon Rawnsley's suggestion, the gift of the 3rd Lord Leconfield of the summit of Sca Fell, England's highest mountain, into the care of the National Trust (1920) as a monument to those lost in the War. Later, Great Gable was bought as a war memorial for the Fell and Rock Climbing Club.

Almost every British community commemorated the First World War, but the northwestern counties, from Birkenhead to Workington, display the country's most solemnly impressive group of stone monuments, in the form of cenotaphs accompanied by bronze reliefs or statuary combining graphic realism with idealised symbolism. Sculptors included Gilbert Ledward (he incorporated a family cat in his frieze of enlisting workers at Blackpool); Hermon Cawthra (at Bootle and Bury); and the Liverpool sculptor H. Tyson Smith, whose stone carvings distinguish monuments at Accrington, Fleetwood, Southport, and Birkenhead.

Workington's ashlar column by Sir Robert Lorimer has the Roll of Sacrifice cemented behind a block which was removed for the addition of Second World War names, then ceremoniously resealed. The first unveiling was performed by a Workington woman who lost four sons and a brother to the trenches. Bronzes by Alexander Carrick include circular reliefs of steel workers and miners.

Apart from the causes of reform and war, monuments of all categories fit into the northern industrial scenery, the wild tops and the secluded valleys of the 'North Countree'. The first English poet, Caedmon, is

Port Sunlight War Memorial (1914–18).
Sculptor: Sir W. Goscombe John (1921).
Location: village cross roads,
Port Sunlight.

remembered near Whitby Abbey ruin by Charles Hodges' carved cross, organised by the indefatigable Canon Rawnsley (who wrote the hymn for the unveiling); a whalebone arch marks Whitby's former industry, and another trade is recalled in Captain Cook's bronze by John Tweed on the West Cliff. It carries a relief of the Whitby collier Resolution, in which the great navigator made his second and his third (final) voyage.

Cook's Memorial Museum in Grape Lane occupies the student lodging house where Cook's serious nature won over the housekeeper, who maintained his supply of candles for winter study and, when Cook returned as a celebrity, forgot her instructions to greet him in dialect, 'Oh honey James'.

All along the coasts are reminders of our sea power and of the sea's destructive force. A small pillar at Flamborough has a worn marble carving of a coble, and dedications to the rescuers and crew who failed to weather the storm; at Bamburgh churchyard, Grace Darling's stone effigy under a rich canopy shows her hair draping her shoulders, and an oar under her arm: at Tynemouth, Admiral Col-

lingwood's column, and statue by John Lough (1845), was long used as a seamark, standing out from a skyline of jagged priory ruins, lighthouses and roof tops above the grey mouth of the Tyne. Collingwood's bust decorates the site of his birthplace, in Newcastle.

At South Shields a Jubilee clock tower lauding the inventor of the lifeboat, William Wouldhave, shows deference to a rival claim by including the carved-relief profile of Henry Greathead. The first rescue boat's completion is wrongly inscribed as 1790, the year of the first rescue; the boat was built in 1789. Stone-carved reliefs make vivid visual records of stormy rescues.

South Shields's Edwardian Baroque Town Hall with its statuary, and the grand steps dominated by Toft's bronze of 'Victoria, Queen and Empress' (flanked by nude cast-iron torch-bearing maidens, 'Day' and 'Night'), remains a prime example of prestigious public architecture which, with the works of eminent sculptors, announced the northern towns' achievements to their rivals and to the world. These improving ensembles later fell foul of city renewal

Monument to Queen Victoria (1819–1901); (l) front, (r) back showing 'Maternity'. Sculptor: Onslow Ford (1901). Location: Piccadilly, Manchester.

and traffic schemes: four of the 'Town Hall Hussies' now raise their torches in South Marine Park.

Bronzes of Queen Victoria in majestic old age included works by masters such as Alfred Turner, whose full-length figure of Victoria with head bowed at Sheffield's Endcliffe Park has the same unsettling honesty as his sombre matriarch enthroned at Tynemouth (1902). A cast of a bronze sent to Delhi, this is claimed as the northeast's first statue of Victoria, and is also reminiscent of Sir Alfred Gilbert's acclaimed work outside Newcastle Cathedral (1904).

Other imposing bronzes of Victoria were set up in the northwest, in satellite towns as well as leading cities like Manchester, whose enthroned, richly-robed and ornamented figure by Onslow Ford is matched in opulence by Frampton's colossal throned statue (erected 1906) in the glass-producing centre, St Helens on Merseyside. Surrounded by stately period buildings of Victoria Square, the elderly Queen has a child's rounded features repeated in Frampton's imperious full-length bronze at Southport seafront further north.

All the northern towns enriched their stately public buildings with sculpture, some by leading artists such as William Calder Marshall, who made Bolton's statue of Samuel Crompton in 1862, and

the garlands and cherubs on the Town Hall in 1870. H. Tyson Smith and other Liverpool sculptors collaborated with the city's architects to enhance the port's prestigious commercial buildings in the early 20th century.

This art form can be studied from Preston to Sheffield, where the Town Hall facia shows a frieze of arts, crafts and trades, including sculptors, cutlers, ivory turners and electro-platers; Thor and Vulcan support the city arms, a small statue of Queen Victoria presides over all, and the Town Hall campanile is crowned with a statue of Vulcan. (The latest 'Vulcan', of glass fibre and copper by the Sheffield sculptor Wendy Ball, was installed on the Lyceum Theatre's copper dome in July, 1990.)

In older cities like York, Chester and Carlisle, such swaggering accessories are obviated by city history. York sculptor G.W. Milman's marble statues of George Leeman, railway promoter, and the painter William Etty, depict two citizens who passionately defended the medieval walls threatened by 19th-century planners.

Carlisle's local sculptor M. L. Watson carved a stone statue of the Earl of Lonsdale, subject of Wordsworth's poem after the Lord Lieutenant had discharged debts owed to the poet's father John, chief law-agent to Lonsdale's father; clad in garter robes (1845), he stands outside Smirke's County Courts of 1810–11. Returns from local mines rebuilt Lowther Castle in 1806–11, also by Smirke. In Carlisle Cathedral, a tablet to the sculptor recalls 'The elegance, purity and simplicity' of Watson's work, which failed to fulfil its potential as a result of his early death in 1847.

Much of Chester's black-and-white architecture, with prolific wood carving, was masterfully recreated in the 19th century, but the best decoration is Charles the Martyr's statue, thought to be contemporary, in Bridge Street. He is flanked by amusing panels and texts on a robust biblical theme. Chester does have some commemorative statues, notably Baron Marochetti's fearless portrayal of Sir Stapleton Cotton, 1st Viscount Combermere (1773–1865), a disagreeable old Field Marshal astride his horse, modelled from life in Combermere's last, and 93rd, year. As a cavalry officer under Wellington, his glittering uniform attracted the French tag 'Lion d'Or'.

Chester's true treasure is the rough, fleeting form of Minerva with her owl, a survival from Roman times, faintly discernible on the red rocky outcrop of 'Edgar's Cave' near the river. Another northern treasure is Cumbria's 10th-century Gosforth Cross with its beautiful carvings – like the Jedburgh and Easby crosses, a prototype for Victorian Celtic Revival monuments throughout England.

An ancient curio, at Knaresborough in North Yorkshire, is an oversize figure of a knight carved in the cliff face outside the Chapel of the Rock. The original is lost in successive reworkings (using cement), but the tradition is centuries old.

Curios belong to all periods and many localities; Bolton's stone statue of Disraeli rivals 'Lang Jack of Whickham' for mad staring eyes. Recently restored and resited in Front Street, this lugubrious head and shoulders immortalises John English, 6' 4" Durham stone-mason and lusty champion of the Reform Bill, a local Sampson who carted his own stone to build a cottage on the Gibside Estate. (*Note*, near the Gibside Chapel (NT), a column of local stone built by estate workers, 1750–57, its statue reputedly carved *in situ* by Christopher Richardson, who received £10 for his efforts. 'Liberty's' vase, in local legend, holds gold coins.)

Further south, Birtley commemorates bushy-bearded iron master Colonel Moseley; on his gardener's dismay at the appearance of a sulphur ball, Moseley remarked 'it will be a bad day for Birtley when there is no smoke in it'. His marble statue was erected in Durham Road soon after his death in 1871

which, as announced by the *Gateshead Observer*, had 'fallen like a thunder-bolt upon society'.

A real rarity is Tynemouth's Wooden Dolly with her creel, a wonderfully hard-bitten fishwife, from the workshops of the Yorkshire 'Mouse man' Robert Thompson. The original Dolly, thought to have been a collier-brig's figurehead, was pared away by sailors who kept the parings for luck. This version was unveiled in 1958 on the 100th birthday of M.E. Spence, creator of the fourth replacement.

Thrusting industrialists are no longer approved subjects for commemoration. Northern Counties' women never were: exceptions include heroic Grace Darling; the graceful Annie Jerningham with floppy hat and hound, in marble, at Berwick-upon-Tweed, and Mrs Gaskell, whose elegant head and shoulders adorn a crazily-carved memorial tower at her Cheshire birthplace, Knutsford, featured as *Cranford* in her novel (without the tower).

Recent northern unveilings reveal unassuming citizens like the great Thomas Chippendale (1718–1799), modelled as an apprentice with his 'splat' at

Thomas Chippendale (1718–1719). Sculptor: Graham Ibbeson (1987). Location: Manor Square, Otley.

his Yorkshire birthplace, Otley, by Graham Ibbeson in 1987. This popular sculptor, formerly a miner, has a starkly-realistic work (his most creditworthy) in the mining disaster monument outside Conisborough Library, South Yorkshire. Anything but heroic, it has provoked pained reaction, but has been strongly defended locally.

At the Lanes Shopping Centre in Carlisle, Judith Bluck's bronze figure of the street musician Jimmy Dyer has

'A face like the moon, sober, sonsy, and douce,
And a back, for its breadth, like the side o' a house',

as he wrote in his *Life and Times*, published in 1870.

The overall picture of Northern Counties' monuments shows a wealth of individualistic works in rural landscapes to north and south of the industrial Pennines, and a fine collection of 19th-century worthies immortalised in the working cities and towns, reflecting the period when textiles ruled, reform was on the agenda, and public sculpture augmented city architecture in lofty town plans. Each new statue gave the city fathers a unique opportunity to preside over each others' unveilings with elaborate public ceremonial, speechifying and banquets in which workers and their masters could bolster their town's successes, and the mayor or sheriff got his name on the pedestal credits.

Robert Ascroft (1847–1899). Sculptor: F. W. Pomeroy (1903). Location: Alexandra Park, Oldham.

Many are now farmed out to parks, not all to disadvantage, as at Alexandra Park in Oldham, laid out in the cotton famine of the early 1860s, where munificent Lancastrian industrialists John Platt MP (1817–1872), textile manufacturer and educationalist, and Robert Ascroft MP (1847–1899), solicitor, ornament the top terrace in bronze – Platt's group most elaborate and grand, by D.W. Stevenson 1878, and Ascroft THE WORKERS' FRIEND honestly portrayed by F.W. Pomeroy. (*Note* also at the far end of the park the sandstone statue of Blind Jo the Bellman, in top hat and frock coat, with bell and stick – these are kept in the museum; and on Oldham Town Hall, the mysterious 'Lady Wrigley'.)

Sir Francis Sharpe Powell (1827–1910) wrote the inscription for his agreeable statue by E.G. Gillick at Wigan's Mesnes Park. Relaxing in a chair, he is gaudily green through verdigris, but the toe of his shoe has been polished bronze by children since the unveiling in 1910.

A more formal ritual takes place annually in the Brougham Dole, bestowed with a field for its distribution by Lady Anne Clifford, restorer of Westmorland family castles. A beautiful stone pillar marks Lady Anne's last parting with her 'good and pious mother, in 1615. Richly painted with symbols and sundials, it illuminates the A66 west of Penrith.

Thomas Bland's spectacular junketings, held in his 'sculpture garden' at Reagill in deepest Westmorland, were a feature of Queen Victoria's Accession anniversaries in the Lyvennet Vale. This eccentric self-taught sculptor put up a stone Accession monument of Britannia on a column, in 1842, with gutsy relief decoration at the base; it is a landmark at Shap Wells. He also carved a fleshy profile of Charles II which stares from a lichened obelisk at the source of the Lyvennet, on Black Dub where the king, marching from Scotland *en route* to defeat at Worcester 'regaled his army and drank of the water' in 1651. Reached by a lonely tramp across the grouse moor, these rough, heartfelt carvings and inscriptions signal high hopes and lost causes long past.

No less touching is a personal monument of 1893, lost in long grass under tall trees at Lawton Hall, Church Lawton in Cheshire. It is a miniature slate tombstone with chiselled lines by M.P. Lawton:

On the Death of a Bullfinch
that sang "God Save the Queen"
when bidden to do so . . .

King, bullfinch or Workers' Friend, each has inspired the impulse to commemorate his cause, and to enrich the varied northern landscape with a work of monumental art.

North Eastern Counties Gazetteer

(Note: The Northeastern Counties appear in loosely topographical order. Within each county, monuments are listed under their locations, which appear in alphabetical order. Letters after a location indicate its country of origin – i.e. (ER) East Riding; (WR) West Riding; (NR) North Riding; (Co.D) County Durham, and (N) Northumberland.

Yorkshire & Humberside

HULL (ER)

City Feature:

William III (1650–1702)
Gilded lead equestrian statue on stone pedestal
Sculptor Peter Scheemakers
Location Market Place

'King Billy' on his excellent horse is the pride of Hull's statuary. His gilded image is modelled in the style of the Roman Emperor Marcus Aurelius, and his steed seems poised to trot over the glass roofs of the Gentlemen's conveniences, past Holy Trinity Church, and along Market Place on the southern approach to the town. Carved into the large stone pedestal are the words:

To the Memory of
KING WILLIAM The Third
OUR GREAT DELIVERER

Hull raised the sum of £893.10s. to purchase the statue, which was installed on the 47th 'Town-taking Day' when the townspeople celebrate the seizing of the Catholic Governor and his garrison a month after Dutch William's arrival at Brixham, on November 5th, 1688. The installation was performed with 'great solemnity'; also, according to the *Gentleman's Magazine*, with much festivity in which the

William III (1650–1702). Sculptor: Peter Sheemakers (1734). Location: Market Place, Hull (Note the statue has been restored since photography).

citizens drank to King William's memory 'till they lost their own'.

Since 1734 'King Billy' has stayed in place, although not without incident. A thistle under the horse's foot was stolen by Jacobites; the railings, an obstruction to carriages, were removed, and gas lamps installed, and regilding was carried out in 1821, 1834 and 1865. During the Second World

War the statue was evacuated to Houghton Hall, to be reinstated by the Corporation 'with the generous help of Wm Broady, Coppersmith of this city' in 1949. Broady performed the unveiling ceremony.

Almost 40 years later, routine repair work uncovered serious deterioration of the statue's lead core and its lead and pewter coating. As Hull prepared a Dutch theme for its tercentenary Festival, the statue was undergoing an 'intensive and costly' overhaul which included regilding, recutting the inscription, and replacing the pedestal's fringe of protective iron spikes. Also replaced were the 'Victorian' lamps, and the cast-iron lion's head water spout, which had been stolen, was returned to working order. Thus the glittering figure of the Great Deliverer, with laurel wreath and toga, continues to enrich one of Hull's draughtier corners.

Hull Selection

One of the country's oldest public commemorative statues is a worn stone seated figure of Dr John Alderson (1757–1829), by Sir Richard Westmacott (1833). Senior physician at Hull General Infirmary, Alderson wrote essays on *Apparitions*, the *Improvement of Poor Soils*, the *Contagion of Fevers*, and other matters. He now appears under trees outside the General Infirmary tower block in Anlaby Road.

Hull's only commemorative bronze is of Queen Victoria enthroned, by H.C. Fehr (1903). 'Her Most Gracious Majesty' presides over the handsome railings of public conveniences in Victoria Square, but stately, sculptured public buildings, including the Ferens Art Gallery, make a proper setting. In Pearson's Park is a sadly damaged marble of the young, wifely Victoria, carved in 1861 by the Hull sculptor Thomas Earle, reputedly assisted by the Prince Consort. Earle's marble of Albert, carved after his death, stands in a nearby rose thicket.

Hull's most conspicuous statue, that of William Wilberforce (1759–1833), was raised on a mighty Doric column after a public meeting passed the resolution (noted on the pedestal) 'that it would not be creditable to the character of the town, which justly glories in having been the birth place of such a man, and in having first sent him into Parliament, to suffer him to sink into his grave without raising some lasting monument of its veneration and lasting affection for his memory'.

The Leeds-based architect John Clarke designed the column, but the statue, an afterthought, is of unknown origin. The first stone was laid as slavery was abolished in the British colonies (August 1

1834), near Monument Bridge, site of Sir John Hotham's denial of entry to Charles I. Later resited, it now overlooks Queen's Gardens and the Peace Statue (1968), a bowed, seated form in smooth bronze, designed by the Glasgow 'lifer' Jimmy Boyle and cast by members of the Gateway Exchange as part of Boyle's work with young offenders.

In the cramped courtyard of his birthplace, now a museum, is a marble statue of William Wilberforce by William Day Keyworth the younger – a good likeness, judging by contemporary portraits inside. Amongst anti-slavery relics can be seen working models for the same sculptor's statues of Andrew Marvell, now standing outside the Hull Grammar School, and of William de la Pole near Victoria Pier (a cross between Richard Branson and the Principal Boy); also Rysbrack's model for his equestrian figure of William III at Bristol.

From here, street clearance and road schemes have created a long view of the majestic Guildhall, with its symbolic sculptures outlined on the parapet; below is the robed marble figure of ship owner Charles Henry Wilson, 1st Baron Nunburnholme, '35 years MP for Hull', carved by F.Derwent Wood in 1913. Wilson's brother was host to the Prince of Wales at the time of the baccarat scandal in 1890.

Hull's 20th-century statues have charm where others have pedigree. Edward VII, dome-headed and unmistakable in marble, holds a helmet with plumes like a bunch of bananas outside a small office in Anlaby Road; carved for one of Edward's visits, the statue lay in Albert Leake's stone yard after the entrepreneur went bankrupt, and was rescued only in 1972. Just south in Hessle Street is Leake's marble statue of Skipper George Henry Smith, who with other members of the Hull fishing fleet died (one of fright) when their lights off Dogger Bank were mistaken by the quick-shooting Russian Navy for the enemy Japanese in 1904. The cryptic details are logged on the rich, red granite pedestal.

Under the façade of the Pearson Shopping Precinct is Amy Johnson's smiling statue in flying gear, with a medallion of her biplane. She was carved by Harry Ibbetson and unveiled by Sheila Scott, OBE, in 1974. Her gauntleted hand rests on the copper citation of her birth date in 1903 at St George's Road, Hull, with her record solo flights: 'She died on active service, Jan 5th 1941. May her fame live on'. Her Portland stone image, likened to a jelly-baby, adds to Hull's repertoire of homespun works.

In Holderness Road someone's front garden has a marble statue of a true Victorian worthy, honoured for 'devotion to the welfare of the city'. James Stuart,

Amy Johnson (1903–1941). Sculptor: Harry Ibbetson (1974). Location: entrance, Prospect Street Shopping Centre, Hull.

JP (1836–1922) was carved by W. Aumonier for Thomas Ferens, himself a great Hull benefactor who gave the site for the Ferens Art Gallery in Victoria Square. His friend's statue and most of its companions would be out of place in the gallery, but Hull would be a lesser city without its street sculptures.

Sledmere (ER)

Village Feature:

Waggoners' Memorial (1919)
Spired Portland stone cylinder on stepped octagonal base with decorated columns and carved reliefs
Designer Sir Mark Sykes
Sculptor Carlo Magnoni
Mason A. Barr, Sledmere Estate
Location Junction with B1253 and road to Kirby Grindalythe

'Good lads and dames our Ridings pride
These steanes are set by this road side
This tale your childrens bains to tell
On what ye did ewhen war befell . . .'
This extraordinary roadside monument is one of a series that ornaments the land outside the walls of the Sykes's Sledmere estate. The Sykes name, famous for horse breeding and land improvement, has dominated this locality for generations. The monument was erected by its designer Sir Mark Sykes to honour 'the Waggoners' Reserve "A" Corps of 1000 drivers raised by him on the Yorkshire Wold farms in the year 1912'.

The Corps served with transport columns in Normandy carrying anything from pit-props to bacon. The farm workers' understanding of horses guaranteed expert care for animals exposed to the rigours of war; promotion to NCO was usually refused, since the men were too attached to their pairs.

The horse handlers' story is carved on this columned, spired drum, which is the most original of the Sykes monuments and has no equivalent in England or Wales. Its Byzantine flavour comes from Sir Mark's interests as an Orientalist, its turrets and columns smack of Victorian revivalism, its inscribed

Waggoners' Memorial (1914–1918/19). Designer: Sir Mark Sykes (1919). Sculptor: Carlo Magnoni. Location: Sledmere.

verses by Sir Mark are in Saxon letters and the detailed scenes carved in relief speak graphically if artlessly of the Woldsmen's Great War, from enrolment to confrontation on alien soil.

The sturdy Woldsmen with their horses, families, dogs and chattels all feature, some in fearful scenes of pillage and flames. The German soldiers are depicted as villainous, and this caused complaint in the 1930s, when the Sykes family refused a request from the German Embassy for the monument's removal. But although they depict savagery, it is hard to see how these rather humble and passive carvings, sited deep in rural Yorkshire, could inflame.

Sledmere Selection

In the estate Church of St Mary a Book of Remembrance preserves names of the Great War dead from all the Yorkshire regiments. The memorial was unveiled in 1919, but Sir Mark Sykes died before its completion.

Amongst other Sledmere monuments, the earliest is the Rotunda of 1840, formerly the estate village well (*note* its fox-in-flight weathervane, and the cast-iron figures of boy hornblowers on the main gate piers opposite). The 4th Baronet Sir Tatton Sykes built it in tribute to his father Sir Christopher, thought to be architect of Sledmere which was judged by Pevsner 'a fusion of grandeur and common sense uncommon in 18th-century planning'. The inscription records Sir Christopher's 'assiduity and perserverance in building and planting and enclosing the Yorkshire Wolds, in the short space of thirty years', by which a bleak and barren landscape was converted to cultivated fields.

High on the Driffield road is a rocket-like Victorian-Gothic tower, liberally endowed with carved biblical texts and stone-carved rustic scenes. Sir Tatton inspired this tribute from 'those who loved him as a friend and honoured him as a landlord', and he appears here on horseback. The sculptor was James Forsyth, the architect J. Gibbs (1863). A key once obtainable from the cottage opposite gave access to a view in which all from the middle-distance was Sykes land. The top six feet recently fell down, but have been replaced.

Continuing west from the Waggoners', at the Malton turn, is a beautiful 'Eleanor Cross', based on the original at Hardingstone near Northampton. Designed by Temple Moore in 1895, it was erected by Sir Tatton Sykes, 5th Baronet, and altered by his son Sir Mark to include 'medieval' brasses portraying local men killed in action during the Great War.

Shown full-length, with details of their lives inscribed, the servicemen in their battle uniform as of medieval knights make curious contrast with the serene statues of Queen Eleanor in the higher stages.

On this grassy corner, a memorial seat to Sir Mark's son Richard (1905–1978), father of the present Sir Tatton, remembers 'a good and generous landlord'; Dame Virginia Sykes (1916–1970) is also remembered with affection by 'The people of Sledmere and the East Riding'. 'Humberside' may be a reality of regional government, but the warmer tradition of Sledmere and the East Riding endures.

South Yorkshire

Barnsley (S)

Town Feature:

Oaks Explosion Monument
Stone obelisk on base with capital, supporting bronze symbolic figures
Sculptor Not known (possibly George Wade)
Design Wade & Turner
Location A635 Doncaster road, Kendray

The price of coal is marked by this winged figure of Athene, her owl at her feet, bearing aloft a wounded warrior. The association of an idealised sculpture with the carnage of the Oaks explosion, in 1866 Britain's worst mining disaster, would not have seemed out of place when the monument was erected by Samuel Joshua Cooper in 1913, the year of the Senghennydd disaster in Wales.

The green-tinged bronze figures, in their purity of line and grace of form, reinforce the stark message of the dedication below. Plain tribute is paid to Parkin Jeffcock and other rescuers lost 'owing to further explosions', and to 'the signal bravery' of John Edward Mammatt and Thomas William Embleton who descended the pit the following day, December 14th, and rescued the sole survivor. Twenty-seven rescuers, many from neighbouring collieries, perished in the secondary explosions. Out of 340 miners lost, 334 were killed by the initial blast.

The monument stands about one mile southeast of the town centre, opposite the dour red brick of Kendray Isolation hospital, on a gloomy bank overlooking a busy road. Its small paved garden has

Monument to the Oaks Explosion (1866). Sculptor: not known
(possibly George Wade). Design: Wade & Turner (1913).
Location: Kendray, Barnsley.

seats and miniature firs, and the obelisk of warm stone has recently been cleaned. The architects, Wade and Turner, designed many of the late Victorian buildings in Barnsley, including the NUM Headquarters of 1874 (which has a plain granite monument unveiled in 1905, honouring officers of the Yorkshire Miners Association).

The gleaming white Town Hall is prominent in the view from waste ground behind the Oaks Athene. Black Barnsley's football ground and the new leisure centre are also visible. To the east spread Retford's National Glass, and Grimethorpe Colliery, with the winding gear of the Oaks Colliery (now Barnsley Main) in the foreground, and the ruin of Monkbretton Priory lost among gantries, chimneys and shafts. In the centre itself, the 1930s-classical Town Hall by Briggs and Thorneley makes a suitable backdrop for Barnsley's imposing First World War

monument showing a tin-helmeted soldier, also recently cleaned.

Barnsley Selection

West of the Oaks Monument off the A634, Locke Park's grand gates open on to a hilly elysium decorated with classical pillars from Barnsley's Commerce Buildings, and with Marochetti's bronze of the railway engineer Joseph Locke (1866), whose widow gave the park. Her memorial, erected on the highest ground by her sister Miss McCreery, is a sculptured belvedere designed by R. Renee Spiers in 1877. The children's joy is Lion Grotto, the stone lion of which was salvaged from the parapet of Dillington Hall, built c.1830 and demolished in 1937.

Four miles west in Silkstone churchyard a pyramidal sandstone pillar, inscribed with biblical texts, admonishes 'READER REMEMBER Every neglected call of God, will appear against Thee at the Day of Judgement...' The Husker Pit Disaster Memorial names 26 children (the youngest aged seven) trapped against closed ventilation doors when storm waters flooded the entrance to the 'day-hole' as they came off shift. The God-fearing inscription includes details of burial: '... The mortal remains of the females are deposited in the graves at the feet of the Males...'

An enquiry was ordered by the Queen, and four years later Lord Shaftesbury's Commission established laws preventing child labour underground (1842). In the church, a stained-glass window commemorates the pit owner, R.C. Clarke. In Knabb's Wood on Silkstone Common near the site of the disaster, the 150th anniversary was marked by a monument formed as a stone replica of the day hole, with crouched statues of escaping child miners: unveiled in July, 1988. Along the Dove Valley Trail, carved 'Heritage Stones' show relief figures of miners.

At Kirkheaton churchyard near Huddersfield, a stone pillar with flame finial records 'the dreadful fate of seventeen children who fell victims to a raging fire at Mr Atkinson's factory, Colne Bridge'. It was erected in the same year, 1818. A chiselled stone slab nearby lists the 14 whose remains could be buried: '... One dreadful flash – one fhriek of woe Left all but namelefs duft below ...'

The fire broke out after the foreman went home for the night with the key in his pocket. The flames could not destroy the iron rings that chained Mary, Martha and others to their work benches. At this date 10,000 workless men were on parish relief, whilst children were paid 2/- for a 96-hour week. 'Victorian hypocrisy' was rife before Victoria was born.

West Yorkshire

Birstall (WR)

Town Feature:

Joseph Priestley (1733–1804)
Bronze full-length statue on marble pedestal
Sculptor Frances Darlington
Location Market Square

The inventor and dissenting theologian Joseph Priestley makes a familiar figure by 'Town Hall Steps', where his statue was unveiled in 1912. After the effort of the steps Birstall's Town Hall never materialised, but plans were afoot by 1970 for the market square to be 'dug up, raised, flattened, paved, pedestrianised, trees planted' and, according to the *Birstall News*, the statue moved. Shopkeepers, however, would have none of it and the square remained a car park and 'Old Joe' retained his site. By eschewing plant tubs and pedestrianisation, Birstall's sloping, cobbled square and its work-worn buildings (with smartened shop fronts) preserve their rough-edged charm.

*Joseph Priestley (1733–1804). Sculptor: Frances Darlington
(1912). Location: Market Place, Birstall.*

Frances Darlington of Harrogate modelled Priestley's head on that of Alfred Drury's bronze made for Leeds in 1899, but Birstall's figure, in accordance with its surroundings, is less stagey than that of City Square. Both Leeds and Birmingham had statues before Priestley's native town, the citizens of which resolved to open a subscription fund 'in the Memory of the late Dr Joseph Priestley' in 1910.

The statue was cast by Alexander Parloti and unveiled by Priestley's biographer, the chemist Sir Edward Thorpe. Later attempts to remove it three-quarters of a mile to Priestley's birthplace, Fieldhead (not the one featured in Charlotte Brontë's *Shirley*) were abandoned in the face of 'a lot of bother'. For the 250th anniversary of his birth, Priestley's statue was cleaned and restored.

As in Leeds and Birmingham, Birstall's statue shows Priestley at the threshold of modern chemistry, discovering oxygen. During his ministry at Mill Hill Chapel in Leeds, the untutored chemist studied gases by observing fermentation processes in a brewery next door to his home; by 1772 he had discovered the principal of aerated waters, and in 1774 he was demonstrating his oxygen experiments to Lavoisier and other French scientists in Paris.

Priestley's radical politics were unpopular in England, and his support for the French Revolution brought the Birmingham mob to his door in 1791. The house with its library, apparatus and manuscripts were destroyed. After three years in London he sailed for America, where he spent his last years.

Priestley's bronze image in wig and habit now attracts the Birstall felt-tip mob (and worse), but this small moorland mill town engulfed in urban sprawl would be a lesser place without Old Joe.

Bradford (WR)

City Feature:

Samuel Cunliffe Lister, Lord Masham of Swinton (1815–1906)
Full-length Sicilian marble statue on polished granite pedestal with bronze reliefs, and ornamented with carved industrial emblems
Sculptor Matthew Noble
Location Lister Park (south entrance)

This model of Victorian self-assurance, massively carved in marble, is one of Bradford's few Victorian commemorative statues to occupy its original pos-

Samuel Cunliffe Lister (1815–1906). Sculptor: Matthew Noble (1875). Location: Lister Park, Bradford.

ition – in the park which Lister gave to the town. Performing the unveiling ceremony was W.E. Forster, MP for Bradford, who with Samuel Lister belonged to the town's coterie of notables whose attendance could be guaranteed at the inauguration of each other's monuments in front of the banners and crowds. Lister himself was present at the ceremony, in May 1875.

The Lister fortunes were built on mechanisation of worsted-wool combing, and bronze reliefs on the pedestal record this vital technological change which also changed Bradford's fortunes; one panel shows hand-combing by skilled men, and another shows semi-skilled women, lower paid, minding one of Lister's wool-combing machines. As sharp an investor as an inventor, Lister bought up patents of failed mechanisation attempts, and with the help of local craftsmen created the world's first reliably-workable wool combing machine.

Lister went on to further fortune by mechanising production of velvets and plushes from silk waste. Other monuments to his wealth and skill remain in the name 'Lister velvet', which means 'high-quality', and in the Manningham Mill which dominates the skyline and is still partly worked by the Lister company. Modelled on the San Marco campanile in Venice, the chimney was built broad enough to take a coach and horses. The land for Lister Park was bought by Bradford Corporation three years earlier, in 1870; 20 years later came Lister's peerage, and in 1898, the Freedom of Bradford.

Bradford Selection

'Essentially a city of the Victorian era', was the Prince of Wales's comment on Bradford at the unveiling of his grandmother's statue (1905). As if to guard this important heritage, a stately bronze of Queen Victoria by Alfred Drury commands a prime site between the Alhambra and the Museum of Photography and Film. Other statues, like Lister's honouring 19th-century industrialists and reformers, have been packed off to quiet backwaters during Bradford's long regeneration as a city of the technological and tourist age. Today's marriage of Victorian Italianate Gothic with glass and concrete blocks, contriving to create spaciousness without soullessness, would make a good environment for a Revival of the Relegated, if ever funds allowed.

Of these five open-air statues, only Samuel Cunliffe Lister's originated away from the city centre. In his park stands Cartwright Hall, art gallery and museum, built in the grounds of Lister's old home as his memorial to Edmund Cartwright, clergyman (1743–1823), whose invention of the power loom in 1784 revolutionised the weaving industry on which Lister and others built fortunes. H.C. Fehr's marble seated statue of Cartwright can be seen in the museum.

At the park's castellated memorial gate (northern entrance), stands Bradford's answer to the Albert Memorial: an extravagently canopied Carrara marble statue of Sir Titus Salt (1803–1876), second mayor of Bradford. Erected against his will ('So they wish to make me into a pillar of Salt!'), it was unveiled in front of the Town Hall in 1874; the *Bradford Observer* noted the absence, on this occasion, of W.E. Forster who, now enjoying a national reputation, was 'doubtless engaged on work of urgent importance'.

Salt also declined an invitation to the unveiling, although he had agreed to sittings. He is shown formidably bearded, seated uneasily under the fabulous Gothic canopy designed by the architects Lockwood and Mawson to harmonize with their Town Hall. The canopy was carved from Cliffe Wood stone by Farmer and Brindley of Westminster.

Two years after unveiling, at Salt's funeral procession, the hearse paused at the black-draped statue before continuing its journey between silent crowds to the family mausoleum at the model township Saltaire, Salt's true monument, created for his workers away from the Bradford smoke. Its street names belong to members of Salt's family; beside the Aire stand his alpaca mill and beautiful Congregational Church, with a marble bust of 1856 — beardless – by Thomas Milnes. (In Victoria Road, are Milnes's four lions intended for Trafalgar Square, although much smaller than Landseer's.)

A bronze of Sir Titus by F. Derwent Wood, with pedestal reliefs of the llama (alpaca) and goat (angora), is in Roberts Park. Twenty years after unveiling, Salt's Bradford statue was moved to ease traffic flow.

Bradford's first public statue, on the high main terrace of Peel Park, shows the park's donor standing on a handsome cylindrical pedestal between two sooty but winsome nymphs, Spring and Autumn (given by local branches of the Band of Hope in the 1860s). Like its predecessor at Leeds, Sir Robert Peel's bronze was created by William Behnes and cast in one piece (1855). At the unveiling, the Mayor of Bradford declared it the first work of art in town to be placed within reach of the people, at 'the dawn of a new era'. Unlike its counterparts still in the city centre, Peel's figure has not been treated with bronze paint; its more honest hue was created by grime, pigeons and verdigris.

Peel's popularity in Bradford was not always great. On his statue's original town site, before his political change of heart, his effigy had been publicly burned by protesters calling for corn law reform.

The statue which has kept its place is that of the ubiquitous industrialist W.E. Forster (1818–1886), Bradford MP from 1861–86, promoter of primary schooling for all through the Education Bill of 1870. Forster's patriarchal bronze image, created by J. Havard Thomas, occupies the car park in Forster Square; stored for city reconstruction, it was revived in 1967, its red granite pedestal reversed to display details of a distinguished parliamentary career. Forster's widow watched the long procession at the statue's unveiling in 1890 from a warehouse window. It stands at the traffic-bound town edge, sharing the skyline with warehouses and moorland.

William Forster attended the inauguration of the statue honouring Richard Oastler the Factory King (1789–1861), Tory, Evangelical and Radical, ranting champion of factory children and the famous Ten Hour Bill. He was born in Leeds, but Bradford, the centre for the Ten Hour Movement, chief subscriber to the monument fund, was chosen to receive J.B.

Richard Oastler (1789–1861). Sculptor: J. B. Philip (1869, resited 1968). Location: Northgate, Bradford.

Philip's statue, unveiled near the Wool Exchange by the great reformer Lord Ashley, 7th Earl of Shaftesbury, in 1869.

William Forster reputedly criticised the rendering of boy and girl factory workers at Oastler's side; dutifully doleful, they are too well clad and fed to be victims of the debilitating system that Oastler 'sought to humanize'. His statue's coat of bronze paint clashes horribly with its pink granite pedestal. It was moved to a plot in Northgate, 1968.

Statues at the heart of Bradford are the 35 'City Hall Monarchs' (1873), lining the facade of the old Town Hall at third floor level in chronological order, from the Conqueror to the young Victoria. She shares with Elizabeth I pride of place at the entrance, despite her refusal to open the new Town Hall, built to rival Leeds's which she had opened in 1858.

Other building sculptures grace Bradford banks; the 'Wool Exchange Celebrities', show character studies of Salt, Lister, Cook, Columbus and others. Edward III and St Blaise guard the Venetian Gothic arches at the Exchange entrance, Hustlergate.

Monuments created in Bradford's latest 'new era' of regeneration include the memorial to the victims of the football stadium fire disaster in May, 1985. Occupying a garden plot opposite City Hall, the three bronze, hurrying figures 'symbolise the eternal bond between the living and the dead'. Created by Joachim Reisner, they were presented by Bradford's twin city, Hamm, in 1986.

Unveiled in the same year, outside the National Museum of Photography and Film, is Ian Judd's bronze portrait of J.B. Priestley (1894–1984); we are confronted with an affable, portly man, pipe clasped to chest, hand in trouser pocket, coat flying. A long excerpt from Priestley's novel *Bright Day* (1946) describes Bruddersford – Priestley's home town, Bradford as '... grim but not mean. And the moors were always there, and the horizon never without its promise ...'

Priestley's figure strides along a few yards from Alfred Drury's stately Victoria, holding Victory, flanked by lions and forming a set-piece with the World War cenotaph set on the lower slope. All three monuments overlook old and new Bradford, the Florentine campanile of City Hall emerging on the skyline.

Leeds (WR)

City Feature:

Edward, Prince of Wales (1330–1376)
Bronze equestrian statue on polished granite pedestal
Sculptor (Sir) Thomas Brock RA
Location City Square

Leeds's city centre statues are survivals of an arranged marriage between civic art and architecture that set out to rival the great cities of Europe. The artists were Thomas Brock, Alfred Drury, H.C. Fehr and F.W. Pomeroy. Their bronze full-length statues stand in City Square, with Brock's heroic equestrian bronze of the Black Prince (1903) as centrepiece. He is accompanied by eight semi-draped maidens holding aloft torches, created by Alfred Drury to encircle the central figure. They are known in some quarters as 'the Drury Dames'.

The Black Prince (1330–1376). Sculptor: Sir Thomas Brock, RA (1903). Location: City Square, Leeds.

Behind the Black Prince are figures of Joseph Priestley (Drury, 1899) and James Watt (H.C. Fehr, (1898); the Leeds merchant John Harrison (1576–1656), with dashing Cavalier moustache; and 'Dr Hook, Vicar of Leeds' (1837–1859), a man of the people in clerical robes (F.W. Pomeroy, 1902), raising his arm in salutation, whilst keeping his place with a finger in the Bible in his other hand.

Each statue carries the name of its donor, the most generous being 'T. Walter Harding, Lord Mayor 1898–1899', who gave all but two. Principal founder of the City Art Gallery (1888), Harding siezed the opportunity to bring art to the streets after Leeds had achieved city status in 1896. Schemes were afoot for replacing a cloth hall close to the heart of Leeds, but Harding's 'little plan' for this prime site aspired to a city scale and style: it displays turn-of-the-century confidence in English democracy, monarchy and empire that was not espoused by all Leodonians, some of whom envisaged tramway waiting rooms and public lavatories.

Time has obscured the wheeling, dealing and machinations that doubtless furthered Harding's plan. His commission for the centrepiece finally went to Thomas Brock, who proposed a figure of the Black Prince 'The hero of Crecy and Poitiers, the flower of England's chivalry; The upholder of the rights of the people in the Good Parliament'.

The statue was inaugurated with suitable ceremony in 1901 and the accompanying bronzes were formally presented in 1903, the year in which Harding received the Freedom of the City for services to furtherance of the Arts. His city centrepiece and ensemble of distinguished sculptures fitted the vision of a newly-arrived city matching Paris, Rome and New York – but above all Leeds's arch-rival Bradford, and other ambitious northern centres.

Helmeted and spurred, the Black Prince in his chain mail dominates the cobbled centre of the square with a rallying posture which is striking but uninspired. The huge pedestal is handsomely ornamented in art nouveau manner with swags carrying names of illustrious medieval figures, and a leopard's head at each corner. Bronze reliefs on either side illustrate the Battle of Crecy and (it is thought) the sea battle of Sluys. The statue was cast in Belgium and carried from Hull to Leeds by barge, then drawn by six white horses through thronged streets.

The statue was originally encircled by 'Morn' and 'Even', but during a 1960s revamp these elegant maidens were consigned to the City scrapyard. They were redeemed, however, after public protest, to form an avenue of gallery nudes through which the eye is drawn to a brutish modern block filling the site of the old court house.

Still surviving on the east of the square is the Unitarian chapel Mill Hill, its minister from 1767–72, Joseph Priestley, stagily poised with pestle and mortar in Alfred Drury's bronze image. The other figures, in period dress, strike the same daintily-mannered attitudes and this perfectly suits Harding's original concept of a formal ensemble, even though that is now dismantled, and the square no longer matches its statues as a prestigious period piece.

Leeds Selection

T.W. Harding, whose factory campanile's fumes blackened the stately city buildings, explained his scheme at the grand opening: 'Let us by all means be proud of our great factories and workshops, but let us too be able to rise above the sordid and rejoice in the beauty'. Town planners have since removed the sordid, and with it some of the beauty. Apart from Alfred Drury's lovely Circe (with supplicant boars) in Park Square, Leeds's most important Victorian public statues languish at Woodhouse Moor, a public park north of the university.

Amongst the relegations is a historical double first, a William Behnes bronze of Sir Robert Peel, the first large scale bronze to be cast in one piece by a British foundry, and claimed as the earliest bronze memorial statue of Peel. (Bury, his birthplace, unveiled its bronze the following month, September 1852.) At the opposite, southwest corner, is the Duke of Wellington by Marochetti (1855), and at the southeast corner is Frampton's colossal, elaborate bronze of Queen Victoria (1905), crowned and attended by 'Peace' and 'Industry'.

These symbols of civic pride were removed from Victoria Square at the front of the Town Hall in 1937, to make way for a small car park. Yet in 1905 *The Yorkshire Post* had reported with satisfaction the imminent appearance of Queen Victoria's statue, 'which has, not inaptly, been described as one of the finest pieces of modern sculpture in the world'.

Now, daubed with students' paint and slogans, the Queen and her companions on their massive pedestals provide an example of civic embarrassment and bad siting. Deemed too bulky for a crowded city, they lack the formal landscape or stately buildings that would match their size and scale. White elephants put out to grass, their stature is diminished, and their *raison d'être* destroyed.

In Woodhouse Square is a bronze statue by Matthew Noble (1868) of Sir Peter Fairbairn who, when Mayor of Leeds in 1858, had masterminded the Queen's opening of Leeds Town Hall (by Cuthbert Broderick, 1853–8). In the Town Hall foyer, full-length statues by Noble commemorate Victoria, commissioned by Sir Peter in 1858, and Albert (1865). They form a group, on high, cylindrical pedestals, with statues of the Prince and Princess of Wales (1869). The nobility of this scene is destroyed by civic notice boards announcing cultural events.

Leeds's Victorian public buildings have many satisfying examples of decorative sculpture in stone or terracotta, the most prominent being the Town Hall lions by William Day Keyworth the Younger. Obscure but delightful is Mr John Patrick Foley, dyspeptic President of the Pearl Life Assurance Company, elevated with his winged gryphons on a parapet opposite the City Library. City banks and offices have ornamental friezes or portrait heads; all are recorded by the City Art Gallery in its town sculpture guide. The gallery has a fine marble statue of Queen Anne, sheltering after various changes of scene in the foyer, carved by Andrew Carpenter for the Moot Hall, Briggate, in 1712.

Modern civic sculpture in Leeds is most prominently represented by Sir Henry Moore's Draped Reclining Figure, his gift to his Sculpture Study

John Harrison (1576–1656). Sculptor: H. C. Fehr (1903). Location: City Square, Leeds.

Centre in the Headrow. Its dark smooth form, occupying the exterior balustrade, makes a companion to a similar, small-scale work reposing in grittier surroundings outside the Civic Centre at Moore's native Castleford, a coal town at the confluence of the Rivers Calder and Aire. Both works were sited by the artist, who saw setting and display as vital elements in the art of sculpture. There is still much to arouse civic pride in the heart of Leeds.

North Yorkshire

Ripon (NR)

Town Feature:

Aislabie Obelisk (1702)
80ft stone obelisk on tall, simply-moulded base with plaque, surmounted by copper weather-vane
Designer Nicholas Hawksmoor
Location Market Place

Among the parked cars stands the nation's earliest surviving free-standing monumental obelisk, made of warm stone and carrying a weather vane in the shape of the Wakeman's horn. The inscription implies that it was 'erected at the expense of William Aislabie' and dedicated to him in 1781, the year of his death after 60 years as local MP, but in fact William merely repaired the obelisk which by then had lost its decorative lions and sundials.

It was created by Nicholas Hawksmoor in the mayorality of William's politically-ambitious father, John Aislabie MP, who is thought to have borne most of the cost met by public subscription. He paved the market place, in the manner of a Roman forum, and also installed a pillory, symbol of Borough power.

Hawksmoor's obelisk was designed 'according to the most exact antient symetry', as he explained in a letter to Aislabie. He also wrote an 'Explanation of the Obelisk' (now in the archives at Blenheim Palace), with detailed references to Roman prototypes 'as big as all this, in One stone', first brought from Egypt by Constantine. They were re-erected late in the 16th century. Around this time Nonesuch in England received a marble obelisk, as high as the Palace which was destroyed in 1682. Ripon's is the next recorded, with its high plinth intended to prevent graffiti, 'and other Mischiefs and Brutalitys'.

Aislabie Obelisk. Design: Nicholas Hawksmoor (1702). Location: Market Place, Ripon.

The obelisk also displays extracts relating to the town's unique tradition of the Wakeman, upheld on orders from the Archbishop of York in 1598: ' ... the Wakeman according to ancient custom shall cause a horne to be blowne every night at nyne of the clocke at the foure corners of the crosse in the market stead ... ' This is still done by a horn blower in a tricorne hat, and his efforts are echoed in the words of a frieze on James Wyatt's Town Hall (1801): EXCEPT YE LORD KEEP YE CITTIE, THE WAKEMAN WAKETH IN VAIN.

Ripon Selection

The Ripon obelisk was built of limestone from quarries on the Aislabie estate at Studley Royal, and it makes a visual link between the ancient cathedral town and the unrivalled splendour of the park laid out by John Aislabie largely after his involvement in the South Sea Bubble affair brought expulsion from Parliament, and retirement, in 1720.

William purchased Fountains Abbey which then adjoined the park, and from 1768 he arranged the picturesque marriage between the skeletal Cistercian ruin and a man-made paradise of winding river, lake and lawns, classical statues towers and temples, all set against banks of trees on the Skell valley sides. Commemorative features include the Quebec Monument, and an obelisk to John Aislabie, but the Aislabies' supreme monument is the park and the Abbey of carved stone – the same honey tone as the Ripon obelisk. (Studley Royal belongs to the NT.)

A commemorative bronze in Ripon's Spa Gardens shows George Frederick Samuel Robinson, 1st Marquis of Ripon (1827–1908), bushy-bearded, rotund in court dress and Garter robes. He was the North Riding's Lord Lieutenant, and mayor of Ripon; his political career is detailed on the pedestal. His statue by F. Derwent Wood was unveiled in 1912.

(Across the Howardian Hills is the magnificent Baroque palace Castle Howard, designed 1699 by the untrained architect and genius John Vanbrugh, with Hawksmoor as Clerk of the Works. The building of the house is commemorated by Vanbrugh's glorious 100' Marlborough obelisk (1714), a sentinel beyond the entrance to the park, giving only a hint of further splendours, notably the *parterre* fountain from the Great Exhibition, centred on Atlas supporting the globe; the Temple of the Four Winds; Hawksmoor's Pyramid on St Anne's Hill, and his Mausoleum, started in 1731, unfinished at his death in 1736 and called by Laurence Whistler the 'noblest invention of them all'.)

Cleveland

Middlesbrough (NR)

Town Feature:

Henry William Ferdinand Bolckow (1806–1878)
Full-length bronze statue on red granite pedestal
Sculptor David Watson Stevenson
Casting Sir John Steell
Location Exchange Square

The Iron Capital's co-founder, first mayor and first MP – the only one during his lifetime – is shown holding the 'Charter of the Incorporation of Middlesbrough', in a newly-paved space surrounded by robust Victorian building and 1980s Post-Modernism, and the viaduct arches of a new road. The statue

H. W. F. Bolckow (1806–1878). Sculptor: D. W. Stevenson (1881). Location: Exchange Square, Middlesbrough.

had been removed to Albert Park, Bolckow's gift to the town, but in 1986 was reprieved and now presides over the changing face of the old commercial centre as Bolckow presided over the development of the original boom town.

The statue was unveiled in 1881 on land given by the Quaker family of Joseph Pease, founder of the original coal port 50 years earlier and treasurer for the Stockton and Darlington Railway, which his father helped to build. Pease had encouraged the German-born Bolckow and the iron-worker John Vaughan (1799–1868), who had met whilst courting sisters in Newcastle, to set up an iron works at Middlesbrough. Vaughan's statue by George Lawson, erected near Bolckow's in 1884, now stands in Victoria Square. (Lawson, like Bolckow's sculptor Stevenson and the sculptor Sir John Steell, was an Edinburgh man.)

Ironstone was already worked in the Cleveland hills when John Vaughan began prospecting for a good-quality seam to use in developing the iron works. The Eston mines opened in 1850; to the iron works and rolling mills were added blast furnaces and coal mines. The project was supervised by Jackie Vaughan, 'one of the best puddlers that Dowlais turned out', while Bolckow provided the cash.

From 'this reckless venture', as it was judged, came the gigantic growth of Bolckow, Vaughan and Co, accompanied by Middlesbrough's metamorphosis from a village to a town of some 7,500 souls in 1861, and by the Jubilee Year of 1880 an industrial centre of 56,000 inhabitants. The unveiling of Bolckow's statue in 1881 coincided with the Jubilee celebrations, held over because of a decline in the iron trade. At another event, full-length portraits of Vaughan, Bolckow and other leading figures, including Joseph Pease (whose statue by G.A. Lawson stands in Darlington), were hung in the Town Hall.

Today, with a population of c.145,000, most of the heavy industry has relocated at the mouth of the Tees. Some of the old, handsome commercial buildings in Exchange Square are still boarded up; others have taken in new businesses. Bolckow's Middlesbrough, now Cleveland's administrative and cultural capital, is still developing.

Middlesbrough (and locality) Selection

Middlesbrough's other two statues stand in Victoria Square, with the bronze statue of John Vaughan (1799–1868) looking down long formal gardens to that of Sir Samuel Sadler (1842–1911), set against the French-Gothic Town Hall. Three times mayor, Sadler operated a Middlesbrough coal-tar manufactory; his haughty, wax-moustached figure in court costume and mayoral robes, sensitively modelled by Edouard Lantéri, was unveiled in 1913.

Bolckow's mansion, Marton Hall, occupied the site of Captain Cook's birthplace, demolished in 1786 to make way for an earlier mansion. Bolckow put up a stone monument to Cook on Marton Green, and marked the birthplace of the 'world circumnavigator' with a large granite vase. Bolckow's collection of Cook documents was sold to the Australian Government after his death; his art collection was auctioned and Marton Hall was allowed to deteriorate, being demolished after a fire in 1960. In its grounds, Stewart Park, is the award-winning Cook Birthplace Museum (1978).

(At time of writing, the American artist Claes Oldenburg is to create a giant, listing bottle on a theme of a 'Message', inspired by Captain Cook. Constructed by Teesside steel workers, it will stand near Middlesbrough's Central Gardens. The project, sponsored by British Steel and supported by Northern Arts, will be a major addition to the city's considerable collection of modern public sculpture.)

Six miles south, the village of Great Ayton marks the site of Cook's father's cottage, sold to the Victoria Government on the Australian state's centenary in 1934. The capped pillar of blackish stones 'hewn from the rocks of Cape Everard close to Point Hicks' is a copy of that marking the spot nearest to Lieutenant Zachary Hicks's first sighting of Australia, from Captain Cook's Endeavour. Set on a gloomy grassed plot near Bridge Street, the pillar records the ship's log date (19th) and calendar date (20th) of this momentous event in April, 1770.

High on Easby Moor two miles southeast, a grim grey obelisk (1827) commands a view of bleak hills sprawling to the industrial coast beyond Teesside, and pays long tribute to the adventures of Captain Cook, 'massacred at Owyhee, Feb 24th 1779, to the inexpressible grief of his countrymen'. It is reached from a small car park beneath scoop-shaped Roseberry Topping, where Cook's father was bailiff at Thomas Scottowe's farm, Aireyholme, on the lower slopes: here was raised 'a man in nautical knowledge superior to none, in zeal, prudence and energy superior to most'. His bronze statue at Whitby, sculptured by John Tweed, was presented in 1912.

Other notable local monuments include: in Middlesbrough's Albert Park the Sanderson Memorial Clock of painted cast-iron, presented to the town in 1900 by Thomas Sanderson; at the Linthorpe Road entrance the 34ft Cenotaph, with names of the fallen on brass panels set in a screen wall of Portland stone; at Eston, four miles east (a small town swallowed into the industrial connurbation), the ironstone gate piers of Finigan's Hall — ugly, pitted and rust-coloured, they commemorate workers from the Main Seam of Eston Mines, whilst another pair stands outside Langbaurgh Town Hall nearby. A stone soldier of the Great War stands with bowed head at the town's central roundabout, with the moors glowering above; and at Eston Nab, a monument and landmark of ironstone features on Section Five of the 'Langbaurgh Loop', a long-distance walk promoted by the Langbaurgh Business Association.

County Durham

Durham

City Feature:

Charles William Vane Stewart, 3rd Marquis of Londonderry (1778–1854)
Electro-plated copper equestrian statue on large bow-ended sandstone pedestal with stepped base
Sculptor Rafaelle Monti
Plating/casting Rafaelle Monti
Location Market Place

3rd Marquis of Londonderry (1778–1854). Sculptor: Rafaelle Monti (1861). Location: Market Place, Durham.

No solemn-browed, bewhiskered, upstanding patriarch commemorated here; instead we have the 3rd Marquis of Londonderry, soldier and diplomat, landowner and employer, booted and spurred astride a mettlesome horse. His sabre hangs at his side, and he wears the outlandish plumed headgear of a General of the 10th Hussars. Erected in 1861, his large, green-tinged statue is a familiar feature of Durham's market place. The carved inscription, added later, commemorates the 'Lord Lieutenant of Durham, founder of Seaham Harbour'.

Durham people call the statue 'the horse', but the Marquis's place in local memory is that of the hated coal owner, a strike-breaker and rigid Tory who resisted reform. Local surnames recall Cornish tin miners brought in against strikers at Seaham, the model town and harbour designed by John Hobson of Newcastle for Londonderry as an outlet for his Rainton pits on land bought from Byron's father-in-law, Lord Milbanke. The Seaham Letter, threatening local suppliers of strikers, is infamous local history. Recent access to family papers has uncovered a less savage picture, of a hard but not cruel employer who provided housing and education for his men.

Born in Dublin, Londonderry succeeded his half-brother Lord Castlereagh, whose suicide in 1822 ended a brilliant diplomatic and political career. The Marquis himself shone as Wellington's Adjutant General in the Peninsula Wars, and succeeded the Prince Regent as Colonel of the 10th Hussars. British Ambassador at the Congress of Vienna, also accompanied Wellington at Verona in 1822.

At home, the Londonderrys were ostentatious and energetic socialites. They entertained lavishly at Wynyard Park, remodelled for them between 1842–4 by Ignatius Bonomi after a fire in 1841. They drove their guests in procession to the races and appeared, glittering, at society balls, Frances Anne bejewelled but 'dumpy, rum-shaped and rum-faced', as described by a fellow guest. She it was who staged bull roasts seating thousands for miners and estate workers, and organised Christmas festivities for working tenants. After the Marquis's death, a memorial room was created by Thomas Liddell at Wynyard to mark his military successes.

The Londonderry family is still prominent in local memory, if not in local affairs. Wynyard Hall was sold in 1987 for development as a hotel and conference centre, with some public access to the grounds, where a 127ft obelisk commemorates the Duke of Wellington's visit of 1827 to 'his friend' the Marquis. The inscription was removed after a dispute with Wellington over the brilliant but hot-headed Londonderry's army promotion, in which the Iron Duke accused the Marquis of intrigue. The quarrel was later patched up – but not the inscription.

The Durham statue was ordered by Frances Anne in 1854, but siting proved almost as hard as the casting process in which the sculptor (assisted by his brother) soaked the plaster with beeswax and coated it with black lead, then immersed it in water saturated with Copper sulphate. An electric charge precipitated the copper, which settled over the coated parts of the mould. The copper statue was placed on an immense iron frame (coated with tin), and filled with cement.

The earliest large-scale electrotype statue, it was finally accommodated at Durham in 1861. Over 100 years later, in 1952, money was readily raised for restoration of the badly decayed 'Horse' – present-day Durham has affection for the Londonderry image, if not his memory.

Durham Selection

The earliest and most valuable Durham statue is a lifesize lead figure of Neptune, with trident and dolphin, erected on a sandstone pedestal as part of a Market Place 'pant', or drinking fountain (1729). Possibly from the workshops of Van Nost or Andrew Carpenter, it was moved to Wharton Park in 1923; badly vandalised, it was restored in 1987 and displayed in the old gas showrooms at Claypath. It is planned to resurrect the 'Old Man of the Sea' near its original site, on a plinth of Dunhouse stone.

East of the Miners' Hall at Redhills, four marble statues on curved, panelled pedestals represent Durham Miners' Union agents. 'Macdonald' is signed J. Whitehead (1874). The runic cross in the

Cathedral churchyard was erected in 1905 to officers and men of Durham Light Infantry, lost in the Boer War. Designed by C.C. Hodges of Hexham, it was carved by G.W. Milburn of York.

A suggested location for Lord Londonderry's statue was Seaham, where John Tweed's orthodox but honest bronze of the 6th Marquis (1852–1915) now stands outside the town's police station, formerly the Londonderry Offices, near the sea front. When surf plumes over the front, the coastal view of this old coal port on approach from the north is worthy of any seaside resort.

Tyne and Wear

Newcastle-Upon-Tyne (N)

City Feature:

Charles, 2nd Earl Grey (1764–1845)
Doric column carrying full-length stone statue
Architects John & Benjamin Green
Sculptor Edward Hodges Baily
Location Blackett Street

Newcastle has not tidied its *objets* to the parks. The city monuments stand in the city streets, and each blackened statue makes its mark. The best and most famous (neither blackened nor merely a statue) is Earl Grey's column, a great landmark in the town and marvellously sited as a focal point at the top of Grey Street.

Newcastle raised this magnificent column in Earl Grey's lifetime, in recognition of 'the minister, by whose advice and under whose guidance the great measure of Parliamentary Reform was, after an arduous and protracted struggle, safely and triumphantly achieved in the year 1832'. Grey entered Parliament at the age of 22 and became Prime Minister at 66, but his political career is associated chiefly with the Reform Bill passed during his first Whig Ministry of 1830–34.

The redistribution of parliamentary seats embodied in the Bill was particularly popular in the north, where the productive developing industrial towns had no separate representation under a corrupt system unchanged since Tudor times. Members for Nomination boroughs were nominated by the landowner whatever the size of their population,

2nd Earl Grey (1764–1845). Architects: John & Benjamin Green. Sculptor: E. H. Baily (1838). Location: Blackett Street, Newcastle-upon-Tyne.

Academy in 1837, and the whole monument completed in 1838. Under the foundation stone, among other things, lie a purse of coins, and a plan of the monument. The height is 135ft, from the massive square base to the top of the statue's head (which in 1941 was struck by lightning, and replaced by R. Hedley). The original sculptor went on to create Nelson's statue for Trafalgar Square in 1842; the architect designed Lord Durham's temple on Pershaw Hill (1844).

Newcastle's column has an internal staircase of 164 steps, open on Bank Holidays and Saturdays in season, with marvellous views over town and Tyne. On the back of the base is added a renewal of 'gratitude to the author of the great reform bill', inscribed in 1932 'after a century of civil peace'.

Newcastle Selection

Outside the cathedral in St Nicholas Square, Alfred Gilbert's bronze statue of Queen Victoria is a powerful study of the aged queen swathed in majestic robes, holding court from an elaborate throne ornamented with helmeted cherubs' heads. Unveiled by the wife of Earl Grey, it was commissioned to celebrate the 500th anniversary of Newcastle's Shrievalty in 1903; the sculptor produced a work that is amongst the most brilliant of Victoria's innumerable statues, and which he himself judged his best work. (Although he had made a similar, and acclaimed, portrait of the queen in imperious old age for the city of Winchester.)

Facing the cathedral's south front, Milburn House (1905) has a fine niche bust of the wood engraver Thomas Bewick (1753–1828), with stone-worked letters: BEWICK SITE OF WORKSHOP. Over a doorway on the building's north face, is a bust of Collingwood (1750–1810), Nelson's second-in-command at Trafalgar, on the site of his birthplace.

Other commemorative figures include the 'Father of the Railways', George Stephenson (1781–1848), with his back to Central Station, portrayed in bronze (1867) by J.G. Lough. Further along Westgate Street, a bronze of Joseph Cowan (1831–1900) by John Tweed catches the reforming local MP in the heat of debate outside Cross House (1906). Nice keystones feature on the nearby County Court of 1864, the lion and unicorn crowning the arch.

At the northern end of town outside the Hancock Museum, Barras Bridge, Hamo Thornycroft's bronze statue presents the 1st Baron Armstrong (1810–1900) of the Engineering firm Armstrong Whitworth, with his Dandie Dinmont hunting dog.

and Rotten boroughs had so few eligible voters that bribery costs were negligible.

The sweeping recommendations of the Committee on Parliamentary Reform, under the chairmanship of Grey's son-in-law the Earl of Durham, caused gasps of disbelief when presented to the Commons. The first Bill's defeat in Committee stage caused a General Election, conducted amid near-riots which confirmed the Whig cause despite the Rotten boroughs; the second, thrown out by the Lords, again incited the mob; the fate of the third brought Grey's resignation, and his reinstatement (with an undertaking by William IV to create more Whig peers) when the Duke of Wellington was unable to form a government. The Duke and his supporters subsequently withdrew, and the Bill became law.

Five years later, in 1837, work began on Grey's fluted Doric column, which closes the view at the top of Grey and Grainger Streets; all were built in the same ambitious development programme. Baily's statue of Earl Grey was exhibited at the Royal

'Rush to the Colours' (1914–1918/19). Sculptor: Sir W. Goscombe John, RA (1923). Location: outside Civic Centre, Newcastle-upon-Tyne.

Weathered bronze reliefs behind pedestal seats show bridges and shipyards. Armstrong gave £10,000 to the museum, and many other gifts to Newcastle.

War Memorials near Barras Bridge include the Haymarket Victory, a tall column with a figure of 'Northumberland' reaching up from the base steps, and a Roll of Honour, to the fallen in the South African War. Big and impressive, it is signed and dated T. Eyre Macklin, 1907. Just north, the Northumberland Fusiliers' monument, a free-standing stone screen, has granite relief figures of St George flanked by soldiers (1674 and 1919) facing the Civic Centre. On the street side is Goscombe John's dramatic high-relief bronze of Tyneside workers' 'Rush to the Colours'. Headed by drummer boys, and a winged 'Renown', the group is idealised but shows the sculptor's moving humanity. It was given by Sir George and Lady Renwick in 1923. More central, in Eldon Square, a large bronze St George and Dragon by C.I. Hartwell commemorates both world wars.

On a slate-clad facia near the Civic Centre entrance, the massive form of the Tyne God, with water falling from an upraised hand, marks the City's installation of sculpture at the centre (opened in 1968). The smooth bronze of a courtyard fountain, 'Swans in Flight', complements building textures of dense brick and reflecting glass. Both sculptures were made by David Wynne and erected in 1969. The

Seahorses capping the Centre's Carillon Tower (1964–5) are by J.R.M. McCheyne, whose Family Group was erected in 1963 on a housing complex behind the City Hall.

Other monuments include a small carved drinking fountain obelisk on Quayside (south side), erected in 1891 near the spot where John Wesley (d.1791) preached in 1742, and in Blackett Street a pavement ventilator with terracotta cladding – 'Parson's Polygon by David Hamilton – a monument to Sir Charles Parsons (1854–1931), creator of the Turbina, made for Art in the Metro'. Installed in 1984 at the centenary of the steam turbine patent, it is based on a drawing of Parsons' turbine design.

Penshaw Hill (Co.D)

Hill Feature:

John George Lambton, 1st Earl of Durham (1792–1840)
Monument in form of Doric temple
Architects John & Benjamin Green
Location A183 between M1 and Sunderland

Penshaw Monument to 1st Earl of Durham (1792–1840). Architects: John & Benjamin Green (1844). Location: A 183 between M1 & Sunderland.

This is Durham's monument to Durham: a grand landmark on Penshaw Hill, its classical outline visible from the steep red-brick terraced streets of colliery villages like Newbottle and Philadelphia, and from the housing estates and coal-worked farmland spread between Durham and Tyneside. Modelled on the Temple of Theseus at Athens, its massive blackened stones carry no inscription, but they stand as a tribute to Lord Durham's memory, historically as Chairman of the Committee for Parliamentary Reform in his father-in-law, Earl Grey's, Whig administration (1830–34), and as an advocate of colonial independence, and locally as a coal owner committed to welfare and safety in the pits.

'Radical Jack', Durham was rich and aristocratic, with Byronic good looks and youthful waywardness (his first marriage was celebrated at Gretna Green) which matured to involvement in political and social reform. After the stormy but successful passage of the Reform Bill through Parliament, however, Durham with his quick temper and 'bad connections' was posted first to Russia as Ambassador, and later to Quebec as Canada's first Governor General.

On being recalled, Durham wrote the *Durham Report* (1839) proposing the merger of Upper French Canada and Lower British Canada. This was implemented in the Reunion Act of 1840. Durham also advocated Canadian self government, modelled on British administration; this was achieved in 1846 by his son-in-law, Lord Elgin.

Lord Durham's time abroad weakened him, and he died of consumption at 48. His funeral procession is said to have been followed by 30,000 Durham miners and shopkeepers.

The consequences of his political career are still with us, although his temple might be better deserved by legions of national figures; but it still has significance in Durham's locality.

The temple's foundation stone was laid in 1844 by Thomas, Earl of Zetland, Grand Master of the Freemasons of England. The cost, £6,000, was raised by public subscription. (The architects also designed Newcastle's monumental memorial column to Earl Grey in 1837.) On Penshaw Hill they built a roofless shell, correct in classical detail, with stairs (now closed) ascending inside one of the massive Doric columns.

Local walkers point out from the temple's flag-paved base a view encompassing Nissan and Washington New Town among distant flares and fumes of Tyneside chimneys; the Victoria Viaduct, opened on Coronation Day in 1837, and still carrying mineral trains; Lambton Castle; 'Old Jameson's farm',

and, on a clear day, Durham Cathedral. Most of the land around the foot of the hill belonged to Lord Durham.

Local myth says that the temple was one of the sites debated for Lord Londonderry's statue in Durham Market Place. Local memory recalls the two landowners' political and economic rivalry; and local history records the Londonderry Marsden quarries as the source of gritstone for the Durham temple. Both men employed Ignatius Bonomi to remodel their sumptuous homes. The Durham family's local associations are said to be as old as the legend of the Lambton Worm.

Their castle and monument are both subject to mining subsidence. In 1939 the temple was given to the National Trust, with an endowment for its upkeep. In 1982, the Trust bought a further 44 acres for grazing and for the use of people from terraced villages like New Herrington, whose pits are now closed – the long low spoil heap lies at the foot of Penshaw Hill, on the other side of the A183. Far from any Hellenic idyll Lord Durham's temple, weathered black, sits well in its harsh landscape. Floodlit in 1988, it makes a great northern landmark both day and night.

Sunderland (Co.D)

Town Feature:

Jack Crawford (1775–1831)
Full-length bronze statue on Aberdeen granite pedestal
Sculptor Percy Wood
Location Mowbray Park

The sculptor has given us a romantic composition of a billowing flag and a boy:

Jack Crawford, the hero of Camperdown.
The sailor who so heroically nailed
Admiral Duncan's flag to the main-top
gallant-mast of H.M.S. Venerable in the
glorious action off Camperdown on October
11th 1797.

The pedestal has a trim of carved rope, and stands on a mound of volcanic-looking limestone; the whole is set on a hillock overlooking the Civic Centre (1970 red-brick) on the west side of the park.

The battle of Camperdown was fought to prevent a Dutch squadron from reaching Brest, where the French fleet was waiting to assist Ireland in a bid for

Jack Crawford (1775–1831). Sculptor: Percy Wood (1890).
Location: Mowbray Park, Sunderland.

independence. When the mast of the British flagship, *Venerable*, was brought down, Admiral Duncan tore the flag from the remains, and Crawford climbed to the top gallant mast head, under heavy fire, with marlin spike and flag. (The statue's original pistol, replaced with a marlin spike in 1910, was later reinstated).

Crawford's feat made him a popular hero, but he did not take to the role. Cheerful and improvident, he ignored the Victory procession in London, painting the town red whilst an unknown sailor took his place (and rewards) in an open carriage showered with coins from the crowd. Illiterate and therefore ineligible for promotion, Crawford scorned a showman's offers of £100 a week to reinact his feat: 'I will never disgrace the real act of a sailor to act the play fool'. He returned to a feckless existence as a keelman in his native Sunderland.

Later, Crawford was presented to George III, and received a pension of £30 a year; from his town he received a silver medal, which he wore in Nelson's funeral procession (1806). He pawned the medal and later redeemed it, but after his death from cholera, Jack's widow sold the medal for £5. Acquired by

the 2nd Earl of Camperdown (Admiral Duncan's grandson), it now resides in the Borough Museum. The hero's statue, perhaps a more reliable monument, was installed in 1890.

Sunderland Selection

In Mowbray Park, far from the town centre on Building Hill, overlooking town roofs and the sea, is Behnes's large bronze of Indian Mutiny hero Major General Sir Henry Havelock (1795–1857), erected in 1861 near his birthplace (Ford Hall). A second cast, also of 1861, stands in Trafalgar Square.

The central terrace has a bronze of the gaunt-looking John Candlish (1815–1874), Liberal MP for Sunderland, draper, coal exporter, ship builder and founder of the *Sunderland News* (1851); his bottle factory at Seaham was one of the biggest in Europe. Candlish's statue by Charles Bacon (1875) is accompanied on the terrace by sweet Victorian statues of dogs and lions and by rounded, draped figures in white composite, figurative but simplified, by Janet Barry. Serenely occupying plinths once carrying classical statues, they were made for a 1980s park rejuvenation on a Victorian theme. A statue of Victory surmounts a First World War column at the Borough Road entrance.

Moved from the park to Bishopwearmouth Cemetery in 1959 are vandalised remains of a Tragic marble group marking 'the calamity' of the Victoria Hall conjuring show (1883), at which 183 children were crushed to death in a rush for prizes through a too-narrow door. Across the Wear, on Roker seafront, a 25ft granite cross dedicated to the Venerable Bede of Jarrow (d.735) was unveiled by the Archbishop of York in 1904. It was designed by Charles Hodges of Hexham.

Northumberland

Branxton Village

Countryside Feature:

Battle of Flodden (1513)
Granite Celtic cross on rustic cairn, with concrete base, in a railed enclosure
Contractors Bower & Florence, Aberdeen
Location Flodden Field

Cross to Battle of Flodden (1513).
Contractors: Bower & Florence (1910)
Location: Flodden Field, near Branxton.

Dedicated to THE BRAVE OF BOTH NATIONS, the plain stone cross recalls the fateful contest late on a September afternoon in 1513 that left nearly 10,000 Scots dead, including King James IV and most of his nobles. The battle was called to honour James's promise of backing for France against Henry VIII. The cause lay in the old nationalistic strife that erupted regularly among the Border hills from Berwick to the Solway Firth. The awful outcome lingers in Scotland's memory as an unhealed wound.

The English columns under Thomas Howard, Earl of Surrey, were lined up across the slopes and crest of Piper's Hill, where the cross now stands. They had marched north of Flodden Hill, which James had refused to abandon at Surrey's earlier invitation to battle on Milfield Plain.

At news of Surrey's approach, the 30,000 Scots had dragged their cannon to Branxton Hill, one and half miles northwest. Facing the English across the muddy valley, theirs was the largest and best-equipped Scots army ever to cross the border. It included a French contingent who had hurriedly trained the Scots in the use of the Swiss weapon, the long pike, and they had the advantage over the English in numbers and equipment, but James's men under clan leaders such as Montrose, Bothwell, Lennox and Argyle, lacked the cohesion of a common allegiance.

Battle commenced at 4.30pm, and the Scots gained the edge, but once James had abandoned his horse to take up the long pike, descending the wet and slippery hill towards the damaged English right wing which faced them across a bog, he was to find his weighty and brutal weapon hopelessly unwieldy against the English bill. The labouring Scots eventually came under fire from Sir Edward Stanley's archers, who had ascended Pace Hill on their right flank, and within a span of two hours the king and his army were cut to pieces, and the cream of Scotland's aristocracy destroyed.

The cross at Flodden was erected at the initiation of the Berwickshire Naturalists' Club in 1907. The appeal committee included club members from both sides of the Border, and funds were augmented by selling a pamphlet on the battle, bearing the motto *'Olim Hostes, nunc fratres'* (Once Foes, now brothers). At the unveiling in 1910 beneath the Union flag, the Naturalists' Chairman gave a stirring speech, after which an impromptu collection amassed £24 to swell the £350 already raised.

Flodden was the last battle on English soil to be fought in medieval style, with armoured knights commanding archers and swordsmen. The fighting in all its stages is explained on interpretation boards overlooking the fertile fields which replace the bare moors of Tudor days. Below the hill can be seen the small Church of St Paul, restored in 1849, where James's stripped and mutilated body was laid before being embalmed at Berwick and carried south to the English capital for burial. The churchyard accommodated one of the pits into which the dead were tipped in the aftermath of battle.

It is hard to imagine such savagery in these serene surroundings, but it is in this fertile border country, for better or for worse, that the old and not-so-old rivalries might be best understood.

North Western Counties Gazetteer

(Note: The North Western Counties appear in loosely topographical order. Within each county, monuments are listed under their locations, which appear in alphabetical order. Letters after a location indicate its county of origin – ie. (C) Cumberland and (L) Lancashire.

Cumbria

Burgh by Sands (C)

Countryside Location:

Edward I (1239–1307)
Red sandstone capped pillar on moulded plinth,
with moulded cornice surmounted by a cross
(restored)
Mason Thomas or John Longstaff (1685)
Location Sandsend

A side road leads north from the village to a farm track, then to a rough path across the saltmarsh, finally a listing pillar in a field. Larksong and lapwing, and cries of estuary birds echo in the big skies reaching between Criffel in Wales, and Scottish hills across the Solway sands. The sense of desolation is perhaps the truest monument to the many-centuries dead. The pillar was raised to mark the last camp of Edward I, 'Hammer of the Scots', marching to do battle with Robert Bruce in July 1306; it could as well speak for the troubled centuries in which Cumbria's allegiance to one or other side was enforced by armed conflict and bloody border raids.

During Edward I's stabilising reign, he attempted unification of Britain by subjugating Wales and betrothing his son to the Scots king Alexander III's infant grandaughter and successor. The Maid of Norway's death *en voyage* to England, and Edward's subsequent imposition of John Balliol as vassal king of Scotland (1290), led to the bitter Wars of Inde-

Pillar to Edward I (1239–1307). Mason: Thomas or John Longstaffe (1685). Location: Sandsend, near Burgh by Sands.

pendence. During the campaign against Robert Bruce, the ageing Edward, suffering from dysentry, wintered at Lanercost Priory near Carlisle, and later in the year 1307, having offered up his horse-drawn litter in Carlisle Cathedral, his forces headed north.

Two days and four miles on, the stricken king made camp at Sandsend, near Burgh (pronounced 'Bruff'). On his death bed he commanded the Prince of Wales to continue north, carrying his bones into battle, but the new king Edward II carried his father's body to the church at Burgh, to lie in state before starting southward. The 'Hammer' and the 'Law-giver' was buried at Westminster Cathedral in October 1307.

The red, lichened pillar in its main inscription commemorates 'EDOARDI primi Famam Optimi Anglici Regis'; this dates from a restoration of 1803, after floods, effected by 'GULIELMUS Vice comes de LOWTHER'. Another side records further restoration, and enclosure, by the 4th Earl of Lonsdale (1876). The name 'Johannes Aglionby' appears crudely carved on the step. The Lowther family bought the barony of Burgh from Henry Howard, Duke of Norfolk, in 1685, the year that the Duke and Aglionby built Edward's pillar. The County Record gives it as 'red sandstone ashlar; tall square column on moulded plinth, moulded cornice, shaped cap surmounted by cross'.

Hutchinson's *History of Cumberland* in 1794 describes 'a very fair square pillar, nine yards and a half in height', but in 1974 a local writer reporting 'a melancholy artichoke in a bed of old nettles', called for information plaques and viewing identification maps, and the pavings to be weeded and cleared. A cleanup is due, but the full Heritage treatment would as usual annul all romance and sense of personal discovery. At Burgh's fortified church (originally built of stones from the Roman wall), a framed descriptive notice, and a map of the estuary, give unobtrusive information – let this suffice.

Derwent Water (C)

Lakeside Feature:

John Ruskin (1819–1900)
Inscribed, rough-cut slab of Borrowdale slate, featuring bronze roundel portrait
Designer W.G. Collingwood
Sculptor A.C. Lucchesi
Location Friar's Crag

Friar's Crag, in 1922, was purchased for the National Trust as a memorial to one of its founders, Hardwick Drummond Rawnsley. Its chief monument is one that Rawnsley himself raised there in 1900 to a more famous off-comer who settled in the Lake District, the celebrated writer, art critic, lecturer and social philosopher, John Ruskin.

The lakeside path leads past Canon Rawnsley's unobtrusive memorial wall tablet to the end of the promontory where, in a pine grove, a rugged pillar of Borrowdale slate is finely inscribed with Ruskin's words and with the early Christian CHI-RHO symbol. On the side facing the shoreline an unexpected pleasure is a profile of Ruskin, handsome in a bronze medallion, with a prominent nose, and a look of detached amusement.

An only child, Ruskin described an upbringing 'in severe seclusion by devoted parents, at a suburban villa with a pretty garden'; he was educated by his

Stone to John Ruskin (1819–1900). Design: W. G. Collingwood. Sculptor: A. C. Lucchesi (1900). Location: Friar's Crag, Derwent Water.

devoutly-Christian mother and later by tutors, and on summer tours of scenic splendours in the English Lakes, Wales and Scotland, closeted with the elderly parents in a carriage. Whilst a student at Oxford and suffering a broken engagement, Ruskin toured *en famille* the fabulous mountains, lakes and cities of Europe.

Preoccupations with natural landscape, mountains and clouds, geology and architecture coloured his art as a painter and architectural draughtsman, as well as his writing. His early success, Volume I of *Modern Painters*, took up the defence of landscape artists and notably Ruskin's ideal, Turner. It was attributed to 'an Oxford Graduate', but by the time Volume V was completed under his own name (1860), Ruskin was an established writer whose defence of the Pre-Raphaelite Brotherhood had helped turn public opinion to their favour. Apart from his time at Oxford and six years of marriage which Ruskin felt unable to consummate, he lived at the parental home near London until buying Brantwood on the shore of Lake Coniston in 1870.

The portrait shows Ruskin 'in his prime', Canon Rawnsley declared during the unveiling, 'at the time I knew him best, at Oxford, in the early 'seventies'. Ruskin was then first Slade Professor of Art there, and pursuing his social and revivalist schemes, such as spinning and weaving at Langdale. He also set up his collection of Turner paintings in the National Gallery, and worked at his unfinished autobiography, *Præterita* (1885–1889).

At the same time he became difficult, quarrelling with friends like Octavia Hill, a former pupil, whom he had assisted financially in housing projects. In 1895, an influential social reformer, she co-founded the National Trust with Robert Hunter and Canon Rawnsley, whom she had met through Ruskin.

Ruskin died at his home, Brantwood, after a protracted retreat into long-bearded insanity, and his memorial was unveiled the same year in an October gale. It bears his words: 'The first thing which I remember as an event in life was being taken by my nurse to the brow of Friars Crag on Derwentwater'.

The portrait's frame of olive leaves carrying Ruskin's motto *TODAY* refers to his collected lectures on social themes, *Crown of Wild Olives*; the lettering was made by Ruskin's secretary and biographer W.G. Collingwood, the authority on Celtic and Anglo-Saxon crosses. The 'dot and dash' style, according to Rawnsley, 'was a favourite method with the Master'. The inscriptions and symbols express the historical revivalism which Ruskin inspired in Rawnsley and many others.

The Ruskin Cross, designed by Collingwood in the Celtic revival, stands in Coniston churchyard where Ruskin was buried having refused a place in Westminster. The head and shaft are hewn from a single block of slate from Tilberthwaite near Coniston, and from Elterwater respectively. A Mr Miles carved the rich figurative and symbolic decoration, explained in a leaflet of 1902 kept at the Ruskin Museum, Coniston. The Hawkshead war memorial cross was also designed by Collingwood.

Lakes Selection

Various local monuments were set up by Hardwick Rawnsley, churchman, writer, preserver of the Lakes landscapes, reviver of local traditions (toned down), and champion of fresh air for the working man. An example is Peace How in Borrowdale, given by Canon Rawnsley (1917) in response to a National Trust appeal for a tribute to Keswick men who perished in the Great War.

The best-known is the Gough Memorial to a faithful dog (1890), a rough stone cairn overlooking Striding Edge and Red Tarn from Helvellyn's summit. A large inscribed slab carries lines from Wordsworth's *Fidelity*, but most touching, in this immense landscape, are Rawnsley's words: 'Beneath this spot were found in 1805 the remains of Charles Gough, killed by a fall from the rocks. His dog was still guarding the skeleton'.

Wordsworth's intials, and others belonging to his coterie, can be seen on the 'Rock of Names', controversially moved to Dove Cottage in Grasmere (1988) and crazy-paved into a whole by Canon and Mrs Rawnsley from fragments of rock shattered in the Thirlmere Reservoir scheme. At Cockermouth, where the Wordsworth birthplace is cared for by the National Trust, Rawnsley installed in Harris Park an ornamental fountain with a statue of Wordsworth's sister Dorothy as a child.

At Lonscale Fell above Mirehouse, on Bassenthwaite Lake, Rawnsley erected a runic wayside cross to the Hawells, father and son; it quotes a verse from his poem *Great Shepherd*, inspired by these 'noted breeders of prize Herdwick sheep'. Sheep grazing here still bear the 'H' mark retained when Lonscale Farm passed to the Speddings of Mirehouse, in recognition of the Hawells' skill.

By Bassenthwaite, in the grounds of Mirehouse, where Tennyson worked on his *Morte d'Arthur* in 1835, the Tennyson Stone compares in atmosphere with that of Ruskin's (who spent childhood holidays with the Tennysons). The slate slab at the water's edge has metal appliqués showing a grasping hand and sword, swirling waves, and lines ending:

But ere he dipt the surface, rose an arm
Clothed in white samite, mystic, wonderful,
And caught him by the hilt, and brandish'd him
Three times, and drew him under in the meer.

The stone commemorates not Tennyson, but 'the visit to this place of the Tennyson Society, 18th May, 1974'. It could as well have been raised by Canon Rawnsley, who described the Speddings' Mirehouse in his *Literary Associations of the English Lakes* (1894).

Lindale (L)

Village Feature:

John Wilkinson (1728–1808)
Black-painted iron obelisk featuring gilded lettering and medallion
Designer Not known
Location The Grange-over-Sands road

Recently restored but still graceless, the 20-ton obelisk occupies a green rise surrounded by gentle High Furness fells. Dull gold paint picks out a delicate relief profile as of a Roman emperor, made for JOHN WILKINSON, IRON MASTER, whose LIFE WAS SPENT IN ACTION TO THE BENEFIT OF MAN, AND, AS HE PRESUMED HUMBLY TO HOPE, TO THE GLORY OF GOD. This was Wilkinson's version. Local tradition recalls a powerful and ruthless industrialist whose restless, innovative mind was obsessed with exploiting the fullest potential of iron.

Wilkinson is said to have been born in a cart on the way to market, and he developed his pioneering skills at his father's iron works in Backbarrow and later in Lindale, making the first flat irons, and perfecting peat smelting. Operative in early days of industrial expansion, he exploited the new technique of iron smelting by coke, winning riches and power as Father of the south Staffordshire iron trade.

His numerous technological contributions included cylinders for the first successful Watt steam engine, and involvement in the construction of Abraham Darby's first iron bridge (1779); eight years later, his launching of the first iron boat 'convinced the unbelievers, who were 999 in a thousand'.

Afterwards the iron magnate returned to Lindale where he built Castlehead, girding it with limestone battlements and massive iron gates, and reclaiming

Obelisk to John Wilkinson (1728–1808). Design & Sculptor: not known (restored & resited, 1984). Location: Grange-over-Sands road, Lindale.

the salt marshes. Irish labourers – Sunday workers – were summoned by a bell brought from Cartmel Priory. This now hangs in Lindale Church.

Notorious rather than notable, reputedly atheistic and refreshingly non-worthy, 'Iron Mad Wilkinson' supported radical causes such as those of Joseph Priestley, his brother-in-law, made homeless by the Birmingham mob for siding with the French revolutionaries. Widowed early, Wilkinson remarried a woman of 'ample fortune'. The *Dictionary of National Biography* notes domestic arrangements 'of a very peculiar character', and at Wilkinson's death his considerable assets were contested in bitter litigation between his nephews and three natural sons.

His cast-iron coffin, transported from Bradley, sank in Morecambe sands before being interred at Castlehead, where the next owner dug it up. Later it found an unmarked grave in the churchyard. Wilkinson's blunt iron obelisk, his headstone, set up at Castlehead and later removed, rusted by the roadside until 1984 when the parish council organised restoration grants to meet a cost of £10,000. Its big Roman letters glow again: LABORE ET HONORE.

Furness Selection

Further west at Ulverston on Hoad Hill, a tower emulating the Eddystone Light commemorates Sir John Barrow (1764–1848), Under-Secretary to the Admiralty and founder member of the Royal Geographical Society (1830). It is closed, but has a viewing gallery and a marble bust of Sir John.

There is a wonderful marble monumental lighthouse in the cemetery on the Barrow-in-Furness road. Sir John's birthplace is preserved just south of Barrow, the town that usurped Ulverston in importance after the ironmaster William Schneider and the railway engineer James Ramsden, with the backing of local landowners, made Barrow one of Britain's fastest-expanding industrial towns.

When the site for Ramsden's portly bronze statue by Matthew Noble was levelled off with slag and renamed Ramsden Square, Barrow had a rising population of 35,000, and the world's largest steelworks. Faded pedestal reliefs show a village of thatched hovels, and the smoking industrial scene. In the same year (1872) Ramsden, Father of the town, completed his mayorality, and was knighted.

His grid plan of broad avenues and long alleys dates from 1865; in 1867 Barrow became a borough and Ramsden its first mayor, whilst the new Devonshire and Buccleuch Docks were named after their landowner-developers. Ramsden's Barrow Shipbuilding Company of 1869 later became the great Vickers group.

In Duke Street, Barrow's best bronze (1890), by Percy Wood, shows the founder of Barrow's steelworks, William Henry Schneider, also in mayoral attire. Like Ramsden, Schneider (1817–1887) entered parliament, but was twice unseated for 'electoral irregularities' said to have lost him a knighthood. He commuted from his Windermere mansion by private yacht, continuing on Ramsden's Furness Railway, built to carry ore from the fells.

Outside the football ground in Hindpool Road is an appealing bronze of Lord Frederick Charles Cavendish, second son of the Duke of Devonshire, by Albert Bruce-Joy. It was unveiled outside the Duke Street Town Hall in 1885, three years after Cavendish, as Chief Secretary to the Lord Lieutenant of Ireland, was assassinated in Dublin.

In 1948, popular protest prevented relegation of all three statues to a Barrow park. The town still has its docks and shipyards, and most of its original buildings. The founding fathers' bronze personae are part of this scene.

Lancashire

Lancaster

City Feature:

Queen Victoria (1819–1901)
Bronze full-length statue on Furness stone
pedestal and large square base with bronze
sculptural ornamentation, and large relief panels
Sculptor Sir Herbert Hampton
Location Dalton Square

Dominating Dalton Square, Queen Victoria's statue faces the majestic columns of Lancaster's new Town

Queen Victoria (1819–1901). Sculptor: Sir Herbert Hampton (1907). Location: Dalton Square, Leicester.

Hall 1909–16 with its pediment statue of Edward VII. Both were the gift of Lord Ashton the Lancaster lino king. A foible of the millionaire recluse was his aversion to being portrayed in any medium (a likeness in oils, showing a distrustful, bespectacled gentleman, hangs in his town hall). He lives on, however, in the county town's most striking monuments, of which the Victoria Memorial is one.

'Victoria the Good' is sternly enthroned above bronze lions, and heroic statues at the corners of the base. One of these – 'Truth' – looks quite like the youthful Victoria herself. Northwestern towns have especially elaborate monuments to the empress-queen, and Lancaster's compares in excellence, but the monument's reward lies in its base panels, large bronze high-reliefs forming a sculptural catalogue of the great, the good and the glorious of Victorian England, whose statues stare from squares and street corners throughout the land. (The pattern was first established on the Albert Memorial in London.)

Over 40 public figures appear, loosely grouped by occupation or discipline. Prince Albert is on the Arts panel with Henry Irving and Lord Tennyson; sculptors include Sir Hamo Thornycroft, creator of Rochdale's statue to John Bright who is in the front amongst the parliamentarians and reformers. These include Disraeli, Gladstone, Cobden and Peel, all having statues elsewhere in the northwest, the work of prominent or local sculptors.

Only two women belong to the *dramatis personæ*: the novelist George Eliot (Mary Ann Evans), and Florence Nightingale who appears with explorers and men of action. Local worthies include James Williamson, whose Lancaster oilcloth business was built into a mighty linoleum empire by his second son James, later the embittered Lord Ashton.

Hard and exacting, but in some respects a benevolent employer, Lord Ashton carried his extreme form of Victorian paternalism into the twentieth century, clinging to control of his company until his death at 87. Lancaster's Liberal MP from 1886–1895, his peerage was said to be a reward for contributions to Liberal funds. This 'slur', and growing local support for his workers' Trades Union representation, caused an enduring rift with the town. 'Ungrateful Lancaster' unveiled Queen Victoria's statue without ceremony in his absence one morning in 1907.

Lancaster Selection

The year before, work began on Ashton's exotic and ostentatious monument to his second wife, Jessy

(d.1904). Crowning a hill in Williamson Park, John Belcher's Edwardian Baroque (using novel construction methods) has been called the 'Taj Mahal of the North', the 'Jelly Mould', 'Baron's Folly', and 'the grandest monument in England' (Pevsner); Lancastrians call it 'the structure'.

With its staircases, porticoes and domes, the 150ft, £87,000 temple was completed in 1909, the year that Ashton took his third bride. The recently-restored tower holds displays on Ashton's life and times, exterior carvings signify his railway and development schemes, and the viewing gallery has panoramas across the park that his father gave to Lancaster, built on wasteland by textile workers during the Cotton Famine. Tickets are sold in the splendid Palm House nearby.

No memorial directly marks Lancaster's former importance as a cotton town, but not far west, just outside the village of Sunderland Point is 'Sambo's Grave', the original worn epitaph of 1736 replaced with verses by a retired headmaster, James Watson:

Full sixty Years the angry Winter's Wave
Has thundering dafh'd this bleak & barren Shore
Since SAMBO'S Head laid in this lonely *Grave*
. . .

Sunderland Point then was a port, Sambo a Negro servant boy whose master disembarked here, leaving Sambo to pine away uncomprehending whilst he travelled briefly on business. So the story is told; Sambo was buried in unconsecrated ground and

. . . still he sleeps – till the awakening Sounds
Of the Archangel's Trump new Life impart
Then the Great Judge his Approbation Founds
Not on Man's COLOR but his WORTH
OF HEART

St Anne's

Town Feature:

Coxswain William Johnson (d.1886)
Full-length stone statue on 'rustic' stonework
pedestal with stone base
Sculptor Burnie Rhind
Location Pierhead

Carved from dull grey stone that glows ochre in the westering sun, a lifeboatman scans the grey sands of the Ribble Estuary beyond St Anne's seafront. Over his shoulder is a bale of rope, and his left hand rests on a lifebelt; his uniform is a sou'wester and

Coxswain William Johnson (d.1886). Sculptor: Burnie Rhind (1888). Location: Pierhead, St Anne's.

cork lifejacket. His name, Coxswain William Johnson, is carved into the rocky pedestal with those of his 12-man crew.

Their craft the *Laura Janet* was last seen under sail on a December night in 1886, battling against mountainous seas after launching from this beach in response to a distress signal from the German barque *Mexico*. She was foundering off Southport on the Horse Bank, most deadly of the sandbanks and channels at the mouth of the estuary. Two other lifeboats, from Lytham and from Southport across the estuary, had also launched. Next day the *Laura Janet* and nearly all her crew were found washed up on Ainsdale beach. No one lived to tell their tale.

Theirs is the most handsome memorial of the *Mexico* disaster, in which 27 local men were lost. Southport seafront has a small polished granite obelisk carved with a lifeboat, and there is a larger memorial in the town cemetery. Lytham, however, has no memorial, although her men were as brave – their recently-improved lifeboat, *Charles Biggs*, managed to reach the *Mexico's* twelve-man crew and to keep upright in the boiling sea. The Southport lifeboat *Eliza Fernley* later capsized within sight of the abandoned wreck, drowning her Cox'n and 13 of her 15 crew. Many of the *Laura Janet's* crew

had relatives on Lytham's *Charles Biggs*, which re-launched after the rescue in fruitless search of survivors.

The RNLI's then-worst disaster brought rapid modifications in lifeboat design as well as a more hard-nosed approach to lifeboat funding. The Manchester businessman Charles Macara, member of the St Anne's Lifeboat Committee, set up a fund for the bereaved, and later organised the first 'Lifeboat Saturday', with purses offered on poles to people on the tops of Manchester trams. Meanwhile, St Anne's commissioned this statue using a local lifeboatman as model. It was unveiled in May 1888, close to St Anne's newly-built pier.

Southport and the St Anne's lifeboat stations were closed because of silting in 1925, leaving the Lytham lifeboat, and a D class inflatable, to ride the unpredictable seas. The original Lytham boathouse, now a lifeboat museum, displays relics from the *Mexico*.

In the centenary year of the disaster, 1986, a service of remembrance was held near the statue. The surroundings, with the Victorian pier and seafront furniture, are disfigured by cheap utilitarian buildings. The monument reflects its time, but Coxwain Johnson's rather delicate, beard-fringed stone features could as well belong to now as then.

Also true to period, and to the region, is an impressive Great War memorial by W. Marsden (1923) in public gardens off Clifton Drive. The symbolic, outstretched female figure surmounting the stone column, and the relief panels of idealised battle scenes, heighten the realism of the bronze side figures: a gaunt soldier, and a passively-resolute mother with child.

Greater Manchester

Bolton (L)

Town Feature:

Samuel Crompton (1753–1827)
Electro-plated copper seated statue on Portland stone pedestal with stepped granite base
Sculptor William Calder Marshall RA
Location Nelson Square

Ignored and exploited in his lifetime, the unworldly developer of the Spinning Mule was honoured by this fine statue 35 years after his death. On one side

Samuel Crompton (1753–1827). Sculptor: W. C. Marshall, RA (1862). Location: Nelson Square, Bolton.

of the bow-fronted pedestal, *bas*-relief bronzes show the young musician studying calculations in front of the mule. The other side shows 'Hall i' th' Wood', the timber-framed house in which Samuel Crompton laboured to build a machine that would spin cotton yarn of uniform good quality.

By 1775, after five years' trial and error, Crompton had combined his own innovative spindle movement with elements from Hargreaves' Spinning Jenny and Arkwright's water frame into a single revolutionary machine. Crompton's mule could spin fine fabrics beyond the reach of rival cotton manufacturers, but his business naïvety allowed an army of entrepreneurs to develop the 'Hall i'th' Wood Wheel', designed for home working, as a means of mass production. They prospered even as the gentle inventor struggled on unrewarded and unsung.

Agitation for a memorial began with a lecture by the president of the Bolton Mechanics' Institute, G.J. French. The *Bolton Chronicle* reported 'a crowded and deeply interested audience comprising many ladies' who heard the Mule described as 'the Minerva of modern times'; the goddess of spinning and weaving had been worshipped by 'ignorant but grateful pagans', whilst Crompton's name went

unknown by Christians of the very town which had most prospered from his technological genius.

Bolton's conscience lumbered into action. A statue was ordered from William Calder Marshall. His simple but effective figure of Crompton was unveiled with fabulous ceremonial on September 24, 1862.

No member of Samuel Crompton's family, then living in poverty, was invited to the day's junketings. A contemporary newspaper photograph shows the gaunt features of Crompton's son John, then 72, hovering in the crowd behind the mayor of Bolton and invited dignitaries. One wonders what he made of the solemn inaugural processions, the performance of 'The Oratorio of the Creation', the ascent of 'Mr Coxwell's Mammoth Balloon', the Ancient Foresters' Ball, the carriages, banners and crowds; the feasting, speeches, fireworks and festoons, and the richly-burnished statue.

Bolton Selection

Bolton statues' peculiar charm tends to increase in proportion to their sculptor's obscurity. Victoria Square has one bronze on either side of the Town Hall steps (with lions), facing Bolton's cenotaph. Dr Samuel Taylor Chadwick (1809–1876), by C.B. Birch, quite a popular sculptor, was unveiled in 1873. A relief on the granite pedestal shows Mrs Chadwick receiving new arrivals at the orphanage given by the couple whose own children had died in infancy.

An utterly charming statue (erected in 1900) is that of portly Lieut. Col. Sir B.A. Dobson (1847–1898), Chevalier de la Legion d'Honneur and four times mayor. He has a waxed moustache and holds a monocle, and is perpetuated for his 'useful life' by John Cassidy of Manchester (also successful).

Another by Cassidy, on top terrace of Queen's Park, is the Portland stone statue of charitable Dr James Dorrian, now lacking nose, erected to commemorate a 'life of usefulness'; signed 1898. Further along the terrace looms a statue of Disraeli in pinkish stone. The grand pedestal is signed 'T Rawcliffe, Sc., Chorley' in small letters at the base.

Last in line along the terrace, also occupying a handsome pedestal, is the doll-like figure of John T. Fielding, JP, 'For over 20 years secretary of Operative Cotton Spinners' Association and United Trades Council. Unity and equity were the guiding principles of his life'. Reputedly the country's first working class magistrate, Fielding died in 1894 aged 45. By J. William Bowden and of durable Yorkshire stone, the statue was presented 'by the Trade Unionists and Public of Bolton' in 1896.

Manchester (L)

City Feature:

Albert, Prince Consort (1819–1861)
Full-length Sicilian marble statue under gabled
Gothic canopy of York stone
Architect Thomas Worthington
Statue's sculptor Matthew Noble
Canopy stone carving T.R. and E. Williams
Location Albert Square

This proud edifice was commissioned from Thomas Worthington nine months after Prince Albert's death from typhoid in December 1861, and inaugurated in 1867 five years before installation of Hyde Park's far-famed Albert Memorial.

A Memorial Committee under chairmanship of Manchester's mayor, Thomas Goadsby, had taken shape within weeks of Albert's demise; Goadsby it was who offered the cost of a statue by Matthew Noble, and soon all other ideas for monuments were abandoned in favour of a canopy for Noble's statue, planned to show the Prince clad in Garter robes.

With the subscription fund standing at over £2,800 the Committee sent for Worthington, and later selected his Gothic open-arched, four-sided, spired ciborium, based in part on Santa Maria della Spina (c.1230), a sailor's church on the River Arno rated by Worthington 'the gem of Pisa'. As specified, his canopy was also drawn from Edinburgh's Scott Memorial designed in 1844 by the self-taught but erudite architect, G.M. Kemp.

Worthington's plans were inspected and approved by the Queen and a site in Georgian Piccadilly was tested with a full-size timber framework (1863) and rejected in favour of the present one, on condition that space would be cleared for the future Town Hall.

The 1867 inauguration was performed by William Fairbairn, member of the Memorial Committee, after various illustrious personages (starting with the Queen herself) had declined invitations. Mayor Goadsby's wife, by then herself widowed, presented the monument to the Corporation for its perpetual care and preservation.

A bust of Mayor Goadsby by Matthew Noble (1862) forms part of the Town Hall's rich collection of commemorative sculptures, whilst Goadsby's name appears as the donor of Albert's statue amongst the inscriptions on the base of the richly-carved canopy.

The canopy corner piers carry decorative figures each representing an aspect of the Prince's interests, Art, Science, Agriculture and Commerce; carved shields are emblazoned with Albert's arms, and base panels are enriched with his armorial bearings, among them his crests as Duke of Saxony and of Cleves; and medallion portraits show historic giants from the Arts – Michaelangelo, Mendelssohn, Wren and Shakespeare, amongst others.

In 1977, the woefully-neglected monument having become structurally unsound, the city raised some £35,000 for a complete restoration. The resulting work is recorded among the other inscriptions at the base of England's first large-scale Albert Memorial.

Memorial to Albert, Prince Consort (1819–1861). Architect: Thomas Worthington. Sculptor: Matthew Noble (1867). Location: Albert Square, Manchester.

Manchester Selection

Unlike other northern cities, most of Manchester's statues are still *in situ*. However, their sculptors and dedicatees would scarcely recognise today's urban scene, particularly in the teeming, unstructured and run-down space of the once-elegant Piccadilly Gardens, overlooked by the Piccadilly Plaza, a favourite spot for flo-pen graffiti artists. Despite 'TRACY 4 JUSTIN', 'G-MEX' and other sentiments, the city-scale bronzes of national figures, and their counterparts in Albert Square or other Manchester corners, make a fine contribution to the Northern Counties' Victorian tradition of rewarding the great's good works with a public statue.

Within sight of the Albert Memorial, resited from Platt Fields to newly-designated Lincoln Square, is a big bony bronze of Abraham Lincoln, gaunt and ungainly, by G.G. Barnard (1919). Given by Mr and Mrs Charles Phelps Taft, its liberally-inscribed pedestal recalls the stalwart friendship of Lancashire people in the hard days of the Cotton Famine during the American Civil War of 1861–5, after the block-ade of Southern American ports by the North.

In Albert Square, flanking the Albert Memorial, is a line of 'coat and trousers' worthies installed after completion of the Town Hall. The earliest shows Bishop James Frazer (d. 1885) by the pre-Raphaelite Thomas Woolner, facing Princess Street north of the square. (Note the polished pink granite pedestal, matched by later statues, with its fine relief panels showing Frazer as a man of the cloth, conducting a confirmation; also as a man of charity, and of the people.)

Albert Bruce-Joy modelled the marble statues of John Bright (1891) and Oliver Heywood (1894), standing to north and south of Albert. Bright, Richard Cobden's supporter in the Anti-Corn Law League, also became a leading champion of the North in the American Civil War. Like Cobden, whose bronze by Marshall Wood (1867) stands in St Ann's Square, he upheld causes vital to social well being in the northern industrial towns.

At the southern edge of Albert Square near Worthington's Venetian Gothic Memorial Hall of 1866 stands W.E. Gladstone in bronze, sculptured by Mario Raggi.

Northward, in the opposite direction, is Piccadilly where the city statues line up on big, blocky pedestals with supporting symbolic figures, pedestal relief panels, and illustrious names boldly and baldly carved: 'PEEL' (by W. Calder Marshall, 1854); 'WEL-LINGTON' (Matthew Noble, 1856); 'WATT' (the younger William Theed, 1857). Covered with graffiti and going into holes, they are centred on Edward Onslow Ford's majestic bronze (1901) of the aged Queen, enthroned, on a marble-stepped pedestal with a lovely full-length figure of 'Motherhood' in an alcove of mosaic tiles on the reverse side. The whole is crowned with a St George.

In the gardens themselves is an energetic and dramatic bronze group by Manchester's John Cassidy, a sculptor of Irish birth who settled here. On the plinth is the worn statement 'Humanity adrift on the sea of life, depicting sorrows and dangers, hopes and fears and embodying the dependence of human beings upon one another, the response of human sympathy to human needs, and the inevitable dependance upon Divine Aid'. It was given 1908 by James Gresham, who also gave a statue by Cassidy of Edward VII (1913), in Whitworth Park.

In Wythenshawe Park is Matthew Noble's fine stone figure of Oliver Cromwell (1875) on a rustic granite base, resited from outside Manchester Cathedral in 1967 to Wythenshawe's gain.

On the Cathedral porch is a small figure of Queen Victoria sculptured by her daughter, Princess Louise; there is a rare marble statue of the Queen when young, by Matthew Noble, at Peel Park in Salford, inaugurated by Prince Albert in 1857 in front of the handsome Victorian Peel Building and the Art Gallery (both with sculptural embellishment). This, and Albert's marble by Noble nearby, are depressingly dilapidated.

Across the road is the Lancashire Fusiliers' noble monument to the Great War, a cenotaph supporting a sphinx. Of Portland stone, it was constructed by J. and H. Patterson, the firm who had worked on Manchester's Albert Memorial 60 years before.

Cheshire

Winnington (Northwich)

Winnington Works Feature:

Sir John Brunner (1842–1919)
Bronze full-length statue on granite pedestal
Sculptor (Sir) William Goscombe John RA
Ludwig Mond (1839–1909)
Bronze full-length statue on polished granite pedestal
Sculptor Edouard Lantéri
Location Research Laboratories, Winnington Lane

The statues stand outside the Winnington Research Laboratory, close to the chemical works and to the baronial mansion around which the first Brunner, Mond laboratories were built in 1873. The initials B. M. appear in wrought iron over the Laboratory door, and inside is a plaque commemorating the discovery of polythene at Winnington in 1933, five years after the new laboratory was built and six years after the company's merger with three other chemical firms to form the industrial giant ICI.

Based in one of Cheshire's main salt-working areas, the Brunner, Mond Company was founded to develop Mond's method for cleaner, more economic production of soda, the raw material used to manufacture soap, glass, paper and other household goods. John Brunner joined as business manager in 1873, and working on borrowed capital, the partners purchased a part-Georgian mansion at Winnington, and building of the industrial plant commenced in the grounds.

Soda production began in 1874, yielding 838 tons and a loss of £4,300. Ten years later annual production had almost tripled, and by the company's Silver Jubilee year (1898), production and profit were in six figures.

By this time the cosmopolitan Mond had moved from parochial Cheshire to London. With his international reputation as an industrial scientist, Mond counted among his honours and awards Fellowship of the Royal Society and a Ph.D. of Padua University. Winnington Staff called him 'the Doctor'.

John Brunner contributed to local and national politics, built schools and libraries and, the true paternalistic Victorian, consolidated the workers' welfare schemes. He was created 1st Baronet in 1895.

The research laboratory is visible from a public highway too narrow and busy to allow proper appreciation of the statues. Each was erected soon after its subject's death, each mirroring a contrasting and complimenting individualism through the originality of sculptural talent.

Goscombe John's bearded Brunner, full of outgoing vitality, shows the more orthodox character. Lanteri's intense expression of the German-born Mond, who had studied under Bunsen at Heidelberg University, revives a Brunnermondian director's account of the Doctor 'in a long shapeless black overcoat' after a tour of the works, 'wearing a black chaplain's hat with a broad brim, both hat and coat much covered with white dust'. To this then-new recruit, Mond with his stoop, rough beard and damaged left eye was a 'fearsome figure'.

Sir John Brunner (1842–1919). Sculptor: Sir W. Goscombe John (1919). Location: Research Laboratories, Winnington Lane, Northwich.

Ludwig Mond (1839–1909). Sculptor: Edouard Lantéri (1909). Location: Research Laboratories, Winnington Lane, Northwich.

Merseyside

Liverpool (L)

City Feature:

Queen Victoria (1837–1901)
Equestrian bronze statue on granite pedestal
Sculptor Thomas Thornycroft
Location St George's Plateau

Erected in 1870 this is a rare and handsome statue, for which Victoria gave several sittings. England's only other prominent equestrian statue of a female historical figure is Coventry's Lady Godiva.

Like Godiva, Victoria sits side-saddle; neither conforms to the mode of dress adopted for statues of women, who conventionally appear in nursing uniform or in brocade and lace. Victoria wears her riding habit. Thornycroft shows her as she might have looked before widowhood, but the straight-backed posture and imperious stare foreshadow numerous images of the crowned and sceptred matriarch. Here, however, she is crowned with a feathered hat, and wields a riding crop.

Victoria's statue was erected as a companion to the equestrian bronze of Albert 'wise and good prince', also by Thornycroft, erected in 1868 at the south end of the Plateau. Both works cost £10,000. Albert carries a top hat and a silk handkerchief. True to form, both statues inspired criticism. Complaints about Victoria's ('her majesty sits upon a disabled steed') echoed earlier judgement on Albert's, from the same correspondent to the *Liverpool Mercury*.

The sculptor, at the unveiling, had declared St George's Plateau 'one of the finest sites in Europe'; Queen Victoria viewed her statue at his studio, and pronounced herself 'much gratified'. However, neither statue could attract a member of the royal family to perform its unveiling, and among the nation's élite who refused was Liverpool's own W.E. Gladstone, then premier. Even so the mayor, himself unveiling Victoria's in 1870, could still give thanks 'that we are living in happy England, under such a constitution and with such a Queen'.

Liverpool Selection

Like other northern cities, this great commercial port has a significant collection of bronze statues by leading 19th- and turn of the century sculptors, but these can also be set against an unusually-distinguished tradition of architectural decorative art, the work of Liverpool sculptors and architects who set their visual seal on the city from the Victorian and Edwardian periods to the futuristic Jazz-Age of the 1930s.

The most conspicuous contribution is the Royal Liver Building (1908–10) which gives the waterfront its exotic skyline punctuated by the copper-cast Liver Birds; with sea symbols, these mythological creatures make recurring motifs. The waterfront's official buildings have sculptural decoration (closer to the ground), but the richest display is in the commercial centre east of Pier Head, where even the doors of the monumental banks can be works of art. In Castle Street, those of the Co-operative (1892) are decorated with Stirling Lee's bronze sculptures of twins, or bosom friends (this bank was formerly the Adelphi, meaning 'brothers' in Greek).

Queen Victoria (1819–1901). Sculptor: Thomas Thornycroft (1870). Location: St George's Plateau, Liverpool.

In Water Street, the fangs of bronze tigers' heads on the National Westminster, originally the Union Bank (1850), were polished by Lascar seamen for good luck *en voyage*. Martin's Bank (1932, now Barclays) near the Town Hall has sumptuous decor with Egyptian detail and the Midas touch. In local lore the sculptor, H. Tyson Smith, included the head of Midas as a joke which the bankers failed to notice.

Some of the the most ebullient decorations, near the station, are Epstein's three relief panels of raw street urchins, over Lewis store's doorway catty-corners to Ranelagh Place (1956). They mark the store's rebuilding after the Blitz; overhead, 'Resurgence' rises from the prow of a ship.

A 1980s resurgence of interest in the Beatles resulted in the Cavern Walks complex, constructed over their demolished Cavern Club in Mathew Street; this has decorative terracotta work by Cynthia Lennon over the entrance, and John Doubleday's stiff and unlikely bronze quartet inside. A curio is a bronze figure, 'Eleanor Rigby' by Tommy Steel; she sits in Stanley Street.

A building that straddles most of the 20th century is the Anglican Cathedral, where Paul MacCartney once unsuccessfully auditioned as a choirboy and where a memorial service was held for John Lennon in 1981. Commissioned after a competition of 1903, it shows the artistry of the Liverpool sculptor E. Carter Preston, who created monuments and sandstone sculptures that were not too modernistic to make disharmony with the Gothic of Giles Gilbert Scott's lofty and majestic interior.

St George's Hall, acclaimed as one of the world's finest examples of neo-Grecian architecture, has allegorical relief panels, added in 1894; the architect Harvey Lonsdale Elmes, who died aged 33 before completion (in the words of his father, 'a martyr to architecture') had also wanted to introduce sculptures between the pilasters.

At the top of the Hall's broad steps overlooking St John's Lane is a bronze by C.B. Birch of Major General Earle. Killed in ambush marching against the Mahdi to Khartoum, he was commemorated in the same year (1883). Also in 1883, Birch's fine bronze of Disraeli was erected between the stone lions at the foot of the steps, but later moved halfway up to make way for the Cenotaph of 1927 on the advice of the Liverpool architect Sir Charles Reilly, first Professor of Architecture at the University. The high pedestal was replaced by a plinth of Darley Dale stone, matching the material of the Hall.

The Cenotaph of the same stone was designed by Lionel Budden (also a University professor), with bronze relief panels by H. Tyson Smith. That facing the Hall shows '... a great company and a mighty army' marching to war, and symbolises the first day and following years of conflict. The front panel, showing citizens in silent grief, marks Armistice Day, November 11th, 1918.

Budden worked on other local monuments to the Great War, including the Birkenhead memorial, which carries the distinctive work of H. Tyson Smith. The sculptor contributed to the war monuments of Southport, which has one of the stateliest and most solemn; Fleetwood Memorial Park, where the sculptor's odd, symbolic nude statue forms the main part, and incorporates many carved spiritual texts; and at Accrington, where a 16ft female figure, 'Compassion', by Tyson Smith presides over a substantial and moving stone monument by Sir Charles Reilly.

Steeply overlooking this Lancashire cotton town, the big scale befits the communal loss suffered when the town's young men were wiped out as their regiment, the Accrington Pals, went 'over the top' at the Somme.

Liverpool has a fine collection of commemorative statuary, the earliest in style being the equestrian bronze of George III, intended to mark the 50th anniversary of his accession, but which appeared in London Road only in 1822. Westmacott's classical treatment is typical of the period, and so is the 132ft fluted Doric column to Wellington near St George's Plateau, even though it was inaugurated in 1863. The Iron Duke's statue by G.A. Lawson, brother of the architect, is said to have been cast from cannon captured at Waterloo. The battle rages in a relief panel at the base.

Near here in St John's Gardens is a parade of conventional public statuary, Victorian in spirit, but mostly created after 1903 by leading sculptors of the time to portray 19th-century philanthropists, social reformers and local political figures; their good works and slogans speak out from Art Nouveau pedestals. 'The Stoneyard' was created around a disused church (since demolished), to enhance the west façade of St George's Hall.

The Napoleonic prisoners of war who were buried here are remembered on a plaque fixed to a low wall at the centre, which is dominated by Brock's statue of W.E. Gladstone, in an ensemble suitably elaborate for Liverpool's greatest son. Even so, his rival, Disraeli's, simpler bronze is more prominently positioned on the Plateau. Gladstone, who favoured for his own statue a classical form was delighted at Thomas Woolner's treatment of him in that manner. J. Adams—Acton also claimed that Gladstone favoured his rendering, and a colossal statue by Adams–Acton was proposed for Liverpool. His Blackburn statue of Gladstone is decidedly bad, however, so Liverpool was fortunate in Brock's version.

W.E. Gladstone grew up in a Liverpool family dominated by Evangelicism and politics. At the age of three he witnessed the Tory triumph in Canning's first Liverpool election, run from the Gladstone house in Rodney Street. His father John, a Scots immigrant, made his fortune as a merchant and slave-owning planter, and from local property and railway development, among other Liverpool interests.

William Ewart was named after John Gladstone's closest friend, another local Scots merchant. At the end of his life the great Liberal leader was denied freedom of the city by the Liverpool Council, then dominated by its Tory leader A.B. Forwood, whose statue by Sir George Frampton appeared at the top of the gardens one year before Gladstone's, in 1903.

The other statues commemorate philanthropists who witnessed the terrible local living conditions largely created by the rush of Irish immigration during the 'hungry forties'. William Rathbone (by George Frampton, 1899), Unitarian and anti-slaver, established Britain's District Nursing system, as shown on a bronze relief panel. The Presbyterian lay preacher Alexander Balfour (Albert Bruce Joy, 1889), founder of an orphanage for seamen's children, introduced libraries on his ships, and furthered temperance and education.

Two other indefatigable children's campaigners, champions of 'criminals' and 'fallen women', were the friends Mgr. James Nugent ('SAVE THE BOY') and Canon Thomas Major Lester. Their statues by F.W. Pomeroy and George Frampton, both showing figures of needy children, date from the 1900s. Lester's was given by 'citizens of all classes, creeds and parties'. Between them is the King's Liverpool Regiment monument by Goscombe John (1905) commemorating South Africa, Afghanistan and Burma, with a bronze figure of a hollow-eyed drummer boy among the soldiers. The surmounting figure of Britannia carries a seahorse on her helmet.

Also by Frampton is a bronze of the shipowner A.B. Forwood dating from 1904, the same year as the opening of the Gardens to a scheme planned by Frampton as an integration of art and architecture.

Behind the entrance to the Mersey Tunnel, at the lower end of the gardens, the weather house figures of George V, and of Queen Mary with pearl choker and fan, are supported on their upturned robes. The bronzes by Goscombe John were exhibited at the Royal Academy and unveiled in 1939, at the

entrance to the tunnel, by the Duke and Duchess of Kent.

Opened by Queen Mary in 1934, Herbert J. Rowse's architectural scheme for the Mersey Tunnel included buildings and street furniture, to the smallest detail of Egyptian trim on the *art nouveau* lamp standards. A unique period ensemble, it matched practically and aesthetically the then unprecedented structural and engineering progress marked by the £8m project.

One of the Portland stone lodges (nearest the library) carries a medallion relief of Sir Archibald Salvidge, prime mover of the tunnel project, crisply carved in green stone. Signed 'E. Cr. P', it is presumably a rare exterior work by E. Carter Preston.

The scheme's decorative stone carvings are typical Liverpool. Look at the goggled motorcyclist, 'Speed', together with electricity and water motifs, on the big windowless ventilating building near Pier Head. Two small statues, 'Night' and 'Day', have been stolen, found and reclaimed, but these prime examples of 1930s street art are now stored at the Walker Art Gallery, and the niches remain void.

The tunnel still serves, but Rowse's unified, sumptuously-colourful urban plan has been rudely dismembered to accommodate succeeding road systems. Liverpool's early 20th-century glory has been wiped out by mid-century dross.

Both Goscombe John and Tyson Smith worked on marine memorials around Pier Head, including the appealing Titanic monument in St Nicholas Place; its statues of Engine Room Heroes, unusually for Goscombe John, are in stone. His equestrian bronze of Edward VII, intended for St George's Hall, was instead sited on the waterfront after a vigorous campaign led by Sir Charles Reilly.

A period piece of 1913, near the domed Liverpool Union building, shows a relief portrait of 'a ship-owner strenuous in business', promoter of trade with western Africa, Sir Alfred Jones. Frampton's surmounting statue 'Liverpool' is said by some to represent King John. Flanking statues represent 'Research' with a microscope (Sir Alfred founded the Liverpool School of Tropical Medicine), and 'Industry', whose fruits include the banana, popularised by Sir Alfred for the masses as well as the classes, so it was described, by his offering free fruit for costermongers to sell. Sir Alfred began as a cabin boy, and became controller of the Elder Dempster line. (The company's 1914–18 war memorial was sculptured by E. Carter Preston.)

Liverpool's earliest important public monument incorporates an unusual departure for outdoor statues in the early 19th-century transition from classical drapery to contemporary dress. A bronze symbolic group in honour of Admiral Lord Nelson, it presents the victor of Trafalgar, one foot on a prostrate figure and one on a cannon, heroically naked. Nelson's sword receives from 'Victory' a fourth naval crown (his four major battles appear in relief scenes on the circular base), but his torso is pawed by the skeleton 'Death', draped in the enemy flag by which Nelson's mutilated arm is also concealed. His famous signal in brass letters is, as so often, inaccurately quoted.

The sculptural ensemble has occupied Exchange Flags since 1866, but will have new surroundings after a proposed reconstruction of the site. Matthew Cotes Wyatt's design was realised and executed by Sir Richard Westmacott, creator of the country's first, slightly plainer, bronze Nelson memorial in Birmingham. Unveiled in 1809 this predates Wyatt's by four years, even though Liverpool's subscription appeal had opened in November 1805 and closed the same year, it is said, at £9,000.

Liverpool historians have interpreted the figures of naked captives, their chains depending from lions' maws, as slaves; British trading ceased in 1807, but planters based in Liverpool and other British ports worked slaves until Abolition in 1833. The figures could also refer to French prisoners of war then housed in Liverpool's new gaol.

Local sculptors and designers created the Victoria Monument by Charles Allen, in Derby Street. Like many other statues around this time, it was unveiled by Queen Victoria's sculptress daughter, Princess Louise, in 1906. The statue under its dome has been called 'gross', but Tyson Smith rated it higher than Brock's 'marble wedding cake' in London, or the 'introspective' Queen on her 'arty royal throne' in Manchester. Models for the groups around the base were friends of Tyson Smith's; symbolic figures, they have everyday, human features.

Tyson Smith helped Allen on the Florence Nightingale monument, designed by Willinck and Thicknesse, showing the lady and her lamp carved by Allen in granite relief outside the Rathbone Staff College on the corner of Upper Parliament Street and Princes Road (1913). Nightingale was Rathbone's mentor; he declared her 'my Pope'.

Liverpool's statues are remarkably intact, but the city's financial and political difficulties in the 1980s led to closure and disuse of many central buildings, including St George's Hall, the magnificently decorated interior of which, with the famous mosaic floor by Stevens, sculptural decoration and com-

memorative statuary, is shut. The Plateau outside the east façade is a quiet cold place, its wide steps and decorative pavement peopled with monuments awaiting a revival.

Outside the centre, street art is endangered by its isolation; thieves recently lifted all four bronze panels by Thomas Brock from Foley's stone statue of William Forwood Senior, at Sefton Park. The replica in bronze by Frampton nearby has had a rabbit, and a nymphet's head, cleanly removed. Presumably the thieves have removed the municipal bronze paint from their truncated works of art. 'Eros', the only bronze cast of London's Shaftesbury fountain, has as yet survived intact – apart from the paint.

Ensemble to Admiral Lord Nelson (1758–1805). Design: Matthew Cotes Wyatt. Sculptor: Sir Richard Westmacott (1813). Location: Exchange Flags (resiting planned; first resited 1866), Liverpool.

Index

Page numbers in *italic* refer to the illustrations